Special Events

Special Events

THE BRAVE NEW WORLD FOR BOLDER AND BETTER LIVE EVENTS

Eighth Edition

Seungwon "Shawn" Lee, Ph.D., DES

Joe Goldblatt, Ed.D.

VP AND EDITORIAL DIRECTOR	Mike McDonald
PUBLISHER	Lise Johnson
SENIOR MANAGING EDITOR	Judy Howarth
DIRECTOR OF CONTENT OPERATIONS	Martin Tribe
SENIOR MANAGER OF CONTENT OPERATIONS	Mary Corder
PRODUCTION EDITOR	Umamaheswari Gnanamani
COVER PHOTO CREDIT	© Colin Anderson Productions pty ltd/ Getty Images, © dwphotos/Shutterstock

This book was typeset in 10/12 ITC New Baskerville Std by SPi Global and printed and bound by Quad Graphics.

Founded in 1807, John Wiley & Sons, Inc. has been a valued source of knowledge and understanding for more than 200 years, helping people around the world meet their needs and fulfill their aspirations. Our company is built on a foundation of principles that include responsibility to the communities we serve and where we live and work. In 2008, we launched a Corporate Citizenship Initiative, a global effort to address the environmental, social, economic, and ethical challenges we face in our business. Among the issues we are addressing are carbon impact, paper specifications and procurement, ethical conduct within our business and among our vendors, and community and charitable support. For more information, please visit our website: www.wiley.com/go/citizenship.

Evaluation copies are provided to qualified academics and professionals for review purposes only, for use in their courses during the next academic year. These copies are licensed and may not be sold or transferred to a third party. Upon completion of the review period, please return the evaluation copy to Wiley. Return instructions and a free of charge return shipping label are available at: www.wiley.com/go/return label. If you have chosen to adopt this textbook for use in your course, please accept this book as your complimentary desk copy. Outside of the United States, please contact your local sales representative.

ISBN: 978-1-119-34573-2 (PBK)
ISBN: 978-1-119-49821-6 (EVALC)

Library of Congress Cataloging-in-Publication Data:

Names: Goldblatt, Joe Jeff, 1952- author. | Lee, Seungwon (Shawn), author.
Title: Special events : the brave new world for bolder and better live
  events / Joe Goldblatt, Seungwon (Shawn) Lee.
Description: Eighth edition. | Hoboken, NJ : Wiley, 2020. | Includes
  bibliographical references and index.
Identifiers: LCCN 2019056733 (print) | LCCN 2019056734 (ebook) | ISBN
  9781119345732 (paperback) | ISBN 9781119498209 (adobe pdf) | ISBN
  9781119498148 (epub)
Subjects: LCSH: Special events—Management. | Special events—Marketing. |
  Special events—Environmental aspects.
Classification: LCC GT3405 .G65 2020 (print) | LCC GT3405 (ebook) | DDC
  394.2068—dc23
LC record available at https://lccn.loc.gov/2019056733
LC ebook record available at https://lccn.loc.gov/2019056734

SKY10030687_102021

*This Eighth Edition of Special Events, celebrating its
30 years since its first edition is dedicated with my eternal
gratitude to Dr. Joe Goldblatt. He is the father of modern event
management education and mentor to countless event leaders
around the world.*

*I also dedicate this book to my family, Youngseon, Jennifer and
Brandon who unconditionally support me in my journey of life.
– Seungwon (Shawn) Lee*

*I wish to dedicate this eighth edition of Special Events to
Dr. Seungwon (Shawn) Lee, my successor author and to all my
former Event Management students who, like Dr. Lee, fill my
heart with eternal pride. – Joe Goldblatt*

CONTENTS

5   Financial Sustainability   134

Part 3   Event Branding and Bold Delivery

6   Event Vendors as Strategic Partners   167

Part 5　Best Practices an Real World Event Experiences

11　Global, National, and Local Best Practices in Event Leadership　347

FOREWORD

Special Events: has been in publication for over 30 years. This eighth edition reflects recent changes in technology, culture, and commerce, along with an ever-shifting and challenging global zeitgeist. It reflects how these changes have impacted what we do and how we do it.

Future updates will, no doubt, be required. But until the ninth edition a few years down the line, right now this is the definitive industry guide—your essential handbook to understanding, planning, promoting, and producing special events.

The more complex our world becomes, it seems the more we need events and celebrations—to share unmediated moments together in real time, for their immersive physicality; for their ability to connect us; and for their potential to not only soothe our spirits but also to send them soaring up to the stars.

Which brings me to Professor Joe Goldblatt.

Joe is a true industry pioneer. He was among the first in our industry to . . . well . . . to be the first.

Back in the day, there was barely a road, never mind a roadmap for event production. There was no industry as such. It needed to be invented by people like Joe. In fact, the origin of the events industry can be traced back to many other industries and personalities, and its multiple strands of lineage permeate the pages that follow. The book also recognizes that there is perhaps still more inventing to be done.

Joe's in-depth knowledge of the events industry—where it came from, where it is today, and where it might go in the future—is beyond compare. His academic insights are rich and well informed—imbued with his innate wit, personal sense of curiosity, and unbounded enthusiasm for his subject and for life in general.

Joe doesn't impose his personal views. Instead, he navigates and curates for us the best of what's out there. His perspective is international, multifaceted, and holistic. He naturally looks forward and outward (this is no history book).

But Joe's insights and qualifications transcend the academic. He's actually "been there" and "done that," many times and with great success, as a performer, producer, director, and client. His passion for his subject is intoxicating. And, to be clear, even after decades in "the business," his stories—of both grand successes and audacious failures—and his influence, remain vital in every sense of the word.

In working as a practitioner, academic, and "relationship broker" over the years, Joe has spawned a global diaspora of loyal and admiring students and professionals who would queue up to sing his praises as I do here or indeed, to contribute to this book.

I have worked as a director and producer of major international public events and ceremonies for many years. I first met Joe in 2004. He was sitting in the crowd watching the Opening Ceremony of the Athens Olympic Games. As the Project Director for the Ceremony, I had slipped out of the show control room for a few moments—stepping out from behind the glass partition—to hear and feel the crowds' response to the show. And there was Joe simultaneously laughing and crying as the action unfolded on the massive stage before him. Even in that brief first encounter I was moved by Joe's ability to immerse himself in the moment, to watch and feel an experience without ego and with a beautiful generosity of spirit. He was willing to be swept along; willing the production success; willing everyone to feel as he did. He knew all about the "what" and "how" of the experience better than most, but he was also utterly tuned in to and moved by the "why" of it all. And "why?" is perhaps the most important question we need to answer before we set out to create our work and invite our audiences to experience it. This book and its authors are acutely aware of that fact.

Now, it might seem that I'm laboring my obvious respect for Joe. For many, the personal attributes I describe here are not necessarily prerequisites for the author of an academic text.

But here's the thing. On a really good day, special events are a means to an end, an expression and a celebration of our best and fullest "celebratory" potential. They are first and foremost vehicles to tell stories. And Joe Goldblatt is a consummate storyteller.

For decades, events industry students, educators, and professionals have been inspired and guided by Joe Goldblatt and the *Special Events* series. The coauthor of this edition Dr. Seungwon "Shawn" Lee is one of them. Shawn represents the next generation of event practitioners and leaders with his own rich, multicultural insights and remarkable understanding of celebrations and technologies across the globe.

All of this, is what makes the Eighth Edition of *Special Events: Creating and Sustaining a New World for Celebration* such a marvellous resource for those looking to carve a career in events, or who simply want to know what makes events and those who work in events tick.

This essential work will help students and practitioners to really get under the skin of the "what" and the "how" of it all. But, uniquely and critically, it also offers invaluable insight into the all-important "why" of events too.

If you want to be the best, learn from the absolute best, and immerse yourself in this book.

David Zolkwer

Creative Director & Producer

*Project Director & Creative Director,
Athens 2004 Summer Olympic Games,
Opening & Closing Ceremonies*

*Project & Creative Director,
Manchester 2002, Melbourne 2006,
Glasgow 2014, & Gold Coast 2018
Commonwealth Games,
Opening & Closing Ceremonies*

Opening

In the opening scene of Thornton Wilder's Pulitzer Prize winning drama "The Skin of Our Teeth" an old fashioned slide projector is showing slides to the audience of great catastrophes such as the ice age, the great flood and Napoleonic wars that have occurred throughout human history. An actress who is playing the maid has just let the fire go out in the fireplace and she says "It is so cold outside, the dogs are sticking to the sidewalk and the whole world is at sixes and sevens!" The actress playing the maid then drops her character and turns directly to the audience and says "I do not understand this play!"

The same may be said about the miraculous continuous expansion of special events in the early years of the twentieth – first century. We live in an age of uncertainty. In the United States, political upheaval in the Congress is only matched by the chaos of the United Kingdom's government that is on the verge of shutting down their parliament to leave the European Union. In Brazil, the world's lungs are on fire in the Brazilian rain forest and the leaders of their country have refused financial help from the G7.

However, although Wilder's drama was written over 75 years ago, it reminds us, as Dr. Martin Luther King stated, "The curve of the moral universe is long, but it bends toward justice."

It seems the more complex and challenging the world becomes the more popular and essential special events are to our lives. In 2019, the Edinburgh, Scotland Festival Fringe (the world's largest cultural arts festival) announced that despite the uncertainty and turmoil of Brexit they had sold 3 million tickets, which is the largest in their 72 year history. All of the other festivals simultaneously occurring in Edinburgh also showed increases in attendance.

Perhaps the most prescient comment about this success that has occurred in the midst of an uncertain world is from Nick Barley, the director of the Edinburgh International Book Festival that in 2019 attracted over 700 authors and nearly 300,000 audience members. Barley explained that "Numbers are only one way to describe the success of the festival. A far better description is from the people themselves and how their lives are changed through their attendance."

Therefore, the early twenty – first century may be viewed either as the age of uncertainty or the age of adventure. This, the eighth edition of Special Events, prefers to focus upon the possibility and opportunity for adventure.

Special events, now and throughout human history have reflected humankinds best hopes, dreams and aspirations. This eighth edition seeks to provide the examples, tools and techniques to help you created through emerging technologies, ecological best practices and the latest evolutions in social science, in order to bring about a better world for all of us, one special event at a time.

This eighth edition of Special Events commemorates thirty years continuous research and dissemination of knowledge regarding this field that goes on and on with no final act in site. It is now up to you to use this knowledge to write the next lines that shall guide future generations of event planners and their guests to transition from the current age of uncertainty to the future age of adventure. The book you are now holding in your hands or viewing on a screen is your tool for helping to surprise and delight your guests whilst perhaps simultaneously helping to bend the long arc of moral history toward future justice.

You Are the Next Generation of Event Leaders

Throughout this book, you will see numerous examples of how special events have evolved both naturally and strategically to refocus more and more on the leadership skills that are needed for sustainable long-term career success. Furthermore, you will discover how the next generation of event leaders is rapidly conquering the new frontiers of the profession through technology, environmental sustainability, safety, and security as well as a greater focus on events whose purposes now reach far beyond generating economic impacts.

The emerging research within the special events profession continues to validate and confirm the findings of event professionals. There appears to be a newfound body of knowledge linking the modern process of event management with the more established field of project management. Project management requires a clear identification of the goals and objectives of the event and a thorough review and evaluation of each milestone that is established. Event leaders are increasingly being held accountable for understanding and embracing similar competencies. With this book, you will be able to develop and expand your competency as an event professional and, therefore, increase your marketability and career options.

Events Education and Careers

Colleges and universities are offering new undergraduate and graduate degree programs in event management to prepare the industry's next generation. The majority of event education programs are located in North America (the United States and Canada); however, the second-largest percentage of programs is located in what could be easily described on a per capita basis as the world capital for event education, Australia. The third-largest percentage of centers for event education is located throughout Europe. A sampling of schools offering undergraduate and graduate degree event management programs is listed in the online appendices.

Continuing Education and Certifications

Events professionals are increasingly seeking professional development opportunities and certification from recognized bodies within the industry. A list of industry certifications and accreditations is listed in appendices. The Canadian Tourism Human Resource Council developed a global certification through their Certified Event Management Professional (CEMP™) program, which is based upon the recently validated Event Management Industry Competency Standards. This body of knowledge has also been adopted by Meeting Professionals International, whose membership includes global community of 60,000 meeting and event professionals with more than 17,000 engaged members in 75 countries.

Meeting Planners' Compensation

Despite the challenges with finding employment in the special events industry, in the meetings and exhibitions field, according to Professional Convention Management Association (PCMA) Convene's annual Salary Survey (the longest running survey in meeting planners' compensation) in 2019, seven out of 10 respondents said that they are satisfied with their jobs and half reported being satisfied with their annual compensation. While eight in 10 are happy with the business events industry as a whole, respondents expressed that there are high levels of stress due to increased demands, and the long hours often required for their role.

Event Planners' Compensation

Salary.com reported in 2019 that the average event planner salary in the United States is $63,475, and the range of salary is between $54,646 and $74,713 depending on locations. Salary ranges vary widely depending on multiple factors, including education, certifications, additional skills, years of professional experience.

Exhibition Industry Growth

According to the Center for Exhibition Industry research, the exhibition industry shows solid year-over-year growth. Its CEIR total index showed 1.8 percent growth for the first quarter of 2018 compared to the same period in 2017. Although in times some sectors struggle, the exhibition industry is poised for steady growth.

CEIR expects that the exhibition industry will enter into an expansion phase in 2019 and beyond.

Growth of Global Business Events

According to the Event Industry Council's study on the global economic significance of business events, in 2018 business events involved more than 1.5 billion participants across more than 180 countries. The findings concluded that business events generated more than $1.07 trillion of direct spending, 10.3 million direct global jobs, and $621.4 billion of direct GDP.

Creating and Celebrating a Changing World

All industries experience different economic periods over time. Generally, economic downturns in the tourism industry are not long-lasting due to the continued need of human beings to experience periods of leisure. Exogenous shocks, such as the global financial crisis or terrorism attacks or the rising cost of energy (automobilte and airplane fuel especially), could slow the growth of the events industry in the future.

However, the global events industry also has the benefit of providing goods and services that are always in demand as individuals mark and, therefore, celebrate the many milestones (births, deaths, and everything in between) in their lives. The worldwide phenomenon of aging populations is rapidly influencing the modern events industry; more events are celebrated as people are living longer.

Furthermore, the demand for professional event planners may grow due to the increasing work requirements of most adults that leave little time to plan even the simplest of celebrations. Finally, the harder one works often correlates with the level of stress in one's daily life.

Therefore, the forces of aging, increased work leading to greater stress, and reduced time for planning events may help fuel the sustained growth of the global events industry. This industry will need Event Leaders like you to plan and produce these events. To succeed, you will need to continue to learn, grow, and demonstrate, through credentials such as professional certification and successful events, the added value of your efforts.

Many of the readers of this book represent students who are the next generation of event planners, who, individually and together, will push the frontiers of the profession to create and celebrate our ever-changing world.

In the opening scene of Thornton Wilder's Pulitzer Prize–winning drama *The Skin of Our Teeth,* an old-fashioned slide projector is showing slides of great catastrophes to the audience, such as the Ice Age, the great flood, and Napoleonic wars, that have occurred throughout human history. An actress who is playing a maid has just let the fire go out in the fireplace, and she says, "It is so cold outside, the dogs are sticking to the sidewalk and the whole world is at sixes and sevens!" She then drops her character and turns directly to the audience and says, "I do not understand this play!"

The same can be said about the miraculous continuous expansion of special events in the early years of the twenty-first century. We live in an age of uncertainty. In the United States, political upheavals in Congress are only matched by the chaos of the UK government that is on the verge of shutting down its parliament over plans to leave the European Union. In Brazil, the lungs of the world , the Amazon rain forest, are on fire, and the country has refused financial help from the G7.

Although Wilder's drama was written over 75 years ago, it reminds us what Dr. Martin Luther King stated: "The curve of the moral universe is long, but it bends toward justice."

It seems that the more complex and challenging the world becomes, the more popular and essential special events are to our lives. In 2019, the Edinburgh Festival Fringe (the world's largest cultural arts festival) announced that despite the uncertainty and turmoil due to Brexit they had sold 3 million tickets, which is the largest in their 72-year history. All other festivals simultaneously occurring in Edinburgh also showed increases in attendance.

Perhaps the most prescient comment about this success that has occurred in the midst of an uncertain world is from Nick Barley, the director of the Edinburgh International Book Festival that in 2019 attracted over 700 authors and nearly 300,000 audience members. Barley explained that "Numbers are only one way to describe the success of the festival. A far better description is from the people themselves and how their lives are changed through their attendance."

Therefore, the early twenty-first century may be viewed either as the age of uncertainty or as the age of adventure. This book, the eighth edition of *Special Events,* prefers to focus upon the possibility and opportunity for adventure.

Special events, now and throughout human history, have reflected humankind's best hopes, dreams, and aspirations. This eighth edition seeks to provide examples, tools, and techniques to help you create through emerging technologies, ecological best practices, and the latest evolutions in social science to bring about a better world for all of us, one special event at a time.

The closing lines of *The Skin of Our Teeth* are also delivered by the maid as she turns to the audience and announces, "This is where you came in. We have to go on for ages and ages yet. You go home. The end of this play isn't written yet."

This eighth edition of *Special Events* commemorates 30 years of continuous research and dissemination of knowledge regarding this field that goes on and on with no final act in sight. It is now up to you to use this knowledge to write the next lines that shall guide future generations of event leaders and their guests to transition from the current age of uncertainty to the future age of adventure. The book now you are holding in your hands or viewing on a device is your tool for helping to surprise and delight your guests while perhaps simultaneously helping to bend the long arc of moral history toward future justice.

The Corona Virus Pandemic Is a Time for Reflection, Re-Invention, and Resolution

Historically, the live events industry has been among the most resilient of all businesses, even following dramatic periods of disruption such as the Coronavirus COVID-19 Pandemic that started in 2020. The Eighth Edition of Special Events was researched and written prior to the outbreak of this global event and the ultimate outcome of this disruption cannot be fully predicted with any certainty. However, this edition of Special Events may prove to be even more valuable now because of its focus upon technology (including artificial intelligence) and sustainable development. This book, the first ever published in this field, allows you the rare opportunity through its thirty-year trajectory to realize that the human need to meet in person is stronger than any war, disease, or other attack. You shall find, particularly in Chapters 9 and 10, that if you seek opportunities to seamlessly integrate advancing technological change within the planning of your live events, you will find a future that is increasingly resilient, even stronger, and more ecologically and economically sustainable. This is indeed your unique time to use this book to carefully reflect upon how technology and environmental sustainability may allow you to dramatically re-invent the world of live events. It is also a time for you to commit, more than ever before, to showing your unshakeable resolve to give birth to many more positive special events. This has been done many times before. In 1947, following World War II, the founders of the Edinburgh International Festival through reflection, re-invention, and resolve vowed to "create a platform for the flowering of the human spirit." It is our hope that this book provides you with many new tools to build even greater platforms in the future.

Conclusion

Thirty years ago when the first edition of *Special Events: The Art and Science of Celebrations* (1990) was commissioned by the original publisher, the author, Dr. Joe Goldblatt, received a telephone call asking if he could provide quantitative evidence that the term "special events" was indeed a noun as used in the manuscript that he had submitted. The author scratched his head because at that time the new industry of special events production had not developed any peer reviewed academic journals nor were there many authorities who he could call upon to defend his use of the term special events to encompass this new emerging industry.

However, Joe was successful in locating dozens of examples of the term special events being used in consumer literature such as magazines and newspapers from all over the world. He submitted this anecdotal evidence to the publisher, and a few days later received another phone call from an editor.

"We agree with you that special events is indeed a noun. However, we have typeset the manuscript and there is a hyphen between special and events and it appears thousands of times in the new book. To remove this hyphen will be very expensive. How important is this?"

The author argued that as this book was the first ever textbook to be published in this field, that it would in fact profoundly influence all future books and publications, and, therefore, it is critically important that the term special events appear without the hyphen.

A few days passed, and then the editor telephoned Joe with their final decision. As the author held his breath in trepidation, the editor explained that "A new technology has been developed entitled 'global spell check' and we may now make one change and it will be reflected throughout the entire manuscript. The hyphen is gone."

In 1999, the author, Dr. Seungwon "Shawn" Lee crossed the Pacific Ocean with one goal in his mind: Learning about special event management, with the second edition of *Special Events: Best Practices in Modern Event Management* in his hand. The book that he read over and over again in Dr. Goldblatt's class when he was a graduate student at the George Washington University has been the guiding star throughout his journey of learning about the event management along with five more editions of it. The two authors have partnered on many projects over the last 20 years through research projects, publications, and speeches at various global meetings. Now they coauthor this eight edition of *Special Events* with one goal in mind: "Guiding future generations of event leaders from around the world" with innovations, sustainability, security, and ever-changing event technologies.

And so the field of special events was born in part through the evolution of new technology and it will be reborn over and over again with the ideas, inventions, equipment, software, and formulas that you will contribute to the continuing story of special events. Your immediate challenge and opportunity is to not rest upon the laurels of previous generations of special events pioneers, but rather to each day seek new opportunities to amaze, to satisfy, and to improve the lives of your guests through the magic and mystery of the events you produce.

Special events has evolved as an industry from the age of invention to the recent age of reinvention, and now, you have, thanks to emerging technologies and the moral responsibility to serve as a custodian of our fragile planet, an even great responsibility. You are indeed piloting the twenty-first-century mission of special events from a time of uncertainty to a time of boundless new adventures that may bring more and more people together for the common purpose of celebrating one another as a united human family. There may have been no greater mission in your or any previous lifetime. Through the future events you will plan and produce using the ideas in the book, you may be able to one day announce, "Mission accomplished!"

Good luck with your exciting journey toward this very special North Star, and may the eighth edition of *Special Events* and your talent help you arrive safely and with light speed.

ACKNOWLEDGMENTS

This *Eighth Edition* of *Special Events: THE BRAVE NEW WORLD FOR BOLDER AND BET-TER LIVE EVENTS* is actually the work of many hands. We offer my sincere appreciation and gratitude to those faculty members and industry professionals who served as reviewers. Their collective experience and skill as educators and scholars of event management studies provided me with collective wisdom needed to continually improve this work and develop this guide. Therefore, We are most grateful to Queen Margaret University colleagues Dr. Rebecca Finkel and Dr. Cathy Matheson, Dr Marjory Brewster, Mhairi Sumner, MBA, and Laura Sweeney, MSc. Additionally, we wish to acknowledge the wise counsel over many years from Franck Arnold, Johnny Allen, Richard Aaron, Professor Veronica Bamberg, Betsy Barber, Elizabeth Bell, Debra Kaye Blair, Jeff Bland, Glenn Bowdin, Gail Bower, Richard Carbotti, Greg DeShields, Christine Cleaver, Penny Dobson, Graham Ferris, Donald Getz, Professor Alan Gilloran, Dana Giovinetti, Dr. Joseph A. Greenberg, Rob Harris, Dr. Donald E. Hawkins, Duncan Hendry, Michael Jackson, Leo Jago, Professor Richard Kerley, Janet Landey, Susan Lacz, Dion Magee, Guy Masterman, Jeff Montague, Sandra Morrow, Dr. Kathy Nelson, Iddo Oberski, Susi Peacock, Cath Pearson, Dr. Catherine H. Price, Gary Quinn, Eilidh Richardson, Ira Rosen, Rai Shacklock, Ira Shapiro, Jim Sharpe, Patti Shock, Fred Stein, Frank Supovitz, Jodi Waterhouse, Karin Weber, Harith Wickrema, Dr. Brunetta Wolfman, and Dr. Emma Wood.

For the *Eighth Edition*, we were able to interview 4 new Global Industry leaders in various sectors; Frank Supovitz, Michelle Russell, Tracey Stuckrath and Corbin Ball. We are most grateful for sharing their insights with our readers to provide real-world practical experience for the readers. In addition there are 10 recorded interview with 10 past presidents of the International Live Events Association (formerly known as International Special Event Society) that are archived from the series of this book. There is a combined expertise of nearly 500 years within these interviews. Therefore, we are particularly grateful to Richard Aaron, Deborah Borsum, Patti Coons, Peter Cwalino, Arnold Guanco, Duncan Hendry, Michael Loshin, Tim Lundy, Lena Malouf, Carol McKibben, Terry Singleton, Robert Sivek, Frank Supovitz, Joe Van Eron, and Martin Van Keken.

We particularly wish to acknowledge our colleagues Dr. Iddo Oberski and Eilidh Richardson for guidance regarding the principles of constructive alignment that we have used throughout the *Instructor's Manual* and the careful review of the legal documents within this text. Dr. Oberski is an authority in adult learning, and we have greatly benefitted from his wise counsel and Eilidh Richardson is the legal advisor for Queen Margaret University and her experience and expertise have greatly enhanced this edition of *Special Events*. In addition, as a result of Eilidh's expertise in Scots Law, this edition represents both a U.S. and U.K. approach to the construction of the legal documents.

We also with to thank our best friend David Zolkwer for writing the foreword to this book. During our long career we have had the privilege to meet and work with some of the great leaders in this industry. Many are excellent managers. Others are brilliant strategists. A few are both. David represents that rare breed of professionals whose vision attracts others to follow him. We are so proud that he is our best friend, and we would follow him anywhere because we know we would be a better person for the journey.

We thank Mr. Corbin Ball, a leader in event technologies and globally respected technology consultant, who has been advising us about technologies in various academic efforts of the authors over many years. In addition to these gifted educators, we also wish to acknowledge my colleagues at John Wiley & Sons: Elena Herrero, Julie Kerr, David Marshal, JoAnna Turtletaub, Mary Cassells, Jenni Lee, Lydia Cheng, Andrea Brescia, and many others. Their combined commitment to education in the event-planning field is best evidenced through their support for The Wiley Event Management Series, which remains a historic achievement for this industry. Thanks in large part to their vision and determination, within the scope of the past 30 years years, over 25 new books by luminaries in this field have been published, and many have been translated into numerous foreign languages.

Samuel deBlanc Goldblatt, a successful event producer and author in his own right, made many excellent and valuable contributions to previous editions of this book and provided excellent advice and counsel for this edition. Jennifer Lee, majoring in Economics at the University of Pennsylvania, contributed on many global economical and financial environmental scanning and data collections for this edition. For this, and so much more, we are most grateful.

The seven previous editions of this book have greatly benefitted from the contributions and inspiration provided by the following individuals.

Richard Aaron
Brigadier General David Alfrey, The Royal Edinburgh Military Tattoo
Nick Barley, Edinburgh International Book Festival
The Barras Family
Cynthia Bernabe
Clara Bignami
Orit Blatt
Raymond Bremer
Liane Boucher
Alicia Brett
Robyn Brown
Alison and Frazer Campbell
Dianne Devitt
Fiona and Jim Doherty

Joan Eisenstodt
Sir Tom and Lady Anne Farmer
Sir Charles and Lady Ann Fraser
Dr. Rebecca Finkel
Joe Goldblatt
Robin Holt
Anthony Lack
Trevor Laffin
Seungwon "Shawn" Lee
Fergus Linehan, Edinburgh International Festival
Douglas MacLean
Johan MacLean
Sharon McElhinney
Shona McCarthy, Edinburgh International Fringe Society

Andrea Michaels
Charlie and Janet Miller
Philip Mondor
Anders Muller
Dr. Kathy Nelson
Kari Felicia Nestande
Mairi and Brendan O'Keefe
Gerry and Mari Reynolds
Arlene Rush
Ira Rosen
Steven Wood Schmader
Astrid Schrier
Liam Sinclair
Rai Shacklock
Dr. Karen Silva-Sabatoni
Stuart Turner

Liz Glover-Wilson

Cheng So Yin

Tina Jones, George Mason University

Additional Contributors:

Alis Aimone (deceased)

Betsy Barber, PhD

Eva Barkoff

Angelo Bonita

Paul Bush

Richard Butt, PhD

Jeffrey Campbell

Shelia Ann Trapp Campbell

Canadian Tourism Human Resource Council

Professor Anthony Cohen, CBE, FRSE

Sara Cohen

Gene Columbus

Alice Conway, CSEP

Christine Cox

John J. Daly, CSEP

Nina de Courson

Julie Day

Ysabel de la Rosa

Professor Mike Donnelly, PhD

Howard Eckhardt (deceased)

Edinburgh International Conference Centre

Robert Estrin

Susan Faulk

Linda Faulkner

Max Goldblatt (deceased)

Max Darwin Goldblatt

Professor Alan Gilloran, PhD

Rosa Goldblatt (deceased)

Sam DeBlanc Goldblatt

Dr. Joseph Arthur Greenberg

Sir Thomas and Lady Emma Ingilby

Klaus Inkamp (deceased)

Jeffrey Hamberger, J.D.

Dr. Donald E. Hawkins

Linda F. Higgison (deceased)

International Special Events Society

Bertha Jacob (deceased)

Johnson & Wales University

Carola Jacob

Sam Jacob (deceased)

Alex Khripunov

Louise E. Knowles

Leah and Stephen Lahasky

Faith Liddell

Josette Locklar (deceased)

Michael Loshin, J.D.

Tim Lundy, CSEP

Kath Mainland

Jean McFaddin

Dr. Cathy Matheson

Meeting Professionals International

Jeffrey Montague

Bill Morton

Jack Morton (deceased)

National Association of Catering Executives

Dr. Kathleen Nelson, CSEP, CMP (deceased)

Gabrielle Pointer

Leah Pointer (deceased)

Professional Convention Management Association

Queen Margaret University School of Business, Enterprise and Management

Jason Quinn

Ridgewells Caterers

Professor Russell Rimmer, PhD

Allison Russell

Lynne Russell

Ira Rosen, CFEE

Dr. Ira Shapiro

Julia Schiptsova

Steven Wood Schmader, CFEE

Wright K. Smith (deceased)

Temple University

The George Washington University

The International Live Events Association (ILEA), formerly known as International Special Events Society (ISES)

The Professional Convention Management Association (PCMA)

Professor Petra Wend, PhD, FRSA

Harith Wickrema

Sarah Whigham

Dr. Brunetta Wolfman

David Wolper

David Zolkwer

Sarah Gardiner

Mary Miller

Chris Wang

Shona McCarthy, Chief Executive, Edinburgh Festival Fringe Society

Sir Charles and Lady Ann Fraser

Charlie Miller OBE and Jane Miller

Sir Tom and Lady Anne Farmer

Colin Beattie MSP and Lisa Beattie

Nicola Sturgeon, MSP, First Minister of Scotland Peter Murrell

Paul Gudgin

Dongbok Lee & Youngae Kang

Jeane Freeman MSP

Rt. Hon. Frank Ross, Lord Provost of Edinburgh and Hanna Ross, Lady Provost

Fiona and Jim Doherty

Jong-Il Ahn, MTA, Secretary General, Busan Metropolitan City Council

Richard Cooke

Hee-joon Jeong, CEO, Busan Tourism Organization

Gary Quinn

The Balmoral Hotel of Edinburgh, Scotland

Sir Rocco Forte

Finally, we must also acknowledge and thank the thousands of students from five continents who have joined us in our classroom. Each time we experimented with new curriculum or teaching methods, these students from over 100 different countries, willingly served as my test pilots. Because of their feedback and support, I have been able to introduce many of the innovations that are found within these pages. They are truly the power or "wind" beneath my celebratory wings. It is to them that this *Eighth Edition* of *Special Events* is eternally dedicated.

Producing Seamless, Secure, and Sustainable (S3) Events

PART ONE

CHAPTER 1

Welcome to Greener Event Leadership and Economic Success

> "*Architecture is a deeper thing. It is the frame of human existence. We must dedicate this existence more to beauty. For if poetic principle has deserted us, how long are we going to last? How long can civilization without a soul last? Science cannot save us; it has brought us to the brink. Art and religion, which are the soul of civilization, have to save us.*"

—*Frank Lloyd Wright,* **(1867–1959) interviewed by Henry Brandon, The Sunday Times, 1957**

In this chapter you will learn how to:
- Understand and appreciate the importance of economic, social, cultural, political, technological, and environmental sustainability for planned events
- Recognize and understand the economic, social, political, cultural, technological, and environmental changes that are affecting the global events industry
- Identify and benefit from the demographic changes affecting the global event industry
- Utilize the psychographic changes affecting event length, purpose, and outcomes to improve performance
- Recognize and analyze the multitudinous challenges facing the events industry including financial, security, labor, ecological, and other critical areas
- Identify new and emerging career opportunities in this growing field
- Understand why education has become the most important factor in the growth of planned events
- Identify industry certification programs
- Advance your career throughout the twenty-first century
- Develop new ways to sustain your career

Photo by Seungwon Shawn Lee

Destinations that provide various transport and delivery options, such as these electronic scooters or bikes and self-driving robots in Metro Washington, DC, area, not only promote greener transport but also brand their destination as environmentally sustainable.

Frank Lloyd Wright, the renowned postmodern American architect who created the concept of organic architecture, was interviewed by Henry Brandon when he was 88 years of age, 2 years before his death. At this point in his life, he was engaged in a wide range of new architectural projects, including the Guggenheim Museum in New York, a synagogue in Pennsylvania, the Arizona State Capitol, and a mile-high office building in Chicago. Wright had recently given a speech in New York, where over 1,500 people attended to listen to his wise thoughts about organic architecture. As he made these statements, the world had recently entered a time of peace after World War II. It was a time of unlimited promise and opportunity exemplified by increased scientific invention and innovation through manufacturing. It was the beginning of an era within the special events industry, which first began to achieve professional status through legendary event pioneers such as Tommy Walker and Robert (Bob) Jani, the first directors of entertainment and creativity at Disney, who helped Walt Disney welcome the world to Disneyland.

The professional event host knows that the word "Welcome!" is an essential part of the guest experience at any event. Therefore, we warmly welcome you to the Eighth Edition of *Special Events*. However, in the global spirit of this book, allow us to add:

- *Ahlan wa sahlan* (Arabic)
- Aloha (Hawaiian)
- *Bem-vindo* (Portuguese)
- *Beruchim* Habaim (Hebrew)
- *Benvenuto* (Italian)
- *Bienvenue* (French)
- *Bienvenidos* (Spanish)
- *Dynnargh dhis* (Cornish)
- *Croeso* (Welsh)
- *Dobre doshli* (Bulgarian)
- *Dobro pozhalovat!* (Russian)
- *Dobrodosli* (Bosnian)
- *Dobre dosal* (Bulgarian)
- *Fáilte* (Irish Gaelic)
- *Fair faa ye* (Ulster Scots)
- *Fun ying* (Cantonese Chinese)
- G'day (Australian English)
- *Hos geldin* (Turkish)

- *Huan ying* (Mandarin Chinese)
- *Isibingelelo* (Zulu)
- *Kalos orisate* (Greek)
- *Karibu* (Swahili)
- *Khosh aamadid* (Farsi: Iran, Afghanistan, and Tajikistan)
- *Kosh Keldingiz* (Kazakhstan)
- *Kwaribu* (Swahili)
- *Laipni ludzam* (Latvian)
- *mrHba o alf mrHba* (Moroccan)
- *Swaagatam* (India)
- *Svay-ks* (Latvian)
- *Tervetuloa* (Finnish)
- *Tusanyuse Kulamba* (Bugandan)
- *Urakasa neza* (Kinyarwandan)
- *Urseo oh se yo* (Korean)
- *Valkommen* (Swedish)
- *Velkommen* (Danish and Norwegian)
- *Velkomst* (Danish)
- *Willkommen* (German)
- *Witamy* (Polish)
- *Yokoso* (Japanese)
- *Zayt Bagrist* (Yiddish)

Often, the first word a host must offer to a guest is a warm word of welcome. However, this term must be translated into the local language to ensure proper communications. One example of the rapidly changing landscape for special events is the multicultural guests that are attending many events. Therefore, the Internet has rapidly improved our ability to instantly access the proper way to welcome all of our guests in their native language. For example, to learn how to say "welcome" in hundreds of different languages, visit http://translate.google.com.

The local or regional nature of planned events was replaced with lightning speed by global connections throughout the world. We discovered this while seated at my home computer receiving e-mail messages from distant lands. "Thanks for your excellent book—it changed my perspective about the profession," wrote one industry member from the Far East. These types of messages were quickly followed by requests for information and, ultimately, offer to fly us to lands that we had only read about. The Internet has had as much influence as Gutenberg's printing press—perhaps more.

The World Wide Web has woven the Event Leadership profession together into a new global community. As a result of this new "Web," each of us now has far greater opportunities for career and business development than we previously imagined or aspired to. In fact, many of us have become less proficient in handwriting and now excel at thumb texting. We have progressed, in a very short time, from talking to texting, from collaborating to colliding. A new lexicon of terms such as LOL ("laughing out loud" or "lots of love") has, in many cases, enhanced person-to-person bonding with a continuous flow of tweets, Instagram, and Facebook likes.

In the past 30 years, since the first edition of *Special Events*, the field of planned events has also seen numerous changes. A generation is defined as a period of 30 years during which children grow up and have their own children, thereby contributing a new generation to society. Figure 1.1 summarizes these paradigm shifts.

These six aspects of the special events profession reflect how the field has experienced sweeping changes in the past 30 years. The letters above the massive doors to the National Archives in Washington, D.C., read "What Is Past Is Prologue." And so it is with our profession. To go forward, we must first reflect on the historical roots of our field of study.

New Challenges and New Opportunities

Although the field of special events, celebrations, rituals, and rites may date back to the early beginning of humankind, you, as a member of the current and future generation of professional practitioners, may have a greater impact on this field than all those who have come before you. That is why the eighth edition of this 30-year-old

Event Aspect	(1989) From:	(2019) To:
Event organization	Primarily originated from other fields such as catering, floral design, entertainment, and rentals	Professional organization with highly educated professional and integrating technologically in a whole spectrum of business
Event guests	Younger, monocultural, less sophisticated, and less demanding	Mature, multicultural, more sophisticated, and more demanding
Event technology	Elemental and tangential to the event developmental and marketing mark process	User friendly and integrated to all stages of event management with an emphasis on constant interactions between event organizers, vendors, and event attendees
Event markets	Locally based	Globally accessible 24/7 and 365 days
Event education	Nonessential to employment in the meetings and events field	Essential (along with professional experience), qualifications required (certifications and event management degrees valued by employers)
Event evaluation	Narrow and simplistic metrics used for measurement of outcomes	Comprehensive and holistic measurement and evaluation of return on investment, return on marketing investment, return on objective, evaluation of economic, social, cultural, political, and environmental impacts at multiple points of an event (before, during, and after), thanks to online evaluation tools

FIGURE 1.1 Special events at 30: A generation of change.

volume is subtitled *The Brave New World for Bolder and Better Live Events*. The purpose of this book is not just to prepare you for your first job but also to prepare you for your last one.

Throughout your career, you will face many daunting challenges, including the recent rapidly changing global alliance (e.g., Brexit from Europe Union), ecological issues, and continuing security threats. In addition, we are certain that you will face challenges we have not even imagined as of this time.

Therefore, in order to prepare for the future, it is important to understand the past. The history of special events is rich with personalities, innovation, and creativity. During your time, you will add to this lore with your own contributions. However, now, we invite you to take a walk up the Main Street of special event history and meet some of the interesting persons whose seminal contributions developed the field that you will soon help advance into the next frontier.

Once Upon a Time and Not Too Long Ago

The term *special events* may have first been used at what is often described as the "happiest place on earth." In 1955, when Walt Disney opened Disneyland in Anaheim, California, he turned to one of his imagineers, Robert Jani, and asked him to help solve a big problem. The term *imagineer* combines imagination with engineering and was popularized at the Walt Disney Company with a new division that was created to design rides and other attractions, called Walt Disney Imagineering. When Mr. Disney opened Disneyland, he soon discovered that he had a major problem. Each day at 5:00 P.M., thousands of people, in fact almost 90 percent of the guests, would leave the park. The problem with this mass exodus was that Walt's happiest place on earth remained open until 10:00 P.M. This meant that he had to support a payroll of thousands of workers, utilities, and other expenses for 5 hours each day with no income.

To correct this problem, Robert Jani, then director of public relations for Disneyland and later the owner of one of the most successful special event production companies in the world, Robert F. Jani Productions, proposed the creation of a nightly parade that he dubbed the "Main Street Electric Parade." Dozens of floats with thousands of miniature lights would nightly glide down Main Street, delighting thousands of guests who remained to enjoy the spectacle. This technique is used today in all Disney parks, with perhaps the best example at Epcot, where a major spectacular is staged every night. According to the producers, this spectacle results in millions of dollars of increased spending annually. Jani used imagination and engineering to solve this complex problem.

One of the members of the media turned to Robert Jani during the early days of the Main Street Electric Parade and asked, "What do you call that program?" Jani replied, "A special event."

"A special event—what's that?" the reporter asked. Jani thoughtfully answered with what may be the simplest and best definition: A special event is that which is different from a normal day of living. According to Jani, nowhere on earth does a parade appear on the main street every night of the year. Only at Disneyland, where special events are researched, designed, planned, managed, coordinated, and evaluated, does this seemingly spontaneous program take place every night. Jani (who would later produce National Football League Super Bowl half-time spectaculars as well as the legendary Radio City Music Hall Christmas Show [among many other unique events]) was a man whose motto was "Dream big dreams and aim high."

Anthropological and Sociological Origins

Emile Durkheim (1858–1917) was a French scientist whose theories and discoveries helped form the basis of the fields of sociology and anthropology. Durkheim was mainly concerned with how societies maintain their integrity and intactness in the modern era. He believed that the relationship between people and the supernatural being was similar to that of the relationship between people and the community. Durkheim classified religion into four categories:

1. *Disciplinary*: Forcing or administrating discipline
2. *Cohesive*: Bringing people together, a strong bond
3. *Vitalizing*: Making things more lively or vigorous, vitality, boosting spirits
4. *Euphoric*: Conveying happiness, a good feeling, confidence, well-being

It may be argued that planned events, celebrations, rituals, and rites accomplish many of these same outcomes. There is a certain discipline within events: they bring people together; they often boost spirits; and they can lead to euphoria. However, they differ in one significant way from Durkheim's theories. Planned events are designed to produce outcomes.

Seventy years after Durkheim's death, in the first edition of this book, Joe Goldblatt defined a special event as a *unique moment in time celebrated with ceremony and ritual to satisfy specific needs.* Joe's definition emerged from that of anthropologist Victor Turner, who wrote: "Every human society celebrates with ceremony and ritual its joys, sorrows, and triumphs." According to Turner and other researchers whom we studied in our exploration of anthropology, ceremony and ritual were important factors in the design, planning, management, and coordination of special events. When we look into far EAST, like South Korea, while celebration of individual's birthday and wedding in every day of normal life was the core of *jan-chi* ("celebration" or "party" in Korean) its anthropological origin came from ritual to an ultimate power, known as *chon* ("sky"). Ancient Koreans gathered and hosted a memorial to the ultimate power with sometimes sacrifice of animals followed by a feast and celebrations (*Samkukji*). *Jan-chi* is comprised of attendants, venue, costumes, food, music, and dance into one united community. It shows irrespective of the regions (West or East) the core foundation of celebration is similar in the perspectives of anthropology.

The term *event* is derived from the Latin word *e-venire*, which means "outcome." Therefore, every event is, in fact, an outcome produced by a team that is led by an event leader. After interviewing thousands of experts in Event Leadership for the past seven editions of *Special Events*, we have discovered that, while special events may represent many professions, one person is always at the helm of this large vessel. That person is the event leader.

Growth Opportunities

Only seven decades ago, when an orchestra was needed to provide music for a wedding or social event, one consulted an orchestra leader. Very often, the orchestra leader would provide references for additional talent to enhance the event. Mike Lanin, of Howard Lanin Productions of New York City, tells the story of a meeting his father, Howard Lanin, the renowned society maestro, had with a client in Philadelphia during the late 1920s. Having already asked Lanin to provide music for her daughter's coming-out party being held at the Bellevue-Stratford Hotel (now the Park Hyatt at the Bellevue), the client asked that he provide the decor as well. When Lanin asked how much the client would like to spend, the client replied, "Just make it lovely, Howard—just make it lovely." Lanin immediately realized that making this huge ballroom "lovely" might require an investment of five figures. With inflation, the cost of such an undertaking today would well exceed six figures. But Lanin was fortunate to have earned his client's total trust. Without further discussion, the orchestra leader and decorator went to work. Few clients of any era would offer such an unlimited budget, but more and more often, special events professionals such as the Lanins are being asked to provide more diversified services. Although orchestra leaders may have been comfortable recommending decorations and other services and products for social events three decades ago, they and others with specific areas of expertise found that, when it came to events designed to be advertising and public relations opportunities, they required specialized assistance.

Public Relations

Public relations is a proud ancestor of the celebrations industry. Less than 60 years ago, the modern profession of public relations and advertising became an accepted tool in American commerce. When a corporation wished to introduce a new product, increase sales, or motivate its employees, its corporate leaders turned to public relations and advertising professionals to design a plan. Today, the celebrations industry includes tens of thousands of hardworking professionals, who, for the first time in the industry's history, are truly working together to offer their clients the excellent services and products they deserve. As an example of the growth of Event Leadership in the public relations field, consider this comment from the first person in the United States to receive a master's degree in public relations and one of the founders of the Public Relations Student Society, Carol Hills. Professor Hills is a former professor at Boston University, and she states that "My students are extremely interested in events. They recognize that public relations and events are now often inseparable. Event planning is certainly a growth area in public relations practice."

Marketing and Retail Sales

According to the International Council of Shopping Centers (ICSC) in New York, marketing directors who produce events for local and regional shopping centers may earn healthy incomes. Marketing professionals have recognized the need for specialized training and the benefits of certification within their industry. Events help attract and influence consumers to purchase specific products and services from merchants ranging from small retail stores up to major regional shopping centers. In this age of entrepreneurship, the creation of new business is far greater than the growth of established firms. With each new business created, there is a new opportunity to celebrate through a grand opening or other special events. There are millions of new businesses created annually throughout the world that may require an event leader to produce an opening celebration. Although there has been a dramatic shift from brick-and-mortar shopping to the online transactions now easily facilitated by the Internet, special events may be seen as even more critical as part of the marketing mix needed to draw shoppers to actual stores. Therefore, special event leaders who have both strong Internet skills and the ability to use those skills to pull shoppers into the malls or individual stores through live events may be in even greater demand in the future as retailers on Main Street need to compete with the Internet for customers.

Global Business

According to the World Economic Forum, there are 12 pillars of competitiveness within the global economy:

1. Institutions
2. Infrastructure
3. Macroeconomic stability
4. Health and primary education
5. Higher education and training
6. Goods market efficiency
7. Labor market efficiency
8. Financial market sophistication
9. Technological readiness
10. Market size
11. Business sophistication
12. Innovation

These pillars are closely interrelated in any economy. In order for your events business to effectively compete in the global marketplace, it is important for you to identify the countries in the world that are leading in these competitive areas. The World Economic Forum *2017–2018 Global Competitiveness Report* of 137 countries throughout the world listed, in order of competitiveness, Switzerland, the United States, Singapore, the Netherlands, Germany, Hong Kong SAR, Sweden, the United Kingdom, Japan, and Finland as the most competitive economies (*World Economic Forum 2017–2018 Global Competitiveness Report*). As a result of the crisis with the euro in 2012 and the weakened economies of Greece, Spain, and Portugal, these 12 pillars of competiveness required a lucky 13th pillar. The thirteenth pillar will be the use of events strategically to bring nation states together to produce bolder and better human outcomes such as medical discoveries, peace between nations, and more. We believe the thirteenth pillar will be like what we call the eleventh commandment (of the ten commandments) "thou shalt work together for the overall benefit of human society."

According to the 2017–2018 *Global Competitiveness Report* and others, 10 years on from the global financial crisis, an across the board failure on the part of world leaders and policy makers install reforms to improve competitiveness and productivity has prevented a sustain economic recovery. However, event leaders may begin to see new opportunities for event growth and development. The European countries (six out of the top ten) and Asia (three out of the top ten) are demonstrating great competitiveness and provide new and stronger opportunities for event development in the present and in the future.

Leisure and Recreation

According to studies conducted by the International Amusement Parks and Attractions Association (IAAPA), the changing lifestyle trends bear watching. Fifty percent of the new so-called baby boomer or limbo generations now have more discretionary income. Due to increased longevity and what is termed *vacation starvation*, they are spending this income on leisure products.

Many of these individuals are described as "wanderlust singletons" because most are indeed single adults. They are socially aware and environmentally sensitive, support fair trade, and desire nature-based tourism experiences.

They have a strong need to escape a working environment that is increasingly stressful, and therefore they seek experiences in the great outdoors, where there is a greater opportunity for controlled risk through activities such as whitewater rafting with an experienced guide.

One final psychographic change identified by IAAPA was the development of *tribing* and mass customization. Seth Godin in his book *Tribes* states that people form tribes with or without leaders and that the key is for leaders and organizations to work for the tribe and make it something better (Godin 2011).

Affinity or special interest groups—in which individuals can bond with people of similar interests and experience levels—and the need to customize experiences are both growing in importance. The ability to satisfy both needs, tribal as well as that for individual activities, will determine in the future which event leaders will succeed and which may fail.

Demographers believe that India and China will soon emerge as the major exporters of tourists due to population density and rising average income. However, in developed countries such as the United States, a new group nicknamed SKIN is developing. SKIN means "spending kids' inheritance now." As adults find new ways to extend the longevity and quality of their lives, leisure activities, sought through special events, will become even more popular.

An event leader historically was a person responsible for researching, designing, planning, coordinating, and evaluating events, and you will learn about each of these phases in the pages to come. However, the logical question one may ask is: What is the Event Leadership profession?

Greener Meetings and Events

Sam Goldblatt's landmark text, *The Complete Guide to Greener Meetings and Events*, proposed the following theory: Sustainable strategies produce superior experiences. Sounds simple, but it's slightly controversial. Before this book, environmentally friendly practices were thought of as optional extras or fancy design elements of an event. Sam argues that environmentally minded and socially responsible practice should be at the core of every meeting or event.

The concept is taking off. All major industry associations now have sustainable initiatives in place, and top-name event producers are increasingly offering sustainability services. The major conference IMEX leads the way with its Green Awards, recognizing outstandingly sustainable exhibitions. Convention centers like the Moscone Center have industry-leading recycling and redistribution programs. Even music festivals like Coachella are getting on board with carpooling and renewable energy initiatives. Certification in green event planning is gaining attention by organizations and planners who want to be more competitive in career advance. Event Industry Council (EIC) started offering a comprehensive green event practices and certificate through its professional development program.

One thing is certain: The rise of environmentally friendly and socially responsible practices is a long-term industry movement, not a trend.

Photo by Joe Goldblatt

Inflatable outdoor sculpture helps define public space at this closing night party in front of the Dallas Museum of Art in Dallas, Texas, for the Professional Convention Management Association closing event party.

The Event Planning Profession

According to experts in the field of professional certification, all modern professions (those developed at the end of the nineteenth and beginning of the twentieth centuries) are represented by three unique characteristics: (1) The profession must have a unique body of knowledge, (2) the profession typically has voluntary standards that often result in certification, and (3) the profession has an accepted code of conduct or ethics. Event planning meets each of these qualifications. Although it can be argued that, like tourism, event planning actually comprises many industries, increasingly, as data are gathered and scientific tests conducted, it becomes more apparent that Event Leadership represents a unique body of knowledge.

Event planning is a profession that, through planned events, requires public assembly for the purpose of celebration, education, marketing, and reunion. Let us explore this further. The term *public assembly* means events that are managed by professionals who typically bring people together for a purpose. Although one person can certainly hold an event by him- or herself, arguably it will not have the complexities of an event with 10 or 10,000 people. Therefore, the size and type of group will determine the level of skills required by a professional event leader.

The next key word is *purpose.* In daily lives, events take place spontaneously and, as a result, are sometimes not orderly, effective, or on schedule. However, professional event leaders begin with a specific purpose in mind and direct all activities toward achieving this purpose. Event leaders are purposeful about their work. Getz defines events as having experiences (phenomenology) and meanings (hermeneutics). He states that "There are many styles of planned events, produced for many purposes, but in every case, there is the intent to create, or at least shape the individual and collective experiences of the audience or participants" (Getz 2007).

The third and final key component consists of the four activities that represent these purposes: celebration, education, marketing, and reunion.

Celebration

Celebration is characterized by festivities ranging from fairs and festivals to social life-cycle events. Although the term *celebration* may also be applied to education, marketing, and reunion events, it serves to encompass all aspects of human life where events are held for the purpose of celebration.

When one hears the word *celebration,* typically one has an image of fireworks or other festivities. In fact, the word is derived from the Latin word *celebro,* meaning "to honor." Another commonly accepted definition is "to perform," as in a ritual. Therefore, celebrations usually refer to official or festive functions such as parades, civic events, festivals, religious observances, political events, bar and bat mitzvahs, weddings, anniversaries, and other events tied to a person's or organization's life cycle or of historical importance.

Education

From the first event in preschool or kindergarten to meetings and conferences through which many adults receive continuing education throughout their entire adult lives, educational events mark, deliver, test, and support growth for all human beings. This growth may be social, such as the high school prom, or it may be professional, such as a certification program. Regardless of the purpose, a school public assembly may be primarily or secondarily educationally related.

The term *educate* is also derived from Latin and means "to lead out." Through educational events, event leaders lead out new ideas, emotions, and actions that improve society. Examples of educational events include convocations, commencements, alumni events, training at corporations, meetings and conferences with specific educational content, and an activity known as edutainment. *Edutainment* results from the use of entertainment devices (e.g., singers and dancers) to present educational concepts. Through entertainment, guests may learn, comprehend, apply (through audience participation), analyze, and even evaluate specific subject matter. Entertainment may be used to lead out new ideas to improve productivity. However, the term *edutainment* is disputed by Mitchel Resnick of MIT's learning laboratory. Resnick (2004) argues that "Focusing on 'play' and 'learning' (things that you do) rather than 'entertainment' and 'education' (things that others provide for you) is better. My preference is 'playful learning' rather than 'edutainment.' It might seem like a small change, but the words we use can make a big difference in how we think and what we do." In adult learning, the term *andragogy* is often substituted for "pedagogy". Pedagogy is focused upon teaching, and andragogy is focused upon learning. Therefore, in the future, event leaders may help participants learn through designing and facilitating appropriate play experiences. We already see examples of this through ropes courses on which teams learn to work together through physical challenges, and in the future, online gaming experiences may contribute to learning through play as well. The event leader who is adept at navigating both the virtual and the real world of play to promote learning may be best prepared for a sustainable career.

Marketing

Event marketing, according to *Advertising Age*, is an intrinsic part of any marketing plan. Along with advertising, public relations, and promotions, events serve to create awareness and persuade prospects to purchase goods and services. These events may be private, such as the launch of a new automobile to dealers or the public. Retailers have historically used events to drive sales, and now other types of businesses are realizing that face-to-face events are an effective way to satisfy sales goals. The fastest growing types of marketing events are those related to technologies such as computers and mobile phones. The late Steve Jobs, founder of Apple, was a master of using live events to introduce his new products. Jobs would interact with his new inventions as though they were organic and even human. This created a deeply personal and captivating experience for the thousands of Apple customers who anxiously anticipated each new product launch.

Another example was at the 2014 Commonwealth Games, UNICEF was selected as the charity, and during the games, people all over the world texted pledges raising over 30 million dollars for UNICEF.

Reunion

When human beings reunite for the purposes of remembrance, rekindling friendships, or simply rebonding as a group, they are conducting a reunion activity.

Reunion activities are present in all the Event Leadership subfields because once the initial event is successful, there may be a desire to reunite. The reunion activity is so symbolic in the American system that President Bill Clinton used this theme for his inaugural activities. Reunions may include family, school, military, and even corporate groups who wish to reunite periodically. Due to the large number of retirements from corporations by individuals who have worked together for a large number of years, this field may be one that develops rapidly in the future. According to the American Express 2011 survey, 23 percent of American families were planning on attending family or school reunions (Airoldi 2011). American Association of Retired Persons reported that about 50 percent have had at least one family reunion with about 20 percent occurring annually (AARP 2012) as more than 66 percent indicating that spending quality time as a family was the most important part (Hall 2016).

Event Planning Subfields

The desire and need to celebrate are unique characteristics that make us human. The humorist Will Rogers is reported to have said: "Man is the only animal that blushes . . . or needs to!" Human beings are the only animals that celebrate, and this not only separates us from the lower forms but also perhaps raises us to a transcendent or even spiritual level. The growth of event planning subfields certainly reflects this extraordinary capability for celebration to transform individual humans and entire industries.

As noted earlier, anthropology historically has recognized a four-field approach to event planning. However, the profession encompasses many specialized fields: advertising, attractions, broadcasting, civic, corporate, exposition, fairs, festivals, government, hospitality, meetings, museums, retail, and tourism. Event leaders may specialize in any of these fields; however, rarely is an event leader an expert in more than a few of these areas. For example, a director of event planning for a zoological society may plan events for the zoo, and some of those events may involve retail promotions. Therefore, knowledge of education and marketing, as well as administration and risk management, is important.

Getz describes a typology of planned events that include four major groupings. First, he identifies cultural celebrations, public and state events, and arts and entertainment programs. Second, he describes business and trade as well as educational and scientific events. Third, he notes that sport competition and recreational events are significant groups within the typology of planned events. Fourth and finally, he recognizes that private events such as individual birthday and anniversary parties are a major thrust in this typology (Getz 2007). In addition to these four macrogroupings, we have identified a wide range of human celebrations that we refer to as subfields. These subfields are not scientifically categorized—there are many cross-linkages. However, this list provides an overview into the possibilities for event leaders as they seek to chart their future course of study:

- Civic events
- Expositions/exhibitions
- Fairs and festivals
- Hallmark events
- Hospitality

- Meetings and conferences
- Retail events
- Social life-cycle events
- Sports events
- Tourism

Once trained in the fundamentals, event leaders may wish to specialize or concentrate their studies in one or two event subfields. By concentrating in more than one area, they are further protected from a downturn in a specific market segment. For example, if association meeting planners suddenly were no longer in demand, due to outsourcing, cross-training in government or corporate event planning may allow them to make a smooth transition to this new field. Use the descriptions of subfields that follow as a guide to focus your marketing or future employment options. The appendices list contact details for many of the industry organizations.

Civic Events

Beginning with the U.S. bicentennial celebration in 1976 and continuing with individual centennials, sesquicentennials, and bicentennials of hundreds of towns and cities, Americans in the twentieth century created more events than at any other time in the history of the republic. In both Europe and Asia, celebration is rooted in longstanding religious, cultural, and ritual traditions. Civic events may include public demonstrations through planned events such as marches to protest certain laws or policies or to advocate for a cause.

The United States not only blended the traditions of other cultures but also has created its own unique events, such as the annual Doo-Dah Parade in Pasadena, California. This parade has been entertaining local residents and tourists for 35 years. Anyone and everyone may participate in this event, and they do. There is a riding-lawn-mower brigade, a precision briefcase squad, and other equally unusual entries. As the United States continues to age and mature as a nation, its celebrations will continue to develop into authentic made-in-the-USA events.

In Edinburgh, Scotland, the Beltane Festival (which resulted in the tradition known as May Day) is held in early May of each year on Calton Hill and involves hundreds of celebrants recreating ancient Celtic rites and rituals as well as, through contemporary celebration, creating new ones. It is known as a complement to Samhain (All Hallow's Eve), when the otherworld visits us, and Beltane, where we can visit the otherworld. The citizens of Edinburgh and tourists visiting the city observe and participate in this ritualistic celebration that involves reenactment of ancient ceremonies. This reenactment of ancient rituals in a contemporary context often creates discomfort and, therefore, the organizers feel the need to notify the guests of what they may experience. The ticket that is issued for admission clearly states, "CAUTION: After 8 P.M. there may be partial nudity and inappropriate behavior."

Civic events may not always result in civilized activities as expected in the traditional sense, as exemplified by the Beltane Festival. However, the term *civil* suggests that the behavior of the group will conform to the social norm. In the case of the Beltane Festival, the social norm that dates back to the Celtic period is imposed on a contemporary setting with many different reactions from the participants, guests, and media who participate and observe.

Expositions/Exhibitions

Closely related to fairs and festivals is the modern exposition. The first international exposition was The Great Exhibition held in London in 1851. Queen Victoria opened the exhibition, which was conceived of and organized by her husband, Prince Albert.

Although divided into two categories—public and private—the exposition has historically been a place where retailers meet wholesalers or suppliers to introduce their goods and services to buyers. Some marketing analysts have suggested that it is the most cost-effective way to achieve sales, as people who enter the exposition booth are more qualified to buy than is a typical sales prospect. Furthermore, the exposition booth allows, as do all event spaces, a multisensory experience that influences customers to make a positive buying decision. A major shift in this field has been to turn the trade show or exposition into a live multisensory event with educational and entertainment programs being offered in the various booths. Like many others, this field presents a growth opportunity. One of the richest men in America, Sheldon Adelson, earned his fortune organizing computer trade shows during the tech boom of the 1980s. Although some smaller trade shows have merged with larger ones, just as many or perhaps more shows are being created each year. According to the Center for Exhibition Industry Research, despite the challenging global economic conditions and the ascension of the Internet as an alternative to face-to-face selling experiences, exhibitions continue to grow in size and exhibitors continue to value this important sales channel. This spells future opportunities for savvy event marketers who wish to benefit from this lucrative field. One of my former students, a dozen years ago, was introduced by me to a U.S. publishing company in Phoenix, Arizona, and she soon became director of events for trade shows that attract upward of 10,000 persons each year.

Fairs and Festivals

Just as in ancient times, when people assembled in the marketplace to conduct business, commercial as well as religious influences have factored into the development of today's festivals, fairs, and public events. Whether a religious festival in India or a music festival in the United States, each is a public community event symbolized by a kaleidoscope of experiences that finds meaning through the lives of the participants. This kaleidoscope comprises performances, arts and crafts demonstrations, and other media that bring meaning to the lives of participants and spectators.

These festivals and fairs have shown tremendous growth as small and large towns seek tourism dollars through such short-term events. Some communities use these events to boost tourism during the slow or off-season, and others focus primarily on weekends to appeal to leisure travelers. Regardless of the reason, fairs (often not-for-profit but with commercial opportunities) and festivals (primarily not-for-profit events) provide unlimited opportunities for organizations to celebrate their culture while providing deep meaning for those who participate and attend.

Hallmark Events

The growth of the Olympic Games is but one example of how hallmark events have grown in both size and volume during the past decade. A hallmark event, also known as a mega-event, is best defined as a one-time or recurring event of major proportions, such as the Summer or Winter Olympic Games, the National Football League's Super Bowl, and other event projects of similar size, scale, scope, and budget. According to Colin Michael Hall (1989), a hallmark event may also be defined as "major fairs, expositions, cultural and sporting events of international status, which are held on either a regular or a one-off basis. A primary function of the hallmark event is to provide the host community with an opportunity to secure high prominence in the tourism marketplace. However, international or regional prominence may be gained with significant social and environmental costs." From the Olympic Games to the global millennium celebrations, the 1980s and 1990s were a period of sustained growth for such mega-events. Although television certainly helped propel this growth, the positive impact of tourism dollars has largely driven the development of these events.

Birthright Israel, an initiative of the Israeli government to bring young Diaspora Jews from around the world to Israel, produces a similar event, appropriately titled the Mega Event. Held in a large Jerusalem hotel, the Mega Event features singers, dancers, pyrotechnics, lasers, and celebrity appearances, all crafted as a celebration of Israel. When Sam Goldblatt attended in 2008, President Shimon Peres himself took the stage to welcome the Diaspora Jews to the Promised Land. This use of grandiose spectacle to forge national identity and promote tourism shows how the concept of mega-events can be reinterpreted.

Ironically, the World's Fair movement appears to have ebbed in the current era of globalization. This is perhaps due to the fact that the inventions showcased in previous World's Fairs (space travel, computers, and teleconferencing) have become commonplace and because supposedly futuristic innovations actually appeared before some fairs opened. This provides an opportunity to reinvent, revive, and perhaps sustain this hallmark event.

Hospitality

In the modern hospitality industry, hotels throughout the world are expanding their business interests from merely renting rooms and selling food and beverages to actually planning events. Nashville's Opryland Hotel may have been one of the first to create a specialized department for special events as a profit center for the corporation. It was followed by Hyatt Hotels Regency Productions, and now other major hotel chains, such as Marriott, are exploring ways to move from fulfilling to actually planning and profiting from events. According to Maricar Donato, president of WashingTours, cultural sensitivity in hospitality will grow rapidly as events increasingly become multicultural experiences due to the diverse composition of event guests.

ECOLOGIC

Festivals and fairs throughout the world are being carefully scrutinized by government, guests, and media for their environmental practices. The Coachella music festival in Coachella, California, and the Glastonbury music festival in the United Kingdom were both forced to develop strong proactive environmental policies to ensure that their events would remain sustainable in the future. Coachella uses solar energy to power its entertainment, and Glastonbury recruits volunteer green police to help encourage responsible environmental behavior by their guests.

Meetings and Conferences

According to the Event Industry Council (EIC, formerly known as Convention Industry Council), an organization that represents 34 associations whose members plan or supply meetings, conferences, and expositions, these combined industries produce over 1.8 million annual meetings and exhibitions. It is important to note that the EIC changed its name from "Convention" to "Event," which shows the term *event* is now a universally accepted term to represent the whole industry. According to EIC's 2017 Economic Significance of the Meetings, the economic significance is impressive with the creation of a total of 1.7 million jobs, $263 billion in spending, $106 billion contributed to the gross domestic product, $60 billion in labor revenue, $14.3 billion in federal tax, and $11.3 billion in state and local tax revenue. Of the total $708 billion that is spent for travel and tourism, the meetings share of travel and tourism is $263 billion (PriceWaterhouse Coopers 2017).

As a result of this significant contribution, the U.S. convention industry is a large contributor to the U.S. gross domestic product. Since widespread use of the jet airplane began in the 1950s, meetings and conferences have multiplied by the thousands as attendees jet in and out for 3- and 4-day events. These events are primarily educational seminars that provide networking opportunities for association members and corporate employees. Despite the recent challenges of terrorism and environmental concerns over rising fuel prices, the globalization of the economy has produced significant growth in international meetings. As a result, many event leaders are now traveling constantly, both domestically and internationally.

The meeting industry has developed widely recognized credentials for proven meeting professionals. They include 1) Certified Meeting Professional (CMP, governed by EIC); 2) Certificate in Meeting Management (CMM, governed by Meeting Professionals International and Global Business Travel Association); 3) Certified Government Meeting Professional (CGMP, governed by Society of Government Meeting Professionals); and 4) Digital Event Strategist (DES, governed by Professional Convention Management Association). These credentials can enhance salary and competitiveness of meeting professionals. For more information on additional certification and designations in the meeting industry, visit https://www.socialtables.com/blog/event-planning/the-12-meetings-events-designations-you-should-pursue-today/.

Retail Events

From the earliest days of ancient markets, sellers have used promotions and events to attract buyers and drive sales. The paradigm has shifted in this subindustry from

ECOLOGIC

Greener Hotels

Hotels are often at the forefront of the ecotourism movement. Famous chains like Fairmont and Hilton are rapidly implementing environmentally friendly practices. As hotel buildings can be prodigious users of energy and water, trying to conserve these resources makes financial and environmental sense. You may have noticed a small sign in the bathroom of your last hotel, giving you the option of reusing your towel to save water. This is just one of a growing roster of eco-friendly strategies being used.

the early 1960s and 1970s, when retailers depended on single-day events to attract thousands of consumers to their stores. Soap opera stars, sports celebrities, and even live cartoon characters during a Saturday appearance could increase traffic and, in some cases, sales as well. Today, retailers are much more savvy and rely on marketing research to design long-range promotional events that use an integrated approach, combining a live event with advertising, publicity, and promotions. They are discovering that cause marketing, such as aligning a product with a worthy charity or important social issue (e.g., education), is a better way to build a loyal customer base and improve sales. This shift from short-term quick events to long-term integrated event marketing is a major change in the retail events subindustry. As stated earlier, the rapid increase in mobile computing has led to the need for brick-and-mortar retailers to use more in-store events to attract larger numbers of customers. Some of the successful retail events include Macy's Christmas show window decorations, Apple's "Today at Apple" at its retail stores, and LEGO store's brick building contest. For example, Apple won the "Brand Experience and Activation" Grand Prix at 2018 Cannes Lions, a largely ad- and marketing-themed festival, for the "Today at Apple" program at its retail stores.

Social Life-Cycle Events

Bar and bat mitzvahs, weddings, golden wedding anniversaries, and other events that mark the passage of time with a milestone celebration are growing. As the age of Americans rises due to improvements in healthcare, there will be many more opportunities to celebrate. Only a few years ago, a 50th wedding anniversary was a rare event. Today, most retail greeting-card stores sell golden-anniversary greeting cards as but just one symbol of the growth of these events.

In the wedding industry, it is not uncommon to host an event that lasts 3 or more days, including the actual ceremony. This is the result of the great distances that families must travel to get together for these celebrations. It may also be the result of the fast-paced world in which we live, which often prevents families and friends from coming together for these milestones. In addition, growing numbers of intercultural wedding couples are contributing to longer wedding event days and demands for wedding planners who have multicultural understanding of wedding traditions. It is clear that social life-cycle events are growing in both length of days and size of budgets.

U.S. funeral directors report that their business is booming. Coupled with the increase in number of older U.S. citizens is the fact that many people are not affiliated with churches or synagogues. Therefore, at the time of death, a neutral location is required for the final event. Most funeral chapels in the United States were constructed in the 1950s and now must be expanded to accommodate the shift in population. New funeral homes are being constructed, and older ones are being expanded. One significant trend is the development of Life Celebration Centers by the U.S. funeral industry where a wide range of life-cycle events are now conducted. As many individuals are no longer affiliated with churches, synagogues, or mosques, these Life Celebration Centers serve as a local community asset for weddings as well as funerals with numerous family reunions conducted between these two events.

In the first edition of this book, Joe predicted that, in the not-too-distant future, funerals might be held in hotels to provide guests with overnight accommodations and a location for social events. Now we predict that in some large metropolitan areas, due to aging demographics, funeral home construction will be coupled with zoning decisions regarding hotel and motel accommodations to provide a total package for out-of-town guests. With the collapse of the traditional family of the 1950s and Americans' proclivity for relocation, it is not unreasonable to assume that weddings, funerals, and reunions are central to our lives for reconnecting with family and friends. Perhaps one growth opportunity for future event leaders will be to design a total life-cycle event environment providing services, including accommodations, for these important events in a resort or leisure setting.

Social life-cycle events have always been important. While conducting focus group research at a local nursing home, a 97-year-old woman told us: "When you get to be my age, you forget almost everything. What you do remember are the important things: your daughter's wedding, your fiftieth wedding anniversary, and other milestones that make life so meaningful." Increasingly, due to limited time availability, people are turning to event leaders to organize these important milestone events.

Sports Events

One example of the growth in popularity in professional sports is the rapid development of sports hall of fame and museum complexes throughout the United States. The 1994 World Cup soccer craze generated excitement, visibility, and, in some cases, significant revenue for numerous destinations throughout the United States. Before, during, or following the big game, events are used to attract, capture, and motivate spectators, regardless of the game's outcome, to keep supporting their favorite team. In fact, the line has been blurred between sport and entertainment, due largely to the proliferation of events such as pregame giveaways, postgame fireworks and musical shows, and even promotions such as trivia contests during the game. In 2010, Singapore hosted the International Youth Olympic Games and Johannesburg, South Africa, hosted the World Cup. In 2012, London, England, hosted the Summer International Olympic Games, and then Scotland hosted both the Commonwealth Games and the Ryder Cup in 2014. In 2018, South Korea hosted its first ever Winter Olympic games in PyeongChang and it contributed to the hosting cities and South Korea in economic terms; local infrastructure development; and self-esteem to the hosting communities as being a member of a globally recognized sporting event host cities.

Tourism

Since the U.S. bicentennial in 1976, when literally thousands of communities throughout the United States created celebrations, event tourism has become an important phenomenon. According to a study Joe conducted in 1994, those communities that do not have the facilities to attract the largest conventions are turning increasingly to event tourism as a means of putting heads in beds during the off-season and weekends. Whether it is in the form of arts and crafts shows, historical reenactments, music festivals, or other events that last anywhere from 1 to 10 days, Americans are celebrating more than ever before and communities are profiting from event tourism.

From taxpayers to political leaders to business leaders, more and more stakeholders are becoming invested in event tourism. According to studies by the Travel Industry Association of America (TIA), an increasing number of adults visit a special event (fair, festival, other) while on vacation. The Cultural and Heritage Traveler 2013 Report by Mandala Research LLC (2013) reported 71 percent of the U.S. adult population (approximately 170.4 million Americans) are categorized

ECOLOGIC

Ecotourism

The tourism industry began adopting sustainable practices long before the events industry, out of necessity. Tourism and travel have very visible environmental footprints, and the ecotourism movement seeks to replace this negative impact with a positive one. David Fennell defines ecotourism as "a sustainable, non-invasive form of nature-based tourism that focuses primarily on learning about nature first-hand, and which is ethically managed to be low impact, non-consumptive, and locally oriented. It typically occurs in natural areas and should contribute to the conservation of such areas" (Fennell 2007, p. 24).

Ecotourism fulfills the needs of modern travelers seeking unique, authentic experiences. Travel consumers are increasingly sophisticated in their purchases, looking for boutique hotels or out-of-the-way restaurants instead of familiar brands. Ecotourism provides these savvy travelers with the perfect criteria for a truly special vacation. Whether it's a friendly bunkhouse at an organic farm or a five-star luxury eco-lodge, many green travel options are available to the modern vacationer.

as a leisure traveler, and 76 percent of all leisure travelers (129.6 million) can be defined as cultural/heritage travelers, having participated in cultural/heritage activities on their most recent trip or within the past 3 years. They spend more money than noncultural/heritage tourists: ($1,319 per trip vs. $819). Top three favorite activities by them are as follows: 1) visiting historic sites; 2) participating in historical reenactments; and 3) visiting art museums/galleries. In fact, the 2017 U.S. Travel Industry Association reports that domestic person-trips for both leisure and business purposes rose by 27.8 million, a 1.3 percent increase and, specifically for leisure purposes, was the main driver of growth in overall travel to and within the United States in 2016 (U.S. Travel Industry Association 2017). In the period immediately after the terrorist attacks of September 11, 2001, when transportation for leisure tourists rapidly changed from flying to driving, many local events such as agricultural fairs and festivals benefited from nearby visitors who took advantage of the opportunity to experience a local festival, often for the first time.

One of the best examples of this growth is the Homecoming Scotland 2009 program of events. Scotland significantly increased its tourism arrivals through the orchestration of a year-long program of successful tourism events celebrating Scottish culture and heritage. This program was so successful that it was repeated in 2014. Scotland's Year of Homecoming in 2014 generated £136 million for the economy, research commissioned by Visit Scotland reveals and other nations have inquired about how to develop their own national homecoming celebrations.

Some see local event tourism as a growth area. The term *staycation*, or *portmanteau* (stay-at home vacation), was first coined by the Canadian comedian and television star Brent Butt, when he sent his friends exotic post cards while actually vacationing in a field across the street from his place of work. The consulting firm YPartnership identified in 2009 that over 60 percent of U.S. leisure travelers' motivation was to celebrate a special occasion. One other trend identified by this study is described a "togethering" and reflects the need for families who often live far apart to come together to experience a vacation. Among the key actors in this phenomenon are grandparents, who will spend more on their grandchildren during a holiday than they did on their own children (YPartnership 2009).

Stakeholders

Stakeholders are people or organizations that have invested in an event and are thus interested in outcomes of the events. For example, the stakeholders of a festival may include the board of directors, the government officials, the municipal staff, the participants (craftspeople), the utility companies, and others. Event leaders must scan the event environment to identify internal as well as external stakeholders. An internal stakeholder may be a member of the board, the professional staff of the organization, a guest, or other closely related person. External stakeholders may include media, municipal officials, city agencies, or others. A stakeholder does not have to invest money in an event to be considered for this role. Emotional, political, or personal interest in a cause is evidence of investment in an event.

A Professional Model for Event Leaders

The analysis herein, from defining the profession to identifying the principal activities conducted within this profession to listing some of the subfields where event leaders work, is not intended to be comprehensive. Rather, it is a framework within which you can begin to see a pattern emerge. This pattern is reflected in Figure 1.2, a model that depicts the linkages among the definition, activities, subfields, and stakeholders. It will be useful to you as you begin or continue your studies in planned events, as it provides a theoretical framework supporting the organization of this profession. The term *eventology* was first introduced in North America in 2003 by Linda Higgison (1947–2007). Ms. Higgison was a prolific writer, speaker, and successful business entrepreneur. The concept was first explored 20 years earlier by the Institute for Eventology in Japan. This scientific field of study incorporates previous studies in sociology, anthropology, psychology, business, communications, technology, theology, and other more established scientific fields. Eventology is a synthesis of studies conducted in previous fields that advances these fields of study to systematically explore the outcomes resulting from human events.

FIGURE 1.2 Goldblatt professional model for event leadership.

THE PROFESSION
Planned Events
The function that requires human assembly for the purpose of celebration, education, marketing, and reunion
⇓
THE PROFESSIONAL TITLE(S)
(Event producer, director, manager, coordinator, supplier)
The person responsible for researching, designing, planning, coordinating, and evaluating and/or supplying goods and services for an event
⇓
SUBFIELD SPECIALIZATION
Examples of subfields: civic events, conventions, expositions, fairs and festivals, hallmark events, hospitality, incentive travel, meetings and conferences, retail events, reunions, social life-cycle events, sport events, and tourism
⇓
STAKEHOLDERS
Individuals or organizations financially, politically, emotionally, or personally invested in an event

Change, Creativity, and Innovation: The Three Constants in Event Leadership

In 2011, we conducted a study of 400 members of the International Festivals and Events Association. The study confirmed that, despite the severe economic challenges experienced by the profession during the economic recession between 2007 and 2011 in the United States, change, creativity, and innovation remain as three constants to ensure stable navigation toward future success.

Demographic Change

Millions of U.S. citizens as well as Europeans are aging rapidly. As a result of the graying of America and Europe, not only will millions of these citizens celebrate a major milestone (middle age) but event leaders will be forced to rethink the types of events they design. For example, as Americans age, it is likely that they will experience more health problems, such as loss of hearing and vision and restriction of movement. Therefore, we must respond to these changes with improved resources, such as large-type printed and online programs, infrared-assisted listening devices, and event ramps and handrails to accommodate persons with physical challenges. The good news is that, as people age, so do their institutions, creating a multiplier effect for the number of celebrations that will be held. The other news is that event leaders must anticipate the requirements the aging population will have and be prepared to adapt their event design to satisfy these emerging physical and psychological needs.

Furthermore, the cultural composition of society is changing rapidly as well. It is projected that the minority will become the majority in the United States by 2050. The U.S. Census Bureau stated in 2017 that by 2050, 54 percent of U.S. citizens will be nonwhite and the number of U.S. residents who are over 65 years of age will more than double.

Aging and multicultural change will be major factors in the design and planning of events throughout the remainder of the twenty-first century. Those who are attuned to the needs, wants, and desires of older persons attending their events and are sensitive to the myriad of multicultural nuances that will inform their event decisions will be most successful and develop sustainable careers.

Psychographic Change

Tourism researchers have identified the adventurist or allocentric tourist as the fastest-growing market in leisure travel. This projection is further evidenced by the rapid growth in ecotourism programs throughout the world. In both developed and developing countries, event leaders must rethink the approach to events to preserve the high-touch experience for guests. This need for high levels of stimulation may be a direct response to the decade-long fascination with the Internet, which is essentially a solitary endeavor. The Internet may have directly or indirectly created an even greater demand for high-touch, in-person, face-to-face events. By understanding the psychographic needs of event guests and providing high-touch experiences, event leaders may, in fact, have greater opportunities for maximizing the outcomes that guests desire.

Career Opportunities

Figure 1.3 lists 15 established and emerging careers in planned events. No one can determine accurately how many more careers may be added to this list in the near-, mid-, or long-term future. However, using the demographic and psychographic cues identified in this chapter, the event leader may begin to imagine what is most likely to develop in terms of future careers.

It should be noted that the Canadian Tourism Hospitality Resource Council (CTHRC) has recently identified through their Event Management International Competency Standards the following general terms: event coordinator, manager, producer, designer, and/or director. However, there is no official standard set of defined employment vocational terms or definitions and they vary by sector and geographic location as shown in Figure 1.3.

Event Management Position	Background and Experience Typically Required
Attraction event director	Organization, marketing, logistical, human relations, financial, negotiation
Catering director	Food and beverage coordination, organization, financial, supervisory, sales, negotiation
Civic or council event manager	Organization, legal and regulatory research ability, human relations, financial, marketing, logistical, negotiation
Convention service leader	Organization, supervisory, financial, logistical, human relations, negotiation
Cruise event director	Interest in cruising and leisure/recreation, ability to develop and lead leisure activities such as seminars, games, dances, and other recreational activities to create events on cruise vessels
Digital event leader	Understanding the principles of delivery of digital experience, online learning behaviors, digital event format, and digital event technology
Education event manager	Understanding the principles of adult learning and curriculum development, marketing, finance, organization, volunteer coordination
Event curator	Understanding the principles of museum or collection curatorial processes and incorporating live events to animate these attractions
Family reunion manager	Human relations, marketing, financial, organization, supervisory, negotiation
Festival event director	Organization, financial, marketing, volunteer coordination, supervisory, entertainment, cultural arts, negotiation
Fitness event director	Strong background in physical fitness and sports, interest in and knowledge of general nutrition, ability to use events to promote physical fitness through walking, running, and other fitness activities
Fundraising event director	Research, fundraising, proposal writing, marketing, human relations, volunteer coordination, financial

FIGURE 1.3 Planned event positions and background and experience typically required.

Event Management Position	Background and Experience Typically Required
Health/Wellness event manager	Strong background in health and physical fitness as well as nutrition, ability to organize events that produce healthy outcomes such as health fairs and exhibitions
Leisure event manager	Strong background in leisure and recreation, ability to develop events for leisure purposes
Meeting director	Organization, education, marketing, volunteer coordination, financial
Political event director	Affiliation with a cause or political party, volunteer coordination, financial, marketing, human relations, fundraising
Public relations event director	Writing, organization, research, financial, marketing, human relations, public relations, logistical, negotiation
Public recreation event director	Strong understanding of principles of youth and adult recreation, strong human relations skills, good physical condition, ability to coach and mentor others
Retail event director	Marketing, advertising, organization, financial, human relations, logistical, negotiation
School reunion event manager	Research, organization, financial, marketing, negotiation, volunteer coordination
Senior or mature commercial recreation event director	Strong understanding of principles of aging, skilled in commercial recreation methods, respect for and dedication to working with older adults, ability to anticipate, market, engage, and satisfy needs of this population
Social life-cycle event director	Human relations, counseling, organization, financial, negotiation
Sport event director	General knowledge of sport, organization, financial, marketing, negotiation, volunteer coordination, supervisory
Technology industry event director	Develops technology user conferences and exhibitions, produces new product launch events
Tourism event manager	Organization, political savvy, financial, marketing, research
University/college event director	Organization, financial, supervisory, marketing, logistical, human relations, negotiation

FIGURE 1.3 (*Continued*)

The aging population in North America and Europe will certainly require a strong healthcare system to provide a comfortable lifestyle. This growth in the field of healthcare will inevitably create new positions for event professionals in tourism, recreation, leisure, and education related directly to serving older people with programs tailored to their physical abilities and personal interests. When our students ask us what will be the hottest jobs of the future, we always respond, "Anything that helps old people feel better." When they look at us quizzically, we remind them that there will be a lot of old people in the future due to the aging of the population throughout the world, and they need to be prepared to distract, entertain, improve, and engage these people through events.

Technology will also offer many interesting vocational pursuits for event leaders of the next frontier. The rapid technological development we have experienced in the past decades will continue and even accelerate. Professional event leaders must meet the technological challenges of the twenty-first century through a commitment to continuing education. As these new technology platforms emerge, event leaders must improve their skills continually to meet these fierce challenges or risk being left behind as technology advances.

Will we see the emergence of an eventologist, one who combines high touch and high tech to provide a virtual and live event, enabling guests to achieve high levels of customization, speed, and service through appropriate technology and greater emphasis on satisfying each person's unique needs? Although we cannot predict with total accuracy what will occur 1 year from today, much less than 5 years from this moment, we must be prepared by accepting responsibility for harnessing new technologies that best serve event guests.

Gender Opportunities

Meeting planners' compensation has been increasing in the past years. According to M&C 2018 Salary Survey, an average salary of meeting planners has increased by 8 percent since its 2016 study, especially corporate planners to $93,492 (an 18 percent increase from 2016). Association planners have a modest 2 percent increase from 2016, and its average salary is $74,628 in 2018. Although the gender pay gap still exists, but it is narrowing. Female planners earn 89 percent on the male dollar in 2018, up from 75 percent in 2016 (M&C 2018).

Males will continue to enter the profession due to the rich array of career opportunities that await them and the lucrative salaries that are being offered. However, to achieve long-term success, the profession must provide upward mobility for all workers. Upward mobility is tied only partially to compensation. Greater upward mobility specifically requires that, as an event planning employer, you must provide advancement, lifestyle, and training opportunities for event workers, to enable them to achieve professional growth within specific event organizations. Without these internal opportunities, event leaders will continue to seek new employment and take with them the institutional memory and experience they have gained while working for your firm.

Educational Opportunities

When the second edition of *Special Events* was written in 1996, Joe identified 30 to 40 colleges and universities that offered courses, degrees, and certificates in

---

TECH/APPVIEW

Will the rapid use of the smartphone and mobile apps enable event leaders to conduct research, source, request proposals, contract vendor partners, develop timelines and production schedules, manage on-site operations, and even evaluate the event in real time during the event itself?

The cloud-based technologies have become a standard in many event technologies and allow less concern on maintenance and technical problem-solving to event leaders. Some of the early leaders in this field are the firm CVENT, SocialTables, and EventMobi. They offer a cloud-based event planning technologies (diagram, event site search, electronic request for proposal, and event mobile app design), and they also offer free student training programs resulting in online certification.

event-related studies. In a recent search of event management degree programs, the authors identified 218 colleges/universities that offer educational opportunities related to meetings, conventions, and special events. This number is a significant increase from over 140 institutions of higher education that was identified in 1999. More emerge annually around the world, such as The Queen Margaret University International Centre for Planned Events, the UK Centre for Events Management at Leeds Metropolitan University, and many others. In addition, well-developed and effective distance learning tools are removing a physical barrier to take world-renowned event management education, and the fastest growth in event management education has been in the development and delivery of distance learning programs. At the George Washington University in Washington, D.C., hundreds of registrations are received annually for their highly successful distance learning event certificate program.

Finally, the technological advancement we have experienced is directly responsible for the contraction and consolidation of global markets. To ensure future success and career advancement, an event leader must embrace the global market as an opportunity rather than a challenge. Through research, focus, and sensitivity to cultural differences, the professional event leader will be able to reap infinite benefits from the new global economy. In this book, we provide a strategic plan for learning how to identify and conquer these markets to ensure further long-term personal and professional growth.

Certification

Historically, modern professions have used voluntary professional certification as a means to continually improve their practice and to slow or discourage regulatory bodies (e.g., local and state governments) from creating licensing requirements. When a profession demonstrates the ability to regulate itself effectively, government may be less likely to interfere. The profession first addressed the issue of certification in 1985 with the delivery of the first Certified Meeting Professional (CMP) examination. Next, in 1988, the International Special Events Society (ISES, now known as International Live Events Association) announced formation of the Certified Special Events Professional (CSEP) task force to develop a certification that would encompass a broader range of event competencies in addition to meetings and conventions. ISES studied a wide variety of certification programs, including the CMP, to identify models for the rapidly emerging event profession. Ultimately, the Canadian government model (Certified Event Coordinator and Certified Event Manager) emerged as the best template at that time from which to construct the CSEP program. In 2007, ISES revised and improved this program. Current information regarding the CSEP program is available at www.ises.com.

The most recent development in terms of certification is the 2012 Canadian Tourism and Human Resource Council (CTHRC) program, called International Event Management Standards (IEMS), which resulted in the final development of the Event Management International Competency Standards (EMICS), created in conjunction with Meeting Professionals International (MPI). Through MPI, a standard entitled *Meeting and Business Event Competency Standards* (MBECS) was adopted and adapted. This program is the first attempt to create a global standard for the development of education and certification in the field of meetings and events. This emerging global standard first developed through a meeting hosted by Janet Landey in South Africa to begin to identify a global standard for event managers. The Event Management Body of Knowledge project was adapted from The Project Management Body of Knowledge and later through the efforts of international education leaders such as Janet Landey, Julia Rutherford Silvers, Glenn Bowdin, William O'Toole, Matthew Gonzalez, Jane Spowart, Kathy Nelson, Philip Mondor, and Professor Joe Goldblatt. This international standard is finally being accepted by many organizations in countries throughout the world.

Developing Your Career

Now that event planning has finally emerged as a professional career, it is essential that you manage your growth carefully to sustain your development for many years to come. There are numerous challenges in developing any professional career, whether in medicine, law, or Event Leadership. Identifying these challenges and developing a strategic plan to address them is the most effective way to build long-term success. The four primary challenges that professionals encounter are time, finance, technology, and human resources. They are the four pillars upon which you will construct a successful career (see Figure 1.4). This chapter will help you transform these challenges into opportunities for professional growth and better understand the emerging resources available in this new profession.

Mastering Yourself

The first person to be managed is you. Your ability to organize, prioritize, supervise, and delegate to others is secondary to being able to manage your time and professional resources efficiently and effectively. Once you are sufficiently well-managed, you will find that managing others is much easier. Managing yourself essentially involves setting personal and professional goals and then devising a strategic plan to achieve them. Doing this involves making choices. For example, you may want to spend more time with your family, and that will determine in what field you elect to specialize. Certain fields will rob you of time with your family and friends, especially as you are building your career; others will allow you to work a semi-regular schedule. Association

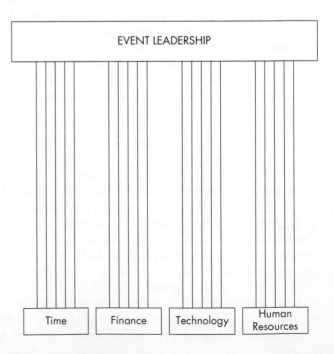

FIGURE 1.4 Four-pillar approach: Foundation for success.

or corporate meeting planning may require that you work 9:00 A.M. to 5:00 P.M. for 40 weeks of the year and 7:00 A.M. to 10:00 P.M. or later during convention preparation and production. Hospitality event planning positions, by contrast, may require long hours every day for weeks on end. After all, the primary resource of the event leader is time. It is the one commodity that, once invested, is gone forever. Setting personal and professional goals has a direct correlation with the type of work you will perform. It is hoped that the fruits of your labors will represent an excellent return on your investment.

Mastering Time Management

One key element in effective time management is the ability to use your time effectively by distinguishing between what is urgent and what is important. Urgency is often the result of poor research and planning. Importance, however, results from knowledge of priorities of time, resources, and the overarching goals of the event. To prevent too many urgent tasks it is important to apply a good project management strategy to keep important tasks on top of a priority list. In addition, it is advised to develop a "time-difference and location-difference proof" approach in any global collaboration on a project.

When we decided to produce the Eighth Edition of *Special Events*, we had to come up with a great time management strategy as we are based in Scotland and the United States with a 5-hour time difference. We agreed to use the "SMART system" to manage our time. We set **S**trategic goals, **M**easured our success by goal attainment, **A**chieved our goals, **R**ealistically set a time schedule for delivery, and **T**imely targets were used to produce the final outputs.

Effective time management must begin with setting personal and professional priorities, especially as this profession is one with a high degree of burnout. Finding a healthy balance among the worlds of work, family, leisure, recreation, and spiritual pursuits is essential to your long-term success as an event leader. This book will not only help you find this balance but also show you how to integrate time management principles into every aspect of your Event Leadership professional career. This integration of time management principles will ultimately allow you more hours for recreation, leisure, and self-improvement while providing increased earnings with fewer working hours. The 10 + 1 suggestions for event time management will help you develop an effective system suitable for your personal and professional style:

1. *Budget your time and relate this budget directly to your financial and personal priorities.* For example, if you value your family life, budget a prescribed period of time to be with your family each week.
2. *Determine, by an analysis of your overhead, what your time is worth hourly.* Remind yourself of the value of your time by placing a small sign with this amount on or near your telephone. Condense extraneous phone calls and other activities that are not profit producing.
3. *Make a list of tasks to complete the next day before you leave the office or go to bed.* Include in this list all telephone calls to be made and carry it with you for ready reference. In the age of cellular communications, you can return calls from anywhere. As each task is completed, cross it off triumphantly. Move uncompleted tasks to the next day's list.
4. *Determine whether meetings are essential and the best way to communicate information.* Many meetings can be conducted via telephone conference call rather than in person. Other meetings can be canceled and the information communicated through memoranda, e-mail, newsletters, or even video or audio recordings.

5. *When receiving telephone calls, determine if you are the most appropriate person to respond to the caller.* If you are not the most appropriate person, direct the caller to the best source. For example, when people contact you for information about the Event Leadership industry, refer them immediately to the ILEA or IFEA websites. Tell them that if they have additional questions, you will be pleased to answer them after they contact ILEA or IFEA.

6. *Upon opening e-mail, mail, or reading faxes, handle each item only once.* Respond to casual correspondence by writing a note on the document and returning it with your business card. Not only is this efficient but is also good for the environment. Respond to business documents upon receipt by setting aside a prescribed time of day to handle this important task. Place a message on your outgoing voice and e-mail letting your clients and others know how soon you will respond to their query.

7. *When traveling for more than three business days, have your mail sent to you through an overnight service.* Doing this allows you to respond in a timely manner and not miss important opportunities.

8. *Prepare a written agenda for every meeting, no matter how brief.* Distribute the agenda in advance and see that each item includes a time for discussion. When appropriate, ask meeting participants to prepare a written summary of their contributions and deliver them to you prior to the start of the meeting. This summary will assist you in better preparing for the contributions of the meeting participants.

9. *Establish a comprehensive calendar that includes the contact name, address, and telephone number of people with whom you are meeting.* Use computer software contact-information programs and a personal digital assistant to consolidate and take this information on the road with you.

10. *Delegate nonessential tasks to capable assistants.* The only true way to multiply your creativity is to clone yourself. A well-trained, well-rewarded administrative assistant will enhance your productivity and even allow you occasionally to take some well-deserved time off.

11. *Use technology to automate and expedite your activities.* Utilize mobile computing, smartphones, texting, event software, and other technologies to simplify and ensure greater accuracy for your program of work.

Mastering Finance

Becoming a wise and disciplined money manager is another pillar upon which you can construct a long-term career. During your event planning career, you will be required to read and interpret spreadsheets filled with financial data. When interviewing students for admission to university programs, we have found that over 90 percent are not comfortable with their financial or accounting skills and do not have a personal budget. However, you cannot entrust this to others. Instead, you must be able to understand their interpretations of these data and then make judgments based on your final analysis.

Sharon Siegel, president and sole owner of Deco Productions in Miami, Florida, has owned her company for over 25 years and understands the importance of prudent financial management. "Watching your overhead is extremely important," she says, "especially if you are constructing and storing props." Siegel, former owner of Celebrations, merged her company with an entertainment firm and provides full-service destination management services, including design and fabrication of decorations. To help control overhead, her firm is located in the building that houses her husband's large party rental operation. Not only does this protect the bottom line, but it also improves gross income through referral business generated through the party rental operation.

Sound financial practices allow savvy event leaders to better control future events by collecting and analyzing the right information with which to make wise decisions. In this book, we look at many ways in which you may become more comfortable with accounting. As a result of your new confidence, you will greatly improve your profitability to ensure a long, prosperous future in this profession. These five techniques will assist you with establishing your own framework for long-term profitability:

1. Set realistic short-, mid-, and long-term financial goals.
2. Seek professional counsel.
3. Identify and use efficient financial technology.
4. Review your financial health frequently and systematically.
5. Control overhead and build wealth.

Mastering Modern Technology

New advances ranging from smartphones, smartwatches, tablet computers, and radio-frequency identification (RFID) to the broadband capability of the Internet itself (social media such as Facebook, Twitter, Pinterest, Instagram, LinkedIn, and other services) have transformed the way in which we conduct business. As an example, most résumés and curriculum vitae that we review describe computer skills and software literacy. Although this is a basic requirement for most administrative jobs, it is surprising that some event leaders are still somewhat intimidated by the computer age.

Overcoming this intimidation through the selection of proper tools to address daily challenges is an essential priority for modern event leaders. These basic tools may include software programs for word processing, financial management, and database management.

Word-processing skills allow you to produce well-written proposals, agreements, production schedules, and other important documents for daily business easily and efficiently. Many successful event leaders incorporate desktop-publishing software with word-processing tools to produce well-illustrated proposals and other promotional materials. Considering that there are still a number of small and individually owned event businesses, a comprehensive skill set of using Excel spreadsheets can be a very useful technology skill. We interview students after their practicum or internship with event firms and they share that Excel is still being used as a main database management for their sites.

Financial spreadsheet software allows you to process quickly, efficiently, and accurately hundreds of monthly journal entries and determines instantly profit or loss information from individual events. These same software systems also allow you to produce detailed financial reports to satisfy tax authorities as well as to provide you with a well-documented history of income and expense. Most importantly, the use of electronic financial management tools will enable you to determine instantly your cash flow to further ensure that at the end of the month, you have enough income to cover bills and produce retained earnings for your organization.

Learning to use these systems is relatively simple, and most event leaders report that they are impressed with the ease of use and efficiency of this technology compared to the days of making pencil or pen entries in financial journals. There are numerous brand name products available for purchase, and we encourage you to determine at the outset your financial management needs and then select software that will meet those needs cost-effectively now and for the immediate future.

A database system will allow you to compile huge amounts of information, ranging from vendors to prospective clients to guest lists, and organize this information for easy retrieval. Event professionals coordinate hundreds of resources per year and the ability to store, organize, and retrieve this information quickly, cost-efficiently, and securely is extremely important for business operations and improved earnings.

There are numerous software systems available; many can be customized to fit the individual needs of your organization. However, event leaders may fail to recognize the time required to enter the data initially and the discipline required to continue to add to the original database in a systematic manner.

Whether for human, financial, or organizational purposes, information technology is the critical difference between an average organization soon in decline and a great Event Leadership firm with expansive growth potential. Use the next five steps to acquire and maintain the right technology to match your needs:

1. Identify the technology needs within your organization.
2. Review and select appropriate technology.
3. Establish a schedule for implementation.
4. Provide adequate training for all personnel.
5. Review your needs systematically on a quarterly basis and adapt/adopt new technologies as required.

Mastering Human Resource Skills

Empowering people is one of the most important human resource skills the event leader must master. Thousands of decisions must be made to produce successful events, and the event leader cannot make all of them. Instead, he or she must hire the right people and empower them to make a range of important decisions.

Although the empowerment of event staff and volunteers is important, the primary reason why most event planning organizations fail is not creativity but financial administration. Perhaps this is why in many companies the chief financial officer (CFO) is one of the best-compensated managers at the executive level.

As professionals become more educated in finance, human resource management, and other business skills, they are actually demonstrating entrepreneurial skills to their current employers. Many employers reward these continuously improving professionals, as they master and exhibit the skills needed to manage a complex competitive environment by working smarter rather than harder.

One of the benefits of mastering skills in event planning is the ability to learn how to run your own business effectively to improve your performance as an employee. In addition, you may be improving your opportunity to one day own and operate your own successful event planning consulting practice. As the chief event officer (CEO), you must empower others to lead as well.

There Is No Substitute for Performance

When meeting with his team and listening to their assurances of improving profits, Harold Gineen, the former chairman of International Telephone and Telegraph (ITT), would invoke the most sacred of all event planning business principles: "There is no substitute for performance." Four pillars of long-term success in event planning—time, finance, technology, and human resource management—must be applied to achieve consistent success. Setting benchmarks to measure your achievements will help you use these pillars to build a rock-solid foundation for your Event Leadership career. According to Sharon Siegel of Deco Productions of Florida and many of her colleagues, all event leaders are ultimately measured only by their last performances. Steadily applying these best practices will help ensure many stellar event performances to come.

Challenges and Opportunities

Three important challenges await you in developing a long, prosperous professional career in event planning. Each of these challenges is related to the other. The environment in which business is developed, the rapid changes in available resources, and the requirement for continuous education form a dynamic triangle that will either support your climb or entrap you while limiting your success. You will find that your ability to master each of these challenges dramatically affects your success ratio throughout your career.

Business Development

Every organization faces increased competition as the world economy becomes smaller and may find that it can no longer compete in a local market. Performing a competitive analysis in your market area is an important step in determining your present and future competitors and how you will differentiate yourself to promote profitability. One way to do this is to thoughtfully consider your organization's unique qualities. After you have identified these qualities, compare them to the perception your current and future customers have of other organizations. Are you really all that different from your competitors? If you have not identified your unique differentiating qualities, you may need to adjust the services or products you provide to achieve this important step. The five steps that follow are a guide to best practices in competitive advantage analysis:

1. Audit your organization's unique competitive advantage: quality, product offering, price, location, trained and experienced employees, reputation, safety, and so on.

2. Survey your current and prospective customers to determine their perception of your unique attributes compared to competing organizations.
3. Anonymously call and visit your competitors and take notes on how their capabilities compare to your unique competitive advantage.
4. Share this information with your staff and adjust your mission and vision to promote greater business development.
5. Review your position systematically every business quarter to determine how you are doing and adjust your plan when necessary.

Whether you are the owner, a manager, or an employee, maintaining a competitive advantage in event planning is the secret to success in long-term business development. To maintain your most competitive position, combine this technique with constantly reviewing the trade and general business literature as well as information about emerging trends.

Relationship marketing has become increasingly important since the development of affinity programs by retailers in the 1950s. Modern organizations are just now learning what buyers and sellers in markets knew thousands of years ago: All sales are based on relationships. Implied in such a relationship is the reality that the buyer and seller like, respect, and trust one another. The higher the price, the more important this process becomes. Event leaders must use events to further this important process.

According to *Advertising Age* and other major chroniclers of global marketing relationships, relationship marketing is the fastest-growing segment in the entire marketing profession. Event professionals must invest the same time that larger organizations do to understand how to use events to build solid relationships that promote loyalty, word-of-mouth endorsement, and other important attributes of a strong customer and client relationship.

Resource Development

As more and more organizations create their own website and Facebook pages, consumers will be increasingly exposed to infinite resources for Event Leadership. Your challenge is to select those resources that fit your market demand and cultivate them to ensure the highest consistent quality. One of the reasons that brand names have grown in importance is consumers' desire for dependability and reliability. Positioning yourself and your organization as a high quality, dependable, and reliable service through your careful selection of product offerings will further ensure your long-term success. Whether you are selecting vendors or determining the quality of paper on which to print your new brochure, every decision will reflect your taste and, more important, that of your customers. Determine early on, through research, whom you are serving and then select those resources to match their needs, wants, desires, and expectations. This may be accomplished in five ways:

1. Identify through research the market(s) you are serving. Use cloud-based electronic tools such as Survey Monkey and MeetingMatrics to collect and analyze your data.
2. Establish a database to collect information about the needs, wants, desires, and expectations of your customers.
3. Regularly review new products (some event leaders set aside a specific day each month to see new vendors), and determine if they meet the standards set by your customers.

4. Match the customers' needs, wants, desires, and expectations to every business development decision. For example, do your customers prefer to do business with you in the evening? If so, stay open late one night per week.

5. Regularly audit your internal procedures to make certain that you are developing new business by positioning your products and services as high-quality, dependable, and reliable resources for your customers.

Lifelong Learning: A User's Guide

If the twentieth century represented the age of innocence in event planning, the twenty-first century may be described as "the renaissance or even second enlightenment." You are part of an era of unprecedented learning and expansion of knowledge in the field of event planning. This book will serve as your primer to direct you to additional resources to ensure that you stay ahead of rather than lag behind the learning curve in this rapidly changing and expanding profession. One way to do this is to establish learning benchmarks for yourself throughout your career. Attending one or two annual industry conferences, participating in local chapter activities, or setting aside time each day to read relevant literature (see appendices) about the profession will certainly help you stay current. Perhaps the best proven way to learn anything is to teach someone else what you have learned. Collecting information that can later be shared with your professional colleagues is an excellent way to develop the habit of lifelong learning. Consider these five techniques for lifelong learning:

1. Budget time and finances to support continuing education on an annual basis. This may often cost you nothing with the thousands of free online resources that are now available.

2. Require or encourage your employees to engage in continuous event planning education by subsidizing their training. Ask them to contribute by purchasing books that are related to the course work.

3. Establish a study group to prepare for the certification examination.

4. Set aside a specific time each week for professional reading. Collect relevant information and then highlight, clip, circulate, or file this information at this time.

5. Participate in webinars and attend industry conferences and expositions to expose yourself to new ideas on an annual basis. Remember that, upon returning to your organization, you will be required to teach what you have learned to others. Therefore, become a scholar of your profession.

When you audit the business environment, select resources that demonstrate your quality, dependability, and reliability, and engage in a program of lifelong learning, you will be far ahead of your current and future competitors. This book will help you understand the profession of Event Leadership as both an art and a science, requiring not only your creativity but also your exacting reasoning ability. However, any book is only a catalyst for future exploration of a field of study. As a result of using this book to promote your future growth, you will have established the rigor required to become a scholar of Event Leadership and an authority in your organization. To maintain your position, you will need not only to return to this book as a central reference but also to begin a comprehensive file of additional educational resources. This book provides several appendix resources from which you may assemble this base of knowledge. Upon completing this book, use Appendix 1 to expand your comprehension of the profession by contacting the organizations listed to request educational materials to improve and sustain your practice. Doctors, lawyers, and accountants, as well as numerous other established professionals, require continuous education to meet licensing or certification standards. Our profession must aspire to this same level of competence. Your use of this book and commitment to future educational opportunities will enhance your competence.

Getting Focused

Although ILEA has identified nearly two dozen professions within the events industry, you must soon decide how you will focus your studies. After reading the preface and this chapter, you should be able to comprehend the macro-profession of Event Leadership through brief descriptions of the many subfields. Now is the time to begin to focus your studies on one or two specific subfields, such as tourism, meetings, conventions, festivals, reunions, and social life-cycle Event Leadership. Use the list of Event Leadership positions described in Figure 1.3 as a tool to get focused, and select the one or two areas where you wish to concentrate your studies.

Did you note the similarities in background and experience in each position? The key to your success in this business (or any other, for that matter) is a thorough grounding in organization, creativity, innovation, negotiation, finance, and marketing. Human relations experience is also essential, as is the related volunteer coordination skill. Increasing in importance is your ability to design, conduct, and analyze research. Throughout the book, each skill is discussed in detail. However, you must now begin to focus on how you will apply these skills to your particular career pursuits.

Event planning is a profession that provides skills for use in a variety of related disciplines. The field is grounded in the science of management, but you will also learn skills in psychology, sociology, and even anthropology as you develop your career. As you move from one subfield to another, these foundational skills will serve you well. They are the portable elements of this curriculum, which you may take with you and apply to a variety of different types of events.

How to Use This Book

Self-Education: The Reading Log

Each chapter of this book represents the sum of many years of professional reading by the authors. Therefore, as you approach a new chapter, look for related writings in industry trade and professional journals as well as general media, such as *The New York Times* (USA) or *The Guardian* (UK). As you identify these readings, save them for your study time. When you complete your two 20-minute study periods, give yourself a bonus by reading the related material and then noting in your reading log the title, author, date, and a short description. Developing this habit during your study period will begin a lifelong process that will reward you richly throughout your career. Make certain that you develop a filing system for these readings for future reference and use the reading log as a classification system for easy reference.

Benchmark Checklists

Self-improvement must be the goal of every successful person. This is a continuous process. Ensuring continuous self-improvement and business improvement requires utilizing an old tradition in a new context. The term *benchmarking* was first used by Xerox Corporation to describe the way its corporate leaders reinvented its organization to compete more effectively. This process was so successful that Xerox won the most coveted award in corporate America, the Malcolm Baldrige National Quality Award. The principles of benchmarking are simple; however, the application requires commitment and discipline.

Benchmarking is a management process in which you study similar organizations to determine what systems they are using that can become quality benchmarks for your own organization. Once you have identified these benchmarks, your organization's goal is to meet or exceed these standards within a specified period of time.

The checklists throughout this book are your benchmarks. They are the result of over 30 years of study of successful individuals and organizations in the profession of Event Leadership. Who knows, perhaps you may be one of the successful persons we study in the future.

EcoLogic

Throughout each chapter, we have provided you with examples of environmental sustainable practices to further develop and sustain your career. Use each of these EcoLogic mini case studies to ensure that each and every event you plan is one that reflects the best sustainable practices through the careful stewardship of the environment to improve the overall quality of your event.

TECH/APPVIEWS and SECUREVIEWS

TECH/APPVIEWS recommends mobile apps that support the chapter content and the adoption of technologically proficient methods to improve your events. SECUREVIEWS to recommend health, safety, and security considerations related to the content.

Critical Connections for Career Advancement

In addition to the numerous tables, charts, and models in this book, each chapter includes four critical connections to help you rapidly advance. The very nature of special events is to connect people through a shared activity; therefore, each chapter includes specific instructions for global, technological, resource, and learning connections. Make certain that you carefully review these sections at the end of each chapter to expand, reinforce, and strengthen your connections in the twenty-first century global Event Leadership profession.

Insights from Global Event Leaders

This edition provides a series of profiles of distinguished event thought leaders. The concept of the thought leader was first developed through high-level and widely viewed conferences such as the Technology, Education and Design conference (TED). This edition of *Special Events* for the first time introduces you to a recognized international thought leader or leaders in each chapter to help you understand through experience and aspiration the infinite opportunities that await you in this rapidly expanding field. This edition includes interviews with event industry visionaries and international past presidents of the world's largest association of event professionals, the ILEA. These thought leaders were selected because of their extensive experience, professionalism, and talent. Even more importantly, they will inspire you with their devotion to the field of special events leadership.

Appendices

The numerous appendices are designed to provide you with extensive resources in one location to use throughout your professional life. Review these listings and determine what gaps you currently have in your operations, marketing, or other areas, and use these resources to add to your knowledge. As event planning is an emerging discipline and rapidly expanding profession, you may notice gaps in the appendices that you may fill. Send us your ideas and resources to slz@gmu.edu, and you will be acknowledged in the next edition.

Role and Scope

This book's role is to expand the knowledge base in the emerging discipline of study, entitled by Getz, as event studies (Getz 2007). The scope of its task is to provide concrete techniques to immediately improve your practice. Your career needs will determine how you use this book to improve your business. However, if you are sincerely interested in expanding the knowledge base in planned events, your practice will improve in equal proportion to your level of commitment. This is so important that it bears repeating. If you are interested in expanding the body of knowledge in planned events, your skills will improve in equal proportion to your level of commitment.

Therefore, as in most professions, the harder you work, the more you will learn. And as is also true in all professions, the more you learn, the more you will earn. We encourage you to become a scholar of this fascinating profession and, as suggested earlier, read this book as if someday, somewhere, you will be requested to teach others. We challenge you to achieve mastery through these pages so that those you will influence will leave this profession even better prepared for those who will follow.

Like you, we are perpetual students of this growing profession. There are new learning opportunities every hour of every day. Nearly three decades ago, Joe stood outside a hospital nursery window, gazing lovingly on his newborn son, Sam. Only a few hours earlier, he had telephoned his cousin Carola in New Orleans to announce the birth and, choking back tears, to tell her and the family that he would be named for his beloved Uncle Sam, her father, who had recently died. Celebrating this new life together, they laughed out loud about the "curse" that might come with his son's name. Would he be as funny, charming, irascible, and generous as Uncle Sam? His potential was limitless. Today, Sam has earned his master's degree in festival management, produces the annual Edinburgh and Glasgow 48 Hour Film Projects, and is the author of his own book *The Complete Guide to Greener Meetings and Events* (Wiley 2011).

The father of organic architecture, Frank Lloyd Wright, without actually realizing it, may have also influenced the development of the postmodern field of special events. This, after all, was and is a time when events have grown from a commercial to a deeply personal experience that create milestone memories for human beings throughout the world. Janet Landey of Johannesburg, South Africa, refers to her work as *event architecture*. The postmodern event leader may indeed design and build organic special events that facilitate experiences that positively influence human lives.

INSIGHTS FROM GLOBAL EVENT LEADERS

ARNOLD GUANCO

Deputy Bus System Manager, Technical Officials, London 2012

(Note: To see the complete video interview, visit the Book Companion Site for this book at www.wiley.com/go/goldblatt/specialevents8e.)

http://goo.gl/kFLJSO

Arnold Guanco was born in the Philippines and later earned his master's degree at George Washington University in Washington, D.C. He was one of the first people in the world to earn a postgraduate degree in events management. Upon graduation, he helped plan the annual meeting for the World Bank and later for the Asia Games in Doha, Qatar. He has served as part of the management team for two Olympic Games in Vancouver, Canada, and London, England. Arnold was interviewed directly after the successful conclusion of the London 2012 Olympic Games.

Q: What motivates you?

A: You must have a goal to go somewhere. Look at me, I came from a small island in the Philippines, and I always had a dream of studying in the United States. Every night I would look out the window and dream about my goal. I did it. I achieved my goal.

Q: What is more important, experience or education?

A: When I began I thought experience was most important. However, now, I believe that education is equally important because by learning from others you may avoid future mistakes and continually improve the future events you plan and produce. Therefore, I think education is really important.

Q: How important is environmental sustainability within the events you have produced?

A: Environmental sustainability is a very important trend. For example, it is important now that the transport for events be as environmentally efficient as possible, so we do not have empty buses running around or idling when stopped.

Q: How important is technology today in the planning and production of events?

A: We need a very reliable and stable technology platform for events such as GPS to help our drivers understand their routes from the very first day. I am very supportive of using cloud technology for managing events, but I am also concerned about the challenges with potential security breaches.

Q: What are the most important skills for an event manager today?

A: A good event manager must also be a good client services manager. You need to be the link between organizations as well as being creative. You must be a thinker.

Q: What do you believe the future of planned events will require from event professionals such as yourself?

A: I want to be a strategist. I do not believe that [what] worked today will work tomorrow. I want to help improve systems as the industry grows.

Q: What will help the special events industry grow and prosper in the future?

A: There has to be more research and understanding of what kind of technology we really need to produce better events. Do we invest the technology money in the planning or in the legacy side or is it consciousness about the climate?

Q: What do event professionals need to know about the future of events?

A: It is not about just producing a show; it is about how you will make this show or event different and better than all others. For example, when London 2012 presented the Olympic Games flag to Rio de Janeiro 2016, they staged a Samba dance. I believe that is what people expected. We must instead also produce the unexpected, so people will remember and tell others what they have experienced.

Confucius declared several thousand years ago that "we are cursed to live in interesting times indeed." Regardless of what road you take in the infinitely fascinating Event Leadership profession, you can be assured of finding many opportunities in these very interesting and challenging times. In the closing lines of his bestseller *Megatrends* (1982), John Naisbitt exalted the world he had spent years analyzing: "My God, what a fantastic time in which to be alive." The future that you and your colleagues will create will carry the curse of Confucius, the joy of Naisbitt, and the final assurance of the French poet Paul Valéry, who wrote: "The trouble with the future is it no longer is what it used to be." Your future is secure, knowing that there are millions of new births annually in the world, people are living longer than ever before, and, therefore, there are many more future events for you to lead.

Summary

Chapter 1 provided you with an overview of the professional field of event planning and leadership. It identified key professional models to help you establish and secure your future career. It has identified the key growth areas to help you best focus your career in the near and midterm. Finally, the chapter provided an overview of how you may best use the book to rapidly develop and advance your career in planned events. Here are three key points you should be able to recall from this chapter:

1. Event planning is a growing profession due to aging populations. The field of study is also growing due to the increased risks associated with this highly sophisticated and complex profession.
2. Event leaders are being carefully scrutinized by government and others as a result of the global economic recession of 2008. Therefore, event leaders must justify their roles to many different stakeholders through careful measurement of return on investment and return on objective.
3. One of the most significant advances in modern event planning is the increased use of technology to research, plan, market, deliver, and evaluate events. Event leaders must remain current with all emerging technologies to create greater efficiency and increase overall quality.

Key Terms

Event: A term derived from the Latin term *E-venire*, meaning *outcome*.

Event studies: An emerging academic field of study and research comprising foundational academic research and theorems from anthropology, psychology, sociology, technology, and tourism.

Planned events: Events that are planned in advance to achieve specific outcomes.

Special event: A unique moment in time celebrated with ceremony and ritual to achieve specific outcomes.

Career Connections

Begin to identify your future career interest in special events based upon demand (aging, leisure, technology, and other growth areas of the economy).

Read Gene Columbus's book *The Complete Guide to Careers in Special Events* (Wiley 2010).

Next Steps

1. Conduct an Internet search and identify five different types of event planning firms in your area and note if they specifically list or promote their sustainability practices regarding the environment. Are these firms practicing EcoLogic?

2. Review *The International Dictionary of Event Management, Wiley, 2001* and *The Convention Industry Council Glossary of Terms, Apex, 2011* and become familiar with the key words and phrases in the profession.

3. List your personal technology strengths and weaknesses and review online to view webinars and tutorials to strengthen your TechnoLogic abilities.

References

AARP (2012) Bulletin poll: Family reunions 2012 comparison of those 18–49 years and those age 50+. Research & Strategic Analysis. Washington, D.C.: AARP.

Airoldi, D. M. (2011, May 10) American families are eager to travel again, per AMEX and homeaway, accessed May 11, 2018: http://travel-industry. uptake.com/blog/2011/05/10/american-families-are-eager-to-travel-again-per-amex-andhomeaway/.

Fennell, D. (2007) *Ecotourism*, Oxford, UK: Routledge.

Getz, D. (2007) *Event Studies*, Oxford, UK: Butterworth Heinemann.

Godin, S. (2011) *Tribes*, London, UK: Piatkus.

Hall, C. M. (1989) The definition and analysis of tourism hallmark events, *Geo Journal*, Vol. 19.3, pp. 263–268.

Lin, K. (2012) *MeetingMatrix Curriculum Study*, Edinburgh, Scotland: Queen Margaret University.

PriceWaterhouse Coopers (2017) *The Economic Significance of Meetings to the U.S. Economy*, Washington, D.C.: Event Industry Council.

Resnick, M. (2004) Edutainment? No thanks. I prefer playful learning. Associazione Civita Report on Edutainment no. 14, accessed May 11, 2018: https://llk.media.mit.edu/papers/edutainment.pdf.

Mandala Research LLC (2013) *The Cultural and Heritage Traveler 2013 edition*, accessed August 12, 2018: https://scholarworks. umass.edu/cgi/viewcontent.cgi?referer=https://www.google. com/&httpsredir=1&article=2032&context=ttra.

M&C (2018) 2018 Salary survey, accessed September 22, 2018: http://www.meetings-conventions.com/News/Features/salary-survey-planner-compensation-research-2018/.

U.S. Travel Industry Association (2017) U.S. travel and tourism overview, accessed September 7, 2018: https://www.ustravel. org/system/files/media_root/document/Research_Fact-Sheet_US-Travel-and-Tourism-Overview.pdf.

Ypartnership/Yankelovich, Inc. (2009) *National Leisure Travel MONITOR*, Chapel Hill, NC: Yankelovich, Inc.

World Economic Forum, Global Competitiveness Report, 2017–2018, accessed September 5, 2018: http://www.weforum.org/reports/global-competitiveness-report-2017-2018.

CHAPTER 2

Changing Paradigms for Greener Leadership and Social Change

> *"Everybody needs beauty as well as bread, places to play in and pray in, where nature may heal and give strength to body and soul."*
>
> — *John Muir, **Environmentalist and the founder of the U.S. National Parks system** (1838–1914)*

In this chapter you will learn how to:

- Recognize and use the five phases of the modern event planning process
- Identify the strengths, weaknesses, opportunities, and threats of your event
- Create an accurate blueprint for your event
- Conduct a comprehensive needs assessment
- Complete a gap analysis for your event
- Communicate effectively with event stakeholders
- Critically integrate corporate social responsibility (CSR) into every event

In 2014, we commemorated the 100th anniversary of the death of the famed environmentalist, John Muir. Muir was born in Dunbar, Scotland, and as a young boy moved to the United States. During his lifetime, he was responsible for giving the U.S. president Theodore Roosevelt the idea of protecting public lands for the enjoyment of people. In Northern California, the Muir Woods stand today as a memorial and testament to his work as an environmentalist. Muir understood that sustainability is a never-ending process as is event planning.

All successful events have five critical stages in common to ensure their consistent effectiveness. These five phases, or steps of successful event planning, are research, design, planning, coordination, and evaluation (see Figure 2.1a). Understanding

Using recycled materials this band performs for the opening night party for the Professional Convention Management Association in Dallas, Texas.

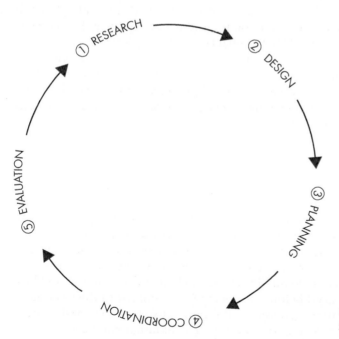

FIGURE 2.1a Event planning five-phase process.

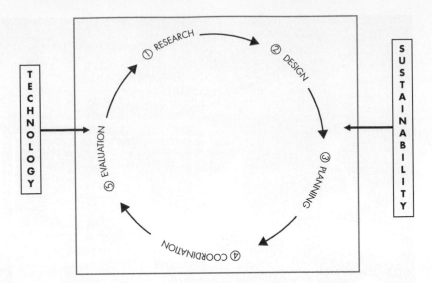

FIGURE 2.1b Lee–Goldblatt Expanded event planning five-phase process.

the business value of sustainability for the event industry is very critical to event leaders. In addition, current knowledge of event technology is key core competencies for event leaders to plan effective events. Therefore, today's event leaders should integrate technology and sustainability into these five stages considering their profound impacts and critical importance to the event industry. We developed an expanded model of the event planning five-stage process that reflect today's event planning (see Figure 2.1b). Throughout this book, we will discuss and share key trends and applicable practices in these two areas in each of five stages.

In addition, underpinning each of these stages should be the principles of social responsibility with its economic and social impact to event communities. In this chapter, we explore each phase to enable you to produce successful and sustainable events every time. For example, the U.S. National Football League created NFL Youth Education Towns (YET) as a means of leaving a lasting legacy in destinations where the NFL Super Bowl is conducted. The first YET center opened in Los Angeles, California, in 1993. Each YET center receives an initial grant from the NFL committee, and this grant is matched by local donations from both the public and private sectors.

Research

Excellent event research helps reduce future risk. The better the research you conduct prior to the event, the more likely you are to produce an event that matches the planned outcomes of organizers or stakeholders. For many years, public relations professionals and other marketing experts have realized the value of using research to pinpoint the needs, wants, desires, and expectations of prospective customers. Government leaders regularly conduct feasibility studies prior to authorizing capital investments. These feasibility studies include exhaustive research. An event is a product that is placed before members of the public with the reasonable expectation that they will attend. Therefore, it is imperative that you conduct careful and accurate consumer research to reduce the risk of nonattendance.

The three types of research that are used for pre-event research are quantitative, qualitative, or a mixed method (using both methods). Matching the research type to the event is important and which is the correct type is determined by the goals of the research, the time allowed for conducting the research, and the funds available. "Start with the end in mind" is very critical in professional event management. "End" means goals and objectives of an event. From the research stage, consider how to deliver the planned outcomes.

Market Research Techniques

Before bringing a new product or service to market, the inventor or manufacturer will conduct market research to determine the needs, wants, desires, and expectations of the target market. Whether your event is a new or a pre-existing product, market research is required to determine how to obtain the very best position in a sometimes crowded marketplace. Typically, qualitative and, in most cases, focus group research is used for this purpose.

Market research will help you determine the target or primary market as well as the secondary and tertiary markets for your event. Market research will also enable you to study the service levels expected by guests as well as the perceptions by internal stakeholders of the services currently being delivered. By studying the market in depth, you are able to spot emerging trends, develop new service-delivery systems, and solve minor problems before they become major catastrophes. One example of this is the event leader who discovered through research that attendees could not register for the upcoming convention during normal business hours due to workplace regulations. Therefore, she rapidly moved her registration channel to the Internet to allow 24/7 access for her members. This new service was a major success, and registrations for the conference increased tenfold.

Quantitative Pre-Event Research

Event leaders primarily use quantitative research to determine demographic information such as gender, age, income, and other pertinent facts about the future market for an event. This research is relatively inexpensive to conduct and easy to tabulate and analyze with computers. Figure 2.2 provides a model of a typical quantitative pre-event research survey.

Questions may be developed in two different styles. As noted in Figure 2.2, Question 4 uses a Likert scale to allow a respondent to select the response that states his or her opinion precisely. Question 5 uses a semantic differential scale to allow a respondent to select a point on a continuum between two opposing adjectives. The number that the respondent chooses indicates the likelihood of his or her attending or not attending an event.

In recent years, a paid panel data service has gained in popularity with event researchers. The challenge of research using surveys (both quantitative and qualitative) is lack of responses (low response rate) and significant numbers of incomplete returned surveys. The paid panel service by commercial companies (e.g., Qualtrics panel service) promotes themselves to guarantee sending surveys to qualified respondents based on researcher's criteria and a collection of a guaranteed number of complete data for a fee.

Qualitative Pre-Event Research

Market research consultants rely on qualitative research to probe for hidden meanings in quantitative studies. Qualitative research tells the research organization what is beneath the numbers in quantitative research and, therefore, is an important step

This survey will enable the organizers of XYZ event to determine the feasibility of producing the following event. Your participation is important in this effort. Answer all questions by checking the appropriate box. Return this survey by January 1, 2019.

1. Gender? ☐ Male ☐ Female
2. Age? ☐ Under 25 ☐ 26–34 ☐ 35–44 ☐ 45–60 ☐ 61 and over
3. Income? ☐ Under $24,999 ☐ $25,000–44,999 ☐ Over $45,000
4. If the event were held during the summer I would: (*Likert scale*)
   ☐ Not attend ☐ Maybe attend ☐ No opinion ☐ Probably attend
   ☐ Positively attend
5. If the event were held during the fall I would: (*semantic differential scale*)
   ☐ Not Attend ☐ 1 ☐ 2 ☐ 3 ☐ 4 ☐ 5 Positively attend
6. If you checked number 1 above, please describe your reasons for nonattendance in the space below: (*open-ended question*)

Return this survey by January 1, 2019 to:

Prof. Joe Goldblatt, Ed. D, FRSA or Queen Margaret University
Queen Margaret University Drive
Edinburgh, Scotland EH21 6UU
UK
To receive a free copy of the survey results, please include your business card or e-mail.
Prof. Seungwon "Shawn" Lee, PhD, DES
George Mason University
University Blvd., MS 4E5
Fairfax, VA 22032
USA

FIGURE 2.2 Quantitative pre-event survey model.

in the research process. This type of research may take the form of a focus group, participant observation, or a case study. Which is the proper methodology depends on your goals, the time available, and the funding.

The focus group typically comprises 8 to 12 people of similar background and experience who assemble for the purpose of discussion. A trained facilitator leads the group through specific questions that will provide clues to the goals or outcomes desired from the research. A focus group may be 1 hour in length, although, in most cases, they last between 90 minutes and 2 hours.

The participant observation style of qualitative research involves placing the researcher in a host community to participate in and observe the culture of those being studied. For example, if you desire to determine whether a certain destination is appropriate for relocation of an event, you may wish to visit that location, participate, and observe for an extended period of time before making a decision. Interviews with key informants are essential to this research.

The third type of qualitative research is the case study. In this style, an existing event is singled out as a specific case to be studied in depth. The event may be studied from a historical context, or the stakeholders may be interviewed to determine how personality, skill, and other factors drive the success of the event.

Photo by Joe Goldblatt

The sign above this sustainable restroom hand dryer reminds guests to complete an evaluation survey.

MeetingMetrics

A leading innovator in measurement, assessment, and evaluation of meetings and events is the firm MeetingMetrics (www.meetingmetrics.com). The founder, Ira Kerns, worked for many years as a producer of meetings and events and recognized the critical need to more carefully and authentically evaluate these programs.

Therefore, Kerns and his colleagues developed the MeetingMetrics system, which incorporates a dashboard of tools, including the discovery, pre-meeting, pulse, and post-meeting evaluation. During the discovery phase, the event leader may convene a virtual focus panel to help develop questions for a pre- and post-meeting/event survey. Discovery uses open-ended questions, similar to the focus panel methodology to help the planner identify issues and concerns that may be addressed later in the quantitatively designed pre- and post-meeting evaluation questions.

One of the major benefits of MeetingMetrics is that, loaded into the software, it has thousands of questions that may be selected for use in any of the survey phases, which simplifies the work of the meeting and event leader immensely. However, any question may be changed or entirely new questions may be submitted as well.

The entire system is Internet driven, so the survey respondents receive an introductory e-mail from the event organizer, alerting them that they are being asked to participate in a survey. The names, contact details, and profiles of the respondents are captured in Excel™ and then uploaded into the MeetingMetrics framework. MeetingMetrics automatically sends out the survey to the respondents within a schedule set by the event organizer. Finally, MeetingMetrics will then automatically produce detailed reports, including charts and graphs to demonstrate the difference between the event attendees' expectations and final perception of the event. Although the most popular phases are the discovery, pre- and post-meeting surveys, the pulse survey may be used to take the pulse of the event if the planning period is lengthy, to make certain the program elements are still tracking closely the needs of the attendees.

MeetingMetrics is a very profound example of how technology is enabling meeting and event leaders to better align their final products with the expectations of their attendees. Measurement, assessment, and evaluation are not only the wave of the future for meeting and event leaders but also the best way to justify future investment in your program and yourself (increased pay, bonuses, and other performance-based rewards).

The case study enables the event researcher to draw conclusions based on the research gleaned from a comparable event.

Mixed Research Methods

In most cases, event leaders use a combination of quantitative and qualitative research to make decisions about future events. Event leaders obtain large volumes of information in a cost-efficient manner using the quantitative method and then probe for hidden meanings and subtle feelings using the qualitative approach.

Effective quantitative research includes elements of qualitative research to increase the validity of the questions. Event leaders should use a small focus group or team of experts to review the questions before conducting a survey. These experts can confirm that a question is understandable and valid for the research being conducted. Figure 2.3 provides a simple way for event leaders to determine what research methodology is most effective for their purpose.

The goals and required outcomes of the research, combined with the time frame and funding available, will ultimately determine the best method for your pre-event research. Regardless of the type of research you conduct, it is important that you take care to produce valid and reliable information.

Goal	Method
Collect gender, age, and income data	Written survey
Collect attitudes and opinions	Focus group
Examine culture of community	Participant/observer
Identify comparable characteristics	Case study
Collect demographic and psychographic data	Combined methods

FIGURE 2.3 Selecting the appropriate pre-event research method.

Validity and Reliability: Producing Credible Pre-Event Research

All research must be defended. After you have decided, "What is it we need to know to be more successful?" and conducted discovery and pre-event surveys, your stakeholders will ask you bluntly, "How do you now know that you know?" If your research has high validity and reliability, you can provide greater assurance that your work is truthful. Validity primarily confirms that your research measures what it purports to measure. For example, if you are trying to determine if senior citizens will attend an event, you must include senior citizens in your sample of respondents to ensure validity. Furthermore, the questions you pose to these seniors must be understandable to them to ensure that their responses are truthful and accurate.

Reliability helps prove that your research will remain truthful and accurate over time. For example, if you were to conduct the same study with another group of senior citizens, would the answers be significantly different? If the answer is yes, your data may not be reliable. Designing a collection instrument that has high validity and reliability is a challenging and time-consuming task. You may wish to contact a university or college hospitality, tourism, and event management research faculty or marketing, psychology, or sociology department for assistance from an experienced researcher in developing your instrument. Often, university faculty will gladly assist you in forming of research project and can arrange a senior-level undergraduate student or a graduate student to help you develop the instrument and collect and analyze the data for college credit. The participation of the university or college will add credibility to your findings. Use software applications such as Microsoft Excel for analyzing data. For more complex analysis, use statistical applications such as SAS, Minitab, and SPSS.

Interpreting and Communicating Research Findings

Designing and collecting pre-event research is only the beginning of this important phase. Once you have analyzed the data carefully and identified the implications of your research, as well as provided some recommendations based on your study, you must present the information to your stakeholders. The way that you do this will determine the level of influence you wield with stakeholders.

If the stakeholders are academics or others who have a research background, using tables or a written narrative may suffice. However, if, as is most often the case, the stakeholders are unsophisticated with regard to advanced research methodology, using graphs, charts, and other visual tools to illustrate your findings can be more effective. To paraphrase Confucius, "One picture is certainly worth a thousand numerals." Use these five steps to present your pre-event research findings to stakeholders effectively:

1. Determine your audience and customize your presentation to their personal communication learning style.
2. Describe the purpose and importance of the research.
3. Explain how the research was collected and describe any limitations.
4. Reveal your findings and emphasize the key points with practical implications.
5. Invite questions.

Distributing a well-produced written narrative with copies of the information you are presenting (e.g., graphs from slides) will be helpful to the stakeholders, as they will need more time for independent study before posing intelligent questions. In the written narrative, include a section describing the steps you have taken to produce research that demonstrates high validity and reliability; also list any independent organizations, such as universities or colleges, that reviewed your study prior to completion.

Communicating your research findings is an essential phase in the research process. Prepare, rehearse, and then reveal your data thoughtfully and confidently. Summarize your presentation by demonstrating how the findings support the goals and objectives of your research plan.

The Five Ws

- WHY is this event occurring? What are the client's motivations? What are the participants' needs? What is the social or cultural purpose for this event? What is the compelling reason for conducting this event?
- WHO is the event for? Who is the client? Who are the participants? Who are the sponsors? Who are all of the event stakeholders?
- WHEN should the event occur? When is most convenient for the client? When is most convenient for participants? When will this event have optimum impact? When comes before where because the date and time of the event may affect feasibility through elements such as cost due to weather conditions.
- WHERE should the event occur? Where is the client? Where are the participants? Where is the best location for everyone?
- WHAT are the outcomes you wish to achieve and the obstacles that you may encounter?
- Once these five questions have been answered thoroughly, it is necessary to turn your deliberations to how the organization will allocate scarce resources to produce maximum benefit for the stakeholders. SWOT (strengths, weaknesses, opportunities, threats) analysis provides a comprehensive tool for ensuring that you review each step systematically.

SWOT Analysis: Finding the Strengths, Weaknesses, Opportunities, and Threats of Your Event

Prior to the start of planning the event, you usually must implement SWOT analysis to underpin your decision-making. SWOT analysis assists you in identifying the internal and external variables that may prevent the event from achieving maximum success. The SWOT analysis is not the first step in research but it must be completed prior to designing the event to make certain you have comprehensively evaluated all of the internal and exogenous variables that could affect your outcomes.

TECH/APPVIEW

Location, Location, Location

Where an event should occur is one of the most important decisions you will make. Consider this: Attendees often spend more time traveling to and from an event than they do at the actual event itself. By reducing their travel time, you may improve their overall experience of the event.

Central locations with multiple transit links make it easy for attendees to get to your event. You may have found an excellent venue with a low hiring cost, but if it's an hour's drive outside of town, the location might put people off. Look for the most central, convenient location first, and only then look for possible venues. Did you know that urban venues can be the most environmentally friendly? Rural venues require car travel and excessive carbon emissions, but urban venues can capitalize on public transportation and mass transit to lower carbon emissions.

One of the technology tools to search for green event resources is The Best Places to Meet Green. It is an easy-to-use website provided by MeetGreen, a sustainable meetings firm, to help meeting planners and clients find sustainable destinations. This catalog of environmentally friendly destinations is continually updated, and uses many different criteria, such as the number of bicycle lanes, public parks, and public transit stations.

Strengths and Weaknesses The strengths and weaknesses of an event are primary considerations that can be spotted before the event actually takes place. Typical strengths and weaknesses of many events are shown in Figure 2.4. The strengths and weaknesses may be uncovered through a focus group or through individual interviews with the major stakeholders. If the weaknesses outnumber the strengths and there is no reasonable way to eliminate the weaknesses and increase the strengths within the event planning period, you may wish to postpone or cancel the event.

Opportunities and Threats Opportunities and threats are two key factors that generally present themselves either during an event or after it has occurred. However, during the research process, these factors should be considered seriously, as they may spell potential disaster for the event. Opportunities are activities that may be of benefit to an event without significant investment by your organization. One example is that of selecting a year in which to hold an event that coincides with your community's or industry's 100th anniversary. Your event may benefit from additional funding, publicity, and other important resources simply by aligning yourself with this hallmark event. Other possible beneficial outcomes, sometimes indirect, are considered opportunities, such as the potential to contribute to the political image of the event's host.

Threats are activities that prevent you from maximizing the potential of an event. The most obvious threat is weather; however, political threats may be just as devastating. Local political leaders must buy into your civic event to ensure cooperation with all agencies. Political infighting may quickly destroy your planning. For example, the film director Steven Spielberg withdrew as artistic director from the 2008 Beijing Olympic Games because of his opposition to China's political positions on human rights. Terrorism and violence have become increasingly important threats to consider since September 11, 2001. The threat of violence erupting at an event may keep people from attending. On the evening of July 14, 2016, a 19-ton cargo truck was deliberately driven into crowds of people celebrating Bastille Day on the Promenade des Anglais in Nice, France, resulting in the deaths of 86 people and the injury of 458 others. The 2017 terrorist bombing attack during a concert at Manchester Arena in

Strengths	Weaknesses
Strong funding	Weak funding
Good potential for sponsors	No potential for sponsors
Well-trained staff	Poorly trained staff
Many volunteers	Few volunteers
Good media relations	Poor media relations
Excellent site	Weak site

FIGURE 2.4 Event strengths and weaknesses.

Opportunities	Threats
Civic anniversary	Hurricanes and tornadoes
Chamber of Commerce promotion	Political infighting
Celebrity appearance	Violence from terrorism
Align with environmental cause	Alcoholic consumption
Tie-in with media	Site in bad neighborhood
Winning elections	Celebrity canceling or not attending
Developing more loyal employees	Food poisoning

FIGURE 2.5 Event opportunities and threats.

England was another example of threats to become a reality. A celebrity canceling or not attending can also create a significant threat to the success of an event. Typical opportunities and threats for an event are listed in Figure 2.5.

You will note that, although strengths and weaknesses are often related, opportunities and threats need not be. Once again, in making a decision to proceed with event planning, your goal is to identify more opportunities than threats. All threats should be considered carefully, and experts should be consulted to determine ways in which threats may be contained, reduced, or eliminated.

SWOT analysis (see Figure 2.6) is a major strategic-planning tool during the research phase. By using SWOT analysis, an event leader can not only scan the internal and external event environment but also proceed to the next step, which involves analyses of the weaknesses and threats, and provide solutions to improve the event planning process.

The research phase of the event administration process is perhaps the most critical one. During this period, you will determine through empirical research whether you have both the internal and external resources essential to produce an effective event. Your ability to select the appropriate research methodology, design the instrument, and collect, analyze, interpret, and present the data will ultimately determine whether an event has sufficient strength for future success. The first pillar of the event planning process—research—rests squarely in the center of the other four supporting columns. Although each phase is equal in importance, the future success of an event depends on how well you conduct the research phase.

Design: The Blueprint for Success

Having researched your event thoroughly and determined that it is feasible, time may now be allotted to use the right side of the brain—the creative capacity—to create a general blueprint for your ideas. There are numerous ways to begin this process, but it is important to remember that the very best event designers are

Known S = strengths		
1. Strong funding 2. Well-trained staff 3. Event well-respected by media	Internal Internal External	
Known W = weaknesses		
1. Weak funding 2. Few human resources 3. Poor public-relations history	Internal Internal External	
Potential O = opportunities		
1. Simultaneous celebration of a congruent event 2. Timing of event congruent with future budget allocation	External Internal	
Potential T = threats		
1. Weather 2. New board of directors leading this event	External Internal	

FIGURE 2.6 SWOT analysis.

constantly visiting the library, attending movies and plays, visiting art galleries, and reviewing periodicals to maintain their inspiration. This continuous research for new ideas will further strengthen the activities you propose for an event.

Brainstorming and Mind Mapping

Meeting and event planning is a creative art. Remember to use your imagination and think outside the box. Begin the design process with a group brainstorming session. Remind your group that there are no bad ideas, and that the goal is to come up with something new. Draw on ideas from art, music, literature, technology, and current events to inspire discussion on new event designs. If one member (or more than one member) tends to dominate the discussion, ask him or her to summarize and then say "Thank you" as you quickly move on to others to solicit their ideas. Use the flip chart to list all the initial ideas, and do not try to establish categories or provide any other organizational structure.

Mind mapping allows an event leader to begin to pull together the random ideas and establish linkages that will later lead to logical decision making. Using the flip chart, ask each member of the group to revisit his or her earlier ideas, and begin to link them to the four Ws and ultimately help you see how the event should be developed. Write Why? Who? When? Where? What? and How? in the center of a circle on a separate page of the chart. From this circle, draw spokes that terminate in another circle. Leave the circles at the end of each spoke empty. The ideas of your team members will fill these circles, and they will begin to establish linkages between the goal (Why? Who? When? Where? What? and How?) and the creative method. Figure 2.7 is an example of a successful event mind-mapping activity.

Mind mapping is an effective way to synthesize the various ideas suggested by group members and begin to construct an event philosophy. The event philosophy will determine the financial, cultural, social, and other important aspects of the

Why?	+	Who?	+	When?	+	Where?	+	What?
What is the compelling reason for this event? Why must this event be held?		Who will benefit from this event? Who will they want to have attend?		When will the event be held? Are the date and time flexible or subject to change?		What are the best destination, location, and venue?		What elements and resources are required to satisfy the needs identified?
				**= How?**				
		Given answers to the five Ws, how do you effectively research, design, plan, coordinate, and evaluate this event?						

FIGURE 2.7 Event Leadership needs assessment.

event. For example, if the sponsoring organization is a not-for-profit group, the financial philosophy will not support charging high fees to produce a disproportionate amount of funds, or the tax status may be challenged. Mind mapping allows you to sift through the ideas carefully and show how they support the goals of the event. As you do this, an event philosophy begins to emerge. Those ideas that do not have a strong linkage or do not support the event philosophy should be placed on a separate sheet of flip chart page for future use.

Dr. Cathy Matheson, a senior lecturer and founder at the Queen Margaret University event management program, uses mind mapping to coalesce and analyze ideas that she identifies while participating in professional meetings. She creates a core theoretical or topical element in the center of her mind map and then links all of the key elements to this core. Finally, she assesses each of the key elements to identify commonalities and linkages. Figure 2.8 is an example of how the mind map process may be used in the event design context.

The Creative Process in Event Planning

Special events require people with the ability to move easily between the left and right quadrants of the cerebellum. The right side of the brain is responsible for creative, spontaneous thinking, while the left side of the brain handles the more

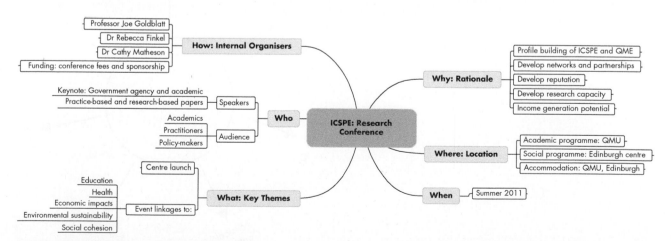

FIGURE 2.8 Mind mapping applied to event design.

logical aspects of our lives. To function effectively, event leaders must be both right- and left-brained.

Therefore, if you have determined that one side of your brain is less strong than the other, you must take steps to correct this to achieve maximum success in Event Leadership. Here are seven tips for continuously developing your creativity:

1. Surf the Internet for new event models, theories, designs, scenarios, products, and services.
2. Visit one art gallery each month.
3. Attend a live performance of opera, theater, or dance each month.
4. Read great works of literature, on a continuing basis.
5. Join a book discussion group to explore ideas about the literature you are reading.
6. Enroll in a music, dance, literature, visual arts, or acting class or discussion group.
7. Play video games that promote creative decision-making.

Apply what you are discovering in each of these fields, where appropriate, to your design of planned events.

Perhaps the best way to stretch your creativity continually is to surround yourself with highly creative people (see Figure 2.9). Whether you are in a position to hire creative people or must seek creative types through groups outside the office, you must find the innovators in order to practice innovation.

Malcolm Gladwell, the author of the bestselling books, *The Tipping Point*, *Blink*, and *The Outliers*, sees the world through a prism of patterns and intuition. He describes his work as that of writing "intellectual adventure stories." For example, Gladwell states that through the process of rapid cognition such as just looking around a person's bedroom, you may learn a great deal about the individual. Gladwell argues in his latest book, *The Outliers*, that, if an individual devotes 10,000 or more hours to mastering their craft, they will rapidly develop greater self-confidence and be perceived by others as an authority.

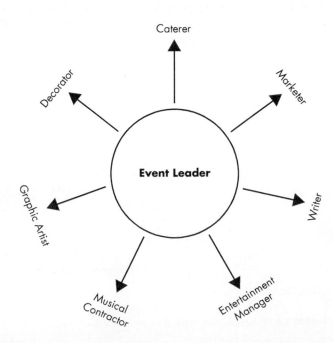

FIGURE 2.9 Creative influences.

Therefore, extensive professional experience (practice) and the acquisition of educational credentials through formal study are both essential, if you are going to design a sustainable career in planned events. The modern events industry demands rapid cognition in order for a person to remain competitive. Therefore, surround yourself with visionaries and gurus like Malcolm Gladwell, and your intellectual and creative bedroom decor will tell the world a lot about your curiosity and continuous pursuit of knowledge and wisdom.

Making the Perfect Host/Guest Match

Once you have completed the brainstorming and mind-mapping activities satisfactorily, it is time to make certain that your creative ideas perfectly match the goals and objectives of your event. This is accomplished through needs assessment and analysis.

Needs assessment and analysis enables you to create an event that closely satisfies the needs of your stakeholders. You actually began this process by asking "Why?" and "Who?" Now it is time to take it one giant step forward and survey the stakeholders to determine if your creative solutions will satisfy their needs.

To accomplish this part of the design phase, develop your ideas into a series of questions, query the key constituents for the event, and determine if the various elements you have created, from advertising to decor, from catering to entertainment, and everything in between, meet their expectations. Once you are confident that you have assessed the needs of the stakeholders adequately and confirmed that you have, through analysis, determined how to meet these needs, you are well-prepared to confirm the final feasibility of your event design.

Is It Feasible? Feasibility simply means that you have looked at the event design objectively to determine if what you propose is practical given the resources available. This is the final checkpoint before actual planning begins and, therefore, must be given adequate time for review. Municipalities often engage professional engineers or other consultants to conduct lengthy feasibility studies before approving new construction or other capital expenditures. Although you may not need a battery of consultants, it is important for you to review all previous steps thoroughly when determining the feasibility of an event plan.

The three basic resources that will be required are financial, human, and political. Each of these resources may have varying degrees of importance, depending on the nature of the event. For example, a for-profit or large hallmark event will require significant financial investment to succeed. A not-for-profit event will rely on an army of volunteers, and, therefore, the human element is more important. A civic event will require greater political resources to accomplish.

Therefore, when assessing and analyzing feasibility, first determine in what proportions resources will be required for the event. You may wish to weigh each resource to help prepare your analysis.

Financial Considerations You will want to know if sufficient financial resources are available to sustain development and implementation of the event. Furthermore, you must consider what will happen if the event loses money. How will creditors be paid? You will also want to know what resources you can count on for an immediate infusion of cash, should the event require this to continue development. Finally, you must carefully analyze the cash-flow projections for the event to determine how much time is to be allowed between payables and receivables.

The Human Dimension In assessing the feasibility of an event, you must not only know where your human resources will come from but also how they will be rewarded (financially or through intangibles, such as awards and recognition). Most importantly, you must know how they will work together as an efficient event team.

Politics as Usual The increasingly important role of government leaders in event oversight must be viewed with a practiced eye. Politicians see events as both good (opportunities for publicity, constituent communications, and economic impact) and bad (drain on municipal services and potential for disaster). When designing civic events, it is particularly important that you understand and enlist the support of politicians and their bureaucratic staff to ensure smooth cooperation for your event. Furthermore, for all events, it is essential that you carefully research the permitting process to determine if the event you have designed is feasible according to the codes within the jurisdiction where the event will be held.

The Approval Process

The research and design phases add to the event history once an event is approved. The approval process may be as simple as an acceptance by the client or as complex as requiring dozens of signatures from various city agencies that will interact with the event. Regardless of the simplicity or complexity of this step, you should view it as an important milestone that, once crossed, assures you that the plan has been reviewed and deemed reasonable and feasible, and has a high likelihood of success. All roads lead to official approval, whether in the form of a contract or as individual permits from each agency. Without official approval, an event remains a dream. The process for turning dreams into workable plans requires careful research, thoughtful design, and critical analysis. This could be called the planning to plan phase, because it involves so many complex steps related to the next phase. However, once the approval is granted, you are on your way to the next important phase: the actual planning period.

Project Management Systems for Event Leaders

According to William O' Toole and Phyllis Mikolaitis, CSEP, the authors of *Corporate Event Project Management* (Wiley 2002), there are several reasons why project management offers you unique resources for improving your practice. Using a project management system will help you establish a systematic approach to all events. Like the Goldblatt–Lee five phases of Event Leadership (Figure 2.1b), the project management system provides you with a superstructure to enable you to systematically approach every event using the same framework.

It is strongly suggested to learn about international sustainable event standards and measurements that can provide guidance in implementing your future events. Event Industry Council launched its certificate course for Sustainable Event Professional in 2017.

Many events, especially those in the social market, are often driven by emotional decisions rather than systematic or logical approaches. The project management system will help depersonalize the event as it provides you with an objective process for reviewing the event development.

> ### ECOLOGIC
>
> #### Is It Sustainable?
>
> Sustainability means looking at the big picture. What impact will your event have on the environment in 100 years' time? Will there be no impact, positive impact, or negative impact? How can you reduce the negative impact? How could you create a positive impact?
>
> For instance, an event that requires excess car travel, uses excess electricity from coal-powered sources, and generates excess landfill waste will certainly have a negative impact on the environment in 100 years' time. By reducing these harmful emissions and pollution, you may be able to reduce your impact. Additionally, you may be able to change the opinions of your attendees, other event leaders, and their descendants for years to come. By showing the world how to reduce environmental impact, your event might change the way events are produced 100 years from now.
>
> When considering sustainability, remember not just to imagine your event in 5 or 10 years' time but also to imagine it in 100 or even 200 years' time. Is your event doing the right thing for future generations?

Communication is critical throughout the event planning process, and the project management system will help you facilitate clear communications with stakeholders from many different fields. Today, electronic communications (e.g., e-mail, text, Twitter, Facebook, and Instagram) have positioned themselves as the main communication channel among planners, attendees, and suppliers. Event apps also integrate communications among stakeholders. Through meetings (both face-to-face and virtual) and documents, project management provides a transparent system to promote better communications.

Planning Consistently Professional Events

The planning period is typically the longest period of time in the event planning process. Historically, this has been the result of disorganization. Disorganization is best characterized by frequent changes resulting from substitutions, additions, or even deletions due to poor research and design. Ideally, the better the research and design, the simpler and briefer the planning period will be. Since events are planned by human beings for other human beings, this theory is fraught with exceptions. However, your goal should be to develop a smooth planning process based on careful research and design procedures. The planning phase involves using the time/space/tempo laws (see Figure 2.10) to determine how best to use your immediate resources. These three basic laws will affect every decision you make; how well you make use of them will govern the final outcome of an event.

Timing

The law of timing refers to how much time you have in which to act or react. The first question that many event leaders ask the client is: When would you like to schedule the event? The answer to that question tells you how much time you have to prepare. Often, that timetable may seem incredibly short.

The length of time available for planning and for actual production will dramatically affect the cost, and sometimes the success, of the event. Equally important, as

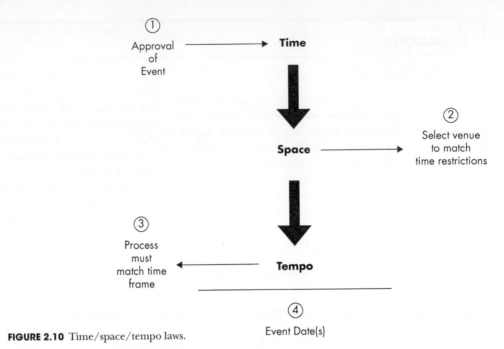

FIGURE 2.10 Time/space/tempo laws.

you discovered earlier, is how you use your time. According to the Greek philosopher Theophrastus, "Time is the most valuable thing a human can spend."

When budgeting time for a proposed event, some independent event leaders estimate the amount of time necessary for pre-event client meetings, site inspections, meetings with vendors, ongoing communications and contract preparations, actual event time from time of arrival through departure, and post-event billable time. You may wish to allocate your billable time to correspond to the five phases of the event process: research, design, planning, coordination, and evaluation.

Because you can only estimate the time involved in these tasks, you must add a contingency time factor to each phase. Mona Meretsky, president of Comcor Event and Meeting Production Inc. of Ft. Lauderdale, Florida (www.comcoreevents.com), believes that using a 10 percent contingency factor will help you cover extra time required but not originally projected.

However, the contingency factor may need to be adjusted based upon the level of uncertainty regarding your final event plan. For example, the London 2012 Olympic Games contingency plan involved millions of pounds. Therefore, one good rule to follow is that the contingency budget should not be so large as to raise suspicion among the stakeholders that you have not carefully reviewed, researched, and justified all expenditures.

Space

The law of space refers to both the physical space where an event will be held and the time between critical decisions pertaining to the event. The relationship of timing to space is one that is constant throughout the entire event process.

For the 1988 Super Bowl half-time show, Radio City Music Hall Productions designed an elaborate show featuring 88 grand pianos. Suddenly, without warning, the day before the actual production, the producer was instructed that his setup time for the production was reduced to only a few minutes. Further complicating matters, the groundskeepers at the stadium raised serious concerns that the movement of the pianos onto the field would affect the turf on the field. In this example and numerous others, the actual physical space governs the time required for various elements of the event.

When selecting a venue for an event, the location and physical resources present will significantly affect the additional time that must be invested. If you select a historic mansion with elaborate permanent decor, less time will be required to decorate the site. By comparison, if you select a four-walled venue, such as a hotel or convention center (where you are literally renting the four walls), significant time and expense must be invested to create a proper atmosphere for the event.

When considering the space for an event, some event leaders prepare an elaborate checklist to review each element carefully. The checklist should reflect the goals and objectives of the event and not merely replicate a form you have copied for convenience.

One of the primary considerations when selecting space is the age and type of guest who will be attending. Older guests may not be able to tolerate extreme temperatures, and this may preclude you from selecting an outdoor venue. For events with young children, you may or may not wish to select a site in a busy urban setting. Go back to the research and needs assessment phase, and review why this event is important and who the stakeholders are, then select a venue specifically to match their needs, wants, and expectations.

The terms ingress (entrance) and egress (exit) are important concepts when reviewing a potential venue. *Ingress* defines the entrances or access to the venue, and *egress* refers to the exits or evacuation routes. When considering ingress and egress, you must consider not only people, including those with disabilities, but also vehicles, props, possibly animals, and indeed any element that must enter or exit the site. You must also keep in mind the time available for ingress or egress, as this will determine the number of portals (doors) that may need to be available for this purpose.

Parking, public transportation, and other forms of transportation, including taxis, limousines, and tour buses, must also be considered when analyzing a site. These considerations should include the number of parking spaces, including those for the disabled, the availability and security/safety of public transportation, and the time required to dispatch a taxi.

Tempo

The final law of event planning is concerned with the rate or tempo at which events take place during both production planning and the event itself. From the moment the client approves an agreement or authorizes you to proceed with planning to the final meeting, you must be aware of the projected rate at which events will happen. Improved technology, such as faxes and online services, has dramatically accelerated the process and the demands of clients to "do it now."

However, "now" is often not as efficient as later. When an event leader is pressured to deliver a product before it is fully developed, the results may be less than exemplary. Therefore, as you manage the rate at which tasks will be completed and events will occur, it is important to consider if each action is being performed at the best time. "Maybe" is not an acceptable response. To determine if this is the best moment for this task to be handled, ask yourself if you have sufficient information and resources to implement it. If not, try to delay the action until you are better prepared.

Establishing the proper tempo is not an exact science. Rather, like a conductor of an orchestra, you must allow your personal taste, energy, and experience to guide you as you speed up or slow down the tempo as required. By analyzing the event site and estimating the time required for a project, the event leader is better able to set the tempo or schedule for the setup, production, and removal of the equipment. Without this advance analysis, the event leader becomes an orchestra conductor without benefit of a score, a musician without benefit of a maestro.

Understanding the needs of guests also helps establish and adjust the tempo during an event. If guests are concerned primarily with networking, a leisurely time frame should be followed to allow for plenty of interaction. For example, while the transition from cocktails to dinner may be brisk when the program is more important than networking, the transition may be slowed when the emphasis is on the connections the audience members make among themselves.

Jerry Edwards, CPCE, past president of the National Association of Catering Executives (Now known as National Association for Catering and Events NACE), and owner of Chef's Expressions, Inc., in Timonium, Maryland, is convinced that the best event leaders are those who are focused on quality outcomes for their guests. "I was very fortunate to own a business in the era of high demand, and I was able to continually upgrade my staff. Now, thanks to The Food Channel and other food-related programming, customers are more sophisticated and demanding," says Edwards.

When Edwards began his catering business, there was little information regarding high-end catering or ethnic menus. Today, due to changing tastes, everyone is concerned with the food components and the final presentation. In terms of changing tastes, Edwards reports that the use of full-liquor bars is up by 21 percent in his events. "Perhaps the nostalgia exhibited by the baby boomers has brought back the name-brand or call liquor consumption. They will actually pay for liquor but may not pay as much for food. Nine out of ten will ask for liquor by brand name. The drink reflects personal taste, sophistication, and success," says Edwards. The three-term president of NACE said that he learned the catering business through the NACE meetings he attended. His involvement in NACE helped take his business from $500,000 to over $2 million per year in revenues.

As Edwards envisioned back then, through professional organizations such as NACE, event leaders now earn credentials from either certifications or college degrees or certificates at both undergraduate and graduate levels and that specific career paths are identified for young people to help them break the glass ceiling that continues to exist in the hospitality industry. Finally, he believes that human nature plays a significant role in developing event leaders and that schools and associations must work more closely to promote leadership development.

"We need to begin developing the next level of event leaders in the catering industry, and we can do this best by working together to help ensure the future for our profession," suggests the man who bought a small lunch counter for $2,000 and then developed a multimillion-dollar off-premise catering enterprise while serving as a leader for one of the industry's major associations.

These three basic laws—timing, space, and tempo—are as old as human creation itself and govern the planning of all events. To become an expert event leader, you must master your ability to manage time in the most minute segments. You must develop the vision to perceive the strengths, weaknesses, opportunities, and threats of every space. Finally, you must be able to analyze the needs of your guests to set tempos that will ensure a memorable event.

Gap Analysis

Too often, event leaders proceed by rote memory to produce an event in a style with which they are most familiar. In doing this, they often overlook critical gaps in the logical progression of event elements. Identifying these gaps and providing recommendations for closure is the primary purpose of gap analysis.

This planning tool involves taking a long, hard look at event elements and identifying significant gaps in the planning that could weaken the overall progression of the plan. An example is an event leader who has scheduled an outdoor event in September in Miami Beach, Florida. September is the prime month of the hurricane season. The event leader has created a wide gap in his or her plan that must be closed to strengthen the overall event. Therefore, finding a secure indoor location in case of a weather emergency would be a good beginning toward closing this gap. Another example can be hosting a national or international event in a city such as Chicago during winter storm season. As its nickname is "Windy City," Chicago's potential winter snowstorms can be a risky weather circumstance to an international event where most attendees arrive by an airplane. Therefore, finding a mild weather destination or hosting a regional event that requires less air or car transportation for attendees can be a plan to reduce a gap.

Use a critical friend—a person whose expertise about the particular event is known to you—to review your plan and search for gaps in your logical thinking. Once you have identified the gaps, look for opportunities to close them. By implementing the findings from SWOT and gap analyses, you are able to begin executing your plan. This execution phase is known as coordination.

Coordination: Executing the Event Plan

As the light turns green, the tempo accelerates, and now you are faced with coordinating the minute-by-minute activities of the event itself. Joe was once asked, "What does it take to be a competent event leader?". "The ability to make good decisions," he swiftly answered. Joe realizes now that it requires much more than good decision-making ability. However, it is also true that, during the course of coordinating an event, you will be required to make not dozens but hundreds of decisions. Your ability to use your professional training and experience to make the correct decision will affect the outcome of the entire event. While it is true that event leaders should maintain a positive attitude and see problems as challenges in search of the right solution, it is also important that you apply critical analysis to every challenge that comes your way. These six steps provide simple but effective ways to make these decisions:

1. Collect all the information. Most problems have many sides to review.
2. Consider the pros and cons of your decision in terms of who will be affected.
3. Consider the financial implications of your decision.
4. Consider the moral and ethical implications of your decision.
5. Do no harm. Your decision must not harm others or yourself, if at all possible.
6. Make the decision and continue looking forward.

Evaluation: The Link to the Next Event

The event planning process, as shown in Figure 2.11, is a dynamic spiral that is literally without end. The first phase—research—is connected with the last—evaluation. In this last phase, you will ask: "What is it we wish to evaluate, and how will we best accomplish this?" You can evaluate events by each part of the event planning process or through a general comprehensive review of all phases. It is up to you and your stakeholders to decide what information you require to improve your planning and then implement effective strategies to accomplish this phase.

Perhaps the most common form of event evaluation is the written survey. Usually, the survey is conducted immediately following the event, to identify the satisfaction level of the participants and spectators. As with any evaluation method, there are pros and cons to immediate feedback. One bias is the immediate nature of the feedback, which prohibits respondents from digesting the total event experience before providing feedback.

Another form of evaluation is the use of monitors. A monitor is a trained person who will observe an element of the event and provide both written and verbal feedback to the event leader. The event monitor usually has a checklist or survey to complete and will then offer additional comments as required. The benefit of this type of evaluation is that it permits a trained, experienced event staff member or volunteer to observe the event objectively while it is taking place and provide instructive comments.

The third form of event evaluation is the telephone or mail survey conducted after the event. In this evaluation, the event leader surveys the spectators and participants after the event through either a mail or a telephone survey. By waiting a few days after the event to collect these data, the event leader is able to glean from the respondents how their attitudes have changed and developed after some time has passed since participating in the event.

A new form of evaluation that is growing in popularity is the pre- and post-event survey. This evaluation allows an event leader to determine the respondents' knowledge, opinions, and other important information both before and after their attendance at an event. This is especially helpful when trying to match expectations to reality. For example, an event guest may state upon entering an event that he or she expects, based on the advertising and public relations, to enjoy nonstop

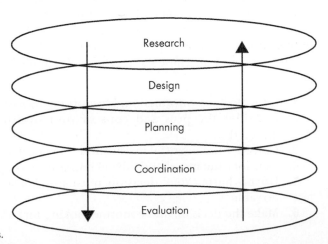

FIGURE 2.11 Planned event process.

entertainment. However, upon completing the exit interview, the guest registers disappointment because of the gaps in the programming. This type of evaluation helps event organizers close the gap between overpromising and underdelivering certain aspects of an event. Registration mail-in rebates and other incentives may be offered for filling out both surveys.

Professor Helmut Schwagermann lectures at the Osnabrück University of Applied Sciences in Germany. A longtime veteran of the global meeting industry, Schwagermann has developed an original theory to control the outcome of events.

He recommends that the control of events take place in three phases:

1. Control the event concept in a pre-event test.
2. Control the event during the process itself using what he describes as the "in-between test."
3. Control the results of the event through a post-test. During this post-test, ask questions such as: Did the event satisfy the economic results and strategic communication goals?

Schwagermann cautions that so-called hard economic facts such as profits are not always justified. Long-term effects, such as changes in opinions and behavior, as well as the effect on remembering and emotional excitement, can be measured with instruments of comprehensive event marketing research.

This event planning process is the conceptual framework for every effective event. The process is dynamic and selective, in that the event leader must determine where to begin and how to proceed to best accomplish the objectives.

One event may be past the research stage, and the event leader may be retained merely to coordinate the elements. Still another may be midway through the planning phase. The effective event leader will immediately recognize that the event process cannot be complete or totally effective unless each phase is considered carefully. It does not matter where you begin the process. What is essential is that every phase be considered, visited, and understood.

ECOLOGIC

The Triple Bottom Line

Leo Jago, deputy chief executive officer and director of research of the Australian federal government's Sustainable Tourism Cooperative Research Center, has similarly conceived and tested a new Triple Bottom Line theory for event evaluation. According to Jago, events cannot be measured or evaluated in strictly economic terms. Rather, he recommends a triple bottom line evaluation process that includes comprehensive analysis of the economic, sociocultural, and ecological outcomes of the event.

The event evaluations standards being established in Australia may be the direct results of the successful Summer Olympic Games of 2000, which were held in Sydney. In preparation for the games, the Sydney Organizing Committee for the Olympic Games developed, in cooperation with the International Olympic Committee (IOC) and Monash University, an information-sharing and knowledge transfer program.

The IOC requires every official organizing committee to provide a final comprehensive report. However, the Sydney Olympic Games were the first time this process was coordinated in a systematic process, which was originally called "Athena" in honor of the Greek goddess of knowledge and wisdom. As a result of the Sydney initiatives, the IOC has formalized the knowledge transfer process as part of their Olympic Games operations plan.

When evaluating your event, remember to also analyze the cultural and environmental impacts alongside the profitability.

TECH/APPVIEW

Research: MeetingMetrics
Design: Pinterest (sharing visual ideas), Google Docs (collaborating on a shared document), MeetingMatrix, SocialTable (floor design), ExpoCad (tradeshow diagram), WebEx (virtual meeting for a collaboration)
Planning: Convene, EventPro (scheduling), CVENT Suppliers Network (site selection)

Coordination: DoubleDutch (attendees engagement and push notifications), on-site volunteer management
Evaluation: MeetingMetrics (ROI measurement), SurveyMonkey (online survey), Qualtrics

Communication: The Tie That Binds All Stakeholders Together

Event planning is a profession whose success or failure ratio often depends on people's ability to communicate effectively with one another. It does not matter whether this communication is oral, written, electronic, or all three. What is important is that event leaders become practiced communicators in order to maintain clear communications with all stakeholders.

Often, both visual and auditory noises provide a barrier to open communication. Visual noise includes those visual distractions that take place when you are trying to communicate with others. Auditory noise may be music, traffic, or other distractions that interfere with others' ability to hear and concentrate on what you are saying. Remove all noise before trying to communicate with others.

Written communications are essential not only for record keeping but also for purposes of mass distribution. It is impossible to transmit an event update verbally to 1,000 people without distortion. (Remember the children's game "telephone"?) Use memoranda, briefing statements, bulletins, and other documents to communicate effectively to one or many others. Memoranda should include an "Action Required" statement to inform the reader how best to respond and in what timeframe.

Bulletins must be sporadic, or you run the risk of becoming the person who cried "wolf" once too often and now is ignored by everyone. Electronic newsletters are a particularly effective tool for communications; however, use caution, as they are extremely labor-intensive to continually write, edit, produce, and distribute on a regular basis. A more contemporary means of communication is through the use of instant messaging (IM), tweeting, and mobile phone texting.

Perhaps one of the best ways to communicate is through an in-person or virtual meeting. When scheduling a meeting, make certain that you prepare an agenda in advance that lists the items for discussion. Distribute this document prior to the meeting to those who will attend and ask them to comment. Use the agenda to guide the meeting, and, as the leader, serve as a facilitator for discussion. Using a flip chart or electronic drawing board will help you capture ideas while sticking to the agenda.

One extremely effective device is to assign participants work prior to the meeting so that they come to the meeting prepared and ready to make specific contributions. Make sure that your meeting does not take much longer than initially planned; otherwise, you will give the impression of being a disorganized person who does not value your own time and the time that others invest in the meeting.

Event Management Body of Knowledge, IEMS, and EMICS

In 2004, the first Event Management Body of Knowledge (EMBOK) Embizo was held at the Edeni Private Game Reserve near Kruger National Park in South Africa. The term *embizo* comes from the Sulu language and means "a gathering." The purpose of this historic meeting was to identify and develop a global model for producing professional live events. Many years earlier, the Project Management Institute (PMI) used a similar process to standardize the project management process. Therefore, the EMBOK participants used the PMI model as a way to standardize the body of knowledge in the global event industry.

The convener for this meeting was Janet Landey, CSEP, the managing director of the South African Institute for Event Management. The event educators included Glenn Bowdin of Leeds Metropolitan University; this author; Dr. Matthew Gonzalez of Events Education; Dr. Kathy Nelson of the University of Nevada at Las Vegas; William O 'Toole of the University of Sydney, Australia; Julia Rutherford Silvers, CSEP of Speaking of Events; and Dr. Jane Spowart of the University of Johannesburg.

TECH/APPVIEW

Communication Technology

Digital technology has made audio and video communication more accessible than ever. Record meetings or dictate your thoughts onto a CD, DVD, or MP3 recorder or even a cassette tape recorder or camcorder. The average person commutes to the office 20 or more minutes twice daily and can use this time to listen to prerecorded information such as meeting minutes or industry news. As more computers come equipped with video-editing software, making your own basic business videos is easier than ever. Thanks to media sites such as YouTube, short user-created (and often made with basic house use video equipment or smartphones) videos are a huge part of today's culture. By creating your own digital audio or video based on your events business, you can generate excitement and capture the attention of staff and stakeholders in a very contemporary and fun way.

While not the most reliable source of information, the blogosphere (the world of personal online journals) and accompanying online forums are certainly the easiest and fastest way to find information on or communicate about specific interests such as events. Google searches will invariably reveal that someone else in the world shares your interest, no matter how obscure, and is communicating about it online. Even when communicating on accredited websites such as those run by *Special Events Magazine*, BizBash, or MPI, use the information as a steppingstone toward more reliable research sources. Remember to stay professional and formal even in anonymous online forums.

Videoconferencing has never been easier, thanks to Web tools such as Skype, a free videoconferencing service, which allows an event manager in Philadelphia to talk face-to-face with a client in Tokyo. For a successful videoconference, prepare the technology and have a backup, choose hours sensitive to the participant's time zone, and treat it like an in-person meeting. Don't make your caller get up at 3 A.M. to call you at 12 noon your time. Don't dress down or multitask while speaking—they can see you! Most importantly, videoconferencing is not always reliable and may result in an interrupted or distorted meeting. Sometimes, a simple phone call will do.

Following several days of intensive meetings and friendly but lively debate, a preliminary model was developed. A second embizo was held in the summer of 2005, also in South Africa, and further work was completed regarding the development of the model and in establishing communications channels to share this valuable information with others. Figure 2.12 demonstrates one example of this

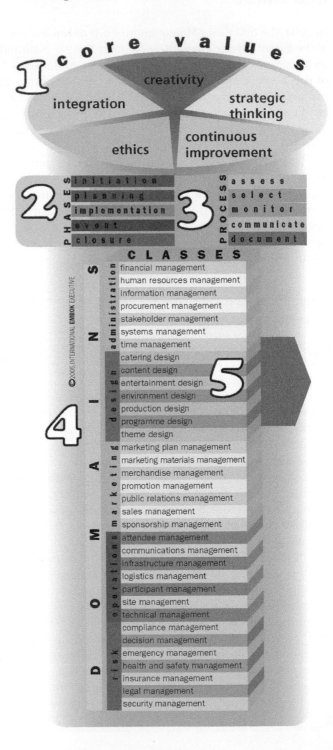

FIGURE 2.12 Model of Event Management Body of Knowledge (EMBOK) project.

model. EMBOK is still very much a work in progress, but it has tremendous potential in creating a set of unifying standards around which event leaders can work together to continuously improve the profession. As a result of the development of EMBOK, the Canadian Tourism Hospitality Resource Council (CTHRC) and Meeting Planners International (MPI) developed the International Event Management Standards (IEMS) and the Event Management International Competency Standards (EMICS). For more information about EMBOK, IEMS, or EMICS, visit their individual websites, which are listed in the appendices.

Synergy: Linking Administration, Coordination, Marketing, and Risk Management

At one time, the Walt Disney Company was the only organization of its size and type with an executive board position called *vice president for corporate synergy*. Due to the diversity in the Disney product line (theme parks, retail stores, movies, recordings, sport, and television), the leaders of this successful organization believe that one person must be responsible for ensuring that there is synergy among all aspects of the business operation.

Up to 1 year in advance, before Disney premieres a new movie, the Disney retail stores are developing new products, the theme parks are planning new live shows, and the other aspects of the corporation are preparing for joint promotion and distribution of the new product. This kind of synergy, even more important now with the recent acquisition of Marvel Comics (owner of Spider-Man and other popular characters) and Lucas films (owner of the Star Wars brand), means that the allocation of Disney's immense resources must be deployed in the most efficient and strategic manner.

Your event also must manage resources efficiently. These resources include your ability to administrate, coordinate, market, and manage the risk for the event. You must link these four competencies together carefully throughout the event process in order to produce the very best and most profitable event product.

The administration process of an event serves as the foundation for the resources you will select and manage during the coordination process. Poor administration will later undermine your ability to coordinate the event. Strong coordination will result in better marketing results. Unless your operations people are aware that today's tickets are discounted, for example, all the advertising in the world will be wasted. The link between coordination and marketing, and for that matter administration, is vital.

Finally, legal, ethical, and risk-management issues form a strong river current that runs through every decision you make in Event Leadership. If your marketing team leader overpromotes or inaccurately promotes an event, he or she will place those who must coordinate event operations at a great disadvantage. In subsequent chapters, we introduce each of these competencies in detail, but at this stage it is important for you to recognize the connection between them. Together, and with the potential adoption of EMBOK, they weave a strong tapestry that will help shield you from future problems and provide you with a rich understanding of how all team members must work together productively.

Today, most established business organizations, including event management firms, have adopted an Integrated Data Management Information System (DMIS), also known as an Enterprise system. It allows multiple departments within an organization to share current and accurate data in real time to support their decision making.

Corporate Social Responsibility (CSR)

The term *corporate social responsibility* has been widely adopted in the past decade by both corporations and local, regional, and federal governments. The term *company* is derived from the Latin root words *cum* (together) and *pani* (the baking of bread). Therefore, when a company plans, organizes, and delivers a special event, it is implicit that they do this in concert with one another and others. David Packard, one of the founders of the computer giant, Hewlett Packard, understood that the mission of a business was greater than financial gain. He stated that "When a group of people get together and establish something called a company they are able to accomplish something collectively that they could not accomplish separately—they make a contribution to society" (Packard 1939).

One of the primary reasons we were attracted to the higher purpose of planning events was the opportunity to draw people together for a positive societal outcome. Today, this is known as CSR. However, Mr. Packard and Joe and other individuals throughout time have described this as the golden rule (do unto others as you would have them do unto you) or as one sage wrote, "If I am not for myself, who will be for me? If I am not for others, what am I? And if not now, when?" (Rabbi Hillel, 30 BC–9 AD).

CSR statements and outcomes now regularly appear in corporate reports as well as in tenders that are offered by corporations and governments. These aspirational and sometimes fundamentally important core values communicate to others what the organization stands for, how they are helping others, and when they are practicing CSR.

One example of CSR in the meetings and events industry is a project entitled Hospitality Helping Hands. This highly successful program has resulted in hundreds of volunteers helping restore and rebuild cities where the PCMA has held their annual conventions for the past several years. In 2009, a group of Scottish students from Queen Margaret University in Edinburgh, Scotland, joined dozens of professional meeting and event leaders in restoring and cleaning the historic cemeteries in New Orleans, Louisiana, after they suffered the ravages of Hurricane Katrina.

1. Devote one morning or afternoon of the event to help clean or restore a children's playground.
2. Use excess funds designated for a cocktail party or banquet to purchase equipment for a children's school or playground.
3. Reuse paper and other products left over from your meeting or event within local schools or community centers.
4. Invite individuals who could not ordinarily afford to attend your event to be your guests.
5. Develop a volunteer team to identify future opportunities for CSR and empower them to conduct research and make future recommendations.

ECOLOGIC

Philanthropy

For the past years, the corporate world has made a steady U-turn from shouting about profit to sharing about philanthropy. Philanthropy means "love of humanity" and a philanthropist is a person or company that contributes to social or charitable causes to improve the quality of human life. Here are just a few companies in the events and hospitality industry that have become effective philanthropists.

Hilton Worldwide has a wide-reaching program of philanthropy, including activities as far afield as helping homeless Egyptian street children.

The Walt Disney Company recently introduced landmark standards for food advertising to promote healthy living for children. Madison Square Garden operates the Garden of Dreams Foundation, which gives children facing obstacles amazing access to this famous venue and the artists and athletes performing inside.

There are innumerable ways in which events may be used to demonstrate CSR. However, it is important to make certain they are carefully aligned with not only the core values of the event organizer but, most importantly, the event sponsor' s mission and values as well. Furthermore, it is equally important to remember that each event has the potential to incrementally improve the world. Therefore, look for the nuggets of gold within every event opportunity as you seek ways to promote fun and foster a better society at the same time.

In a broader and global context, your organization may also wish to consider buying as much of your products and services from local providers, purchasing only Fair Trade products, ensuring that your products are made in an ethical manner, including purchasing only from firms who provide safe and secure working conditions for their workers. In a later chapter, we will explore the potential for greener events; however, every event should be considered an opportunity to reduce the carbon footprint and slow global warming through the planning and delivery of environmentally sustainable programs.

Indeed, as exemplified by the further development of EMBOK, IEMS, and EMICS, the models for global event planning are changing rapidly. As Gladwell suggests, stakeholders in planned events use rapid cognition to make conscious and unconscious decisions about whom they want to work with and whom they want to give their money to for planning events. The positive movement toward CSR can be seen as a critical step in the right direction that will serve as the fundamental underpinning for future event decisions. If events are designed to serve others, one could then ask, how may each and every event repair, improve and advance human society through research, design, planning, coordination, and evaluation? The pioneering environmentalist John Muir may also ask, "How can each and every event through its planning process produce a sustainable outcome?" As a professional event leader, the answers to these two questions must guide future practice.

Summary

The five phases of successful event coordination are research, design, planning, coordination, and evaluation. And those five phases are closely linked with technology and sustainability applications. Qualitative or quantitative research methods, or a SWOT analysis, may help in the initial phase. Brainstorming, mind mapping, and project management may improve the planning. Use time, space, and tempo to coordinate the actual event. Always analyze the triple bottom line of your event, and consider corporate social responsibility in the evaluation phase.

Key Terms

Corporate social responsibility: The corporate commitment to creating and delivering events that promote corporate responsibility by improving economic, social, and environmental impacts for society.

EMBOK: Event Management Body of Knowledge developed by a group of industry professionals to establish standards for the global events industry.

EMICS: Event Management Industry Competency Standards developed by the Canadian Tourism Human Resource Council and Meeting Professionals International.

Gap analysis: Analysis of the planning gaps that may be present before the start of an event.

IEMS: International Event Management Standards developed by the Canadian Tourism Human Resource Council to identify common competencies and standards for event managers throughout the world.

Mind mapping: A process for pictorially linking thoughts and ideas to create a mind map that represents the inputs of various event stakeholders.

Project management: A system composed of commissioning tasks, milestones, closure, and other key elements to provide a common vocabulary and process for managing projects throughout the world.

Qualitative research: Research that uses language and observation to identify and analyze the meaning provided by interviewees.

Quantitative research: Research that may be enumerated in terms of its outcomes.

Reliability: The extent to which your research is accurate.

SWOT analysis: The strengths, weaknesses, opportunities, and threats posed by future events.

Tempo: The pace of the planning and delivery process of the event.

Triple-bottom-line evaluation: A comprehensive evaluation of the social, economic, and environmental impacts of an event.

Validity: The accuracy of the research instrument as evidenced through pilot testing and reviews prior to conducting a full scale study.

Career Connections

Imagine that you have an interview for your dream job. How would you use the five phases of research, design, planning, coordination, and evaluation to describe your project management system for planning events and to ensure a successful outcome from the interview?

Next Steps

Visit MeetingMetrics or Corbin Ball website (https://www.corbinball.com/) to learn how technology is being used to improve and advance the measurement, assessment, and evaluation of meetings and events. What is the latest technology, and how could you incorporate it into your next event?

References

Mikolaitis, P. and O'Toole, W. (2002) *Corporate Event Project Management*, Hoboken, NJ: John Wiley & Sons, Inc.

Packard, D. Goodreads, accessed June 4, 2013: http://www.goodreads.com/quotes/76783-agroup-of-people-get-together-and-exist-as-an.

PART TWO

The New Sustainable Event Algorithms

Composing the Sustainable Event Plan

"By concentrating on precision, one arrives at technique, but by concentrating on technique, one does not arrive at precision."

—*Bruno Walter (1876–1972)*

In this chapter you will learn how to:
- Conduct comprehensive research for your event
- Identify key sources of information for planning
- Design a program creatively with sustainability in mind
- Develop an appropriate theme
- Establish and manage an effective strategic plan
- Use emerging technologies to improve and accelerate your event planning process
- Develop and manage the timeline for an event

Bruno Walter, an Austrian Jew, served as the conductor of the Vienna, Austria, Philharmonic Orchestra prior to the occupation in Germany during World War II. Hitler removed Walter as conductor because he was Jewish. After the war ended, the Edinburgh International Festival was created by Rudolf Bing and others to raise the spirits of postwar Europe. In order to compete with other, more established, festivals in Salzburg and Vienna itself, Bing needed a major attraction to create excitement. Therefore, he asked Maestro Walter if he would reunite for the first time with his beloved orchestra in Edinburgh as a featured part of the new festival. Walter agreed, and the outpouring of emotions by the musicians, the maestro, the audience, and the media made this one of the legendary moments in modern musical history.

The event leader shares many of the same qualities as great musical composers such as Beethoven, Bach, Puccini, and others. The event leader must first conceive the feeling he or she wishes to achieve through the final event performance and then must arrange the notes (event elements) to achieve this outcome. Once a young conductor in Innsbruck, Austria, described for Joe Goldblatt how he achieved

Photo by Joe Goldblatt

Marquee Rents, a professional party rental firm based in Austin, Texas, puts on display its wide range of event rental items.

the best sound from his musicians. "I arrive one hour before the orchestra and sit in most of their seats. I want to be certain they can see me." The conductor went on to explain that by ensuring the musicians could see him, he could more easily communicate with them and therefore collectively they could produce a better performance. The conductor was literally arranging the musicians in an algorithm that would lead to a better outcome.

In fact, it is attention to details such as this one that produce successful and sustainable events. Comprehensive administration is the foundation for all successful events. The administration of an event provides you and the stakeholders with data with which to design the dream that will produce the deliverables you desire. Yuval Noah Harari writing in *Homo Deus, A Brief History of the Future* (2017) states that "Evolutionary science teaches us that, in one sense, we are nothing but data-processing machines: we too are algorithms. By manipulating the data we can exercise mastery over our fate. The trouble is that other algorithms—the ones that we have built—can do it far more efficiently than we can. That's what Harari means by the 'uncoupling' of intelligence and consciousness. The project of modernity was built on the idea that individual human beings are the source of meaning as well as power. We are meant to be the ones who decide what happens to us: as voters, as consumers, as lovers. But that's not true anymore. We are what gives networks their power: they use our ideas of meaning to determine what will happen to us."

Stephen Wolfram in MathWorld defines an algorithm as "a specific set of instructions for carrying out a procedure or solving a problem, usually with the requirement that the procedure terminate at some point. Specific algorithms sometimes also go by the name method, procedure, or technique." The same steps apply to the research, design, planning, coordination, and evaluation of a professional event.

Online search of all kinds of decor and equipment for multiple types of events (Courtesy of CORT).

However, in addition to using the human brain, event managers may now benefit from computer programs to assist and expedite these computations.

During the administration process, the event leader must make certain that data identified during research are used to drive the design and ultimately to produce the measurable outcomes required by event stakeholders:

Research (data) + Design = Planned successful outcomes

Research without the important phase of design will result in a dry, one-dimensional, and perhaps boring event. To produce a multidimensional and multi-sensory event experience that transforms guests, you must research as well as design the event outcome. The research and design phases ultimately produce the tools with which you can construct a blueprint of the event plan. The final event plan is, in fact, a direct reflection of the research and design phases.

Designing the Event Environment with Sustainability in Mind

The playwright's work is restrained by what the theater's limited confines can accommodate. Event leaders face a similar challenge each time they are called on to create an environment. Whether the site is a palatial mansion or a suburban park, the challenges remain the same. How can the site be adapted to meet the needs of guests? Ballrooms with their four bare walls, department stores filled with products, and even main streets upon which parades are staged offer the same problems and opportunities as those confronting playwrights and set designers.

Photo by Joe Goldblatt

This double buffet used matching linens to create an enchanting evening in Göteborg, Sweden.

When creating an environment, the special events professional must return to the basic needs of the guests. To be successful, the final design must satisfy these needs. Lighting, space, movement, decor, acoustics, technology, and even such seemingly mundane concerns as restrooms all affect the comfort of the guests and so play vital roles in creating a successful environment.

Five-Card Draw: Playing the Five Senses

When attempting to satisfy the needs of guests, remember that the five senses are very powerful tools. Like five winning cards in the event leader's hand, combining the five senses—touch, smell, taste, sight, and hearing—to satiate the needs of guests is the primary consideration when designing the event environment. The olfactory system creates instant emotional and creative reactions within your guests. Plus, virtual reality (VR) is being accepted readily to create environments. Currently, VR uses mainly vision, sound, and touch, but engineers are developing next-level VR that utilizes all five senses.

How many times have you walked into a room, noticed a familiar smell, and suddenly experienced déjà vu? Event Leadership pioneer Jack Morton (1910–2004) stated that smell is the most powerful sense because of the memories it produces. In fact, smell may generally be the strongest sense in terms of generating emotional response; however, this will vary among individual guests. Therefore, as the event leader you must actively seek to employ in your environmental design elements that will affect all the senses.

When designing a *Sex in the City*-themed banquet, you may erect a backdrop that evokes memories of the popular television show and movie, play the theme music,

Photo by Joe Goldblatt

A magician at a local event customized one of his magic tricks with a photo of the guest of honor's (Kong Goldblatt) dog to add a very special personal touch.

and even have *Sex in the City* cast look-alikes at the door to greet your guests. However, the settings and actors are still lacking one critical sensory element. When you add the sound effects of honking taxi drivers and street noise found in New York City then the event becomes a total sensory experience. Find the perfect sensory melody and guests will become involved in your event creatively and emotionally.

Five procedures will enable you to survey guests to determine their level of sensitivity as well as their primary sensual stimuli in order to create an effective event sensory environment:

1. Use an online or in-person focus group to determine the primary sensory stimuli of your guests.
2. Identify any oversensitivity or even allergies guests may have that could be irritated by certain sensory elements. Often, cultural considerations provide a clue to what sensory elements might be irritating. For example, Indian guests from the subcontinent may appreciate spicy cuisine, whereas Scandinavian guests may wish to enjoy less spicy foods. However, these are generalizations at best and must be confirmed by surveying the guests in advance.
3. Use the draft diagram of the event environment to identify and isolate the location of certain sensory experiences. Using systems such as Meeting-Matrix Express room diagramming and set software can help you design and communicate these cues to others in advance.
4. Share this design tool with typical guests and solicit their attitudes and opinions. Take time to distribute your ideas to others and solicit their feedback before making your ideas a reality. Consultation is key! Think of this as playing a few bars of music for your guests to gauge their early reaction.

5. Audit the venue to determine the preexisting sensory environment and what modifications you will be required to implement. Venues in the twenty-first century have numerous sensorial devices, from scents to lighting, that may help you, at a nominal cost, enhance the overall guest experience.

Soundscaping

To communicate with the guests at an event, you must design a sound system and effects that are unique and powerful enough to capture their attention. Do not confuse powerful with loud, however. Poignant background music at a small social event has as much power as a booming rock beat at a retail promotion. As with other components of event production, successful use of sound requires gauging and meeting the needs of the audience.

For example, how will sound help support, reinforce, or expand the guests' perceptions of the event? Consider the theme of your event, and devise ways in which sound can be used to convey that theme to the guests. For example, if you are planning a Hawaiian theme event, the use of recorded island-type music at the entrance will help communicate that theme.

Meetings and convention events also place more importance on sound reproduction for their programs. Long gone are the days when a meeting planner was content to use the hotel house speakers for live music. Today, many musical groups carry their own speakers, mixing boards, and operators, or high-quality concert sound equipment must be provided by the event leader.

Visual Cues

Both the baby boomers and generation Y were raised in front of television sets and, therefore, require strong visual elements to assist them with experiencing your event. This includes using proper signs to orient the guests and provide clear direction. Additional visual elements that must be considered are the proper and repetitive use of key design elements such as the logo. A logo is the graphic symbol of the organization sponsoring the event. Not only must this symbol be represented accurately but it also must always appear in the same manner to benefit from repetitive viewing and establish consistency to promote retention. Millennials are the generation of "visual" than any other generations that ever existed. More than 60 percent of millennials say they understand information faster when it's communicated visually, versus just 7 percent who don't (Brumberg 2018). It is not an overstatement saying their language is largely visual. Therefore, it is critical to understand visual cues are much more matter to engage millennial audiences in events.

Touch

Whether you are considering the cloth that will dress the banquet table, the napkins, or the printed program, touch will immediately convey the quality of the event environment. To establish this sense, use several different textures and, while wearing a blindfold, touch the various elements to determine what feelings they promote. When handling the cloth, do you feel as if you are attending a royal gala or a country picnic? When holding the program, are you a guest of the king or

Photo by Seungwon Shawn Lee

Various seating format and furniture types greatly enhance the overall atmosphere and also improve attendees' satisfaction: more colorful and comfortable furniture are used in events and meeting.

the court jester? This blindfold test is carried out to help you narrow your choices and effectively select the right fabric, paper, or other product to properly communicate the precise sense of touch you desire. Today, there are hundreds of different types of linens available to provide a strong sense of touch for your event. One of the largest linen providers is BBJ Linens, which has offices in over 20 different cities in the United States and ships worldwide. Its extensive inventory can be viewed at www.bbjlinens.com.

Smell

Throughout the event environment, a series of scents may be present that will either create the correct environment or confuse and irritate the guest. When conducting the site inspection, note if the public areas are over-deodorized. This smell is often a clue that chemicals are being used to mask a foul smell. Instead, you may wish to look for venues whose aromas are natural and the result of history, people, and, of course, natural products such as plants and flowers.

Taste

The sense of taste will be discussed later; however, the event leader must realize that the catering team members play a critical role in establishing a strong sensory feeling for the event. Consult in advance with the catering team and establish the goals and objectives of the food presentation. Then, determine how best to proceed in combining the other four senses with the sense of taste to create a total olfactory experience for the guests. Keep in mind the age, culture, and lifestyle of the guests. Older guests may not be as sensitive to taste, whereas other guests may require spicier food combinations to engage their sense of taste. The taste sense historically has been linked with a strong sensual experience.

Photo by Joe Goldblatt

Photo by Joe Goldblatt

An unusual venue, such as this secret tasting room at 21 Club in New York City, may be just the attraction you need to attract high-profile guests. One additional benefit is that you may label your own beverage to surprise your guest of honor.

Blending, Mixing, and Matching the Senses for Full Effect

Make certain that you carefully select those event-design sensory elements that will support the goals and objectives of the event. Do not confuse or irritate guests by layering too many different sensory effects in an effort to be creative. Rather, design the sensory experience as you would select paint for a canvas. Determine in advance what you hope to achieve or communicate, and then use the five senses as powerful tools to help you accomplish your goals.

A good example is an event hosted at a sports stadium. The stadium provides five senses—the smell of roasted peanuts (just be cautious with attendees with an allergy) and hot dogs, the vision of a green field, and the sound of PA announcement and roaring cheers. Events can be held on a game day that automatically provides a specific sensory expectation but also can be hosted on a non-game day with a creation of the above senses for attendees. Event attendees gather at player's locker room and walk through a tunnel to a stadium field with the PA announcing their names amidst the background sound of roaring fans. Stepping on a cushioning grass field and high fiving with other event attendees to begin a sport-themed event is a great example of "five-card" event planning.

Bells and Whistles: Amenities That Make the Difference

Once you have established the atmosphere for your event environment and satisfied the basic needs of all guests, you have the opportunity to embellish or enhance their experience by adding a few well-chosen amenities. An amenity is best defined as a feature that increases attractiveness or value. In today's added value-driven business environment, amenities are more important than ever before. These amenities may include advertising specialty items given as gifts at the beginning or the end of the event, interactive elements such as karaoke, and even child care.

One popular way to stretch the decor budget is to transform the guests into decor elements themselves. This is accomplished by distributing glow-in-the-dark novelty items, such as necklaces, pins, or even swizzle sticks. As guests enter the darkened event environment, their glowing presence suddenly creates exciting visual stimuli. Firms such as Oriental Trading Company specialize in providing these types of novelty items.

Karaoke, Japanese for "empty orchestra," was invented in Japan in the 1980s as a way for party guests to sing along with their favorite pop songs. Patrons sing into a microphone over backing tracks, as the lyrics are shown on a TV screen. The growth in popularity was explosive for many years, and it remains a classic event activity. In the twenty-first century, however, karaoke technology has rapidly diversified. Events can now sing, dance, rap, or play musical instruments along with their favorite songs. Dance Dance Revolution (DDR) shows event patrons the dance moves so that they can dance with their pop idols, and Rock Band gives patrons the ability to play electric guitar or drums along with rock stars. The popularity of Nintendo's Wii has shown that consumers demand more physical activity with their video games, and karaoke software remains a beloved party technology. Online gaming itself has become a main event as there are global phenomenon of e-Game tournaments and trade shows and meetings with its focus on e-Games.

Whether dealing with glow-in-the-dark jewelry or karaoke software, you must evaluate consistently the needs, wants, and desires of guests to determine if the communications media you are using are effective and efficient. Using feedback from specific populations will help you achieve this purpose rapidly.

Identifying the Needs of Your Guests

Once you have gathered all the quantitative data from the site inspection, it is time to analyze your findings and determine what implications emerge for your event environment design. Important considerations include the legal, regulatory, and risk-management issues that are uncovered during the site inspection.

Photo by Seungwon Shawn Lee

Whenever possible, name badges should be sent in advance to the delegates either through the mail or electronically. Setting up a well-organized registration area with a self-check-in and badge printing kiosk (shown in the top right corner) at events can speed up registration and improve on-site management. At MEET conference, Washington, D.C.

Provision for Guests with Different Abilities

We prefer the term different abilities instead of disabilities. If the venue is not in full compliance with the U.S. Americans with Disabilities Act (ADA) or comparable regulations in your country, you may need to make certain modifications in your design. Always check in advance with local authorities to determine if the regulations governing your event site require modification of your design. Regardless of the regulatory environment, it is critically important that your design provide a total sensorial experience that all guests may enjoy.

For example, if you are hosting a group of children or adults with visual challenges, you may wish to increase the tactile elements in your event or invite them backstage for a touch-and-feel experience of the costumes prior to the start of the event. If your guests have an auditory challenge, you may wish to augment their auditory experience with more tactile (Braille) or visual stimuli, such as signs or the use of sign language interpreters. For stage spectaculars, hiring an audio describer can provide hearing-impaired patrons a rolling commentary of what is happening visually onstage.

Implications of Size, Weight, and Volume

Let us assume that your design requires massive scenery and that the ingress to your venue is a door of standard width and height. How do you squeeze the elephant through the keyhole? The answer is, of course, "Very carefully." Seriously, make certain that your design elements can be broken down into small units. Using component parts for the construction process will enable you to design individual elements that will fit easily through most doorways.

Weight is an important consideration, as many venues were not built with this factor in mind. Before bringing in elements that have extraordinary weight, check with the facility engineer to review the construction standards used in the venue and then determine if the stress factor is sufficient to accommodate your design. Shifting weight also can cause serious problems for certain venues. Therefore, if you are using a stage platform and simply placing a heavy prop, you may not experience any problems. However, if on this same platform you are showcasing 50 dancers performing high-energy routines, the platforms may not be sufficiently reinforced to handle this shifting weight.

The final consideration is volume. The fire marshal determines the number of persons who can be safely accommodated in the venue. You, however, greatly influence this number by the seating configuration, the amount of decor, and other technical elements that you include in the final event environment. Less equals more. Typically, the fewer design elements you incorporate, the more people you can accommodate.

When Unique Events of Edinburgh, Scotland, created a new event during its 2008 Edinburgh Christmas program, it decided to stage it in an area that had not been used before for live events. The Grass Market is a historic section in the old city of Edinburgh that combines both residential and commercial structures. In order to host this event there, the organizers sought permission from the home dwellers in advance.

There are a number of applications available to help you quickly calculate the square feet/meters required for your event. One of these is Real Measure AR, which uses your mobile phone camera to quickly measure a room (see more in APPVIEW at the end of this chapter).

Do not do this in reverse. Some event leaders create a lavish design first, only to find later that the number of guests will not allow them to install this design.

1. Identify the total number of persons and multiply the square feet (or meters) required for each person. For example:

50 couples × 10 square feet per couple (five square feet per individual) = Total of 500 square feet

2. Subtract the total number of square feet required for the couples from the total space available. For example:

1,000 square feet available for dance floor − 500 square feet required by couples = 500 approximate square feet available for props, tables, chairs, and other equipment (less columns and other permanent architectural elements)

Calculating Required Event Size and Sizing the Event Environment.

This would be similar to a composer creating a piece of music too difficult for the musicians to perform or too long for the audience to listen too without a break.

Securing the Environment

The local or state fire marshal/warden is responsible for determining occupancy, and the police and local security officials will determine how to secure an environment to reduce the possibility of theft or personal injury. When considering the theme and other important design elements, remember that people will be walking under, over, and within this environment, and their safety must be paramount in your planning. Providing adequate lighting for traversing the event environment, securing cables and other technical components with tape or ramps, and posting notices of "Use Caution" or "Watch Your Step" are important considerations when designing beautiful, as well as safe, event environments. These signs should be posted at the bottom near the floor as well as above eye level so that, in case of fire, if persons are required to crawl along the floor they can see the signs easily.

Theft, sadly, is a major concern in designing an event environment. Do not make it easy to remove items from the event environment. Secure perimeter doors with guards or provide bag check stations at the entrance to discourage unscrupulous persons from removing valuable event elements. This is especially important when designing expositions where millions of dollars of merchandise may be on display for long periods of time. Furthermore, do not allow event participants to store merchandise or personal goods, such as purses, in public areas. Instead, provide a secure area for these elements, to ensure a watchful eye.

In today's post–September 11, 2011 world, securing the environment also involves additional considerations. For example, event leaders must ask questions concerning biochemical risks, terrorism threats, communicable disease threats (pandemics and epidemics), and effective crowd-control procedures.

Transportation and Parking Factors

Julia Rutherford Silvers (2011), writing in *Risk Management for Meetings and Events*, states that "Hope is not an action plan." Silvers suggests that every event plan must have a risk management strategy. Often the first and the final experience a guest will have when attending an event will occur in the parking lot. Therefore, a specific strategy is required for this very important area.

Event safety and security expert Dr. Peter Tarlow, in his book *Event Risk Management and Safety* (Wiley, 2002), states that the area that unites security and safety is the parking lot. Tarlow reminds us that parking lots can be dangerous for six reasons.

1. *People tend to drive in parking lots as if there are no rules or laws.* Having parking attendants or traffic directors can help alleviate this problem.
2. *Pedestrians often assume that parking lots are safe and that drivers will follow the rules and see them.* The use of parking attendants will help separate unaware pedestrians from clueless drivers.
3. *Event attendees often lose their cars and may inadvertently set off the alarm of another car that looks like theirs.* This type of behavior could cause a panic, so it is best if signs are posted reminding drivers to note the location of their vehicle.
4. *Catastrophic weather conditions can create dangers for people who have parked in outdoor locations.* Providing enclosed shuttle buses or trams can help alleviate these problems.
5. *Poor lighting has been proven to promote criminal activity in parking lots.* When possible, make certain the parking areas have sufficient lighting and/or adequate patrols.
6. *Children can run off while parents are loading or unloading cars and can easily be injured.* Having a drop-off area for children where they can be safely secured before parents park their cars is an excellent way to mitigate this problem.

The venue may or may not provide easy vehicle ingress. Therefore, well in advance, you must locate the proper door for load-in of your equipment, the times the dock is available for your deliveries, and other critical factors that will govern

Photo by Joe Goldblatt

Golf carts may be decorated as shown here, at Wheaton College in Massachusetts, to provide attractive transport for guests at homecoming and commencement events.

your ability to transport equipment and park your vehicles. Another consideration for transportation relates to approved routes for trucks and other vehicles. In some jurisdictions, such as Washington, D.C., truck and large vehicular traffic is strictly regulated. Once again, confer well in advance with transportation and venue officials to determine the most efficient route.

Whether you are parking your vehicles in a marshaling facility or on the street, security must be considered as well as easy access. Some venues may not be located in the safest of neighborhoods, and, therefore, securing your vehicles and providing safe and fast access to them are important. Well-lit, fenced-in areas are best for parking; however, the proximity of the vehicles to the loading area of the venue is the prime concern.

You may think that transportation and parking have little to do with creating a proper event environment, but these two considerations should be given significant attention. Many events have started late or suffered in quality due to late or lost vehicles and inefficient load-in operations. Remember, you may design the most incredible event environment, but until it is shipped, loaded in, and installed properly, it is only your idea. Proper transportation and installation will turn your idea into a dynamic event environment.

Effectively Manage the Event Environment

Understanding the basic needs of the guest is of paramount importance, especially when you are working with a smaller budget than you would like. In circumstances where the budget is severely restricted, there are ways, using your imagination, to stretch limited funds. Use your budget to enhance the beginning and the end, as these are what the guest will most remember. The following are some considerations for managing the design of an event environment.

Photo by Joe Goldblatt

Bride and groom arrive at church in double-decker bus.

Entrances, Pre-Function, and Reception Areas

The event leader must immediately establish the theme of the event with a comprehensive environmental design. The use of proper signs, bearing the group's name or logo, and appropriate decor will reassure guests that they are in the right place. Consider the arrival process from the guests' point of view. They received the invitation some time ago and probably did not bring it with them to the event. Therefore, they are relying on memory to guide them to the right building and the right room. Once they have located parking, they ask the attendant to direct them to XYZ event. The attendant is rushed, having to park several hundred cars for perhaps as many as six different functions, and cannot recall the exact location of the affair. Should the guests stumble upon your site and not recognize it because the logo is absent or the entrance does not communicate the theme of the party, they will become confused and lost. Providing your own personnel in costume or professional wardrobe will help guests locate your event, as will proper signage. Figures 3.1 to 3.4 demonstrate how to place greeters, or "damage control" hosts, to handle problems in the reception area. In Figure 3.1, the guests have begun to form a second row at the reception table. When this occurs, greeters should immediately invite the second-row guests to step forward to the additional tables set behind the primary tables. Having extra tables available will be perceived by guests as an added courtesy and will help ease heavy arrival times. Note that the guests at the primary tables enter between them so as not to conflict with the guests at the additional tables.

Figure 3.2 shows a solution to the problem of guests arriving without an invitation and without their names appearing on the list of invitees. To avoid embarrassment and delay, the guest is invited to step forward to the courtesy table, conveniently isolated from the general crowd flow. There, the problem can be resolved quietly and courteously, or the guest may be ushered out a back door without disrupting the event.

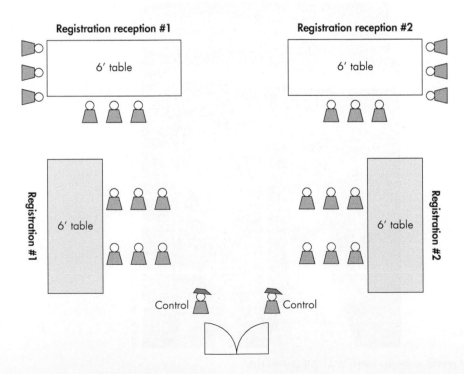

FIGURE 3.1 Registration-reception setup with secondary tables supporting a primary table.

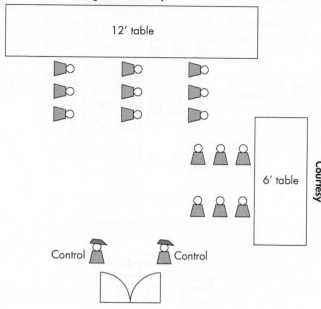

Registration-Reception

12' table

6' table

Courtesy

Control

Control

FIGURE 3.2 Registration-reception setup with a secondary courtesy table.

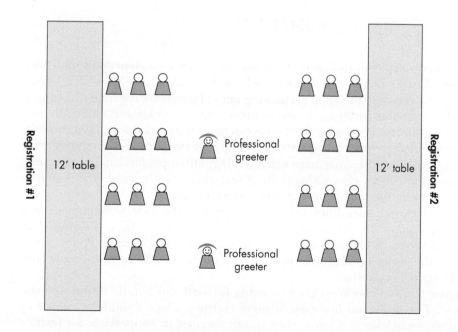

Registration #1

12' table

Registration #2

12' table

Professional greeter

Professional greeter

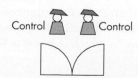

Control   Control

FIGURE 3.3 Reception setup integrating the professional greeter into the flow of guest traffic.

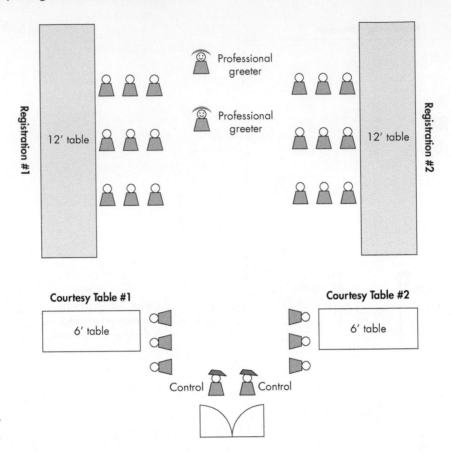

FIGURE 3.4 Reception setup using two additional courtesy tables positioned at an angle.

The scenario depicted in Figure 3.3 is one that every experienced event leader has known. During heavy arrival time, such as the second half-hour of a 1-hour cocktail party preceding the main event, long lines of guests are forming while those staffing the reception tables are trying to greet arrivals quickly and efficiently and keep the line moving. Professional greeters can make the guests' wait less annoying. Their job is simply to greet the guests in line, quietly thank them for coming, and answer any questions they may have while waiting. Often professional performers, such as strolling mimes, clowns, jugglers, or magicians, can be used in this area to entertain, thereby distracting guests while they wait in line.

When you expect long lines over a brief period, the best arrangement is a variation of Figure 3.1. By using two additional courtesy tables, positioned at an angle, as shown in Figure 3.4, you can alleviate crowding. The reception setup integrating the professional greeter into the flow of guest traffic further ensures the ease and comfort of guests.

In Figure 3.4, you can keep guests moving forward and handle disputes at the same time. The hosts and hostesses at these courtesy tables should be trained to resolve disputes quickly and know when to refer a guest to a supervisor for further assistance. Most disputes can be remedied simply, requiring no more than preparation of a name badge, a payment, or other minor business. If handled at the primary table, such tasks become cumbersome. Experienced planners know that the floor plan for the reception area should facilitate guests' arrivals and is critical to the success of the event. The way in which a guest is first received at an event determines all future perceptions that he or she will have about the event program you have designed. Take time to plan this area carefully to ensure an efficient and gracious reception.

Function Areas

The reception area may create the first impression, but the main function area will determine the effectiveness of the overall design. This is the area in which guests will spend the most time, and this is the area where your principal message must be communicated to guests in a memorable manner. Traditional space designs are currently being rethought by meeting planners as well as psychologists to develop a more productive environment. Dr. Paul Radde is a psychologist who has pioneered the development of physical-space planning for conferences that provides a better environment in which to learn. Radde has, often to the chagrin of various hotel setup crews, determined that speakers prefer and often deliver a better talk when there is no center aisle. In the traditional theater, or classroom-style setup shown in Figure 3.5, all of the speaker's energy escapes through the center aisle. When this lane is filled with live bodies, the speaker's interaction is increased, as is the human connection among audience members themselves.

Figure 3.6 illustrates the optimum setup, complete with wide aisles on each side to allow for proper egress. With this setting, each row should be at least 6 inches farther apart than in Figure 3.5, to allow for more efficient egress. Some fire marshals prohibit the arrangement in Figure 3.6 because some audience members will be seated too far from an aisle. An excellent alternative is shown in Figure 3.7, in which the front two rows are solid, with side aisles beginning behind the second row.

Perhaps the best adaptation is shown in Figure 3.8. In this arrangement, all rows except the first five are sealed, and the center aisle is easily reached by latecomers in the rear of the auditorium. Planning an effective seating arrangement

FIGURE 3.5 Traditional theater- or classroom-style setup.

is only the beginning. Masking tape or rope on stanchions can be used to seal the back rows, as shown in Figure 3.8, encouraging guests to fill in the front rows first.

Once the rows are filled with guests, the tape is removed. After 30 years of watching audiences head for the back rows, we experimented a few years ago with this method to determine if we could control seating habits without inconveniencing the audience unduly. Much to our delight, several audience members have thanked us for this subtle suggestion to move up front. Without this direction, audience members become confused and revert to old habits.

Interestingly, once a guest claims a seat, he or she will return to it throughout the event. However, unless we have predetermined that they will sit up front by making the back rows unavailable, all the coaxing and bribing (we once placed dollar bills under front-row seats) will not move audience members from the back-row comfort zone.

Innovative sites

The purpose of creatively designing your environment is to provide a dynamic atmosphere within which your guest may experience the event. One innovative decorator staged a banquet in a tractor-trailer. The guests were escorted up the steps and dined inside an actual tractor-trailer decorated by the decorator's team of artists. The goal of this creative design was to surprise and intrigue guests, who were picked up in limousines and brought to this isolated and inelegant site. Inside the tractor-trailer, they found luxurious decor, complete with chandeliers, tapestries, and fine linens. The decorator stated that the total tab for the 40 guests, including catering, service, and decor, was roughly $16,000.

With the new opportunities for use of public space come increased challenges for decorators, who must now cope with the increased demand for atmospheric props in place of flat scenery, banners, murals, and other more traditional scenic devices. Figure 3.9 (shown in the electronic appendices) includes a sampling of ideas for unusual sites in which to hold special events. Use this list to brainstorm with your

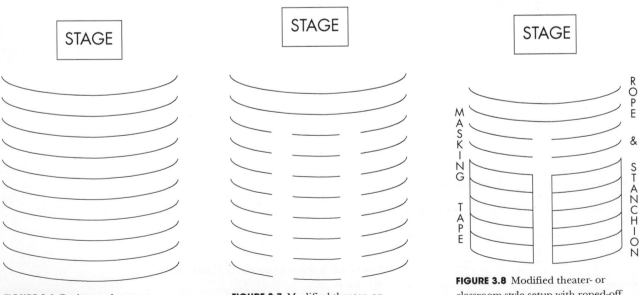

FIGURE 3.6 Optimum theater- or classroom-style setup.

FIGURE 3.7 Modified theater- or classroom-style setup.

FIGURE 3.8 Modified theater- or classroom-style setup with roped-off rear section.

event stakeholders to determine the best venue for your next event. The possibilities for exciting, innovative, and offbeat event sites are infinite. It is important, however, that your selection be logical and practical in terms of location, parking, setup, budget, and use of space.

One important source in North America for identifying a suitable venue for your event is BizBash.com, a publication that promotes the special events industry in key cities including New York, Los Angeles, Toronto, Miami, and others. Additional sources include MeetingMatrix.com and Cvent.com. Wherever you turn, you will find new products and new services available to help you transform an environment for a creative special event. And *UniqueVenues* (www.uniquevenues.com) publishes a list of unique event venues (e.g., museum, sport stadiums/arenas, colleges, and cruise ships) in the United States and Canada.

Amenities and Furnishings

The possibilities for linens, silverware, glassware, centerpieces, and even costumes for servers are greater in the profession today than ever before.

Edible Centerpieces and Displays The centuries-old European custom of including elaborately designed food displays as part of the decor is finally becoming popular—indeed, in some regions, de rigueur—in the United States. This important area of setting design can range from fancy carved crudités for the hors d'oeuvres to elaborate centerpieces carved from thick dark chocolate. The display must be accessible to guests and still look appealing after they are served. If possible, a server should offer the first guests who visit the display a serving of the decorated or carved item. This will help encourage other guests to help themselves. You may wish to prepare two versions of an item: one for show on an elevated, lighted platform and one for serving, placed within reach of guests. This will allow every guest to appreciate the work of your culinary artists throughout the event.

Decorating the Environment Sixty years ago, special events were most often held in private rooms, private clubs, churches, public sites, or hotels. Modern decorators are faced with the challenge of turning almost any conceivable space into a suitable environment for a special event. From football fields to tractor-trailers, today's decorators must display more imagination, creativity, and skill than ever before to keep pace with changing styles and trends. The designer/decorator's craft is one of transformation. Turning a polo field into a castle, a ballroom into the Land of Oz, or a black tent into an extraterrestrial fantasy, decorators transport guests from the ordinary to the extraordinary by creating a world of fantasy.

Regional customs and geographic location may determine, to some extent, what types of products are used for some events. Very often, for example, a client in Florida will request a mariachi theme, and a client from the Southwest will desire a Polynesian holiday. However, expanded delivery services, that allow suppliers to send almost anything overnight, have enabled designers and decorators to obtain almost any product for a special event, regardless of location.

One challenge that decorators face is designing an environment that will satisfy both primary and secondary audiences. Creating designs and products that will translate to television, film, still photography, and Web/SNS posting is becoming increasingly important. Consequently, when formulating design ideas, consider both the primary and secondary audiences: Who will view this event, and in what format? Perhaps the design will be detailed in such a way that it will show well in close up

Photo by Joe Goldblatt

A simple but effective tea pedestal may enhance the event through a proper display of the tea cakes.

photography. Many stock decor items available in today's events marketplace did not exist 60 years ago. Synthetic fibers and plastics have become increasingly sophisticated, enabling the fabrication of countless imaginative pieces. Even as these lines are written, products continue to be developed, providing greater selection at lower cost.

Interactive Decor Today's guests want to be more than just spectators at a special event—after all, movies, television, and Web/SNS provide plenty of opportunities to watch fantastic special effects and see gorgeous set designs and wonderful performances. To provide more than just a passive viewing experience, the event designer must create an environment that allows the guests to participate—to be actors in the decorator's dream world.

In Atlanta, Georgia, Joe experimented with this idea of interactive decor with an audience of prestigious and somewhat jaded professional catering executives. The challenge was to show these hospitality professionals something new, working, as always, within a specific budget. The theme of the banquet was "Starship NACE" (National Association for Catering and Events). As the guests entered the foyer, they passed between two giant television screens that featured a close-up view of an extraterrestrial's face. As each guest passed, the alien greeted him or her by name and offered a warm welcome to the event. Joe stood in the shadows, out of sight, and watched the guests' reactions—they suddenly stopped and laughed, clearly baffled by how an image on a screen could recognize and greet them. In actuality, an actor was hidden in a side room. As each guest stepped into the reception area, a technician using a two-way radio revealed the name to the actor, who in turn announced the name on television. Fog machines were set a few feet beyond the television monitors; just as the guests were recovering from one experience, they would receive a small blast of dry chemical fog to surprise them again. Throughout the cocktail reception, a prerecorded endless-loop cassette tape featuring space sounds and a professional narrator making pre-boarding announcements was played. When the time came to open the ballroom doors for dinner, four astronauts dressed in white jumpsuits, with NACE embroidered on their breast pockets, and blue and white space helmets, also featuring the NACE emblem, appeared in front of each door. As the doors were slowly opened, more fog seeped from the ballroom into the cocktail area. The guests entered the ballroom via a tunnel constructed of black pipe and drape and hundreds of miniature white lights. They tiptoed over a moonscape atmosphere, created by thousands of Styrofoam peanuts covered by ground cloth. Walking through that tunnel, the guests were entering another world. Once inside the ballroom, a robot welcomed the guests from the dance floor and instructed them to "be seated quickly, as the starship will be departing soon." Richard Straus's *Also Sprach Zarathustra*, the music used in the movie *2001: A Space Odyssey*, played in the background, and the sound effects of sonic blasts were added, projected through four speakers to create a true sense of surround sound. One-dimensional scenic pieces of planets were hung from the walls, and miniature strobe lights created the effect of moving starlight.

In another example of interactive decor, Joe's firm was involved in designing a theme event titled "A Dickens of a Christmas," in which the streets of Victorian London were re-created to bring the feeling of Charles Dickens's England to a hotel exhibit room. Since one of Dickens's best-known tales is *A Christmas Carol*, we decided to employ a winter setting and scattered artificial snow throughout the hall. The client was delighted to see the usually staid guests kicking the snow throughout the room as they traveled down each lane, participating actively in the setting. We also included a group of street urchins (actually, professional boys and girls with extensive Broadway credits), who were instructed to attempt to steal food from the lavish buffets throughout the room. Each time they snatched a scone, the waiters would grab them and say, "All right, if you want to eat, you must sing for your supper!" The children then proceeded to sing a 10-minute medley of holiday carols. The guests reacted first with surprise when the waiter reprimanded the children and then, within seconds, became emotionally involved as the adorable and talented children sang for their supper. A life-sized puppet of Ebenezer Scrooge was also used. As guests wandered by his house (a display piece), he popped his head out and shouted, "You're standing on my kumquats! Get out of my garden now! Bah, humbug!" The guests, of course, loved this Christmas nemesis. Those who were recognized by the puppeteer were called by name, much to their delight and the delight of their friends. Mr. Scrooge created gales of laughter, once again emotionally stimulating the guests.

Inside the New World of Event Design

When the Barack Obama Presidential Inaugural Committee required an experienced and award-winning official decorator for their balls and parade, they turned to Hargrove, Inc., which has been providing this service for over 50 years.

Hargrove, Inc., of Lanham, Maryland, was founded in the late 1930s by Earl Hargrove Sr., who specialized in what was then called window trimming, decorating store windows of retail establishments in the Washington, D.C., area to promote sales. With the advent of television, Hargrove's clients began to funnel their advertising dollars into the new medium, and his business soared. When Hargrove's son, Earl Jr., returned home from a stint in the Marine Corps in the late 1940s, he joined his father's company. Earl Jr. wanted to pursue the new and lucrative field of convention and trade-show display and exposition decorating, but his father wanted to remain solely in the specialty decorating market. Although they separated

Maximizing the surroundings of an event destination can drastically enhance the outcome of events. This photo shows a welcome sign sand sculpture at the entrance of reception held at Atlantic Ocean beach for WEC by PCMA.

for a time, Earl Jr. pursuing the convention market and Earl Sr. struggling in the specialty decorating market, they eventually rejoined forces.

Today, a third-generation Hargrove, Carla Hargrove McGill, helps lead the organization that provides decor for major casinos, corporations, and associations, as well as private individuals who seek decorations for their bar and bat mitzvahs, weddings, and other celebrations. McGill believes that her mission in the social-event field is to bring the client's theme to life through decor. Doing so today, however, is trickier than in past years, in part because of more stringent fire regulations. According to McGill, "Many states have particularly tough fire laws governing interior decor, and others are following. Every product we use must be flame-proofed, which in the balloon industry, for example, is very difficult to accomplish, largely due to high manufacturers' costs." When Earl Jr. began with his father, the available materials were paper, cloth, and wood. Today the Hargrove firm and other event designers enjoy many more options, including foam, fiberglass, a wide selection of flame-proofed fabrics, and a full range of plastics, to mention only a few. Forty years ago, guests were content merely to view the decoration. Today, Hargrove, Inc., is challenged to give guests a feeling of participation and interaction with the decor.

Therefore, according to Hargrove, it is always important to consider these points when choosing decorations:

- What will the venue (site, building) allow in terms of interior/exterior decor?
- What are the policies regarding installation? What are the policies or laws of the local municipality regarding decorating materials?
- What is the purpose of the decor?
- Are you conveying a specific theme?
- Is there a specific message?

- What period or style are you attempting to represent?
- What are the demographics and psychographics of your attendees?
- Are they spectators or participants?
- What are the budgetary guidelines for the decor?
- How long will it be in use?
- Which existing scenic pieces can be modified to fit your theme or convey your message?

Stretch It During the 1980s, Joe proposed that the audio visual industry that they develop a series of videos that could be projected onto the neutral walls of hotel ballrooms to create changing atmospheric conditions of clouds, rain, sun, and also establish mood through images of iconic architectural buildings such as the Eiffel Tower and others. His idea was too early for the technology to be available to achieve this level of sophistication. However, in the early part of the twenty-first century, there is an emerging innovation of using stretch fabrics within event venues combined with video projection to create phenomenal moving images. Rather than only projecting on a static flat screen, today, video projection for text, moving images and mood lighting is projected on a wide range of shapes of stretched fabric.

Project It The dramatic 3-D digitally mapped video projections seen on the façade of Buckingham Palace for the 2012 Diamond Jubilee celebrations of HM Queen Elizabeth II further confirmed how important this technology is for creating spectacular decor during major events. The moving images amazed and entertained hundreds of thousands of celebrants as major performers, such as Sir Paul McCartney and Sir Elton John, performed below on stage. These projections were staged by Trunk Animation through mapping the architecture of the exterior of Buckingham Palace to create precise images of the Queen and iconic figures.

In 2018, Sony and multiple leading electronics and A/V companies launched its home theater system for small scale (including home and small event spaces) with its IMAX-enhanced projectors and IMAX-certified TVs. These types of technologies will contribute to creating ultimate immersive environments for event environment design. For more details, see www.digitaltrends.com/home-theater/sony-imax-enhanced-projectors-tvs-cedia-2018/.

Parades and Float Design Starting with the original Cherry Blossom parade in Washington, D.C., the Hargrove artists have been recognized as leaders in the U.S. float design and construction industry. Many nationally known parades, including the annual Miss America parade in Atlantic City and the 1987 We the People parade in Philadelphia, celebrating the bicentennial of the U.S. Constitution have featured Hargrove floats. Designing, building, transporting, and operating floats can be a costly enterprise. But the rewards for the sponsor, in terms of publicity, can be priceless, provided that the right steps are taken. These questions should be addressed before contracting to design a float:

- What does the parade committee or organization allow in terms of size, materials, and thematic design?
- Under what meteorological conditions and in what climate will the float be used? (Some float builders specialize in designs suitable for particular climates.)
- Will the float appear on television?

Photo by Seungwon Shawn Lee

Parades are always a favorite to many event goers. July Forth Independence Day parade on Pennsylvania Avenue in Washington, D.C.

- What investment will the sponsor make?
- What constraints are imposed by the parade itself regarding construction, size, weight, materials, and themes? (For example, spatial constraints may limit a float's dimensions.)
- What message does the sponsor wish to convey?
- Where will the floats be stored prior to the parade?
- What is the physical environment of the parade route?

Parade floats are a perfect example of the need to consider the ultimate viewership of your design. Corporations sponsor floats in an effort to develop positive publicity and influence consumers to buy their products and services. Since only a few parades are televised nationally, most floats need only ensure that the sponsor's theme is conveyed to the live audience viewing the event. Many floats include people—pageant queens, actors, actresses, costumed characters, and celebrities—in their design. When planning the float design, it is essential to consider their place in the display. The wardrobe color of the person riding on the float, for example, will affect the total look of the float and, therefore, is an important design concern. Additionally, the lighting at the time of the parade will determine, to some extent, which colors and materials will best convey your message.

Say It with Flowers Flowers are usually more costly than stock rental decorations (props) because of their perishable nature. According to some designers, the markup for floral is often four times the cost. If the cost of the floral centerpiece is $20, the designer will sell it to the client for $80 or more to recover his or her labor, materials, and overhead costs, plus retain a margin of profit.

John Daly, of Santa Barbara, California, began his career as an award-winning event designer providing floral products for major events all over the world. He suggests that when designing vertical centerpieces, these guidelines should be observed: "The centerpiece height should not exceed 14 inches unless it is loose and airy, therefore see-through, over the 14-inch mark. This, of course, does not apply to the epergne arrangement. An epergne is a flower holder, such as a candelabra or mirrored stand, that raises the flowers from the table. When using the epergne, the base of the floral arrangement should begin at least 24 inches above table height."

Daly believes that event design has truly matured into both a fine art and a science because of the new materials available and the speed at which they can be obtained. Today, a wider range of floral products is available because of the advances in transportation and shipping. With the advent of overnight delivery systems, Daly can have virtually any product he wishes for any event in any location in the world. Daly is a designer for events in Seoul, South Korea; the Virgin Islands; and throughout the world, and this advantage has increased his ability to use fresh and exciting ideas in many far-off event sites.

Daly has taken his design skills in a new direction and now is president of The Key Class, an organization that teaches etiquette and career planning to at-risk young people. John has recently evolved his firm from designing events to helping at-risk young people and others redesign their lives for greater success.

Balloon Art Balloon decor can range from a simple balloon arch to more elaborate designs, such as three-dimensional shapes or swags of balloons, intertwined with miniature lights, hung from the ceiling. Balloons can create special effects, such as drops, releases, and explosions. Balloon drops involve dropping balloons over the audience from nets or bags suspended from the ceiling. Releases, including setting helium-filled balloons free outdoors from nets, bags, or boxes, are commercially available. Explosions might include popping clear balloons filled with confetti or popping balloons mounted on a wall display to reveal a message underneath.

From centerpieces to massive walls of balloons, such as the U.S. flag displays that Treb Heining (Balloonart by Treb) created for the city of Philadelphia, balloon art has become an established part of the special events industry. Organizations such as the National Association of Balloon Artists (NABA) and Pioneers Balloon Company's Balloon Network are working to educate both balloon professionals and their clients to the uses of this art form, as well as to ensure greater responsibility in employing it.

Balloon art has become an integral part of event decor largely because of the innovations in the 1980s and 1990s by Treb Heining of California. From creating an enormous birthday cake for a 10h-anniversary celebration at a shopping mall to supervising the balloon effects for the opening and closing ceremonies of the Los Angeles Olympic Games to orchestrating the mammoth balloon drops for the U.S. national political conventions and coordinating the New Year's confetti blizzards in New York's Time Square, Heining has been at the forefront of his profession for many years. He began by selling balloons at Disneyland in Anaheim, California, and later used the same products for decoration at both social and corporate events.

In recent years, there has been much discussion regarding the effect of balloon releases on the environment. Marine biologists have determined that wind currents cause balloons to drift out over bodies of water, where they lose velocity and eventually fall into the waters below. They are concerned that sea animals may ingest these products and become ill or die. Although there is currently no conclusive evidence that balloon releases have harmed marine animals, what goes up must eventually come down, and both the balloon professional and his client must act responsibly. Electric power companies in some jurisdictions throughout the United States have reported incidences where foil balloons have become entangled in power lines following a release, causing power failures due to the conductivity of the metallic balloon. All balloon professionals disapprove of foil balloon releases, as well as releases where hard objects are included in or on the balloon itself. Although it is impossible to regulate a balloon's final destination after a release, it is possible to design and stage releases that will not adversely affect the environment. A tethered release—where the balloons are released on long tethers and not allowed to float freely—may be one alternative. In some jurisdictions, the Federal Aviation Administration requests notice of balloon releases in order to advise pilots in the area.

Tents: Beyond Shelter Is Decor One example of a new adaptation of a classic environment is in the tenting industry. Developments in materials and workmanship in this industry have multiplied the design possibilities of tents. Half a century ago, the standard tent available for a special event was a drab olive U.S. Army tarpaulin. Flooring was rarely considered, and lighting was most elementary. Today, however, thanks to significant pioneers such as Bob Graves, former owner of the Van Tent company, Harry Oppenheimer, the founder of HDO Productions, and major innovators such as Edwin Knight, CERP of EventQuip, the tent/marquee industry has truly come of age. Oppenheimer describes his service as "essentially solving a space problem. For that special occasion, such as a 50th anniversary, you don't have to build a family room to accommodate your guests. You can rent a tent with all of the same comforts of a family room."

Oppenheimer once stated that the successful tenting professional prepares for the unforeseen, imagining the structure in snow, wind, rain, and perhaps hail. Most professionals in the tenting industry will not only carefully inspect the ground surface but will also bore beneath the surface to check for underground cables and pipes that might be disturbed by the tent installation. When Oppenheimer receives an inquiry for tenting from a prospective client, he first dispatches an account executive from his firm to meet with the client in person and view the site. Once the site has been inspected, the account executive is better prepared to make specific recommendations to the client. HDO Productions uses a computer network to track the client's order. The computer will first tell HDO if equipment and labor are available to install the tent on the date requested. The computer then lists the number of employees needed for the installation and prints the load sheet for the event.

Today's tent fabrics are synthetic rather than muslin. Synthetics provide a stronger structure that is easier to maintain and aesthetically more pleasing. Oppenheimer introduced such innovations as the parawing tent structure, which can be used indoors as well as outdoors in venues that need aesthetic enhancement to mask unfinished portions or obnoxious views. A parawing tent or marquee is a triangular or rectangular piece of fabric that is used to create a shelter for an event. It is stretched at each corner (tension point) to create a bold and often times dramatic covering for a stage, a booth, or other event area. The addition of lighting to these sail-like images will make the event even more aesthetically pleasing. Furthermore, video projection may be used on the interior or exterior to create exciting moving images to establish and sustain mood and atmosphere.

Heating, air conditioning, and flooring are also used and often essential within tented environments. Each of these important elements can help ensure the success of your tented event. A competent tent contractor will survey your installation area and determine if flooring is advisable, or perhaps essential, because of uneven topography. Listen carefully to his or her recommendations.

Joe Goldblatt had the misfortune of watching 3,000 women remove their fancy dress shoes as they sank into ankle-deep in mud under a tent. The client had refused to invest in flooring, although the additional cost was quite minimal. Pouring rain started just before the guests stepped under the canopy, and it flooded the public areas of the tent. It is a wonder that the client did not have to replace 3,000 pairs of ruined shoes. From wooden floors to Astroturf, your tent contractor can recommend the most cost-efficient ground surface for your event. In some instances, the location for the tent may require grading or other excavation to prepare the land for effective installation. Most tent contractors provide a preliminary evaluation and recommendation at no charge in order to prepare a proper bid for an event.

Heating or air conditioning can greatly increase the comfort of your guests, thus helping increase attendance at your tented event. Once again, your tent contractor will assist you in determining whether to add these elements and what the cost will be. If you elect to air-condition or heat your tent, make certain that the engineer in charge of the temperature controls remains on-site during the entire event. The temperature will rise as the tent fills with guests, so the heating or air conditioning must be adjusted throughout the event to ensure comfort. When you use a tent, you not only take responsibility for ensuring the comfort and safety of the guests but in some jurisdictions you are actually erecting a temporary structure that requires a special permit. Check with local authorities.

A tent provides a special aesthetic appeal; like balloons bobbing in the air, white tent tops crowned with colorful flags seemingly touching the clouds signal an event to your arriving guests. Few forms of decor make as immediate and dramatic an impression as a tent does. With a competent tent contractor, the problems you might anticipate are easily manageable, and the possibilities for an innovative event, year-round, are limitless.

Decor Costs When hiring a design professional for an event, expect to cover not only the cost of labor, delivery, and the actual product but also the designer's consultation fee. In some cases, this consultation fee may be included in the final bid for the job. If you are soliciting many different proposals, it is best to outline your budget range for the project to the prospective designers up front. This openness may dictate the selection of products for your event. Labor is a major component of design charges because the designer-decorator's craft is so time-consuming.

The complexity of the design will affect costs, as will the amount of time available for installation. The longer the time allowed for installation, the fewer persons required. We have seen decor budgets double when less than 1 hour was allotted for installation of a major set. Allow enough time for the designers to do their work from the very beginning, alleviating the need for extra last minute labor to complete the job. While many variables are involved in pricing decor, a typical margin of profit above the direct cost of materials and labor is 40 percent. This does not include the general overhead associated with running a business, including insurance, rent, promotion, vehicles, and the like. Therefore, today's designers must be very careful when quoting prices, to ensure that costs are recovered adequately and allow for a profit. When purchasing design services, remember that each designer possesses a unique talent that may be priceless to your particular event. This perception of value may, in your estimation, overrule the pricing formulas already described.

Themed Events

The theme party or theme event originated from the masquerade, where guests dressed in elaborate costumes to hide their identity. From these masquerade events, a variety of themes were born. Today, it is typical to attend western-, Asian-, European-, or South and Central American-themed events, as themes are often derived from destinations or regions of the country or world. Robin Kring, author of *Party Creations: A Book of Theme Design* (1993), says that "theme development and implementation are really very easy. Themes can be built on just about any item you can think of."

Themes usually are derived from one of three sources. First, the destination will strongly influence the theme. When guests travel to San Francisco, they want to enjoy a taste of the city by the bay rather than a Texas hoedown. The second source is popular culture, including books, movies, and television. Whether the theme is popular such as from a hit movie (*The Hunger Games*) or classic (*Gone with the Wind*) or topical such as preserving the environment, the idea is usually derived from popular culture. The third and final source is historical and current events. Themes reflecting the Civil War, World War II, or the landing of a human being on the moon, as well as the collapse of the Berlin Wall, have strong historical or current significance and may be used to develop themes. It is also important to note to avoid any potential controversial themed events (e.g., uninhabited island by aircraft crash). Such theme may bring a negative experience to those who suffered such tragedy themselves or by close relatives/friends. See the examples of themed events in Figure 3.10 (in electronic appendices).

An important consideration when planning theme parties is to understand the history of the group. Themes can be overused, and it is important that you rotate themes to maintain the element of surprise. When planning theme parties, ask your client these questions:

- What is the history of your organizations theme parties? What did you do last year?
- What is the purpose or reason for this event?
- Is there a specific theme you wish to communicate?
- To convey the theme, is food and beverage, decor, or entertainment most important for your group's tasks?
- Remembering that first and last impressions are most important, what do you want the guests to most remember from this event?

The answers to these questions will provide you with ample instructions to begin your planning of a terrific themed event. The list of themes in Figure 3.10 is by no means exhaustive. However, it does reflect a sample of the top themes currently in use in American events. When selecting a theme, make sure you are certain that the theme can be communicated easily and effectively through decor, entertainment, food and beverage, and, of course, invitation and program design.

The Ultimate Planned Event

John P. Tempest, a funeral director in Leeds, England, notes that, while fashions come and go when planning "the ultimate final tribute," tradition governs the format of most funeral rites. For example, Tempest notes that, in Great Britain, many families engage a funeral director to arrange for the burial of their deceased family member. The services Tempest provides include providing essential staff, preparing all official documentation and liaising with the proper authorities, making and receiving all necessary telephone calls, arranging for the attendance of the minister for the funeral service, placing obituary notices in newspapers, and making the necessary disbursement payments on behalf of the family. In addition, his firm will supply a traditional coffin with fittings for cremation (more frequently selected as a burial option in Great Britain than in the United States), vehicles and professional fees for the director.

Photo by Seungwon Shawn Lee

Unusual venues, such as this elephant house at the National Zoo in Washington, D.C., may help enhance the theme of an event.

When planning this important final event, Tempest suggests that most families select a traditional service rather than deviate from the norm. After the funerals of public figures, such as Princess Diana, Tempest noted that, for a short time, certain new customs are adopted, such as the use of white flowers, in an effort to emulate the funeral rites of the departed celebrity. However, these are the exceptions to the rule, in a country where hundreds of years of tradition and precedent govern most decisions.

Deviation from tradition resulting in further customization will increase the costs. Event leaders may elect to use the formula of basic pricing for standard services that is customary in the funeral industry to create standard packages and improve efficiency when providing price quotations. Although every event represents the unique tastes and sensitivities of the host/purchaser, many standard steps can be priced well in advance to ensure consistent profit when providing individual quotations.

According to the National Funeral Directors Association, many funeral homes are rebranding as *celebration centers* to host baby namings, weddings, and family reunions as well as funerals. In the future, event suppliers may find this market one they wish to attract, as it appears to be a growth industry in the United States and perhaps, soon, due to aging baby boomers, throughout the world.

Big Theme Success with Small Budgets

Even the slightest budget can achieve big results through a carefully planned theme event. First, you must decide what elements are most important because it is not likely that you will be able to fund equally everything you desire. If your guests are gourmets, the largest percentage of the budget will be dedicated to food and beverage. However, if they are creative, fun-loving people who are only slightly interested in the menu, you will want to shift your expenditure to decor and entertainment. Make certain that the first impression (entrance area) is well decorated, as this not only sets the tone for an event but is often the most photographed area. Next, include a series of surprises, such as a dessert parade or the arrival of a guest celebrity as your auctioneer, to keep guests on the edges of their seats.

Finally, share your resources with others. Check with the director of catering at the hotel and find out if other groups are meeting in the hotel before, during, or following your stay. Ask for permission to contact their event leader and determine if you can produce the same event and split the costs for decor and entertainment. You will find that you can afford 50 percent more by allocating your scarce resources in this manner.

Trends in Theme Events

Interactive events are transforming couch potatoes into fully participating guests. The late David Peters was a well-regarded pioneer in the field of interactive games and activities for planned events. His firm Absolute Amusements, in Orlando, Florida, and Las Vegas, Nevada, annually produces hundreds of interactive events, ranging from corporate celebrations to social events. The firm provides interactive equipment for activities such as sumo wrestling (where participants wear giant foam rubber suits), the Velcro wall (where the participants wear Velcro-covered jumpsuits and jump and land in various positions on a large wall covered with Velcro), and virtual surfing (where surfers stand on boards attached to electronic terminals and see themselves on a large video monitor as they roll, slide, and sometimes tumble into the virtual ocean). When designing interactive events, it is critically important keep in mind the safety of the participants.

One of the firm's top inventions is a product called PopNoggins® (www .popnoggins.com). PopNoggins allows guests to have a personalized video made of themselves dancing to a popular song. Their faces appear on the video but their bodies are replaced by voluptuous dancing torsos.

Alcohol will, of course, increase the margin of risk for a guest when participating in an interactive activity such as faux sumo wrestling. Some event leaders require guests to sign hold harmless waivers to acknowledge the risk involved with the activity.

One of fastest growing themes and interactive activities in events is eGame theme with integrated technologies. Characters, dance, and costumes from popular eGames, such as recent mega hit eGame, Fortnite® (www.epicgames.com/fortnite), have become very popular theme for events, especially with younger attendees.

Your event environment is the opportunity to explore dozens of opportunities in decor, entertainment, and other elements to make every moment unique and memorable. Every event leader has essentially this same opportunity. By understanding how the various pieces fit together to solve the puzzle that is the event environment, you provide a finished picture that will be remembered by your guests for years to come. Your ability to design, balance, and mold this collage will be rewarded by the guests' total immersion in the environment, leaving an indelible impression for many years. Especially in the new world of Event Leadership, you must be sensitive to the cultural, political, and other unique factors represented by your event guests. Remember, this is one reason why you are so valuable. You are the artist and scientist; use your experience, sensitivity, good taste, and talent to create and plan this unique moment in time.

Environmental Ecological Sensitivity

Environmental and ecological sensitivity are important for two major reasons. First, they are the right thing to do. When allocating scarce resources for an event, remember that no resource is as scarce as the environment in which we live, work, and play. Second, clients are increasingly requesting that every event meet or exceed certain environmental standards. Major corporations have been criticized by their customers for not demonstrating enough sensitivity to the environment. Therefore, when these corporations retain you to manage an event, they want you to reflect their renewed commitment to environmental concerns.

One example is by American Chemical Society (ASC) meetings. ASC's sustainable event planning includes implement impactful carbon and waste reduction, eliminating waste streams such as plastic water bottles, printed paper usage (down from 15,000 registration packets per event to a current 3,000), and soon-to-be-integrated event app leading into zero printing. These steps in event planning can spread throughout an organization's core culture. ACS's sustainable event planning has inspired the pursuit of Platinum Leadership in Energy and Environmental Design (LEED) designation for the ACS building near The White House.

Still the best way to accomplish this is to clearly define the organization's environmental policy and then incorporate these policies into your event environment design and operations. Event sponsors who practice recycling in all likelihood will want recycling bins at an event they sponsor. Event sponsors who do not use foam products for disposable serving utensils will not want you to specify these items in your catering orders. Meet with the key environmental policy person for the organization sponsoring your event and determine, with his or her help, how to incorporate such policies within the event environment.

Why not create your own policies? To ensure that events enjoy sustainable growth, it is important for you to establish your own environmental policies that will demonstrate to prospective event sponsors your knowledge and sensitivity regarding these issues. These policies need not be repressive. However, they must be consistent. Do not alter your policies merely to satisfy the budget considerations for the event. Instead, seek creative solutions, such as finding a sponsor for the recycling station, to make certain that your environmental ideals are well protected at every event.

Recycle Your Success

In the exposition event field, a growing trend is the recycling to local schools of leftover materials such as paper, pens, pencils, and other reusable supplies. Usually these items end up in the dumpster when, only a few blocks from the venue, there may be a school with children who cannot afford these basic supplies. You may wish to incorporate this program in your agreements to inform your sponsor of your policy of recycling your success to help others.

Many event sponsors recycle leftover food products to local homeless shelters or food distribution agencies. Doing this assures your guests that you are committed to sharing the success of your banquet with those less fortunate. Some venues require the recipients to sign a hold harmless form; however, regardless of the legal technicality, this opportunity to feed others should be seized for every event.

Still another way to recycle your success is to build into your event a project to benefit a local organization. Some event organizers schedule a day before or after the event for attendees to use their skills to clean up a local playground, paint a school, or perform some other community service. To arrange this activity, contact the volunteer center in the local community. The office of the mayor is a good place to start to locate the local volunteer-coordinating organization. Tell the office what resources you are bringing to their destination, and then apply your success to help others.

Inspiration and Perspiration

The inventor Thomas Alva Edison reportedly once stated that success is 10 percent inspiration and 90 percent perspiration. Although the design phase provides inspiration, it also expands and tests the limits of research. At the conclusion of the design phase, the event leader should have a clear idea of the needs and desires of event stakeholders. The goals and objectives that were identified in the research phase represent the skeletal structure in the anatomy of an event, and the flexible elements identified in the design phase represent the musculature needed to move event research forward. Now it is time to add the cardiovascular system to give and sustain life for the event. This is the beginning of the event's life, and the primary organ that will sustain this life is the event strategic plan.

Event Strategic Planning

The event strategic plan is similar to extrasensory perception (ESP) in that it provides the definition for event stakeholders of the steps, people, time frame, and other critical elements needed to ensure that an event reaches a successful outcome. Your ESP can be compared to the tracks driving a locomotive. Without tracks, the train cannot reach its destination. Without a workable plan, an event cannot achieve the optimum outcome and arrive at the destination that you and the stakeholders desire. Often event planning students use the phrase "we hope to find sponsor." We remind them that hope in and of itself is not a strategy.

The planning phase is a direct result of the data collected during research, and the color, luster, and texture mixed into the process during design. The plan must be reasonable (as confirmed during the research phase) and match the expectations of the stakeholders (as identified during the design phase). The planning phase involves the key informants or leading stakeholders who will manage the event. During the planning meeting, it is important to involve those people who

TECH/APPVIEW

Use cloud technology to improve the planning and on-site coordination of your event. Firms such as EventMobi and many others now provide mobile technological solutions for event leaders to offer their guests enhanced and superior experiences. In addition, the rapid adoption of global positioning systems (GPS) tools and Google Maps enables event organizations who rely upon transport to more precisely route and track their vendor partners and guests.

have not only the responsibility but also the authority to make decisions. The plan will reflect those decisions, and these important stakeholders must be included to ensure that they take ownership in the creation of the plan. These key informants should be involved in the planning process:

- Admissions coordinator
- Advertising coordinator
- Assistant event leader
- Audiovisual coordinator
- Caterer
- Corporate social responsibility (CSR) coordinator
- Decorator
- Entertainment coordinator
- Environmental/ecological sustainability coordinator
- Event coordinators
- Event leader
- Exposition coordinator
- Facility manager
- Fire department
- Food and beverage coordinator
- Insurance coordinator
- Legal advisor
- Lighting, sound, and technical production coordinator
- Logistics coordinator
- Marketing coordinator
- Medical coordinator
- Municipal, state, and federal officials
- Police/public safety
- Public relations coordinator
- Registration coordinator
- Risk management coordinator
- Safety coordinator
- Security coordinator
- Sponsorship coordinator
- Technology coordinator
- Transportation coordinator
- Ushering coordinator/house manager
- Volunteer coordinators
- Weather and meteorological experts and officials

Planning to Plan

Tom Kaiser, author of *Mining Group Gold, Third edition* (2010), suggests that prior to any meeting the participants should be assigned prework to prepare them to participate actively in the meeting. The scope and level of the prework is determined by the event leader based on the skills and responsibilities of the planning team members. The planning team members should, however, be prepared to contribute empirical information in addition to their opinions as a result of their preparation.

The planning process begins with the announcement of the planning meeting. This announcement should include a time and date for the meeting that is convenient for the planning team members. One of the most common mistakes is to schedule this meeting without consulting with the participants in advance. An effective planning meeting requires that the planning team members be fully committed to the process. This commitment requires advance approval of the date, time, location, and format. Another common mistake is not allowing sufficient time for the first meeting. Prior to scheduling the first meeting, you should assemble a small group of senior members of the team to actually plan the planning process. This planning to plan (or preplanning) is a critical part of the ESP process.

The length of the event planning meeting will ultimately influence the productivity. The maxim "less is more" is appropriate for planning meetings. Limit meetings to 90 minutes maximum. If the meeting must last longer than 90 minutes, schedule frequent breaks. The agenda for the ESP meeting will guide the team toward their eventual goal: the production of a workable and sustainable plan. Therefore, the agenda should be developed during the preplanning process and distributed to the full team in advance of the first planning meeting. A typical agenda for the ESP meeting follows:

    I. Welcome and introduction of team members
    II. Review of goals and objectives of event
    III. Review of critical dates for event
    IV. Reports from team members from prework
    V. Discussion of event preproduction schedule
    VI. Consensus regarding event preproduction schedule
    VII. Discussion of production schedule
    VIII. Consensus regarding production schedule
    IX. Final review of plan to check for any illogical elements, gaps, oversights, or other issues
    X. Adjournment

Confirming Validity, Reliability, and Security

After the planning meeting or meetings are concluded, the event leader must make certain that the event plan is valid, reliable, and easily communicated to a wider group of stakeholders. Prior to distribution of the plan, make certain that your event plan passes the "grandmother test." Show the plan to those stakeholders who were not directly involved in the planning process. Ask these stakeholders pointed questions, such as: "Is this logical? What is missing? Does the plan support the goals and objectives of the event?"

Once the plan is validated and prior to distribution to a wider group of stakeholders, make certain that there are no security implications of this release.

For example, if a very important person (VIP), such as a high-ranking elected official or celebrity, is included in the plan, you may wish to assign the individual a pseudonym or limit the distribution of the plan to preserve the security of your event.

Timeline

The tracks that your event train will travel to reach its successful destination are reflected in the instrument known as the event timeline. The preparation of the event timeline literally reduces to writing the major decisions that will be included in the event from the beginning of research through the final tasks involved in evaluation.

Often we are asked, "When does the event timeline begin?" After many years of experience and literally thousands of event experiences, we can state that it must begin with the first inquiry about the potential or prospective event. For example, the first telephone call from a prospective client researching your availability to manage an event or from an event leader who is researching information about your catering services may quickly lead to design, planning, coordination, and, finally, evaluation.

Therefore, we suggest that you begin the construction of the timeline when you first hear that unmistakable sound that telegraphs curiosity and enthusiasm or that twinkle in the eye that immediately and firmly announces that a potential spectacular is hiding just around the corner (from research and design). In fact, the only distance between you and the ultimate realization of the event may be a few hours, days, weeks, or months. To best control this period, it is essential that you construct a realistic timeline.

One reason that many events fail is insufficient time to effectively research, design, plan, coordinate, and evaluate them. When time is not sufficient to research an event properly, you may end up paying more later, due to insufficient or incorrect information. When time is not sufficient to design an event, you may overlook some of the more creative elements that will provide you with the resources to make the event magical and, therefore, memorable.

Each event leader should construct a timeline that begins with the research phase and concludes with the evaluation phase. The timeline should cover each

TECH/APPVIEW

Event space calculation

Meeting/Banquet Space Calculator
Real Measure AR (room measurement)
Meeting Room Capacity Calculator
Banquet and Meeting Room Calculator

Event diagram design

MeetingMatrix
ExpoCad

SocialTable
Dolce Meeting Room Setup
Hotel Planner
Banquet Tables

Event Timeline

Planning Helper Event Planning
Timeline Planning Helper
Gantt Project Management Sourceforge
Barry Seidenstat of Multimedia By Design Peer

TECH/APPVIEW

Today, event leaders do not need a thick binder with hundreds of documents. The use of the tablet computer is becoming more common on-site during events as event leaders use the technological cloud to retrieve and store their critical documents for each event. However, it is still important to have access to a hard copy just in case your technology fails during the event.

aspect and component of the event. It should include the start and ending times for each activity or task. It must be comprehensive and incorporate the individual timelines established by auxiliary organizations, such as vendors and government regulations. The event leader should carefully collect individual timelines from all vendors and other service providers. The timeline should detail the elements or components that appear in other people's timelines. This process of purging and merging the various timelines into one master production instrument is essential for communication between all parties.

Prior to distribution of the final copy, the event leader should seek consensus among all stakeholders before codifying the final results. The timeline must be acceptable to all stakeholders. One way to ensure the careful review and approval of each critical stakeholder is to require that the stakeholders initial the final document, indicating their acceptance. The final timeline should be distributed to all stakeholders as well as appropriate external officials (i.e., police, fire, media) to ensure timely service and provide effective damage control. By providing media and other external stakeholders with accurate information in a timely manner, you may avoid problems with innuendo and hearsay that cause erroneous reporting of your event planning process.

The way you depict your timeline ultimately will determine its effectiveness in communication to the broadest possible number of event stakeholders. Figure 3.11 in the electronic appendices shows a typical event timeline in summary form. Although the information in the figure is presented in summary form, it demonstrates that the timeline must be a comprehensive instrument that provides a separate column for each task, list of participants, and start and end dates and time. For example, in the evaluation phase, only the quantitative survey evaluation is listed as the task to be performed. In fact, as you will discover later in the book, evaluation is a comprehensive process, and in this phase you will also evaluate factors ranging from finance to timing. Each of these factors will be listed on a separate task line with specific participants assigned to supervise this process.

The timeline provides the event leader and event stakeholders with a precise tool for managing the event. It is the comprehensive map that results from the event planning process. Just as with any map, there may be shortcuts; however, you must depict the entire map to ensure accuracy to provide the traveler with the best choices for gaining efficiency during the journey. The same may be said of the timeline. Once you have created this master planning document, in subsequent meetings, you may adjust the timeline to gain speed and save time and money, ensuring that you will also ultimately reach your destination in order to achieve your goals and objectives.

The process of planning—from preplanning through the essential corrective planning during the coordination phase—forces the event leader and his or her team to logically assemble the best ideas to produce added value for the client.

INSIGHTS FROM GLOBAL EVENT LEADERS

PATTI COONS, CSEP

Chairman, Nalu Creative, Volcano, Hawaii Past President, International Live Events Association

(Note: To see the complete video interview, visit the Book Companion Site for this book at www.wiley.com/go/goldblatt/specialevents8e.)

Patti Coons is one of the world's leading designers of special events. Her career began by designing for television shows, theater, and rock and roll productions, which she did for 10 years in Hawaii; working predominately in the rock and roll business. Before that she was involved in regional and community theater and designed for comedy television specials. One day she was doing a show at a local hotel in Waikiki, and a friend was delivering scenery for a special event. Patti turned to her friend and said, "Ask your boss if he has an opening for me." Her friend called her boss and he said that he indeed did have an opening, and according to Patti, 1 week later she was head of the theme party and special event division of this company.

http://goo.gl/0oobDC

Q: What do you recommend for individuals who wish to enter the special events industry?

A: When I teach a design class I tell all of the students to go volunteer at a local community theater. Through this experience you will learn upstage, downstage, and the language of theater as well as what the lighting director and technical director does and then this knowledge will be accepted worldwide.

Q: What impact do you believe environmental sustainability is having on event design?

A: The event designer is often designing props and other items that may be reused. If it cannot be reused, then it must be disposed of properly. There was a product 10 or 15 years ago, you added it to water and it looked something like crushed ice. I was working in St. Thomas and St. John in the U.S. Virgin Islands, and I found out that this product is incredibly toxic. To get rid of it after the event, we had to take it to a special dump site for toxic waste.

Q: What advice do you have for new or emerging leaders in the special events industry?

A: When a new president is coming into office they often ask me what advice do you have, and my answer is always the same: listen. First, get everyone else's ideas before you jump in with your individual opinion or idea. Listen to everyone else. I think it is the ability to take everyone's ideas, think them through, and come up with a negotiable solution. It is important to leave room for everyone to have an acceptable place at the table because you have listened and incorporated their ideas where possible. You never walk into a room as an event leader and say "This is how it is going to be." Rather, you first listen and then work with others to find the best solution.

Q: How has the special events industry changed since you started your career?

A: The special events industry is actually very old. I think what organizations such as the International Special Events Society have done is taken people from around the world and made it cohesive so that we may all communicate effectively.

Q: Can special events actually help change the world?

A: I think that whatever the size of the special events, one of the things that must happen is to show respect for others. Never produce and event that ever puts any group or person down in any way. It is important to show respect for the products, the people, the passion for the group you are leading. If you respect them and what they are doing and help them show respect, well, that is the main quest of what we do.

In addition, the planning process must result in a document or instrument that will guide and memorialize the journey of the stakeholders. From a legal standpoint, the timeline, organizational chart, and production schedule can be used to show illogical planning or, even worse, gaps in the planning process. As an expert witness in numerous trials involving negligence by event professionals, we often see attorneys use these three documents to prove that the event leader and his or her organization did not meet or adhere to the standard of care generally accepted in the modern profession of event planning.

As the modern profession of event planning advances into the twenty-first-century global marketplace, Event leader s must not only meet and exceed the standard of care that is generally accepted in developed countries but also use these instruments to begin to communicate a global standard for the worldwide event industry. Through standardized planning instruments and processes, event planning will join other well-developed professions, such as medicine and engineering, in establishing protocols that will lead to better communication, increased safety, and higher-quality performance wherever event leaders research, design, plan, coordinate, and evaluate professional events.

Summary

Chapter 3 provided you with the understanding needed to compose a future event masterpiece by understanding the needs of the audience as well as your other key stakeholders. The three key learning outcomes from this chapter include the following:

1. Event administration, design, and decor are changing rapidly and require attention to detail as well as continuous research to remain on the cutting edge.
2. Event leaders are responsible for using safe, secure, and appropriate decor elements for their events to satisfy the needs of their increasingly diverse guests.
3. One of the most significant advances in event decor is the use of projection and video to create ambiance.

Key Terms

Administration: The planning, management, and control of the event outcomes by the event leader.

Decor: The elements that create and sustain the atmosphere of the event.

Environmental sustainability: The use of decor items that provide sustainable strategies and superior experiences for your guests.

Parade: A moving pageant or procession involving self-powered and motorized floats, automobiles, animals such as horses, large inflated balloons, and individuals dressed in colorful costumes.

Career Connections

Begin to identify emerging event planning templates and decor resources to continually improve your practice. Become familiar with the use of stretch fabrics and video projection as well as using a wide range of thematic ideas to compose your future event programs.

Next Steps

1. Conduct an Internet search and identify five different types of event decor including stretch fabrics, projection, sensory devices, and traditional scenery.
2. Review *The Art of the Events* (Monroe 2006) for additional ideas on how to create award winning decor for your next event.

3. List the environmental sustainable policies that you will use to administer the selection and implementation of decor for your event.

References

Brumberg, R. (2018) Study: Millennials crave visuals, accessed May 12, 2019: https://www.ragan.com/study-millennials-crave-visuals/.

Harari, Y. N. (2017) *Homo Deus: A Brief History of Tomorrow*, New York, NY: Vintage.

Monroe, J. (2006) *The Art of the Event*, Hoboken, NJ: John Wiley & Sons.

Silvers, J. (2007) *Risk Management for Meetings and Events*, Hoboken, NJ: John Wiley & Sons.

Silvers, J. (2011) *Professional Event Coordination*, Second Edition, Hoboken, NJ: John Wiley & Sons.

The UK Event Safety Guide (1999) Health and Safety Executive, United Kingdom, accessed June 4, 2013: http://www.hse.gov.uk/pubns/books/hsg195.htm.

CHAPTER 4

Event Leadership and Human Resources Management

"The supreme quality of leadership is unquestionably integrity. Without it, no real success is possible, no matter whether it is on a section gang, a football field, in an army, or in an office."

Dwight D. Eisenhower **(1890–1969), 34th president of the United States**

"The global event planner must wear many hats in various leadership roles. One role is the creator, another is the communicator, another is the visionary, and still another is the problem solver. The successful event planner must not only wear these hats and many more but must also become adept at continually changing hats to achieve the goals and objectives of the event."

—Linda Higgison **(1947–2007), former Chair and CEO of the TCI Companies and Curriculum Designer for the Temple University Event Leadership Executive Certificate Program**

In this chapter you will learn how to:
- Identify different leadership styles
- Solve problems with a six-step system
- Use mirror etiquette and e-etiquette
- Improve communication skills
- Establish a human resource recruitment and orientation plan
- Use technologies as an enhancement or replacement of traditional human resources
- Recruit the best staff and volunteers
- Educate, inform, train, and inspire staff and volunteers
- Create organizational charts
- Champion equality and accessibility

Linda Higgison recognized that event leaders must communicate effectively with a myriad of different players. From the client to the special guest to the janitor, an event leader must effectively communicate to each person with a thorough consideration of different languages and cultures. This chapter is about how to work effectively with the different personalities you may come across in the special events industry.

It is extremely important that the event planner carefully identify the human resources required for each event and then properly recognize their contribution throughout the event planning process. Joe Goldblatt produced the *Salute to the First Lady* in 1989 at the John F. Kennedy Center in honor of Barbara Bush, following her husband's election as President of the United States. He recalls how Mrs. Bush took time, following the production, to thank every person who was involved in its production. From the doorman to the visiting duchess, Mrs. Bush made certain that everyone who had contributed to the success of its production was properly acknowledged.

Event Planner as a Leader: Leadership Styles

The three classic leadership styles may be demonstrated with a simple game. Gather a group of friends, some crayons, and three sheets of paper. Then start drawing.

For the first sheet of paper, give everyone a crayon and let them draw whatever they want, wherever they want. Some might scribble, others doodle; some might write words, others might draw detailed and realistic portraits of celebrities, and others may draw right over those portraits. You might end up with a Jackson Pollock canvas of splattered colors or even something that looks like graffiti on a public bathroom wall. It might be beautiful; it might be horrible. This is the laissez-faire style of leadership, where everyone gets an equal say, and there is no leader.

For the second sheet of paper, give everyone a crayon but yourself. You are the leader, and you will tell them exactly what to draw, and how to draw it. Tell the group to draw a detailed outdoor landscape, and have them each fill in a different section. Be as detailed as possible in your instructions. You may end up with a beautiful landscape, but it depends on the talent of your group and your talent as a leader. Did you choose the right person to draw the trees, and the right person to draw the sky? Did the team respond well to your instruction, or did they rebel? This is the autocratic style of leadership, where one person is in charge of all.

Before you use the final sheet of paper, discuss with your friends what they would like to draw. Find out who is good at which area of drawing, and what they feel inspired to draw. Vote for what to draw. Now vote for who will draw each area. Vote for who will shade, and vote for who will outline. Discuss a schedule, a timeline for completion, and take a vote on it. Once everyone feels that they have been heard and that the process for drawing is fair and proper, you may begin. This might just be your best drawing of all—each friend has contributed to the best of his or her abilities, and each person has really shone as an artist. The only problem is that this last drawing took hours to complete! This is the democratic style of leadership.

Leadership Characteristics

Throughout ancient and modern human history, a number of people have been identified by historians as effective leaders. Some of these people became leaders due to a defining moment or event in their lives, while others sought leadership opportunities to cause positive change. In Figure 4.1, the general

Traditional Leaders	Event Leaders
1. Communication	1. Integrity
2. Confidence	2. Confidence and persistence
3. Courage	3. Collaborative decision-making
4. Decision-making	4. Problem-solving
5. Enthusiasm	5. Communication skills
6. Integrity	6. Vision
7. Persistence	7. Social and environmental responsibility
8. Problem-solving	8. Fiscal responsibility
	9. Delegation and Empowerment

FIGURE 4.1 Event leadership characteristics.

Perception of	Perception of	Low Integrity Evidence	High Integrity Evidence
Consistency	Punctuality	Tardiness	Communications
Inclusiveness	Participation	Absenteeism	Intolerance
Participation	Consistency	Inconsistency	Participation
Tolerance	Inclusiveness	Exclusive Favoritism	Exclusiveness
Punctuality	Tolerance	Intolerance	Inconsistency

FIGURE 4.2 Integrity quotient.

traits associated with effective leaders are compared to those specialized characteristics that Ms. Higgison identified within successful event leaders. Not all leadership characteristics are equal; however, integrity is paramount. Integrity is the value that determines the external perception by others. External perception by others can be called as a "brand." Each individual has his or her own brand. Successful sports event marketing firm guru Michael Smith says, "People tend to be associated with people with positive branding and positive branding is the most important asset in business world."

Integrity

The event leader must set the standard for integrity. If he or she does not exemplify integrity in performance and decision-making, event stakeholders will soon lose faith not only in the event leader but also in the event organization. If an event leader reminds his or her staff that it is inappropriate to accept gifts from vendors and then is seen by subordinates receiving a substantial gift from a vendor, the credibility of the person, as well as that of the organization, may be shattered. The leader who exhibits high integrity will not only refuse the gift but will communicate to his or her colleagues that the gift has been refused and why it would be inappropriate to accept this gift. Figure 4.2 demonstrates perceptions of high and low integrity by event stakeholders. Therefore, students and young professionals in the event industry should use this table (Figure 4.2) to identify their strength on "integrity" and use it as a tool to improve weaknesses in "integrity" for their career building.

Confidence and Persistence

When your back is against the wall, will you have the confidence and persistence to forge ahead? Most events have a reality-check point, where funds are low, morale is even lower, and impending disaster seems just around the corner. During these times of trial and tribulation, all eyes will be on the event leader. Your ability to stay the course, maintain the original vision, and triumph is what is expected by your event stakeholders.

Let us suppose that you are responsible for acquiring sponsors for your event. Only a few weeks before the event, your biggest sponsor backs out. There is no time to replace the sponsor. In addition, the neighbors whose houses are near your event venue are starting to make rumblings in the media about noise, traffic, and other disruptions that they believe will result from your event. A traditional manager would collect all the necessary information and perhaps assign each problem to an appropriate subordinate after making a decision as to the best course of action. An event leader, however, will turn these challenges into opportunities for the event organization to implement problem-solving skills and prove how great the event leader and organization is to the event stakeholders. The event leader may ask members of the board, as well as staff, for recommendations on how to replace, or at least mitigate the damage that could be caused by, the missing sponsor. Furthermore, the event leader will meet with the neighbors or their association and work collaboratively with his or her staff to offer the assurances they need to provide new and long-term support for the event. Event leaders use their confidence and persistence as teaching tools to positively influence other event stakeholders.

Collaborative Decision-Making

Since Frederick Winslow Taylor (1856–1915) created the management methods used to propel industrialized America (as exemplified by the rapid production of the Ford motor car), most management theory has focused on achieving efficiency to maximize profits. As workers began to organize into labor unions, they challenged this approach and sought an equal share in the decision-making process, regarding not only the type of work they do but also how they do it. Event organizations are not linear organizations like factories. Instead, they are pulsating organizations that may start with a small staff, swell to a large part-time and volunteer organization as an event grows near, and then rapidly deflate to the original small staff as the event winds down. This type of organization requires close collaboration between the event leaders and those who will encounter event guests in various event service deliveries that can shape the final perception of the event by the guests.

Collaborative organizations or quality teams have been used for the past three decades by numerous for-profit and not-for-profit organizations to achieve high quality and, consequently, better financial results. Event leaders should always perceive their associates (permanent and part-time staff), volunteers, and others as collaborators who share a mutual goal of producing a successful event. All decisions should be preceded by close collaboration among the stakeholders. However, there are also times when the event leader must lead by making timely decisions without consulting all affected stakeholders. For example, during Dr. Lee's 2018 Winter Olympic study abroad program, he was notified that one of the program attendees was about to enter a gender-separated lodging section when the central office closed. He had to stop the attempt and collect the information of the staff. Then he contacted the central office handling violations of lodging policy via e-mail to seek their input. Then he followed up first thing in the morning when the office opened. In addition, the details of how the incident was handled were shared with related stakeholders and other staff to prevent such an incident from happening again and shared steps/decisions to be made in the future.

Problem-Solving There are various versions of problem-solving steps in general business environments. The number of steps to take varies from four to eight. No matter the number of steps, most of the solutions have commonalities. A colleague once said that she counted thousands of potential problems during the development of an event and, therefore, concluded that events consist of a series of problems whose solutions determine the level of success achieved by event stakeholders. Few event leaders continue in the field unless they are comfortable with their ability to solve problems. This six-step list provides a framework for event leaders to understand, analyze, and solve event problems:

1. UNDERSTAND the size, scope, and time sensitivity of the problem.
2. IDENTIFY the key informants and stakeholders affected by the problem.
3. Determine if there is a MODEL or comparable problem whose solution could be used for this problem.
4. TEST the potential solution by seeking the collaborative input of those affected by the problem. If the problem is urgent and requires an immediate response, use a precedent or other model to frame your response.
5. Document the problem-solving agreement(s).
6. Once a decision has been made, MONITOR the impact to determine if anything further must be done to mitigate future problems resulting from your decision.

Let us take, for instance, an outdoor festival faced with an environmental problem. A famous outdoor music festival has welcomed thousands of visitors to engage in music, spirituality, and environmentalism for many years, but recently there was a very nasty article in the press criticizing the festival for allowing visitors to drive to the festival, thus burning fossil fuels and creating a carbon footprint.

The festival organizers first needed to UNDERSTAND the size, scope, and time sensitivity of the issue. After meeting with their stakeholders and senior management team, they realized that they were faced first with a publicity issue and, secondly, with a much greater question about their environmental credentials. The publicity issue was time sensitive, whereas the environmental question was not immediately time sensitive.

The management team IDENTIFIED the stakeholders upset by this problem. First, they needed to publicly respond to the media outlets that had questioned them. Second, they needed to create a greater conversation with their attendees, their fans, their business partners, and their staff.

They had never received such bad publicity, so there was no MODEL for responding; however, they did have a model for talking to their community about sustainability. A similar festival in Australia had created a successful environmental campaign that their attendees had adopted with great enthusiasm.

They TESTED their response to this news article by posting a short article on the festival's website, acknowledging the issue and pledging that they would work to reduce car traffic to and from their event. As this post received positive feedback from both journalists and attendees, the management team decided to proceed with an environmental campaign.

After the model is implemented, event leaders must DOCUMENT details of the problem-solving agreement(s). Relying on memory is a bad idea. Make sure to put them in writing as it will help event leaders and stakeholders to think through all the details and implications for the current event and in the future. Circumstances can change and "if-then" event leaders now have a tested model to apply with some adjustments. This festival now provides group transportation, partners with public transit corporations, and promotes carpooling as a way to reduce car traffic to and from their event. They MONITOR both car traffic and the carbon footprint of their event, and they also survey their attendees to better understand their attitudes about sustainable travel alternatives.

It would have been easier for this festival to react swiftly and passionately to this negative news article, but they may not have made such a considered and rational decision. By employing these six steps, the festival ensured a thoughtful and effective solution that would guide the festival toward continual improvement.

Communication Skills

Communication is quite simply the way we, as human beings, interact with one another. More than just speaking, communication includes written words and body language. Do you know when to use an exclamation point in an e-mail and when not to? When do you shake hands, and when do you hug? Do you make eye contact? Do you wait for your turn to speak? Each of these courtesies has its place. Most importantly, remember the golden rule: treat others as you would like to be treated. Similarly, your etiquette should mirror that of the person you are interacting with. Figure 4.3 describes how to use mirror etiquette.

Every person is an individual, and we all have our peculiarities. We each like to be treated in our own special way. Try your best to understand the way someone wants to be treated by mirroring their behavior.

- If a colleague is formal and businesslike, maintain formal and businesslike communication.
- If a colleague is informal, you can be informal.
- Handshakers want handshakes. Huggers want hugs!
- Always return pleasantries. If a colleague always says "please" and "thank you," then offer that person the same courtesy.

Carefully observe others when you are in unfamiliar human territory. Their behaviors may be mirrored by you to ensure you are communicating and fitting in within a new social situation.

FIGURE 4.3 Mirror etiquette.

ECOLOGIC

Through using electronic communications you will reduce your carbon footprint. It is estimated that over 40 percent of the carbon footprint for meetings and conferences may be from paper waste. Therefore, whenever possible use e-programs or e-conference proceedings to enable you to reach even more people with a lesser carbon footprint being derived from your event. Event Industry Council (EIC, formerly known as CIC) has developed the Events Industry Council Templates (formerly APEX) for standardization of many event practices. EIC has developed Events Industry Council Templates environmentally sustainable practices in nine key areas for the event industry. It has partnered with the American Society for Testing and Materials International (ASTM) and it is called Events Industry Council Templates/ASTM Environmentally Sustainable Meeting Standards. One of the nine areas is communications, and it provides a useful framework to identify sustainability practices in communications among staff, vendors, and attendees. It specifies standards for evaluation and selection of communication materials for environmentally sustainable events.

TECH/APPVIEW

E-Etiquette

The vast majority of business communication now is not spoken, but typed. Most office workers spend the majority of their day on e-mail, but what are the protocols or rules of etiquette for these electronic messages?

Mirror etiquette holds true with e-mail. Always try to reflect the tone and formality of the e-mail you are responding to—this goes for the opening salutation and the closing signature line. If unsure, the safest way is to copy your correspondent's phrasing–if it's good enough for them, it should be good enough for you. For instance, if they open with "Dear Mr. Lee" and sign off with "Kindest Regards," then your safest option is to copy these phrases in your response.

It is always best to err on the side of formality. A CEO is less likely to be offended if you address her as "Dear Dr. Higgins," than if you use "Hello Jane!" even if she does prefer to be called by her first name. It is her place to say, not yours, so wait until she signs off an e-mail with "Jane" before using her first name.

Deduce the general tone of the e-mail to craft your response. Formal language needs a formal response. Jokey e-mailers can handle a jokey response,

as long as it is all in good humor and suitable for work. Avoid emoticons such as ☺ unless you are closely acquainted with your correspondent and know that he or she appreciates these.

Finally, the correct way to correspond with professionals is through official business e-mail and office phone numbers. Do not use Twitter or Facebook to contact colleagues about work-related matters. While your event marketing may extend to social media, your internal communication should stay private and within official channels. If you do use social media sites to communicate with coworkers or clients, set up a separate SNS account clearly indicated as a business SNS account. Jin, Lee, and Daniels (2017) studied wedding planner in the United States, and their findings indicated that half of the leaders use Facebook daily followed by Instagram for their business marketing communication. And more than one-third of the leaders use WeddingWire, Pinterest, Facebook, and LinkedIn at least once a week. It is important to know which SNS toll is most widely accepted by its communication partners and identify any specific channel that is used in a certain field to maximize the effectiveness of e-communications.

Open and Continuous Communication

Without open and continuous communication, event stakeholders cannot form the collaborative team needed to achieve common objectives. To promote open communications, the event leader must listen, analyze, and act. To listen effectively, an event manager must be intuitive, set specific criteria for the analysis of facts, and, when necessary, act quickly and decisively to unblock communications among stakeholders.

Julia Rutherford Silvers recognizes that coordinating events require a complex set of skills, including effective communication. She states in *Professional Event Coordination* (2003), "Creating and producing events is an exhilarating and sometimes exhausting occupation, but it is always rewarding emotionally, spiritually, and often economically. The professional event coordinator must be flexible, energetic, well-organized, detail-oriented, and a quick thinker. As a professional event coordinator you must understand the integrated processes, plans, and possibilities specific to each event you coordinate so that you will be a better planner, producer, purchaser, and partner in delivering the special event experience that exceeds expectations."

Vision

One important element of communications strategy is the event leader's presentation of the vision of the event to his or her team. The professional event leader must clearly demonstrate that he or she has a vision of the event's outcome. During early meetings with the stakeholders, the event leader must describe in a visual manner the outcome that will result from the event. For example, the event leader may state: "On the opening day, thousands of guests will line up to buy tickets and, once inside, they will smile, participate, and have a good time, all due to your efforts." Furthermore, the event leader must "lead" the stakeholders toward that vision of the event by asking leading questions, such as, "Can you see this happening? Are you prepared to help me make it happen? What will you do to help us achieve this goal?"

Social and Environmental Responsibility

Social and environmental impacts of events have been bigger than ever, and they will only continue to increase. Therefore, event leaders' knowledge in these areas and responsibility are now very critical part of event leadership. No person is an island. You belong to a rich and diverse society, and also a vibrant ecosystem, and every action you take affects both your society and your environment. Because events are gatherings of many people, the social and environmental impacts of events are magnified. If you forget to recycle a soda can, it's a small issue; if you forget to provide recycling facilities at an event with 1,000 soda cans, it's a big issue.

All events carry the opportunity to create a real, positive change in the community and environment they occur in. Event leaders will identify these opportunities and maximize them. Corporate events can inspire economic development in an era of recession. Cultural events can support equality and showcase neglected communities.

ECOLOGIC

South by Southwest (SXSW)

South by Southwest (SXSW), colloquially referred to as South By, is an annual conglomerate of film, interactive media, music festival, and conference that takes place in mid-March in Austin, Texas. SXSW first started in 1986 and celebrated its 31st event in 2018. The economic impact on the Austin economy from SXSW in 2017 was $348.6 million.

SXSW acknowledges and takes responsibility for its environmental impact. Learn more about their efforts to integrate principles of environmental sustainability into organizational practices.

SXSW understands its environmental impact, and its sustainability statement clearly indicates its focus on ecological sustainability of the events.

"We will demonstrate leadership in efforts to integrate principles of environmental sustainability into our organizational practices. We strive to implement solutions that limit and mitigate the environmental effects of our operations and events."

As the host city, Austin has a strong record of thriving environmental stewardship, conservation, and clean tech. Among its series of events, the annual SXSW ECO, a sustainability and energy conference, is one of the organization's newest features. The programming relates to urban ecosystems, food waste, climate change, and social justice. During March of each year, the city hosts its world-renowned music festivals with an environmental consciousness to match it. Public transportation includes its Metro train stops right outside the Austin Convention Center. SXSW selects a number of sustainable hotels as its partner hotels for its events. For instance, the award-winning Habitat Suites Hotel has a commitment to ecology and sustainable business practices.

Sources: www.sxsw.com/about/sustainability; and www.sxsw.com/wp-content/uploads/2016/07/HabitatSuites-Sustainability.pdf.

Fiscal Responsibility

Event leaders are responsible for ethical and sustainable budgeting and cash flow. A great event is not so great if it makes a financial loss. There is greatness on the stage, and greatness on the page of your bankbook. Did you budget wisely and carefully? Did you spend appropriately, and charge a fair price? Never forget your responsibility to pay your staff and vendors fairly, accurately, and on time. This includes your own payment. Have you budgeted a salary that reflects your work on this event? Can this salary sustain you, and if not, how will you source extra income? A great event is one where everyone gets paid at the end, and you can afford to produce an even better event next.

Delegation and Empowerment

An event leader is not able to do everything. It is important for an event leader to focus on key responsibilities while delegating tasks to others. Assigning tasks to the correct staff is an important skill set of an event leader. Assign tasks to your staff and evaluate their performances. In the meantime, an event leader should provide all the resources that the staff needs to accomplish the tasks. In addition, there are times an event leader can empower his or her staff based on evaluations and can motivate them, thereby making them excel in the delegated tasks. If such assignment and empowerment are not given to your team members, it may result in a lack of trust. Most importantly, the event leader will not have sufficient time and energy to focus on critical tasks nor perform at the highest level.

Human Resource Management

You are the locomotive that makes the event train move forward. The human resources (HR) for your event represent the fuel that will drive the successful outcomes for your program. This fuel represents scarce resources that must be conserved and carefully deployed to achieve maximum benefit for your events organization. Southwest Airlines refers to its HR department simply as the "people" department. In fact, the event industry's most important resource is and always will be its people. Julia Rutherford Silvers, CSEP, in *Professional Event Coordination* (2003), describes how using "reverse scheduling" assists event planners in realistic scheduling of human resources. According to Rutherford Silvers, "When estimating the time required for each task is defined, you must consider all constraints, assumptions, capabilities, historical information, and mandatory dependencies (the tasks that must be completed before another task can begin)."

Fairness

Life is not fair, but it is our responsibility as human beings to strive for fairness. In a work situation, people make or influence decisions about the employment, payment, and treatment of others. These decision makers have a responsibility to employ, pay, and treat others fairly.

In terms of employment, qualified candidates should have a fair chance of getting the job, regardless of their race, sex, or background. Employees should receive a fair wage for the work they do. They should be provided with a happy, healthy

Photo by Seungwon Shawn Lee

Students from George Mason University and Virginia Tech volunteer at the 2018 PyeongChang Winter Olympics/Paralympics in South Korea. Highly dedicated volunteers like them are valuable resource for HR management.

work environment, and given the resources required to do their job in a safe manner. These are the essentials of human resources.

Job opportunities should be posted widely in your community so that all persons have the chance of applying. At least two members of staff should collaborate in selecting candidates for interviews, based on established criteria relevant to the job description. At least two staff members should be present in the initial interview, and interview questions should be relevant to the job. The person in charge of hiring should get feedback from other staff members before making the final selection.

Salary should be based on the job criteria, the average industry salary for this position, and the living costs in your region, with some flexibility built in for a specific candidate's experience. Do not guess at salaries based on your budget, or else you will end up overpaying when you are flush, and underpaying when you are not, creating inequality in the workforce. Research the proper rates in your industry.

ECOLOGIC

Fair Trade

The fair trade movement seeks to champion workers' rights and stand up for a fair wage and fair working conditions, especially in the developing world, where few government regulations exist. The Fairtrade Foundation includes the following criteria in their definition of fair trade:

- Fair pricing that reflects the value of the labor
- Investment in improving the environment of the working location
- Mutually beneficial long-term relationship between workers and traders
- Establishment of socially, economically, and environmentally responsible working conditions

Look for the Fairtrade label when purchasing products, and ask your event vendors about their fair trade practices.

Equality

In addition to fairness, equality is a core concept of human resources. Every person deserves to be treated equally regardless of their age, sex, race, religion, economic or social background, romantic lifestyle, or political belief. The only thing that should matter is: Can they do the job?

All too often exceptional candidates are left out of the application process because of personal bias. This bias may be overt, such as sexism, or unconscious—perhaps the hirer was put off by a hard-to-pronounce name and didn't even realize it. One way to ensure equal opportunity is to insist on anonymous job applications, without any picture or personal details except for a last name. This way the hirer will not know the age, gender, race, or religion of the candidates.

You may wish to include an Equal Opportunities Monitoring Form with each job application. Applicants may volunteer demographic details such as age, gender, race, or religion on a separate sheet, returned separate from the application to an HR person, who can then track the demographics of those who have applied to better understand if your company attracts a diverse pool of applicants.

Does your company's diversity match that of the region? Are you primarily hiring men? Are all of these men over 40 years? Is it all men with long white hair and beards over 40 years? If you work in a magical land of wizards such as in *The Hobbit* or *Harry Potter*, this demographic may be appropriate. However, if you work in other locations, you may want to enquire why you have no women or no young persons as members of your staff.

Rarely will a company's diversity exactly match that of its community, but if you notice a huge discrepancy, you may want to try advertising your jobs to a wider audience. There may be hugely qualified candidates who have not yet noticed your company because they live in a different neighborhood or read different newspapers.

It is extremely important to be sensitive when communicating about equality and diversity. Saying that you would like to hire people belonging to a certain demographic can be just as offensive as saying that you would *not* like to hire that same demographic. The important thing is that everyone have a fair shot, and a person's demographic or personal details have nothing to do with his or her potential work for your company.

Do Say	Don't Say
Persons with disabilities	The disabled, the handicapped
Mentally disabled	Retarded, slow, crazy
Persons with physical disabilities	Handicapped, crippled
Visually impaired	Blind
Hearing impaired	Deaf
Persons of short stature	Midget, dwarf
Wheelchair user	Wheelchair bound

FIGURE 4.4 Accessible terminology.

Accessibility: ADA and Global Policies

According to the latest U.S. Census Bureau's *2014 Survey of Income and Program Participation* (SIPP), 6.5 percent of Americans under age 65 years have a disability. If your next meeting or event reflects the national average, nine out of one hundred attendees may have a disability. Accessibility is no longer an option; all events must be accessible to persons of all abilities.

Begin with understanding the correct terminology. Figure 4.4 shows both the correct terms and those that are deemed offensive and hurtful. Some terms are common sense; others are more complex. The important thing is to treat all people with the respect and dignity that they deserve.

Once you know the language, learn the best practices in accessible communication. Do not raise your voice, as if you are speaking to a child, when speaking with persons with mental disabilities. Try to engage wheelchair users at eye level, leaning or crouching when necessary. Offer your hand as a guide to visually impaired persons, and describe where you are leading them. These are simple tips that should be shared with all staff.

The more difficult part of this process is building improvements. Is your building or event site accessible? Here are just a few of the guidelines for building accessibility required by the U.S. Americans with Disabilities Act (ADA):

- Clear all accessible walkways and parking spaces of debris.
- Provide accessible pathways at least 3 feet wide.
- Provide ramps for any elevated pathways.
- Provide accessible countertops low enough to suit wheelchair users.
- Ensure that all signs include a Braille translation.
- Provide audio enhancement services.
- Provide captioning and audio description.

Today we have events with a global representation in both event staff and attendees at locations all around world. That requires event leaders to possess a broad understanding of international laws and regulations in regard to accessibility and equality. At the international level, there are binding and nonbinding international human rights instruments adopted by the General Assembly of the United Nations that explicitly protect the rights of disabled persons. At the regional level, the Organization of American States (OAS) and the European Union (EU) have passed strong equality legislation on disability. For example:

- The Europeans with Disabilities Act was developed and implemented by the Council of Europe and the European Union.
- The Law of the People's Republic of China on the Protection of Disabled Persons establishes the China Disabled Persons' Federation, which has the responsibility to represent and protect the rights and interests of disabled persons in China.

Photo by Joe Goldblatt

Successful event team acknowledges applause from audience.

The topics of accessibility and equality are very important and complex matters to an event leader. Therefore, it is strongly advised that event leaders consult with their HR department or HR specialty lawyer in key issues while striving to pay the best attention to the people with a disability. Accessibility is an exciting issue for public events that is constantly developing. Begin learning the basics now and you will stay ahead of future regulation.

The Relaxed Performance

On December 13, 2012, Edinburgh's Festival Theatre hosted the first ever Relaxed Performance in Scotland. No, it's not a show where you get a pillow and have a nap. A Relaxed Performance is aimed at children with profound and complex learning needs, who have little opportunity to attend theater and events because they may make disruptive involuntary noises, may not be able to sit still, have complex physical needs, and may not cope well with the darkness of an auditorium or with loud music.

Unlike a traditional show, this relaxed performance featured:

- No black-outs in the auditorium and reduced sound levels
- Provision of hoists and changing beds
- Break-out spaces for those feeling overwhelmed
- Removed seating to accommodate more wheelchair users
- Accommodations for dealing with food, medication, and transport
- Extra ramped emergency exit provision

Thanks to the Festival Theatre's efforts, hundreds of children from special schools across Scotland were able to enjoy a very special performance of the Christmas classic *The Snowman*. For many children, this was the first time they had ever seen a live theatrical show. A brand new musical production of *Dr. Dolittle* returns to the stage in 2019, featuring a cast of amazing puppets and incorporating a petting zoo for children with autism, allowing them to actually experience the animals.

Volunteer Coordination

Volunteers are the lifeblood of many events. Without volunteers, these events would cease to exist. In fact, the vast majority of events are entirely volunteer-driven. Effectively recruiting, training, coordinating, and rewarding volunteers is a vital part of many event operations. Although challenging, the recommendations that follow will help you streamline this critical function.

Many event leaders are now turning to corporate America to recruit legions of volunteers for their events. First, the corporation is asked to serve as an event sponsor, and as part of its sponsorship, the corporation may provide key executives to give advice and counsel or a team of 100 or more volunteers to manage the beverage booths, games, or other aspects of the event. A good source for volunteer leadership through corporations is the office of public affairs, public relations, or human resources. Toni McMahon, former executive director of the Arts Council of Fairfax County and producer of the International Children's Festival, goes right to the top. "I start with the chief executive officer. If I can get this person to buy into the event, others will surely follow," McMahon says. Her track record speaks for itself, with literally dozens of major corporations providing hundreds of volunteers for this annual event.

Other sources for volunteers are civic and fraternal organizations. Part of the mission of these organizations is community service, so they will be receptive to your needs. A related organization is that of schools, both public and private. In many school districts across the United States, high school students are required to complete a minimum number of community service hours in order to graduate. Do not overlook colleges and universities. Many institutions of higher learning have dozens of student organizations that also have a service mission and may be willing to participate in your event.

Social consumer-generated media, such as Facebook, Twitter, and MySpace, have become critical to the recruitment process. Encourage your current employees and family, as well as friends, to post on these sites about opportunities to work with your event. These sites now reach a wide range of diverse stakeholders, whose talents may be well used for your upcoming event.

The key to attracting these groups is the WIFM ("What's in it for me?") principle. When you contact these organizations, learn a little bit about their needs and then use the objectives of your event to help them fulfill their needs. Jeff Parks, president of ArtsQuest, the producer of the Bethlehem, Pennsylvania, award-winning MusikFest, works with numerous community groups to produce everything from food and beverage stands to maintaining the porta-johns; in turn, each group raises thousands of dollars to support the good work for their not-for-profit organization. These groups know exactly what's in it for them: cash. This cash enables them to do good work all year long. Determine what's in it for them, and you will quickly find volunteers standing in line to help your event succeed.

All volunteers must be trained. This training need not be time-consuming, but it must be comprehensive. One way to reduce the amount of time required is to publish a handbook for volunteers that summarizes event policies and procedures. Training may take the form of a social gathering, such as an orientation, or it can be a formalized instruction in the field at the actual event site. It does not matter

TECH/APPVIEW

Recruiting Volunteers with Social Network Services

As the popularity of social media continues to rise with no sign of slowing down, the ways it can be used have increased dramatically. It is no longer simply a means to stay connected with friends and family. Now, social media is a news resource, a way of promoting products and services, a fundraising platform, and even a recruitment tool.

If you run a nonprofit, you can use social media to attract and engage volunteers. In fact, every follower is a potential volunteer. Follow these tips to recruit individuals who are as passionate about your cause as you are.

To optimize social media for your volunteer recruitment, an event leader must understand the characteristics of SNS users. Most people tend to skim through their newsfeeds without pause unless something sticks out. Therefore, your event and newsfeeds must include multimedia; simple and professional looking image to hold people's attention.

Post interesting, eye-catching content consistently. Consider what your audience will find most compelling to transform followers of your SNS into volunteers.

Once you have a number of volunteers signed up via SNS, the next key step is screening and training them to be an invaluable asset to your event. Here again, an event leader must be sure to consider the characteristics of the SNS-recruited volunteers; they are pro technology and feel comfortable in settings with many activities. Online training is an effective training channel for them. For instance, the 2018 Winter Olympics volunteers were recruited via online channels (e.g., its official website and SNS sites), and the majority of extensive screening and training sessions were conducted online. Before, during, and after, event volunteer management was seamlessly run by its online volunteer managing platform.

The 2020 Summer Olympics in Japan has launched its SNS volunteer application campaign and is successfully progressing its application process using social media channels.

---

how you deliver this training, as every group of volunteers will require a different method in order to help them learn. However, what is important is that you test for mastery to make certain that they are learning and applying the skills you are imparting. Testing for mastery can be done through a written exam, observation, or a combination of both.

The on-site management of volunteers entails coordinating their job performance to ensure that you are accomplishing the goals of the event. Depending on the skill level of the volunteers, you must assign team leaders or supervisors in sufficient number to oversee their performance. Remember that the coordination of volunteers involves coaching and mentoring. Make certain that your team leaders or supervisors are skilled in these areas.

Don't wait until the end of the event to say "thank you." Some organizations publish volunteer newsletters; others host holiday parties to thank the volunteers for their help during the annual summer festival. Giving volunteers early, frequent, and constant recognition is a critical component in developing a strong and loyal volunteer team. You may wish to create an annual contest for Volunteer of the Year or some such recognition to encourage good-natured competition among your team members. Make certain that you carefully research with your volunteers how to effectively recognize and reward their service to the event.

Contract Temporary Employees

You may incorporate cost-efficient human resource management with cost control by contracting temporary employees for peak seasons. This will allow you to keep in place only those employees whom you need all year long. This will also help you to retain your permanent staff longer, since you will be in a better position to extend your resources to a smaller number of permanent staff. The biggest downside of this strategy is the challenge of attracting qualified personnel for short-term assignments. You can minimize the risk of having to deal with unprofessional behavior by hiring hospitality and event students from your local colleges and universities or by establishing long-term trusting relationships with a specialized staffing agency. Your collaboration with local schools can be based on offering shorter- and longer-term professional internships. Such programs can also be helpful for screening your potential future employees.

Organizational Charts

Although not all organizations have their organizational charts in document form, all organizations have an internal structure that determines important things such as promotion and growth and that simply regulates everyday operations. Even if you have never seen an organizational chart, you know to whom you report, who reports to you, and at what level of responsibility and authority you are at a certain point in time.

However, it is important to be able to evaluate organizational charts from the employer and employee standpoints. Figure 4.5 represents a typical "flat" organizational structure with little opportunity for growth and significant power in two managers' hands. Although these structures exist, it is important to realize that employee retention under this structure is likely to be low, since most people would like to see a potential for growth and promotion within their organization. If they do not find it, they will soon start looking for other opportunities elsewhere. The few managers in such organizations share high power and probably will keep their positions for a lengthy time period.

In some cases, the organization structure cannot be changed; therefore, you may develop loyalty in your employees by creating incentive programs, improving the work environment, and increasing compensation. Figure 4.6 represents a more dynamic and complex organizational structure that offers its employees better growth potential, higher titles, and more focused work assignments. In this kind of organization, you can offer your employees cross-training opportunities that will add to their professional growth. You can clearly see identifiable departments, which will make it easier to form teams.

Less frequently, you can find other types of organization structures (see Figures 4.7 and 4.8). For example, some organizations have one subordinate reporting to three supervisors. This kind of situation rarely works out successfully and often leads to frustration for both employee and manager. Many small event organizations run into difficulties when they hire very few people to complete a vast variety of tasks

FIGURE 4.5 Flat traditional organizational structure.

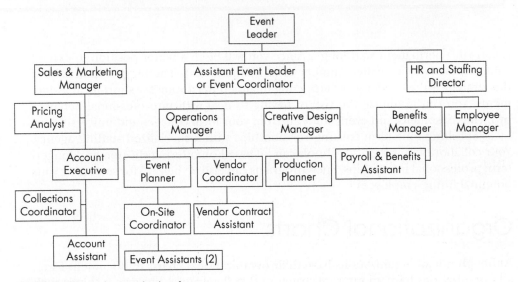

FIGURE 4.6 Dynamic organizational structure.

due to limited financial resources. If the relationship is built on trust and mutual cooperation, such alliances can be beneficial for either party for a limited period of time. However, when the company gains more business, the situation needs to be changed. If an employee is overscheduled with work and is not physically able to complete it due to the lack of help, this employee will probably quit and look for another job. You have to remember that valuing your employees, investing in their development, and building their loyalty will be more financially rewarding to you in the long run than saving money on employee incentives and generating extra costs for recruiting and training.

FIGURE 4.7 Top-down organization.

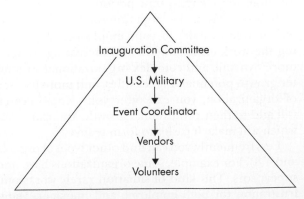

FIGURE 4.8 Bottom-up organization.

Baby Boomers	Generation Y	Generation Z
Compensation (salary and benefits)	The values of the organization are aligned with those of the worker	When their opinions and input are valued as collaborator
Title (position name)	Flexible hours	Important issues to them (e.g., human, gender, racial, and sexual orientation equality)
Promotion opportunities	Travel opportunities	Want to change the world a better place Security and money
	Education	Cool product over cool experience
	Compensation	
	Career advancement	

FIGURE 4.9 Motivations for special event human resources by generations.

Retired or soon-to-be-retired baby boomers (1.72 billion) and generation Y (2.5 billion) have defined modern workplaces. Event leaders engage with and understand generation Y and Z—an increasingly important group of customers and workforces who shape the present and the future. Although the baby boomers were primarily motivated by compensation packages, generation Y employees are motivated by different incentives. Figure 4.9 demonstrates the similarities and vast differences in motivation between the baby boomers and generation Y.

As Figure 4.9 demonstrates, the motivations for the generation Y and Z workers are vastly more complex than those for the baby boomers. It is likely that you will be supervising multi-generations so it is important to understand the motivations of all types of workers so that you can address these issues through recruitment and meet their expectations to ensure retention. For further information about generation Y, visit www.generationwhy.com and playbook.amanet.org/training-articles-characteristics-motivations-generation-z/. For generation Z, visit www.forbes.com/sites/deeppatel/2017/09/21/8-ways-generation-z-will-differ-from-millennials-in-the-workplace/#5787b34a76e5.

Developing Policies, Procedures, and Practices

The best organizational chart will not completely communicate to your stakeholders the precise actions they should take in specific situations before, during, and following the event. This is why it is important that you carefully develop policies, procedures, and practices that reflect the culture of your event organization.

Everyone benefits from well-written policies and procedures. First, the internal stakeholders benefit from having a clear process through which to make decisions. Second, the external stakeholders benefit from using a tool to help them understand the organization and the decision-making process of the event team. Finally, the guests themselves benefit. Although they may never see a copy of the policies and procedures, in the event of a life-threatening emergency, thanks to this document, lives may be saved.

This document is used in a variety of ways. It may be given to all full-time staff and volunteers as a reference tool. It may be distributed to members of the board of directors to guide the development of future policies. Most importantly, it may be used by the event leader to implement the board's policies through carefully developed procedures.

Policies are conceived of and approved by the sponsoring organization's trustees. Typically, the trustees are the owners of the event, such as a private businessperson, a corporate board of directors, or the trustees of a not-for-profit group. The policies that are developed and approved reflect the vision and mission of the organization as well as comply with local, state, provincial, and federal laws.

Procedures are the implementation tactics for policies. Policies may be broad, overarching rules of conduct, whereas procedures are the regulations that administrators or event leaders use to implement policies. Both policies and procedures are essential to produce and sustain successful events.

Many events have well-crafted policies and procedures that can serve as a model for an organization. Contact another event organization of similar size and scope, and ask it to share a copy of its policies and procedures. In addition, ask the company how it most effectively communicates these policies and procedures to its stakeholders.

Carefully review your vision and mission statement, and use your event strategic plan as a litmus test for every policy and procedure you create. Appoint experts in a variety of event fields, including volunteer coordination, risk management, sponsorship, and others to help you review and create the final draft of your policies and procedures.

Convene a focus group composed of typical event stakeholders to make certain that what you have written can be implemented easily and effectively. Next, survey a wider group to sample their opinions. This group should include external stakeholders, such as government, police, fire, and other officials.

Make certain that your policies and procedures are fully in compliance with local, state, provincial, and federal laws. Retain an attorney to review your document to ensure compliance. Your document may be beautifully written, but unless it is in full compliance with all laws, it will be of no value.

Finally, regularly evaluate and revise your policies and procedures. Laws change, events mature, and other changes require that your policies, procedures, and practices document be revisited annually to look for gaps and provide updates to close these gaps. One example of this is the massive revisions that were required after the implementation of The U.S. Americans with Disabilities Act. A typical event policy and procedure can be outlined as follows:

I. Media conferences. Media conferences will be held prior to the annual event and at other times as required. (Policy)
   A. The event manager will schedule the media conference with staff. (Procedure)
      1. The public relations coordinator will implement the media conference. (Practice)
   B. Participants will include but not be limited to credentialed members of the media, members of the board of trustees, and invited guests.
      1. The public relations coordinator will issue these credentials.
   C. The chair of the board of trustees will serve as the official spokesperson for the event organization at all media conferences. In the absence of the chair, the event leader will serve in this position.
      1. The official spokesperson will prepare in advance copies of his or her written remarks and distribute the copies for comment to the board.
      2. An audio recording will be made of each media conference.
      3. The public relations coordinator will be responsible for recording the media conference and providing a written transcription.

Linda Higgison further noted that event leaders wear many hats, creating a culture of professionalism, quality, and yes, fun. You will not only educate and inform but even occasionally inspire your event team to exceed the expectations of your guests.

GLOBAL EVENT THOUGHT LEADERS

TERRY SINGLETON, CSEP

President and COO, CCP Events Inc., Past President, International Live Events Association

http://goo.gl/qf5XsR

(Note: To see the complete video interview, visit the Book Companion Site for this book at www.wiley.com/go/goldblatt/specialevents8e.)

Ms. Singleton started her career working for Xerox Corporation as a product manager responsible for product launches, team building, sales contests, and other events. During that period of her career she was exposed to a casino night party and met the owner and was soon helping produce these types of parties as a hobby. Five years later, she realized she loved the special events industry, packed up her family, and moved to Atlanta, Georgia, and used her life savings of $20,000 to start a new business in a town she had never lived in before. Today, she has a warehouse with 25,000 square feet of equipment and eight full-time employees, and a turnover of about US $2.5 million per year.

Q: How is the special events industry different today from when you started?

A: I think that thanks to people who have been doing this for a long time we have become legitimized and recognized as a true profession. In addition, young people today are focusing upon educating themselves and finding high-quality mentors who are experienced industry professionals. Young people must have an extreme depth of knowledge due to the trend of the one stop shop being rapidly developed. Caterers are becoming decorators and decorators are becoming conference planners so the people they hire have to know how to do much more than in the past.

Q: Do you see environmental sustainability as an important trend in the events industry?

A: Absolutely, we do things now we would not have done years ago. As an example, when we design floral [arrangements] we do not dump the waste water, instead, we repurpose it. Our clients want to know if the flowers are locally grown. What pesticides were used in the growing process? They want to know what you are doing as an event professional to promote ecologically sound programs.

Q: How is technology affecting the special events industry today?

A: No longer do you put out pads and pencils at conferences. Clients now want devices where they can record the entire program. iPads and even charging stations are more and more becoming the norm for events. Clients want to be able to blog and tweet during the event. Registration for many events is now almost universally online. I recently attended a seminar describing using 3-D mapping to create visual images on the facades of buildings. This kind of thinking was unheard of when I began in this industry.

Q: How is the style of special events changing?

A: I think we are diving toward more minimalist events. It used to be about the big prop, the big wow factor. Now it is being driven by lighting and technology. One of the reasons for minimalism is that clients want it to look like they spent less even if they spent more.

Q: How do you become an effective Event Leader in the special events industry?

A: People do things and follow your lead because the leader inspires them to want to do that. I believe the leader must first be someone who inspires [people] to connect with others, to learn, to grow personally and professionally, and to become a great leader by following through example. I think great leadership is all about inspiration.

Q: How would you like to be remembered for your contributions to the modern special events industry?

A: I made a difference and that I inspired people and as a result of that they became better professionals at what they do.

Q: If you were to write a LinkedIn recommendation for the special events industry 25 years in the future, what would you say?

A: I would say the special events industry has grown to be recognized as a legitimate and valuable industry, and that by using professionals you will have flawless and creative events that help to grow companies and organizations and project images of what they wish to be.

Q: What will the future hold for the special events industry?

A: Today, companies and organizations are developing events that have a cause-related focus. I think that they will continue to be involved in social awareness and continue to give of their time, talent, and resources, and that events will continue to be a celebration of those successes.

Summary

People planning and management, and effective communication are essential skills for leaders in the events industry. The three major styles of event management are autocratic, democratic, and laissez-faire. Critical leadership characteristics include integrity, confidence, communication, vision, and social, environmental, and fiscal responsibility. Create policies, procedures, and practices to anticipate problems that may occur among your staff and volunteers. Event leaders are responsible for establishing equality and accessibility within all of their events. Volunteers and temporary employees are the lifeblood of most events, and you must find out what is in it for them, as they are motivated differently from staff who receive paid compensation.

Key Terms

Accessibility: Every event must be accessible to the widest possible audience and group of stakeholders.

Autocratic leadership: Leadership that is driven from a central command or top down.

Bottom-up structure: Where volunteers and other stakeholders lead the organization producing the event, as in a not-for-profit organization or association committee.

Democratic leadership: Where the event leader consults with the members of the event planning organization and considers their opinions before acting.

Dynamic structure: An event organization such as The Olympic Games that begins with a small team and then escalates to a large group and then returns to its small size following the delivery of the event.

E-etiquette: The use of thoughtful, accurate, and respectful language when utilizing e-mail.

Laissez-faire leadership: When the event leader allows the stakeholders to widely discuss the event ideas and plans, and waits for them to reach consensus before he or she offers their opinion.

Mirror etiquette: When an individual observes persons during a meal or other function and then mirrors their behaviors to ensure they are using proper etiquette in each setting.

Organizational chart: A pictorial tool for notifying the stakeholders who reports to whom within an organization.

Temporary employee: An individual who is appointed to a position for a fixed period of time.

Time management: The ability to efficiently and effectively use the time allotted to produce the event to achieve the best possible outcomes.

Top-down structure: The organizational chart design used in hierarchal organizations such as the military where there is a strong central command and all stakeholders follow a central leader.

Volunteer: A person who is not financially compensated for the work they contribute to an event but is instead motivated by a complex set of desires including the opportunity to support a cause, to network with others and to advance their own career by gaining further experience.

Career Connections

Analyze the eight leadership characteristics and how they apply to your previous experience in work. Which areas are you most confident in and which areas do you need to work on? Ask a friend or colleague for his or her perspective on these characteristics. Look for opportunities to develop your skills in the areas that you are lacking.

Next Steps

Check out *The Complete Guide to Careers in Special Events*, the first comprehensive guide to careers in special events by Gene Columbus. Gene served in a wide variety of managerial positions for Walt Disney World for nearly 40 years. During this time, he was instrumental in interviewing, hiring, coaching, and mentoring thousands of event leaders and professionals in other fields. His experience, expertise, advice, and wise counsel are priceless, and we recommend that you review this book for more information about your own human resource development and career development.

References

American Management Association (2018). PLAYBOOK: Your source book for practical workforce. Accessed: October 11, 2018: playbook.amanet.org/training-articles-characteristics-motivations-generation-z/.

Degener, T., Quinn, G., and Disability Rights Education & Defense Fund (2012) *A Survey of International, Comparative and Regional Disability Law Reform*, Berkley, CA.

Festival & King's Theatres, Edinburgh: www.edtheatres.com

Jin, N., Lee, S., and Daniels, M. (2017) Wedding planners' use of social media, *Event Management*, Vol. 21, pp. 515–521.

Patel, Deep (2018) 8 Ways generation Z will differ from millennials in the workplace, *Forbes*. Accessed October 1, 2018: www.forbes.com/sites/deeppatel/2017/09/21/8-ways-generation-z-will-differ-from-millennials-in-the-workplace/#5787b34a76e5.

Rutherford Silvers, J. (2011) *Professional Event Coordination, Second Edition*, Hoboken, NJ: John Wiley & Sons.

Taylor, F. (1911) *The Principles of Scientific Management*, Create Space Independent Publishing Platform.

Financial Sustainability

"It is not from the benevolence of the butcher, the brewer, or the baker that we expect our dinner, but from their regard to their own self-interest."

"To feel much for others and little for ourselves; to restrain our selfishness and exercise our benevolent affections, constitute the perfection of human nature."

—*Adam Smith,* **Father of Modern Economics, (1723–1790)**

In this chapter you will learn how to:
- Understand basic event planning financial and accounting terminology
- Maintain event financial records
- Understand and interpret the event balance sheet and income statement
- Calculate the break-even point and profit margin for your event
- Forecast projected revenues and expenses for your event
- Estimate reliable budget goals for your event
- Provide a pro forma, a forecast and to re-cast the budget to satisfy final revenue goals
- Examine financial contingency plans for overcoming low ticket sales, business interruption due to disasters
- Increase cash flow
- Identify sustainable funding for your event
- Identify alternative funding for your event
- Manage your event during turbulent economic times
- Plan and allocate your event budget

Photo by Seungwon Shawn Lee

Sponsorships make event finances strong in both good and bad economies. The photo shows the main sponsor recognition poster at the IMEX America in Las Vegas.

During the great economic turbulence of the early twenty-first century, one might assume that Adam Smith's theory of self-interest in business would be sufficient to correct the problems of the past. However, Smith, a philosopher as well as the father of the first theory of modern economics, also believed that no business might be sustainable in the long run if it did not also do good in order to do well. By this, he meant that businesses have a responsibility to all of society and not just for their own personal benefit. Throughout the development of the field of event planning, many early planners have given economics, finance, and accounting less attention than is needed in order to develop sustainable enterprises. It appears that only severe economic stress, such as that experienced from the global financial crash of 2008, is the catalyst for refocusing upon the fundamental necessity of carefully managing the financial side of the event planning enterprise.

The most common deficiency we have identified in many event planners and students who major in event management relates to the area of financial management. Event planners, by nature, rely on the right side of the brain and often ignore the important logical-thinking abilities that help ensure long-term success. In Dr. Lee's Meetings and Convention and Event Management courses at his university, he often asks students, "Do you like accounting or finance courses?" Answers from students are consistent: "NO!!!!" Then he follows up with "Do you like to make money in your career and event business?" Everyone shouts out unanimously "YES!!!!" Wait a second here. They want to make their future career or business to be profitable, but are not interested in doing good job with finance nor accounting. By simply asking these two questions, we can easily see the deficiency starts earlier in their career building up. Whether you use the services of a professional bookkeeper and/or accountant or not, knowledge of financial management is essential to the practice of modern event planning. This knowledge is not difficult to master. With modern software systems, it is actually simple and, many say, fun to practice. This chapter will introduce some of the reputable and widely used budgeting, financial software for event planners. Whether you enjoy financial management is not the issue. Few people enjoy studying for and taking their driver's license exams. However, can you imagine what the streets would be like without this baseline of knowledge? Accidents, death, and destruction everywhere might result from this lack of rigor. Financial ignorance can just as easily wreck a creative, successful event planning business and destroy your reputation, as well as have serious legal ramifications. This chapter is essential if you are planning not only to make money but to keep it. Additionally, as your business ages along with you, this chapter will help you learn how to work a little less and earn a little more.

Budgeting

The budget represents a strategic action plan that each successful event planner must carefully develop far in advance of the actual event. Budget preparation is probably the most challenging part of financial management since the entire preparation is usually based on limited information or assumptions. To complete the budget preparation, you should come up with estimates based on assumptions.

The event budget is the most important tool you will use to manage the financial decisions within your event planning business. Each event represents a separate budget. All individual budgets are combined into an annual budget. Your daily business operations also require an annual budget to reflect your earnings and expenses. Event planners should use the expression "staying within the budget" every day and for every project.

Each budget represents first and foremost the financial philosophy of the event. Since different events are designed for different purposes, they may fall into one of three categories:

1. *Profit-oriented events*: In this type of event, revenue exceeds expenses. Typical examples are events produced by corporations for the purpose of generating new sales.
2. *Break-even events*: In this type of event, revenue is equal to expense. A good example is an association conference. In this case, event professionals should budget the event, keeping the break-even assumption in mind. Admission fees should be calculated at the rate that will cover all expenses and break even.
3. *Loss leaders or hosted events*: These events are designed from the very beginning to lose money. Good examples of such events are university graduations or governmental celebrations. These events usually are organized for the purpose of promoting a cause or agenda and not designed to break even or generate a profit.

If your event is a charitable endeavor, your financial philosophy will be markedly different from that of a commercial venture. First, determine what is the financial philosophy of your event before you begin the budget process. A budget represents the income and expenses of your organization or the individual event. An event budget is based on five factors:

1. Marketing projections and estimates
2. The general history of previous identical or similar events
3. The general economy and your forecast for the future
4. The net profit or excess you reasonably believe you can expect with the resources available (return on investment)
5. The type of financing that you choose to use to finance your event (borrowed funds, prepayments, existing funds)

Financial History

The best financial history is that which occurs over a 3-year period. In some cases, it is not possible to construct a precise history, and the event planner must rely on estimates or on what is known at the time the budget is prepared. In still other cases, the event planner will have to rely on events of similar size and scope to develop the budget because his or her event is a first-time venture and no history exists. Not only is it important to base your budget on history, it is equally important that you develop controls to begin collecting financial data on the event budget you are currently preparing. These data will become the next event's historic information and help you construct a better budget.

The longer you are in the planned events industry, the more accurate your estimates will be. A good technique used for developing income projections is high–low. The logic is that an event planner compares two scenarios: the best and the worst. Next, the event planner decides whether the losses that may occur under the worst-case scenario are bearable. If so, the project is accepted. If not, the project is refused. This method is especially beneficial to small and midsized planned-events businesses that operate under financial constraints and do not have much margin for error.

General Economy in the United States and the World

Event leaders should make efforts to stay current with trends in the general domestic and international economy so they can use general economic data to assist you with the development of your budget. Reams of secondary data are available about the local, state, and national economy from offices of economic development as well as the U.S. Department of Commerce. No event takes place in a vacuum. Whether you are managing the International Special Olympics in New Haven, Connecticut, or the local food and wine festival, your event's success will be affected by the general economy. Indicators of strong economic health usually include low unemployment, a steady rate of inflation, and healthy retail sales. Other indicators include new-home-building activity, new industry, and capital investments by local, state, or federal government. Before finalizing your budget, consult with an economist from a local college or university, a representative from the local office of economic development, or the editor of the business section of your local newspaper, and ask for his or her opinion on the health of the economy.

After the 2008 global recession, excluding a handful number of countries, the U.S. Bureau of Labor Statistics assumes U.S. economy to fully recover from the recession by 2020 with its labor force returning to full employment; however, the projected slowdown initiated by the trade wars started in 2018 and 2019 is being a concern to many. However, the inflation rate is expected to remain in the 2 percent range for the next several years.

Global companies are cautiously monitoring the uncertainty resulting from the trade war between the United States and other countries.

Based on a report by World Economic Forum, global economy forecasting is more complex. Reached in its peak of Eurozone growth in 2017, it has been steadily decreasing. Political uncertainty, including Brexit, challenges faced by France's government, and Germany's chancellorship changes have contributed to a decline in EU business. China's economy is expected to begin decelerating. Emerging markets face a number of changes, too. They include slowing growth in advanced economies; their weakening currency to the U.S. dollar; and rising political uncertainty in Brazil and Mexico.

Economic environments will constantly change, but one key rule is that event leaders stay focused on trends in general domestic and international economies and use them to assist your budget development.

Reasonable Projected Income

The Greek word *logos* (or logic) means to "act reasonably." A budget based on certain logical assumptions of projections of income is one that is within reason. To logically project revenue based on the resources available, you must consider market research as well as a general knowledge of the economy. For example, if your city festival is being held this year on the local payday from the area's largest industry, does that mean you can reasonably expect that spending will be increased for your event? The only way to test this theory is with research. You may wish to contact other events of similar size and scope and evaluate their experience with similar circumstances. Furthermore, you may wish to survey some of the workers to determine if they are more likely to attend the event this year and, if so, if they will be inclined to increase their spending due to the coincidence of their payday and the event date. Making reasonable assumptions about projected revenue is one of the most important decisions that you must handle as you begin the budgeting process. Gather all the facts, seek objective opinions and counsel, and then conservatively project the revenue you hope to achieve.

Sustainable Funding

Kuan-wen Lin, Ph.D. and assistant professor at Chung Hua University, Taiwan, and Vice President for Industry Relations of Asia Pacific Institute for Events Management (APIEM), studied the budgets and financial reports of the major festivals in Edinburgh, Scotland, over a 10-year period. His study found there was no correlation between public funding for events and a successful financial outcome for the organization. Rather, his study found that the more mature the event, the more likely the financial outcome would be successful. Using Dr. Lin's study as a base, Drs. Rebecca Finkel and Joe Goldblatt interviewed public leaders in both Glasgow and Edinburgh, Scotland, to identify potential alternative sustainable funding for their cultural events, including festivals. The majority of persons they interviewed supported voluntary donations from individuals at the time of ticket purchase (such as an optional £1.00 per ticket) or an optional donation at the time of purchase of a product or service that directly benefits from the cultural event (restaurant meal, hotel room night, or other business whose income may be somewhat derived from the events). The public officials stated that redirecting the tax that is already collected from these businesses would not be as successful.

Furthermore, the overall reaction by most officials in both Glasgow and Edinburgh was that future public funding for the cultural sector will be less than in the past. It will also be erratic as it will reflect the current turbulence in the general economy. Therefore, finding alternative funding is critically important. Sustainable funding for your events should come from a variety of streams including the public purse, corporate sponsorship, philanthropy, and earned income from ticket sales, merchandise, food and beverage, and other sources. The greater the diversity of your funding, the less likely you will be strapped for cash if one of your streams dries up.

Typical Income Categories

Due to the wide range of events represented by the subfields within the event planning profession, it is difficult to categorize every type of income. However, there are some general items that most budgets include:

- Advertising revenues (event program, Internet website)
- Concession (food and beverage and merchandise sales)
- Consulting fees
- Donations/philanthropy
- Exhibit or exposition booth rental fees
- Gifts in kind (actual fair market financial value)
- Grants and contracts
- Interest income from investments
- Management fees
- Merchandise sales
- Registration fees
- Special events ticket sales
- Sponsorship fees
- Technology income (from advertising)
- Ticket sales
- Vendor commissions (hotels)
- Venture capital and venture philanthropic investment

Expenses

When preparing your budget, the first thing you will note under the expense category is how many more items are listed as compared to income. Darwin T. Lynner, a successful businessman in Des Moines, Iowa, once stated, "The income comes in through one or two doors, but the expenses can leak out of many doors." In the strange economic times of the mid-1990s, organizations placed greater emphasis on monitoring expenses because it was easier to control costs than to project revenue. Lynner also recalled that Benjamin Franklin observed some 200 years ago, "A penny saved is a penny earned." Developing solid, predictable expense categories is critical to sound financial management. These expense items often come from historical data or comparing your event to other events of similar size and scope. The actual amount budgeted for each expense line item is what you and your advisors believe to be reasonable based on the information known at the time the budget is prepared. Therefore, the more you know, the more precisely you can budget for expenses. This is another reason why record keeping is so vital to the success of your financial management operations. The general expense categories for most events are as follows:

- Accounting
- Advertising
- Advertising specialties
- Audiovisual equipment rental
- Audiovisual labor
- Automobile mileage reimbursements
- Automobile rental
- Awards and recognition
- Bonds
- Brochure and other collateral design
- Brochure and other collateral mailing
- Brochure and other collateral mechanical preparation
- Brochure and other collateral printing
- Complimentary registrations or admission
- Consultants
- Corporate social responsibility (social, economic, environmental)
- Décor
- Ecological sustainability
- Entertainment
- Evaluations
- Food and beverage
- Gratuities
- Guest transportation
- Insurance
- Legal counsel
- Licenses
- Lighting equipment rental
- Lighting labor
- Local, state, provincial, and federal taxes
- Materials shipping/freight fees
- Miscellaneous or other
- Percentage of administrative overhead
- Permits
- Photocopying
- Photography
- Postage
- Proceedings editing, design, and printing
- Public relations
- Registration contract labor
- Registration materials
- Report preparation and publishing
- Research

- Risk management corrections
- Signs
- Site office furniture rental
- Site office supplies
- Site rental
- Site telephone expense
- Sound equipment rental
- Sound labor
- Speakers' fees and/or honoraria
- Speakers' travel
- Staff travel
- Taxes (federal, state, local)
- Technology including Web design and Web hosting and telecommunications
- Videography
- Volunteer appreciation activities and gifts
- Web design and management

Structuring Account Codes

Each income or expense item must have a corresponding account code. Accounts are those general budget categories where items of similar type and impact on the overall budget are grouped together for more efficient analysis. For example, in the administration category, these items would appear:

- Décor
- Insurance
- Site telephone expenses

Under the account category "staff/volunteers," these items would be grouped together:

- Staff accommodations
- Volunteer accommodations
- Volunteer appreciation activities and gifts

TECH/APPVIEW

Tracking the budget throughout your event is important. Technology can help event planners meet financial goals through exchanging current and accurate financial information with their event team.

Cloud-based financial software can transfer financial data to communicate and collaborate with your event team. Its major benefit includes access to the information and to be able to manage your financial operations anywhere and anytime.

There are a number of helpful technology solutions in the market that will support you in budgeting. They include Expensify (www.expensify.com);

FreshBooks (www.freshbooks.com); Certify (www.certify.com); and Aventri (www.aventri.com/products/budget-planner).

Key determinants to make a selection for your team include the following: 1) if the technology solution can be easily implemented; 2) how much training does it require; 3) what type of technical support is available (ideally 24/7); 4) capability of budget tracking, forecasting of event expenses over several events; and 5) discussion with key stakeholders of your events who may need access to financial information through a technology.

Each account code has a numerical listing to make it easy to find individual entries. The general categories start with the 100 series. For example, administration would be 100, marketing would be 500, and so on. Each item would have a separate sequential numerical listing:

100 Administrative
500 Marketing
501 Advertising
502 Advertising specialties
503 Brochure and other collateral design
504 Brochure and other collateral mechanical preparation
505 Brochure and other collateral mailing
506 Brochure and other collateral printing
507 Public relations

Finding and Supervising an Accountant

Contact your local chamber of commerce, society of chartered or public accountants, or local business association to obtain a referral for an accountant who may be familiar with event budgets or service businesses. Once you have prepared a draft budget, seek the counsel of the accountant to review your budget and help you with establishing the various line items and account codes. Your accountant will be able to interpret the tax codes for you to make certain that your accounts match the terms and requirements for the local, state, provincial, and federal tax authorities.

Make certain that you discuss billing and fees in advance with your accountant. You may retain the accountant to handle specific operations or to coordinate all of your financial procedures. Obviously, the cost will fluctuate greatly based on the number of tasks you ask the accountant to perform. Using accounting software may help you reduce your costs and provide you with better, faster information.

Accounting Software

Since the invention of the spreadsheet program for computers, accounting has never been the same. Commercial software packages such as Quicken have allowed small business owners to record their journal entries quickly, accurately, and cost-effectively. What once required many hours with a pencil and eraser has, thanks to modern computer science, been reduced to a fraction of the time. Microsoft Excel is still a very effective tool in budgeting and creating financial projections for many small-sized event firms. Many college students who return from their semester-long internships at various types of event planning firms share that MS Excel is still widely popular for basic budget and financial reporting. They also express that there are a lot more that they should have learned about features of MS Excel to effectively utilize it. Therefore, we encourage you to spend some time familiarizing yourself at least with basic functions of this software.

Although using commercial software is time-efficient, it does require certain additional safeguards. First, make certain you always back up your data on a back-up data storage on both hardware and cloud and store this information in a safe, fireproof location. Next, regularly send a copy of your data to your accountant so that he or she can prepare your monthly, quarterly, and annual financial reports. Consult with your certified professional accountant to determine the best type of software to invest in because, to a large extent, you will be partners, and you should be using software that will allow you to communicate effectively on a regular basis.

Producing Profit

The financial purpose of every for-profit business is to produce a fair net profit. The term *profit* means the earnings over and above all expenses.

Profit = Revenue – Expenses

Not-for-profit organizations do not, for obvious reasons, use the term *profit*. Instead, they refer to this excess of income over expenses as *retained earnings*. In fact, the earnings are not retained for long, as the organizations are required by the tax code to reinvest the earnings in their business operations rather than distribute them to shareholders, as some for-profit businesses do.

Producing a fair net profit is challenging but possible for event planning businesses. The challenge is that event planners must work with a wide range of clients, and it is difficult to budget for each event carefully to ensure a net profit. There are too many variables to ensure that this happens every time. However, if the business is to remain healthy at year end, the business activities must result in a net profit.

Although there is no average for net profit, let us consider, for the purposes of discussion, that your financial goal is to achieve an annual net profit of 15 percent. To do this, you must guard all fixed overhead expenses carefully. All expenses may be divided into two major categories: (1) fixed overhead expenses and (2) variable expenses. Although both of these categories are expenses, the methods you use to manage and control them are different. To understand how you can minimize your expenses, you should be able to make a distinction between these two categories.

Fixed Overhead Expenses

Fixed overhead expenses of an organization are those predictable items such as rent, salaries, insurance, telephone, and other standard operating expenses required to support the event planning business. The better you are able to achieve a lower cost of sale, the greater net profit you will achieve. To lower your cost of operations, it is imperative that you try to reduce your fixed overhead expenses. Many event planning firms have suffered great losses or have even gone out of business entirely because they tried to expand too rapidly. Expansion brings increased cost of sales, and increased cost of sales means that you must produce much greater income. As we discussed earlier, due to the volatility of the world economy, this is not always possible. Once you have cut your fixed overhead expenses to a level that allows you to maintain quality but at the same time produce a fair net profit, you must return your attention to variable, or direct, expenses.

Fixed expenses of an individual event do not depend on the number of participants. For example, rent is a fixed expense. Rent expense usually does not vary when the number of participants increases or decreases slightly. The expense of live music is similar. If an event planner contracts a local band to entertain guests, the cost of this entertainment is fixed. Variable costs are the costs that depend on the attendance (e.g., food and beverages). Food and beverage expenses for 100 people will be approximately twice as large as if only 50 people attend the event.

This example will help you to understand the difference. The event planner of a midsized corporation has to budget expenses for a reception. He or she is not sure about the exact number of guests; however, the minimum and the maximum numbers of guests are known. The minimum number is 200 guests and the maximum is 400. The catering company has provided the event planner with its price quote of $25 per person for food and $15 per person for beverages. The event planner creates the expense calculation shown in Figure 5.1.

Variable Expenses

Variable expenses are more difficult to predict because often they relate to items that are purchased at the last minute from vendors, and the prices may fluctuate. Variable, or direct, expenses include audiovisual rentals and labor, registration materials, proceedings design and printing, and other items with a total cost that relies on the final number ordered and your ability to negotiate a fair price. Due to last-minute registrations and an increase in walk-up guests for a variety of events, it is extremely difficult to wait until the last minute to order certain items. Printing, as well as advance notice for audiovisual equipment rental and labor, requires a sufficient window of time to deliver a high-quality product. This means that your ability to use historical data to project the volume of items you will need or to order less with an option to obtain additional supplies rapidly will greatly help you reduce your variable or direct expenses. In addition, your ability to negotiate the best deal for your event organization will have tremendous impact on these items.

Net Profit versus Gross Profit

Event planners endeavor to produce a fair net profit. The difference between net profit and gross profit is the percentage of fixed overhead expenses that was dedicated to producing a specific event. Fixed overhead expenses dedicated to the individual event include a percentage of staff salaries and benefits, a percentage of the office expense, and other shared expenses. This percentage will fluctuate, but by using time sheets you can easily calculate the staff time directed to the event. The other expenses, such as rent, insurance, and telephone, may be given a percentage based on the time recorded from the time sheets.

Break-Even Point

To understand the break-even calculation, you have to understand one more term: *contributional margin*, the difference between the revenue received from a single person and the variable costs incurred for one person. For example, if an event planning company receives revenue of $50 per person, but the total variable cost

Number of people	200	400	
Food $25 per person	$5,000	$10,000	Variable
Beverages $15 per person	3,000	6,000	Variable
Rent / hire expense	2,000	2,000	Fixed
Entertainment expense	1,000	1,000	Fixed
Total expenses	$11,000	$19,000	

FIGURE 5.1 Fixed and variable expenses.

	Loss	Break-even	Profit
Number of people	290	300	310
Revenue:			
$50 per person	$14,500	$15,000	$15,500
Expenses:			
Variable expenses:			
Food $25 per person	7,250	7,500	7,750
Beverages $15 per person	4,350	4,500	4,650
Fixed expenses:			
Rent expense	2,000	2,000	2,000
Entertainment expense	1,000	1,000	1,000
Total expenses:	$14,600	$15,000	$15,400
Profit (revenue – expenses)	$(100)	$—	$100

FIGURE 5.2 Break-even analysis.

for one person is $40 ($25 food and $15 beverages), the contributional margin is $10 per person:

Contributional margin = Revenue per person – Variable costs per person

The final step to calculate the break-even point is to divide the total fixed costs by the contributional margin:

Break-even point = Total fixed costs/Contributional margin

For example, if the total fixed costs are $3,000 and the contributional margin is $10, the break-even point is 300 people:

300 = $3,000/$10

or

300 × $50 = $15,000

If fewer than 300 people attend the event, it loses money. It turns profitable once the attendance exceeds 300 people. Therefore, the break-even point is achieved when you collect $15,000 in revenue. Figure 5.2 demonstrates the break-even analysis.

Controlling and Reducing Costs

As an event planner, your ability to cut costs rapidly to ensure consistent profits is one that will serve you well throughout your career. To decide which costs may be cut without sacrificing the integrity of the entire event, you must begin with the budgeting process by prioritizing expenses. Seek counsel from your stakeholders and honestly determine what, in the worst-case scenario, they would like to preserve and what they could give up to ensure a profit. Although this is a difficult decision process, it is wise to make such decisions free from internal and external pressures during the final phases of the event planning process. Typically, these costs are associated with variable or direct expenses. Therefore, the expenditure is not made until later in the event planning process. Cutting your event's costs is one way to help improve your cash flow.

Ensuring Positive Event Cash Flow

It is not enough to just have profitable operations. Many event planning companies were unsuccessful because they were always out of cash. These companies showed profit on their books but had an empty checking account. This situation is called *insolvency* and may lead to bankruptcy or administration. The best way to avoid insolvency is to execute sound cash-flow management.

Cash flow is the liquidity that allows you to pay your bills, including salaries, in a timely manner. When this liquidity is gone, your reputation may not be far behind. To ensure a positive event cash flow, two measures are necessary. First, you must prearrange with your vendors payment terms and conditions that will allow you to collect revenues adequate to honor these obligations. Second, you must diligently collect those funds that are due and payable to you in a timely manner in order to meet your obligations to your vendors.

Payables are those financial accounts that you have established with vendors (money that is owed by you to others for work that has been ordered, delivered, or performed). These are funds that are due according to the agreements you have arranged with individual vendors. Receivables are those funds due to your event organization from others such as commercial sponsors and advertisers by a certain date. Aging receivables are simply those funds that were not collected at the time they were due. Five simple techniques for collecting your event receivables are shown here:

1. Log on your calendar the precise day the receivable is due.
2. Telephone early in the morning (before 10 A.M.) to ask when your payment will be processed.
3. If possible, arrange to pick it up in person or have it wired directly to your bank account.
4. If it is not possible to pick it up or have it wired, offer to provide an overnight mail service.
5. Courteously, but firmly, request payment every morning until it is received.

One of the challenges with the value of event planning services is that there is often rapid depreciation as soon as the curtain rises. Consider this scenario. Your client has invested $50,000 with your firm to produce a gala awards dinner. Midway through the dinner, the client's spouse notices a cigarette burn in the tablecloth. Later, he or she comments on "skimpy" floral arrangements. Finally, he or she complains loudly about the inferior music and food. Before long, the client locates you and wants to discuss the bill. Ironically, only 3 hours earlier, the client walked through the ballroom and event planning. Those providing leadership services and products are not usually experts in your profession. That is why they have retained you. Because the purchase of event planning services and products is sometimes an emotional decision, the buyer may easily be influenced by others. The only leverage you have as the professional provider of these services is to collect your full fee as soon as possible, because otherwise the value of your performance will deflate rapidly. As in medicine and other established professions, the old maxim "people only value what they pay for" is absolutely true in this profession.

Effective management of accounts receivable is only half of the equation needed for solid cash flow. The second half requires that you become knowledgeable about typical accounts payable agreements and learn to negotiate for the best possible payment terms. The best policy is to collect cash as fast as possible but pay off your bills on the last day allowed by the contract.

Accounts Payable: Finding the Best Terms

When establishing relationships with vendors, it is important that you learn as much as possible about the size, scope, and nature of their business. You will want to know if they own or lease their equipment. You will also want to know when they may have periods of slow business. Their off-season can produce favorable terms and perhaps discounts for your event. You will also want to know if a vendor could benefit from exposure through your event. Some event planners have a stringent rule about not letting vendors promote themselves directly to their clients. However, it is our belief that these hard-and-fast rules may prevent you from providing your client with the products and services your vendor may be able to offer.

The key to negotiating excellent terms with vendors is first to establish professional friendships (vendor partner relationships) and conduct business in an atmosphere of mutual respect. The more you know about your professional partners (vendors) and the more they know about you, the easier it is to do business. There are typical accounts payable customs and traditions in the event planning profession; however, your ability to make friends and provide assistance to your vendors will alter these customs to your benefit.

Typical Accounts Payable Customs

One accounts payable custom is for the vendor to require a deposit of 50 percent of the final contracted cost as a deposit and receive the full balance plus any additional agreed-upon charges immediately following the event. Entertainment vendors, especially those representing major celebrities, are even more stringent. They may require full payment in the form of a certified check prior to the first performance as a guarantee.

Another accounts payable custom is for the vendor to require a small deposit (as low as 10 percent) and then invoice you for the balance due net 10 or 30 days after the event. Still another custom allows you to pay your balance on account. In this custom, typically you are a regular good customer of the vendor, and the company allows you to pay off the balance monthly or within a reasonable amount of time without interest, late charges, or other penalties. Sometimes vendors even provide small discounts if you pay off your balance faster than required. There is a special terminology for this situation. For example, if a vendor offers you a 3 percent discount if you pay off your balance within the first 10 days, you may hear this formula: "3/10, net 30." This means that if you pay off the balance within 10 days, you receive 3 percent off your total bill; otherwise, you have to pay the entire balance within the next 30 days.

The final custom is for the vendor to extend credit to your organization, allowing you to authorize purchases and be invoiced by the vendor at a later date. This is the best scenario, as you are able to negotiate credit terms well in advance. Although most accounts are due within 30 days of the date of the invoice, I have heard of some arrangements where the vendor will extend credit for 60 or even 90 days to maintain the account. It is up to you to negotiate the best possible terms.

SECUREVIEW

"Master Account," sometimes interchangeably called the master bill, is a record of all charges made during an event, with the resulting balance paid by the event host.

The biggest advantage of having a master account for your event is that it allows event planners to track and reconcile charges securely and more easily than searching and sorting a specific charge.

Sometimes there can be multiple master accounts for one event if the event is city-wide with multiple event venues or event planners want to separate master accounts per expense categories (e.g., room, food and beverages, or incidentals). But the bottom line is "the lesser number of master accounts, the better to manage your budget."

It is critical to address key information (e.g., credit to and names of authorized personnel who can charge on the master account) of the master account at the start of contract negotiations to avoid any hassle during an event and at the end of it.

Negotiating Accounts Payable

Always negotiate from a position of strength. Strength in the area of accounts payable means that you have collected as much information as possible about the vendor with whom you need to negotiate. The answers to these six questions will enable you to negotiate favorable terms for your accounts payable:

1. How important is your business to this vendor?
2. During what time period is your business most needed?
3. Are your clients the types of organizations your vendor would like to do business with? How well-funded/capitalized is your vendor?
4. How does your vendor market his or her services and products? How sophisticated are your vendor's business operations?
5. What are your vendor's standard and customary accounts payable terms?
6. Most importantly, can you speak with other clients of this vendor to determine what types of terms they are receiving?

Once you have the answers to these questions, it is time to ask your vendor for more favorable terms. To do this, you will need to provide your vendor with documentation about your own business health. Testimonials from recent clients, a list of accounts receivable, and other financial data will also help you create a favorable impression. Once you have established your credibility with the vendor, ask for the most favorable terms. You might ask for credit and 90 days. The vendor may counter with 30 days, and you then agree on 60 days. Do not play hardball. Remember, this vendor will be serving your clients, and maintaining their goodwill is of supreme importance. However, you have a responsibility to your event organization to negotiate the most favorable terms and must remain firm in your pursuit of what you believe to be a fair agreement.

Your vendor may ask for a trial period, after which he or she may extend better terms once you have demonstrated your ability to meet your obligations consistently and provide the benefits your vendor expects. We cannot emphasize enough how important your relationships with your vendors are in the full spectrum of your event operations.

Controlling Purchases

The most common device for approving purchases is the purchase order (PO). No purchase should be authorized without an approved PO. This form specifies the product or service approved for purchase, the number of units, the price per unit, and the total amount due, including taxes and deliveries. The type of shipping and date and time of arrival should also be clearly specified. The PO should also state the payment terms. Instruct all your vendors by letter that you will be responsible only for purchases preceded by a valid PO. Include this statement on each PO: "Vendor may not substitute or alter this order without the written permission of the purchaser." This statement helps you avoid the creative vendor who is out of red tablecloths and believes that you will accept blue instead at the same price.

Finally, the PO must have a signature line that grants approval and the date of the approval. The PO is the most important tool you have to control your purchases and, therefore, monitor those numerous doors where expenses leak and potentially drain your event economic engine. Since your PO is a very important financial document that can hold you or your company liable, it is important to ensure a safe procedure for issuing and approving all POs. All your vendors should be informed as to who in your company is authorized to sign POs. A PO signed by the authorized person should be mailed to a vendor at the beginning of the transaction. This PO procedure is very important, and it can help save you money when you compose the final invoice.

Barter/In-Kind Payment

As the general economy tightened in 2008 and 2009, many event planning firms turned to the ancient practice of barter (providing in-kind products and services in place of cash) to help increase their cash flow and remain profitable. Barter simply means that you trade services or products with a vendor partner. For example, you may agree to provide event planning services for a corporation in exchange for the products you need (lighting, sound, audio visual, décor) to produce a future event. Although cash is not exchanged, there may still be some tax implications related to the value of the goods you barter. Therefore, check with your accountant to determine how you report these exchanges to avoid any surprises at tax time.

Common Event Financial Challenges and Solutions

The planned events profession is a business. As in other businesses, there are common problems and solutions. When planned events business owners assemble for annual meetings and conferences, they can be heard discussing many of the same challenges year after year. As one wag said, "The problems don't change, the solutions only become more difficult." Perhaps by reviewing the examples that follow you will be able to anticipate some of these challenges and thereby take measures to avoid them entirely.

- **Challenge**: Negotiating employees' salaries and benefits.

  Solution: Collect information from the *Convene Magazine* (Professional Convention Management Association) annual compensation survey, International Festivals and Events Association (IFEA) compensation study, Salaries.com (www.salaries.com), or from other event planning firms in similar market areas. Use this information to determine a market basket figure from which you can negotiate up or down based on the potential value of the employee to your firm.

Photo by Seungwon Shawn Lee

In-kind payments from sponsors are critical for successful event budgeting. The photos show a closing reception sponsored by Las Vegas CVB and MGM Hotels & Resort at the WEC by PCMA and their promotional giveaway items for event attendees.

- **Challenge**: Proper compensation for event planning salespeople.

    Solution: Three methods are customary. First and most prevalent is the draw against commission. This approach requires that you provide the salesperson with a small stipend until his or her commissions have equaled this amount. After he or she has equaled the amount of the draw, the stipend stops and the salesperson receives only sales commissions. The second approach is straight commission. In this case, usually the salesperson has existing accounts and is earning commissions immediately. Typical commissions range from 3 to 7 percent of the gross sale. Therefore, a salesperson who produces $500,000 in gross revenue will earn $35,000. The final custom is to offer the salesperson a salary plus bonuses based on sales productivity. This bonus is typically awarded after the salesperson reaches a certain threshold in sales, such as $1 million. A typical bonus is 1 or 2 percent of sales. A salesperson earning a salary of $50,000 could earn an additional $20,000 based on a 2 percent bonus on $1 million in sales.

Straight salary as compensation is the least desirable because it provides no financial incentive, and salespeople typically are driven by financial incentives. Whatever arrangement you agree on, do not change it for 1 year. You will need 1 year of financial data on which to base your review and future course of action.

- **Challenge**: Client is slow to pay balance of account.

  Solution: Inquire how you can help expedite payment. Can you pick up the check? Is there a problem, and could the client pay the largest portion now and the rest later? Are other vendors being paid? Does the client have a history of slow payment? What leverage do you have? Can you suspend services until the balance is paid or payment on account is made? Can you speak with one of the owners or principals and solve this problem? Can you find a creative solution, such as the one where the event planner had his dog deliver a collection notice, complete with begging for food and a paw print.

- **Challenge**: Out of cash.

  Solution: With prudent management of accounts payable and receivable, this problem should not occur. Assuming that a business emergency has caused this unfortunate situation, you must contact vendors immediately and notify them of your intent to pay. Then, notify all past-due accounts receivable and accelerate collection. Reduce or stop spending with regard to fixed overhead. Next, contact your lenders to access a line of credit based on your receivables until you have sufficient cash to meet your expenses.

- **Challenge**: Vendor promotes himself or herself to your client directly.

  Solution: Do you have written policies and procedures outlining what is and what is not permissible by your vendors? Realistically, how will this promotion injure your business? Can you negotiate with your vendor to receive a commission from any future sales to this client since you were the first contact?

- **Challenge**: Employee is terminated, starts own business and takes your clients.

  Solution: Does the employment agreement forbid this practice? Assuming that it does, you can have your attorney send a cease-and-desist letter. This rarely helps because clients have no constraints on whom they do business with. Either way you lose. Instead, suggest to the former employee that he or she may wish to provide you with a commission on the first sale he or she makes with your former client, as a courtesy for providing the first introduction. This way you can release the client and also receive some compensation for your effort in first identifying the account. If former employees refuse to provide you with a commission, chances are that their bad business ethics will eventually alienate them from enough industry colleagues that it will limit the amount of sales that they are able to achieve and reduce significantly the level of services they receive from vendors suspicious of their behavior.

- **Challenge**: Vendor partners enter into bankruptcy (administration).

  Solution: Immediately contract the bankruptcy or administration attorney in writing and officially register your claim for payment. In some cases, you may be offered a settlement that is lower than your claim and in other cases there will be no funds available to settle your claim.

- **Challenge**: Unauthorized charge placed on a master account.
  Solution: Make sure to schedule daily meetings with the event property's accounts receivable department while you are on-site. It allows event planners to double-check daily charges to the master account and if there is any error or question, it can be addressed quicker than you do it when you return to your office.

These common challenges and typical solutions should serve as a framework to guide your decision-making. Although most of the solutions in modern business still rely on common sense, we have noticed that there is nothing as uncommon in today's business environment as common sense. You will want to test each of these solutions with your business advisors (attorney, accountant, mentor) before implementing it to make certain that it addresses your particular problem and provides the most logical solution. There is no such thing as a general solution for a specific problem. All business problems are specific in nature, and you must seek a solution that addresses your precise problem.

Foreign Exchange Rates

It is important in this global world that you understand exchange rates, their fluctuations, and the differences that international exposure brings to your financial operations. Remember that although large international event planning companies depend greatly on global changes that occur regularly in various countries, midsized and small event planning companies are also affected by these changes. Event planning today is a global economic enterprise. Food and beverages that you purchase in the United States or elsewhere are often produced outside of the country in which they are sold. Payments that your organization makes or receives from overseas can be conducted in either local or foreign currency.

The foreign exchange rate is the price of one currency expressed in another currency. For example, EUR 0.881/1 USD means that for 1 U.S. dollar (USD), the market requires 0.6896 euro; USD 1.130/EUR means that for 1 euro, the market requires $1.448. The currency exchange rates vary in the same way that stocks do. Changes are usually not significant for small and midsized businesses and affect mainly large banks and investment companies. Exchange rates generally are affected by market conditions and government policy and also by national disasters (especially for small countries).

For accurate currency exchange rates, event planners should use an online currency converter. One widely used tool is XE Currency Converter (https://www.xe.com/currencyconverter).

Market Conditions

The general rule is that currencies of countries with strong economies are in greater demand than currencies of countries with weak economies. If the economy of country A is getting stronger and stronger, but the economy of country B is getting weaker and weaker, the exchange rate between the currencies of these countries will favor the currency of country A.

The change in U.S. dollar's currency exchange rate can be attributed to the global economic factors. Factors can include, but are not limited to, the International Monetary Fund (IMF) forecast of global economy, the economic slowdown in

China, or low oil prices. Another ongoing circumstance is Brexit with its still ongoing debate and voting on it. It surely has been affecting the UK's event industry in areas of HR, accounting, and finance. It is expected to continue this way until Brexit is concluded. Political uncertainty in Europe could be negative for the euro and pound sterling. It is expected that the euro will stay weaker to the U.S. dollar until the uncertainty clears. At the same time, the Chinese yuan is predicted to stay steady as a result of the Chinese government's desire for financial stability.

Government Policy

The currency of countries with strong governments that have predictable policies is always preferred over the currencies of countries whose governments have unpredictable policies. While the U.S. dollar rose to its highest following Donald Trump's 2016 victory in the presidential election, the U.S. dollar exchange rate was not greatly affected because the United States is known for its predictable domestic and foreign policy. Major financial newspapers, such as the *Financial Times* and *Wall Street Journal*, contain daily information about currency exchange rates and projections. You should monitor journals to forecast the economic conditions in countries where you will be doing business.

Changes in exchange rates affect all companies. Large businesses are affected directly; small businesses are affected indirectly. In one example, a large event planning company based in the United States signs a contract with a UK-based corporation to produce a large event in London. The U.S. event planning company is paid in pound sterling (£). The total cost of the contract is £400,000. Let's run a simulation of currency exchange rate and its impact on income statement. The contract is signed on June 1 and the event is to be held on December 21. The contract says that the UK company must make a 50 percent advance payment in June with the balance payable on the day of the event. On June 1, the British pound was worth $1.658. If the exchange rate between the pound and the dollar stays unchanged until December 21, the income statement of the event would appear as shown in Figure 5.3. Note that since the event planning company is U.S.-based, all expenses that it incurs are in U.S. dollars and total $500,000.

The gross profit is calculated to be $163,000. This represents a 25 percent profit margin ($163,000/$663,200). Obviously, the project looks very attractive. The question is how attractive the project would be if the exchange rate were to change by December 20. Suppose that, due to the strong economy in the United States, you predict that the U.S. dollar will appreciate (its value will increase). Now suppose

TECH/APPVIEW

Use online currency calculators such as Oanda.com or XE Currency Converter (www.xe.com/currencyconverter) to identify the fluctuation of currency on a specific date so that your payments are evidenced and date stamped with the correct conversion amount. By looking back to the time the expense was incurred and identifying the exact currency value on the date of the transaction, you may save hundreds of dollars when it is time to pay your bills. Banks in Asia offer a banking app with a premium currency rate. This type of app would be beneficial for relatively small amounts of currency exchange for event staff travel and miscellaneous expenses and tips.

	UK pound	U.S. dollar
Revenue		
50% advance on June 10	£200,000.00	$331,600.00
50% payment on December 20	200,000.00	331,600.00
Total	400,000.00	663,200.00
Total expenses	n/a	(500,000.00)
Gross profit	n/a	$163,200.00

FIGURE 5.3 Income statement: No exchange rate fluctuation.

	UK pound	U.S. dollar
Revenue		
50% advance on June 10	£200,000.00	$331,600.00
50% payment on December 20	200,000.00	300,000.00
Total	400,000.00	631,600.00
Total expenses	n/a	(500,000.00)
Gross profit	n/a	$131,600.00

FIGURE 5.4 Income statement: With exchange rate fluctuation.

that the exchange rate in December will be $1.5 for £1. Figure 5.4 shows how this change could dramatically reduce your margin of profit. Due to the exchange rate change in December, £200,000 will be worth only $300,000 but total expenses are still $500,000 (since they occurred in U.S. dollars). Therefore, the gross profit dropped to $131,600 and the profit margin dropped to 20 percent.

The more expensive the U.S. dollar becomes, the less profit the U.S. organization makes from its overseas events that are paid in foreign currency. This means that the U.S. organization can purchase fewer dollars for the amount of foreign currency earned. To attain the same level of profitability, the organization should start charging more for its service event; however, if it does so, it becomes less competitive. Alternatively, when the U.S. dollar depreciates, services provided by U.S. event planning organizations overseas become less expensive, hence more competitive. Global event leaders should pay close attention to global economy, trade, and government relations as these can impact foreign exchange rates, which in turn can directly impact their financial statement. For example, the recent trade war between the United States and China and the events of Brexit have impacted the exchange rate of the Chinese yuan and British pound against the U.S. dollar.

Typical Events Budgets

Your budget is a general guide to the income and expense projected for your event. It may be adjusted as necessary, provided that you can justify these changes and receive approval from the stakeholders. For example, if your revenue projections are way ahead of schedule, your variable costs will also increase proportionately. Use the budget as a valuable tool that may be sharpened as needed to improve your percentage of retained earnings.

The sample budgets shown in Figure 5.5 will serve as a guide as you develop your financial plans for various events. Each budget has the same structure; however,

AWARDS BANQUET

Income

100	Registrations		
101	Preregistrations	$	25,000
102	Regular registrations		50,000
103	Door sales		5,000
	Subtotal	$	80,000
200	Marketing		
201	Sponsorships	$	15,000
202	Advertising		10,000
203	Merchandise		5,000
	Subtotal	$	30,000
300	Investments		
301	Interest income		1,000
	Subtotal	$	1,000
400	Donations		
401	Grants	$	5,000
402	Individual gifts		10,000
403	Corporate gifts		25,000
	Subtotal	$	40,000
	Total income	$	151,000

Expenses

500	Administration (fixed expense)		
501	Site office furniture rental	$	1,000
502	Site office supplies		1,000
503	Site rental		3,000
504	Site telephone expense		1,000
	Subtotal	$	6,000
600	Printing (fixed expense)		
601	Design	$	3,000
602	Printing		5,000
603	Binding		1,000
	Subtotal	$	9,000
700	Entertainment (fixed expense)		
701	Talent fees	$	10,000
702	Travel and accommodations		1,000
703	Sound		2,000
704	Lights		2,000
	Subtotal	$	15,000
800	Food and beverages (variable expense)		
801	300 dinners @ $50	$	15,000*
802	Open bar for 1 hour		3,000*
803	Ice sculpture		500
	Subtotal	$	18,500

FIGURE 5.5 Sample budgets.

900	Transportation (variable expense)		
901	Staff travel	$	1,000
902	Valet parking		750
	Subtotal	$	1,750
1000	Insurance (fixed expense)		
1001	Cancellation	$	1,000
1002	Host liability		500
	Subtotal	$	1,500
	Total expenses	$	51,750
	Total variable expense	$	29,250
	Total projected income	$	151,000
	Total projected expense		51,750
	Gross retained earnings	$	99,250
	Percentage of fixed overhead		25,000
	Net retained earnings (reinvestment)	$	74,250

MUSIC FESTIVAL

Income

100	Ticket sales		
101	Regular advance	$	50,000
102	Student advance		25,000
103	Regular door sales		100,000
104	Student door sales		50,000
105	Group sales		25,000
	Subtotal	$	250,000
200	Marketing		
201	Sponsorships	$	50,000
202	Advertising		25,000
203	Merchandise		30,000
	Subtotal	$	105,000
300	Investments		
301	Interest income		3,000
	Subtotal	$	3,000
400	Donations		
401	Grants	$	10,000
402	Individual gifts		0
403	Corporate gifts		25,000
	Subtotal	$	35,000
	Total income	$	393,000

Expenses

500	Administration (fixed expense)		
501	Site office furniture rental	$	500
502	Site office supplies		500

FIGURE 5.5 (*Continued*)

503	Site rental		10,000
504	Site telephone expense		1,500
	Subtotal	$	12,500
600	Printing (fixed expense)		
601	Design	$	1,000
602	Printing		5,000
	Subtotal	$	6,000
700	Entertainment (fixed expense)		
701	Talent fees	$	50,000
702	Travel and accommodations		5,000
703	Sound		5,000
704	Lights		5,000
	Subtotal	$	65,000
800	Transportation and parking (variable expense)		
801	Staff travel	$	500
802	Parking lot rental		3,000
	Subtotal	$	3,500
900	Insurance (fixed expense)		
901	Cancellation	$	1,000
902	Host liability		500
903	Comprehensive general liability		2,000
904	Pyrotechnics rider		1,000
	Subtotal	$	4,500
	Total expenses	$	51,750
	Total variable expense	$	29,250
	Total projected income	$	393,000
	Total projected expense		91,500
	Gross retained earnings	$	301,500
	Percentage of fixed overhead		150,000
	Net retained earnings (reinvestment)	$	151,500

CONFERENCE AND EXPOSITION

Income

100	Registration		
101	Early-bird discount	$	100,000
102	Regular		50,000
103	On-site		25,000
104	Spouse/partner		10,000
105	Special events		15,000
	Subtotal	$	200,000
200	Marketing		
201	Sponsorships		10,000

FIGURE 5.5 (*Continued*)

202	Advertising	15,000
203	Merchandise	10,000
	Subtotal	$ 35,000
300	Investments	
301	Interest income	$ 1,000
	Subtotal	$ 1,000
400	Donations	
401	Grants	$ 5,000
	Subtotal	$ 5,000
500	Exposition	
501	200 booths @ $1,500	$ 300,000
502	50 tabletops @ $500	25,000
	Subtotal	$ 325,000
	Total income	$ 566,000

Expenses

600	Administration (fixed expense)	
601	Site office furniture rental	$ 1,500
602	Site office supplies	500
603	Site rental	30,000
604	Site telephone expense	1,500
	Subtotal	$ 33,500
700	Printing (fixed expense)	
701	Design	$ 2,000
702	Printing	10,000
	Subtotal	$ 12,000
800	Postage (fixed expense)	
801	Hold this date	$ 1,000
802	Brochure	5,000
803	Miscellaneous	500
	Subtotal	$ 6,500
900	Entertainment (fixed expense)	
901	Talent fees	$ 5,000
902	Travel and accommodations	500
903	Sound	0
904	Lights	0
	Subtotal	$ 5,500
1000	Transportation and accommodations	
1001	Staff travel	$ 1,500
1002	Staff accommodations	1,500
	Subtotal	$ 3,000

FIGURE 5.5 (*Continued*)

1100	Insurance (fixed expense)		
1101	Cancellation	$	3,000
1103	Comprehensive general liability		2,000
	Subtotal	$	5,000
1200	Speakers (variable expense)		
1201	Honoraria	$	10,000
1202	Travel		3,000
1203	Accommodations		1,000
1204	Complimentary registrations		3,000
1205	Per diem		1,000
	Subtotal	$	18,000
1300	Audiovisual (variable expense)		
1301	Rentals (general sessions)	$	25,000
1302	Labor (general sessions)		10,000
1303	Rentals (breakouts)		2,000
1304	Labor (breakouts)		1,000
1305	Prerecorded modules		5,000
	Subtotal	$	43,000
1400	Exposition (variable expense)		
1401	Pipe and drape	$	10,000
1402	Aisle carpet		20,000
1403	Signs		5,000
	Subtotal	$	35,000
	Total projected income	$	566,000
	Total projected expense		161,500
	Gross retained earnings	$	404,500
	Percentage of fixed overhead		199,000
	Net retained earnings (reinvestment)	$	205,500

*Include taxes and gratuities.

FIGURE 5.5 (*Continued*)

you will note that in the case of not-for-profit organizations, the term *retained earnings* has been substituted for the term *profit*. Use these budgets as a model as you endeavor to create consistently effective financial management systems for your organization.

Although most event planners find that financial matters are the least interesting aspect of their role and scope of their jobs, you now understand that to sustain long-term success, it is critical that you firmly control this important management area. The better you become at watching the bottom line, the more resources will become available to you for other more creative activities.

Julia Rutherford Silvers, CSEP, believes that financial goals, objectives, and tactics must be considered when evaluating the event elements being deployed. In *Professional Event Coordination* (2003), Rutherford Silvers puts this concept into perspective by offering this example. "Suppose you are coordinating a conference for your professional association. The costs to a delegate may include a registration fee of $600, an airline ticket at $500, a hotel room at $600 (four nights at $150 per night), and meals, business center services, and other incidentals that may add up to $400. Add to that $900 for a week away from work (a factor too many organizers ignore), and the cost to the delegate is $3,000. To achieve a positive return on his or her investment, the delegate will have to come away from the conference with a $3,000 idea."

How to Manage Your Finances during Turbulent Economic Times

The fundamental rule for surviving and thriving during turbulent economic times is to first ensure you have enough liquid assets to support your business for at least 12 months. A bank loan should not be considered a liquid asset because the bank may call it at any time. Further, it may be difficult to find a reasonable loan during a turbulent time. Therefore, having access to cash is the best plan.

The second rule for ensuring you will thrive during a difficult time is to renegotiate all payments with your vendor partners. During a difficult economic climate hotels, caterers and others may be more amenable to lowering their costs and being more flexible with their payment terms.

Third, and finally, do not panic. A recessed economy may be just the right time to actually grow your business through savvy investing. There will be fewer people advertising, and that means lower rates and less competition. Use this time to go out and market your business aggressively.

During the Great Depression of 1929, many U.S. businesses failed because of panic. Those that thrived were the ones whose management steered their ship with a steady hand on both receivables and payables. Further, they were the ones who knew that the customer is king and queen and that that was a good time to get closer to them and find more ways throughout one's unlimited talents to fill their needs.

It is an old maxim, but it is true: Tough times do not last, but tough people do. We would add that in addition to being tough, being prudent with your investments, flexible with your vendors, and devoted to your customers will pay even bigger dividends in the future.

Contingency and Scenario Planning

It is critically important for all event planners to have scenario plans A, B, and C with regard to income and expense. This requires that you carefully research macro- and microeconomic conditions and think about the best- and worst-case scenarios at all times. For example, what would you do if the local major employer suddenly went into administration and you could not sell tickets to their employees? Or what would you do if the cost of obtaining fuel doubled, and this increased your transport costs for products and people? Each of these scenarios has actually happened during the past 4 years. Your ability to forecast these scenarios and plan accordingly will ultimately determine how you will manage to successfully achieve an on target budget for your event.

INSIGHTS FROM GLOBAL EVENT LEADERS

Lena Malouf, CSEP, AIFD, Creative Director/Designer at Lena Malouf Consultancy, Sydney, Australia; Past President, International Live Events Association

(Note: To see the complete video interview, visit the Book Companion Site for this book at www.wiley.com/go/goldblatt/specialevents8e.)

Lena Malouf was born into a business family in a very small Australian country town. She was weighing up potatoes at seven, running around doing deliveries at ten, and filing invoices for her dad at twelve. Because she came from a business family it was inevitable that she went into business. In the early 1960s she opened a flower shop in Australia. In the 1970s she was called into Technical and Further Education (TAFE) to start forestry programs. In 1982 she became involved with the American Institute of Floral Designers, which was the start of her international connections in special events. In the 1990s her event design business was very good, and she became known as a celebrity designer. She also became involved with the International Special Events Society in the 1990s. According to Lena, there has been no stopping her career since then, and she is a great believer in giving back to the special events industry.

Q: How has the special events industry changed since you began your career?

A: We had no specific event management education opportunities when I started my career. Therefore, I think today, people who want to be in the special events industry should first partner with other successful event professionals and follow them around. I also believe that professional certification is essential for future success.

http://goo.gl/2aB2Xk

Q: What is required to be a successful special event planner?

A: I do not think I have ever met a person who does not dream of being an event planner. What they have to realize is that it is hard work with meticulous detailing required. The need to have the knowledge of creating a budget as well as how to pull back a budget. It is also a matter of continual learning and learning from every single event you produce.

Q: How has environmental sustainability affected the special events industry?

A: I always pre-cycle by asking what are the second and third uses for my design products.

Q: What are the essential factors for being successful in the special events industry?

A: In my field, as a designer, the star has to go under the mat. I have to be a team player. Therefore, every event producer wants to have a highly professional team to lead.

Q: How can event planners be more successful?

A: I know many event planners who will start work without a deposit. It is important that we are businesspeople and know the budget and conduct ourselves as businesspeople. If you do not do the paperwork, do not do the party.

Q: Do you believe events can help change the world?

A: I believe that events give us a purpose in life and that carries into the workplace as well.

Summary

Chapter 5 provided you with the knowledge required to develop a strategic budget for your event and to manage and control your finances in order to achieve financial sustainability. The three key learning outcomes from this chapter are as follows:

1. Developing an accurate budget is critically important to the overall event planning process. The budget should be based upon history or accurate assumptions.
2. Event planners are responsible for their fiduciary outcomes and therefore must carefully balance receivables and payables to maintain sufficient cash flow.
3. Searching for new and alternative funding sources, such as venture philanthropy, is critically important to provide sustainable financial success. Venture philanthropy is defined as taking concepts and principles from venture capital in finance and business and applying them to achieving philanthropic goals. A venture philanthropist will invest in a good cause and instead of expecting a financial capital return on their investment, they will expect to see an increase in social capital.

Key Terms

Account Codes: The enumeration system listed in the far left column of the budget to allow you to easily track income and expense.

Accounts Payable: Funds that are due from you to others for work orders, delivered or performed.

Accounts Receivable: Funds due to you from others for work you have agreed to perform or have performed.

Barter: Where the event company accepts an in-kind equivalent product or service in lieu of cash. In the case of a hotel client this may mean rooms or food and beverage credit.

Budget: The tool that forecasts, manages, and helps control income and expenditure for the event.

Deposit: A portion (usually 75 to 90 percent) of the total final amount due to the event planning company.

Hold Back: A small portion (usually 10 percent or less) held back from the total fee amount due to the event planning company until the work is performed.

Master Account: A record of all charges made during an event, with the resulting balance paid by the event host.

Payables and Receivables: Money that is due to others such as suppliers and money that is due to the event organization such as sponsorship fees, registration, and advertising income.

Venture Philanthropy: Investment from private organizations who desire a social return on their investment rather than a financial one. Therefore, if a venture philanthropist provides your event organization with $10,000, they may desire evidence that you have made a significant contribution to the social welfare of your stakeholders.

Career Connections

Practice developing model budgets, reading spreadsheets, and financial reports such as cash-flow statements, balance sheets, income statements, and other forms so that you may demonstrate your financial skills to future employers. Practice recasting your budget based upon different scenarios such as lower ticket sales, lower sponsorship revenue, increased transport, or audiovisual costs.

Next Steps

1. Conduct an Internet search and identify five different types of event budgets for a wide range of events, including for-profit, break-even, and profit-making.

2. Review all legal requirements for annual financial reporting in your jurisdiction to make certain you are complying with all regulations.

3. Develop five budgets using account codes for different types of events, and clearly identify fixed versus variable expenses.

References

Attrill, P., and McLaney, E. (2010) *Finance and Accounting for Non-Specialists*, New York, NY: Prentice Hall.

Rutherford Silvers, Julia (2012) *Professional Event Coordination, Second Edition*, Hoboken, NJ: John Wiley & Sons.

Smith, Adam (1995) *The Wealth of Nations*, London: UK: Pickering & Chatto.

World Economic Forum (2019). 10 Predictions for the Global Economy in 2019, accessed June 2019: https://www.weforum.org/agenda/2019/01/what-to-expect-for-the-global-economy-in-2019.

Event Branding and Bold Delivery

Event Vendors as Strategic Partners

A brand is not a product or a promise or a feeling. It is the sum of all experiences you have with a company.

—*Amir Kassaei (1968–)*

In this chapter you will learn how to:
- Develop and implement the design for your event
- Develop appropriate resources
- Coordinate catering operations
- Use trends in event catering
- Coordinate technical resources, including lighting, sound, and special effects
- Conduct and analyze the site inspection and introduce virtual and artificial reality technology enhanced site visit
- Develop and construct the production schedule
- Anticipate and resolve operational conflicts
- Recognize and comply with standard and customary event regulations and procedures
- Read, understand, and evaluate legal event documents
- Use green riders and corporate social responsibility clauses in emerging contractual agreements
- Access, plan, manage, and control potential event liabilities
- Obtain necessary permits and licenses to operate events
- Develop and manage risk management procedures
- Understand and comply with environmental regulations governing events
- Comply with regulations governing sponsorship of conferences and meetings
- Maintain documentary evidence of compliance procedures
- Incorporate new forces and trends in event catering

MGM Events in Las Vegas, Nevada, demonstrates how effective it may be to swag fabric to create an elegant effect for the opening night party of the Professional Convention Management Association

Amir Kassaei is the international creative director of the international advertising agency DDB. DDB is one of the largest advertising agencies in the world. Amir was 13 years old when the war broke out in his native homeland of Iran. He fled in the trunk of a car to safety in Turkey and then to Austria. He performed community service in Austria, including looking after people in a dying station. He has won over 2,000 awards for his advertising creations. Kassaei well understands that it is often the event marketing team that works together to create the experience that the customer or, in the case of event planning, the guest recognizes as great value.

The International Live Events Association (ILEA) annually awards several Esprit prizes for excellence in the spirit (*esprit*) of teamwork. This is the only awards program that we are aware of in the hospitality, meeting planning, and related industries that salute achievement through high-quality *team*work. The awards are primarily bestowed on teams that are responsible for innovative, excellent event production. ILEA members understand that great events are the result of great people working together to achieve a common goal. Great events are indeed the sum and substance of everyone on the event team working together to deliver a great and memorable guest experience. A positive event experience means satisfied attendees, exhibitors, and sponsors who would like to be back and and bring their colleagues and friends. Multiple stakeholders' expectations on positive expediences can be delivered when the right balance between those is met. The experience management and industry, which is creating satisfying experiences for customers, is now a widely adopted term to define today's event management and industry. For example, PCMA and many higher education hospitality and event management programs that used to use terms like, convention, event, hospitality management are now re-naming/re-branding their core business as an experience design or management.

Creating and Implementing the Design for Your Event

Once the design has been developed and the plan finalized, the two must be merged to begin the implementation process. During the coordination phase, we arrive at the intersection of research, design, and planning and, through the convergence of these three phases, begin to operationalize the event itself. The coordination phase provides us with the opportunity to see the results of our early labors in research, design, and planning. It is also the opportunity to ensure that we preserve the integrity of our early efforts. Too often, changes are made during the coordination phase that negatively affect the outcome of the event because they do not preserve the integrity of the design and planning process. One technique for ensuring that you continually preserve the integrity of your event design is to appoint one person to monitor the coordination and make certain that there is an obvious relationship between the design, the plan, and the final version of the event. Another method is to develop a series of written or graphic cues, such as design renderings or goals and objectives to make certain the stakeholders hold fast to the early vision of the event.

Developing Appropriate Resources

Event resources generally include people, time, finances, technology, and physical assets. Although each is important, each is also extremely scarce. Occasionally, someone will tell me that he has unlimited resources for his event. I am skeptical about this because of the economic theory, which states that you must learn to allocate scarce resources to achieve maximum benefit. No matter how many resources you have, the fact is that they are always limited. The way you stretch your resources is through careful and creative allocation.

The event leader must first identify appropriate resources for his or her event during the proposal stage. It is not unlikely that you may receive a telephone call one morning at 9 and be told that you need to deliver a proposal by noon to be eligible to earn the right to produce the event. Given this short timeframe, the event leader must be able to identify appropriate resources quickly and accurately. Figure 6.1 provides a general guide to where to find these important resources.

Category	Examples	Sources
Money	Starting capital, contingency funds	Investors, credit, vendors, and sponsors
People	Volunteers, staff, vendors	Convention and visitors' bureaus, destination management companies, schools, colleges, organizations, public relations, event alumni, and advertising firms
Physical	Transportation, venue, catering	Destination management companies, school districts, caterers, convention and visitors' bureaus
Technology	Software, hardware	Internet and industry organizations
Time	Scheduling, organization	Scheduling software and delegation strategies management, and expanded time and tactics

FIGURE 6.1 Event resources and where to find them.

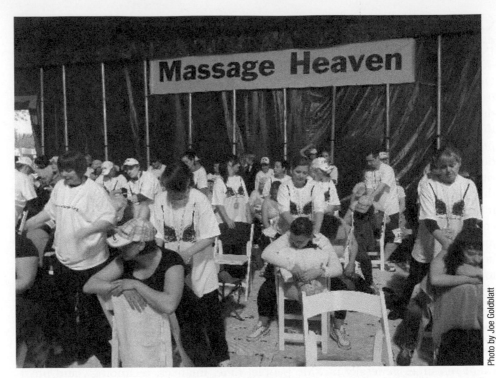

Photo by Joe Goldblatt

The Edinburgh Moonwalk provided dozens of professional massage therapists to help the walkers relax before they began their 13- and 26-mile walk to raise money for breast cancer.

The event leader must be able to identify quickly the most appropriate resources for the event. Furthermore, the event leader has to attest that these resources are reliable. This is not always possible, due to time constraints. Therefore, after every effort is made to verify the quality of an event resource such as entertainment or catering or venue, the event leader may wish to include this statement in the proposal to reduce his or her liability: "The information contained herein is deemed to be reliable but not guaranteed." It is impossible to verify and confirm every resource within the brief time constraints imposed by most events. Therefore, the event leader should do what is reasonable and inform the client of the status of the level of reliability of the information that he or she is providing. The most common method for identifying appropriate resources consists of these 10 steps:

1. Conduct a comprehensive needs assessment.
2. Determine the projected budget allowing for contingencies.
3. Develop the request for proposal (RFP) document and evaluation criteria.
4. Identify appropriate firms or individuals to submit proposals.
5. Distribute a RFP.
6. Review the proposals.
7. Select the suppliers.
8. Negotiate with the suppliers.
9. Develop and execute contracts with the suppliers.
10. Monitor contract performance by vendors and event staff.

Steps 1 and 2 are critical in order to proceed to develop an effective RFP. They may be conducted during the research phase and will include using historical as well as comparable data. The RFP must include the history of the event and/or the goals and objectives, as well as the budget parameters. You may wish to establish a

Using performers to provide free hugs, like this charity worker in London, may provide guests with a highly personal and memorable experience.

broad list of qualified organizations or individuals to receive the RFP. These lists can come from the resources shown in Figure 6.1 or through historical or comparable information. Regardless of how you acquire these lists, it is wise to qualify them further by calling each potential proposer to ask if he or she would like to receive the RFP. The initial list of proposers may be lengthy; however, the final list should not include more than five organizations or individuals. Typically, no more than three proposers receive the RFP.

The average event leader responsible for a large event, such as the one described in Figure 6.2 in the electronic appendices, may have dozens of proposals to receive and review. Therefore, it is important that you develop a methodology or system for receiving, reviewing, and responding to these proposals. Figure 6.3 in the electronic appendices provides an example of how to manage this process. Coordinating the flow of documents is the first step in this phase of managing a successful event. The system shown in this figure will help you track these important documents and evaluate the qualifications and value of each proposer. This system will also help you develop a historical profile for each vendor, so you can plan more efficiently in the future.

William O'Toole and Phyllis Mikolaitis report in Corporate *Event Project Management* (2002) that the ideal situation for contracting goods and services is with the use of the black-box view system. The black-box view dictates that the way in which the vendor accomplishes the deliverable is usually of no interest to the event leader. According to O'Toole and Mikolaitis, "Only the results matter." Using the black-box approach, the inputs include the event charter, the design specifications, the performance specifications, and the contract additions. These requirements are given to the vendors, who process these components into outputs or deliverables, which are the event goods and services. In order for this process to be successful, you must first clearly and accurately communicate to your vendors the requirements for your event.

Working with Suppliers and Vendors

Your ability to work with your vendors to satisfy the needs of your guests will ultimately help determine the level of success you achieve as an event leader. There are innumerable vendors, for example:

- Advertising agencies
- Advertising specialty providers
- Amusement-games providers
- Animal providers
- Audiovisual providers
- Balloons
- Caterers
- Clowns
- Corporate social responsibility consultants
- Decor specialists
- Destination management companies
- Dietary consultants
- Environmental specialists
- Entertainment providers
- Envelope addressers
- First-aid providers
- Flag providers
- Fundraising consultants
- Florists
- Government agencies
- Health and safety experts
- Hotels
- Insurance brokers and underwriters
- Invitation designers
- Legal counsel

Korean traditional marching band welcome and entertain guests at 2018 Pyeongchang Winter Olympic (at Kangreung Olympic Park).

- Lighting providers
- Magicians
- Medical personnel
- Mobile technology providers
- Printers
- Public relations counselors
- Puppeteers
- Pyrotechnic designers
- Security providers
- Simultaneous interpreters Social Network Service (SNS) designers
- Special effects providers
- Technology (computers, Wi-Fi) specialists
- Translation providers
- Valet parking providers
- Venue lessors and operators
- Web designers and managers

RFP Using standard format that is widely accepted by planners and vendors, such as the EIC Industry Insights, formerly known as CIC APEX, or individual websites of suppliers such as major brand hotels, attractions, suppliers. It is now common to submit a request for proposal electronically (e-RFP) using a standard format or customized format and receive responses within a few business days or, in some cases, even less than an hour. You may wish to include the following requirements in your RFP for technical production (audiovisual, lighting, and sound) specialists.

1. Equipment and labor for video magnification and sound for two general sessions with 1,000 persons using rear projection.
2. Equipment and labor for seven breakout sessions with an assortment of equipment, including slide projectors, video projectors, personal computers with PowerPoint, front projection screens, microphones, flip charts (pads and markers), and laser pointers. Average audience size is 55 persons. Audience size will range from 30 to 75 persons.

Upon arriving at Fyvie Castle in Aberdeenshire, Scotland, guests of the National Tour Association (NTA) have their photos taken in their costumes.

Submission requirements. All proposers must follow these guidelines to be considered for this assignment:

1. Company/organization profile and history, including names of owners or principals as well as persons assigned to coordinate the event.
2. Itemized list of equipment and labor that will be provided, including redundant (backup) equipment.
3. Complete listing of all costs, including taxes if applicable.
4. Evidence of insurance company and evidence of commercial general liability with minimum limits of $2 million per occurrence.

Contracting Your Vendor Partners

Once the vendor partners have been selected for your event, it is essential that you prepare and execute proper contracts to further clarify expectations related to performance, identify roles and responsibilities, and reduce risk.

In the United States and other countries, some type of official permission is required to conduct most public events. The larger the event in terms of attendance or technical complexity, the more official oversight is usually required. Official review may come from local (town, city, county), state or province, or federal agencies. There are numerous reasons why an event must comply with existing laws and regulations. The four primary reasons are to protect your legal interests, to abide by ethical practices, to ensure the safety and security of your event stakeholders, and to protect your financial investment. For example, the city of Chicago Mayor's Office of Special Events provides a comprehensive event planning policy, regulations, and permission and review processes in one-stop service through its

TECH/APPVIEW

Through Sustainable e-RFP Model

Electronic RFP (e-RFP) transactions have increased exponentially over the past years due to its supposed quick turnarounds and ease of use. It is certain that the electronic model of RFPs and sharing information electronically reduce the carbon footprint by incorporating environmentally sustainable practices. However, there is a rising concern in another face of suitability: substitutability of e-RFP business model. Efficiency of the e-RFP system is being questioned, and suggestions for sustainable e-RFP systems are discussed by event industry stakeholders. EIC's white paper on e-RFP efficiency by Bondurant (2016) suggests the following to event leaders:

Include your event history.

-Disclose your budget: you start pricing transparency FIRST.

-Identify "make or break" items/services.

-Indicate the number of properties included in the e-RFP; limit number of cities and properties (three cities and five properties in each).

It is suggested to limit a total number of cities and properties to be reasonable in an event leaders' e-RFP submission. Since e-RFPs have adopted as one of its mainstays of the venue search process with its nature of easy to use and no cost , the number of e-RFPs has drastically increased and many event venues dedicate tremendous time and labor to respond quick to those; however, its success measured by a conversion rate to actual sales is not as high as it is expected.

Due to mass distribution, challenges include difficulties for vendors/venues to respond to leads in a timely and complete manner and the declining probability of business materializing from those leads. It is perhaps the vendors, however, that face the most challenge in the e-RFP process. A small number of staff on their meeting and events team are handling hundreds of RFPs. The loss is resulted on both sides: vendors waste their time and resources on increased numbers of not-fitting/qualified e-RFPs that should be spent on customized event production to respond to these requests; event leaders receive less comprehensive proposals that can contribute to a success of their events with less back-and-forth communications to get more details.

To create sustainable e-RFP procedure for vendors and event leaders, they have to remember that the number one goal is to produce great events. And it can start from reasonable and responsible e-RFP submission approach.

official website and resource guide (https://www.chicago.gov/city/en/depts/dca/supp_info/resource_guide.html).

Protecting Your Legal Interests

Preparing proper contracts, researching the permits and licenses that are required, and complying with other legal requirements help ensure that your event can proceed without undue interruption. Contracts or agreements may range from a simple letter or memorandum of understanding to complex multipage documents with lengthy riders (attachments). The event leader should utilize the services of competent legal counsel to review all standard agreements, such as hotel contracts, to ensure validity prior to execution. Furthermore, when writing new agreements, local legal counsel must make certain that the contract conforms to the code of the jurisdiction where it is written and executed (usually where the event takes place). Lawyers are admitted to the state bar in the United States and must be experts on the state code (laws). Therefore, it is important to use an attorney who is admitted to the state bar where your event is being held or where, in the case of litigation, the case may be tried.

The majority of permits and licenses will be issued by local agencies. However, some state, provincial, or federal authorities may also issue licenses for your event. Therefore, it is wise for you to audit past and similar events carefully to identify the customary permits and licenses that are required for an event.

The permitting and licensing process may require weeks or even months to accomplish, so you must carefully research each jurisdiction where you will produce an event and meet these time requirements. For example, any street closures for outdoor events must be requested a minimum of 72 hours in advance according to Chicago's Mayor's office of special events. The cost for permits and licenses is typically nominal. However, some larger or high-risk events (such as Grand Prix auto racing) may require the posting of expensive bonds.

The major reasons why you must convince your event stakeholders of the importance of legal compliance and the need to obtain all necessary permits and licenses are as follows:

- Event leaders are legally required to obtain certain permits and licenses to conduct many events. Failure to do so may result in fines, penalties, interest, or cancellation of an event.
- You have a fiduciary responsibility to event stakeholders to plan, prepare, and provide evidence of compliance. Avoiding compliance can have dire economic consequences.
- You have an ethical responsibility (as stated by various industry codes of ethics) to comply with all official regulations and to provide written agreements.
- Although an oral agreement may be binding, the written agreement usually takes precedence. Written agreements provide all parties with a clear understanding of the terms, conditions, and other important factors governing the event.
- One of the primary ultimate responsibilities of an event leader is to provide a safe environment in which to conduct an event.

Although developed countries have many more regulations and compliance requirements, developing countries are rapidly instituting controls to ensure the safe and legal operation of events.

Honoring Ethical Practices

One of the primary definitions of a profession is adherence to a code of ethical/professional conduct. As event planning has emerged as a modern profession, a code of ethics has been developed by professional associations such as Meeting Professionals International and the International Live Events Association (ILEA). The code of ethics is different from biblical moral laws and from legal codes voted by governing bodies.

A code of ethics reflects what is standard and customary in both a profession and a geographic area. In that sense, it is somewhat elastic in that it is applied in various degrees as needed for different circumstances. For example, when a hotelier offers an event leader a complimentary lunch at the first meeting, should this be construed as a bribe by the event leader and, therefore, refused? Attorney Jeffrey King, an expert in the field of meeting, convention, and event legal procedures, advises his event leader clients always to pay for their lunch when meeting with a hotelier or other supplier for the first time. "This immediately lets the hotelier know that the relationship is equal and represents a business transaction," according to King. It also sets an ethical standard for future discussions and the building of a relationship. Some geographical parts of the world, such as Asia, consider "relationship," known as "Guanxi (關係)," is very important to build professional and long-lasting partnerships. Guanxi can be a very subjective ethics rule depending on time, location, and business case and sometimes can cause a major problem in certain types of event businesses (such as government or municipal hosting events). For example, in 2016 a law has been passed that government officials in South Korea cannot be treated with a meal worth over 30,000 Korean won (US $26) or gifts over 50,000 Korean won (US $45), and violation of the law can lead to a criminal offense. This case shows the importance of being updated with international policy in related to gift or treating event business partners.

Although many professional societies, including ILEA, enforce their code of ethics with a grievance procedure, in most cases it is up to the event leader to determine what is and is not appropriate ethical behavior, using the code of ethics as a guide. Robert Sivek of The Meeting House Companies, Inc., suggests that event leaders use the front-page-of-the-newspaper rule. "Ask yourself if you would like to wake up and see your decision or action plastered across the front page of the newspaper," says Sivek. This may quickly determine whether your proposed action is one that is acceptable not only to you but also to others in your events community.

Henderson and McIlwraith, in their book *Ethics and Corporate Social Responsibility in the Meetings and Events Industry*, state that corporations and event organizations must take responsibility for all of their actions in the community. They argue that CSR must not be seen as an add-on; rather, it must be a strategic part of every organization's core purpose. One of the critical components in terms of taking responsibility for your actions is the contract.

Key Contract Components

The contract reflects the understanding and agreement between two or more parties regarding their mutual interests, as specified in the agreement. A binding contract must contain the following four components described in this section.

1. **Parties**

    The names of the parties must be clearly identified. The agreement must be described as being between these parties, and the names that are used in the agreement must be defined. Typical event agreements are between the event leader and his or her client or the event leader and his or her vendor. Other contracts may be between an event professional and an insurance company, an entertainment company, or a bank or other lending institution.

2. **Offer**

    The offer is the service or product tendered by one party to another. The event leader may offer consulting services to a client, or a vendor may offer products to an event leader. The offer should list all services that an event professional offers to provide. Any miscommunications here may lead to costly litigation in the future.

3. **Consideration**

    The consideration clause defines what one party will provide the other upon acceptance of an offer. Consideration may be either cash or in-kind products or services. Therefore, a sponsor may offer an event property complimentary products or services in addition to cash to pay for their sponsorship.

4. **Acceptance**

    When both parties accept an offer, they execute (sign) the agreement confirming that they understand and agree to comply with the terms and conditions of the agreement.

Other Components

Although the key components are the parties, the offer, consideration, and acceptance, event planning agreements usually include many other clauses or components. The most typical clauses are listed next.

Terms The terms clause defines how and when the funds will be paid to the person extending the offer. If the event leader offers consulting services, he or she may request a deposit in the amount of the first and last month's retainer and then require that the client submit monthly payments of a certain amount on a certain date each month. These terms define the financial conditions under which the agreement is valid.

For some large events, payments are made during a specified period. In this case, or in case of another complicated payment arrangement, a separate payment schedule should be attached to a contract. This schedule should be treated as an essential part of the contract and signed and dated by both parties. If advance payment is mentioned in the payment term section, special attention should be paid to the provisions of how the deposit is returned in the case of event cancellation. For example, is the deposit credited toward future transactions within a specific time period, or is a cash refund offered?

Within the events industry, event professionals are increasingly concerned with reducing internal or operational risk in order to improve the profitability of their enterprise. Internal risk issues include theft, slippage, and the need to safeguard intellectual property. Event professionals must work closely with colleagues to put in place procedures aimed to reduce internal risks.

Cancellation Special events are temporal in nature and, therefore, always subject to cancellation. Therefore, it is important to provide for this contingency legally with a detailed cancellation clause. Usually, the cancellation clause defines under what circumstances either party may cancel, how notification must be provided (usually in writing), and what penalties may be required in the event of cancellation. Another key point of a cancellation clause and beyond is that "Cancellation-by-you clause." This type of clause is common in the hospitality industry and is known as a cancellation-by-hotel clause. So it is wise to include a by-you clause, too. In the event planning contract, include the scenarios that allow event leaders to opt out. One wise piece of advice on cancellation of event contract is "Any contract should have an exit clause or at least make best efforts to include it."

Force Majeure (Act of God) In the force majeure clause, both parties agree on which circumstances, deemed to be beyond their control, will permit an event to be canceled without penalty to either party. The force majeure clause must always be specified to reflect the most common or predictable occurrences. These may include hurricanes, earthquakes, floods, volcanic eruptions, tornadoes, famines, wars, or other catastrophic disasters such as terrorism.

Arbitration It is common practice to include in event planning agreements a clause that allows both parties to use arbitration in place of a legal judgment when they fail to agree. The use of arbitration may save the parties substantial costs over traditional litigation.

Billing Because many events involve entertainers or are theatrical events in and of themselves, the agreement must define how entertainers will be listed in advertising and in the program. Generally, a percentage, such as 100 percent, is used to describe the size of their name in relation to other text.

Time Is of the Essence The time-is-of-the-essence clause instructs both parties that the agreement is valid only if it is signed within a prescribed period of time. This clause is usually inserted in order to protect the offerer from loss of income due to late execution by the purchaser.

SECUREVIEW

The eco-rider is a type of contract rider that requires that specific activities take place to reduce the carbon footprint that is created at a concert or other entertainment production. The eco-rider may specify that food and other supplies be locally sourced to reduce travel and fuel or that recycling, reuse, and reduction policies be enacted across the entire event. An artist, such as a band or speaker, may specifically request an eco-rider to perform at your event. For more information about eco-riders visit the Live Earth Green Guidelines website or contact the Event Industry Council, formerly known as Green Meetings Industry Council (listed in the electronic version of the organizations appendices too).

Assignment As employees have shorter and shorter tenures with organizations, it is more important than ever that agreements contain clauses indicating that the contract may not be assigned to other parties. For example, if Mary Smith leaves XYZ Company, the agreement is between XYZ Company and the offerer and may not be transferred to Smith's successor, who may or may not honor the agreement as an individual. Therefore, Mary Smith has executed the agreement on behalf of XYZ Company.

Insurance Often agreements detail the type and limits of insurance that must be in force by both parties, as well as a requirement that each party coinsure the other. Some agreements require copies of certificates of insurance that name the other party as additional insured in advance of the event date.

Hold Harmless and Indemnification In the event of negligence by either party, the negligent party agrees to hold the other party harmless and to defend it (indemnify) against harm. For example, if the hotel where you are conducting your event causes harm to a guest through its negligence, the hotel will be responsible for defending the event leader and his or her company from the future action. In many event agreements, the provision for hold harmless and indemnification is mutually shared by both parties.

Reputation The production of an event is a reflection of the personal tastes of the event organization and sponsors. Therefore, some event leaders include a specific clause that recognizes the importance of the purchaser's reputation and states that the event leader will use his or her best efforts to protect and preserve that reputation during management of the event.

Complete or Entire Agreement Typically, the complete agreement is the final clause and states that the agreement constitutes the full understanding of both parties. Figure 6.3 (shown in the electronic appendices) demonstrates how a complete agreement is used in a typical event planning consulting agreement.

Rider

A rider is an attachment to a main agreement and usually lists the important ingredients that support the main contract. These may include sound equipment and labor, lighting equipment and labor, F&B, transportation, housing for artists/entertainers, or other important financial considerations other than the artist's fee (e.g., a payment schedule). The rider should be attached to the main agreement, and it should be initialed or signed separately to signify acceptance by both parties.

Changes to the Agreement

Most agreements will require negotiation prior to execution, and the result of these executions will be changes. If only two or three insubstantial changes are made, you may choose to initial and date each change prior to returning the agreement for execution by the other party. Your initial and date signify your acceptance of the change but do not obligate you to fulfill the entire agreement until you have affixed your signature. If there are substantial changes (such as in the date, time, venue, or fees) or more than three changes, it is best to draw up a new agreement.

Terms and Sequence of Execution

First and foremost, always require that the purchaser sign the agreement prior to affixing your signature. Once both signatures are affixed, the agreement becomes official. If you sign the agreement and forward it to the other party, and the purchaser makes changes and signs it, you may be somewhat obligated for those changes. It is always wise to request the purchaser's signature before affixing your own.

Second, refrain from using a verbal agreement or a facsimile. Should you be forced to litigate the agreement, most courts will seek the "best copy," and that is usually an original. You may use a facsimile for an interim memorandum of understanding, but binding, official agreements must be originals. Interestingly, in Scotland, Scots law recognizes verbal agreements if both parties have a common agreement and they both seek to create a legal relationship. However, in most legal jurisdictions, an original signed agreement is considered the best copy and evidence of agreement.

Third, take the time to sign the agreement with the other party in person. Explain to the other party that the terms implied in the agreement are only as valid as the integrity of the persons signing the document. Offer your hand in friendship as you jointly execute this agreement.

Other Agreements

These agreements, along with many others, may be required to ensure the professional operation of an event. To identify all the agreements that may be required, check with other event organizers and local officials as well as your vendors to determine the critical documents that must be executed prior to the start of the event. These agreement templates may be found in the electronic appendices. Figure 6.4 (as shown in the appendices) depicts a typical event consulting agreement.

Other Types of Agreements

Most jurisdictions where your event will be conducted will require you to obtain various permits in advance of the event being promoted and held. The following permits and licenses should be reviewed and secured prior to publicly announcing the event.

Permits

Permits are issued by local, state, provincial, or federal governmental agencies and allow you to conduct certain activities at your event. Figure 6.5 (shown in the electronic appendices) details the typical permits that may be required. Allow sufficient time to obtain the permits. A permit may be issued only after you have submitted the appropriate documentation and have paid a fee. Determine well in advance what type of documentation is required by the issuing agency and how funds are accepted.

Permits/Licenses	Source
Alcohol	Alcohol beverage control boards (usually at the state level in the United States) or within the local authority in Europe or the national and local level Tax/Revenue Service Offices in Asia
Business	Economic development agency; recorder of deeds
Entertainment	Local authority, council
Food	Local or state health department
Music	American Society of Composers, Authors, and Publishers or Broadcast Music, Inc.
Pyrotechnics	Local or state fire department/service; the U.S. Bureau of Alcohol, Tobacco, and Firearms

FIGURE 6.6 Typical event leadership licenses and where to obtain them.

Remember that permits are not issued automatically. A permit reflects that an agency is permitting your event organization to conduct certain activities provided that you conform to the regulations established. Make certain that you are able to comply with these regulations prior to applying for the permit. If you are denied a permit, you may consider appealing your case. In some cases, event leaders have sued an agency to obtain permission to conduct an event. However, since most event leaders rely on the goodwill of local agencies to conduct an event successfully, litigation should be the absolutely final resort.

Licensing

A license is granted by a governmental institution, a private organization (as in music licensing), or a public entity to allow you to conduct a specific activity. The difference between a permit and a license may be slight in some jurisdictions. Usually the requirements for obtaining a license are much more stringent and require due diligence (evidence of worthiness) prior to issuance.

Figure 6.6 lists the more common permits/licenses required for events and their sources. Additional licenses may be required for your event. To determine what licenses are required, make certain that you examine the event's history, check with organizers of similar events, and confirm and verify with the appropriate agencies that issue these licenses.

One of the best sources of information will be your vendor partners. Audit your vendors, especially in the technology field, and determine if licenses are required (as in the case of laser projection) or if the event leader must obtain a license. And event leaders also should be updated with new regulations with new technologies, such as drone and its flying permit and regulation for events.

For many events, both permits and licenses must be secured. The larger the event, the more likely the number of permits and licenses will increase. Remember that licenses and permits are the government's way of establishing a barrier to entry to protect its interests. And it is important to follow up on any changes or new ones in event-related regulations and policy, especially for international event organizers and attendees. For example, Thailand, one of the most popular destinations for MICE in January 2019 through its Thailand Convention and Exhibition Bureau (TCEB), announced its new event regulations related to permit requirements, drone usage, and importing/exporting of medical devices (Singapore is a very popular destination for medical tourism/events). Work closely with government agencies to understand their procedures, time frames, and inspection policies. A close working relationship with the agencies that issue licenses and permits will help ensure the success of your overall event operation.

Environmental Regulations Increasingly, local government bodies are requiring that event leaders submit an environmental plan with their other required documents for the event to be approved by the government agencies. This requirement is due to citizen pressure to reduce the carbon footprint and the environmental damage caused by large-scale and hallmark events.

Therefore, event leaders must be prepared to comply with all environmental regulations, including recycling, reuse, reduction, waste management, and even, where possible, on-site composting of waste matter. You might be asked to submit a separate environmental management plan for your event or might be required by a local government to provide additional funds to restore the area to its original state.

Regardless of the requirements by local authorities, it is important that you think well in advance what may be required and then put the procedures in place to minimize environmental damage as a result of your event.

Sponsorship Regulations Since 2008, U.S. healthcare organizations have been required to only accept funds from corporate sponsors when those funds directly support the educational mission of the organization. The requirements for accepting funds have dramatically limited the capacity of some healthcare organizations to provide traditional hosting services for doctors, nurses, and other medical providers because the pharmaceutical companies are now severely restricted in what they may provide.

Although these regulations are not mandated by a government body, they have been widely accepted in the healthcare industry as a way to improve public perception of their industry and to not unduly influence doctors or others through lavish hosting was traditionally done by the pharmaceutical companies.

According to *Medical Meetings* magazine in 2009, "The Pharmaceutical Research and Manufacturers of America's updated Code on Interactions with Healthcare Professionals, takes effect in January 2009. The new, voluntary code places a strict focus on science and education. When it comes to medical meetings, resorts and non-educational gifts are out, and the watchword for everything from venues to menus is 'appropriate'."

In 2012 the Event Industry Council announced that they were developing an additional certification for medical meeting planners to further enhance the well-established Certified Meeting Professional certification. This development was deemed necessary and essential due to the numerous increased regulations self-imposed by the medical and pharmaceutical industries, both in the United States and increasingly throughout the world.

SECUREVIEW

Why not promote your exceptional environmental planning and management record? Proudly announce in well-targeted publications how you have worked with the local authorities to reduce the carbon footprint of your event. Erect a stand or booth at your event and share information with your guests about your positive environmental practices. Let your stakeholders know that you are promoting sustainable event management and that each year you are moving closer to the goal of one day achieving carbon neutrality. Reducing the carbon footprint at events can be achieved through responsible planning and implantation and some cost to offset it. Start with calculating offset costs of your event carbon footprint. There is a very useful event carbon footprint offset cost calculator. It is an easy and straightforward tool; just enter the square footage of an event venue, total days of event, number of attendees, and location. The link to the free and online calculator is https://nativeenergy.com/for-individuals/calculators/#Events.

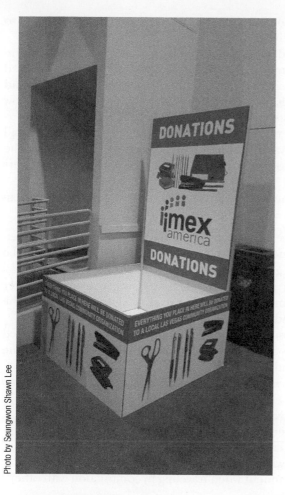

Photo by Seungwon Shawn Lee

Sustainability and environmental regulations are important in all types of events. This donation box on the IMEX America show floor collects items from exhibitors to donate to local community organizations.

However, when deciding how to comply, the interpretation of the term *appropriate* is very difficult to understand with these new regulations. However, the responsibility for compliance is firmly in the hands of the pharmaceutical companies. Therefore, medical and healthcare event leaders should work closely with their pharmaceutical colleagues to determine how best to appropriately position themselves and their financial support within the planned event. Perhaps the new professional certification being developed in this area will further help clarify what is considered appropriate in the future.

Travel Documents, Visas, and Work Permits Following September 11, 2001, many countries have tightened their visa procedures to ensure that only individuals who have valid reasons for entering the sovereign nation state may do so. Typically, when one country raises the threshold for entry into it, other countries reciprocate. For example, in recent years Brazil has required that American citizens be fingerprinted upon entering Brazil as a direct response to the United States implementing the same requirement for Brazilian visitors.

Therefore, it is very important that event leaders check with the consulate or embassy of the country where they will be conducting their event to determine the types of visas and work permits that will be required for their workers and guests. Generally, guests from the United States attending an educational meeting may enter certain countries for a specified period of months and without a special visa. However, it is best to check first as these rules and policies are extremely fluid. Workers or staff who are being paid by the country where they will be working will be required to have a work permit or other credentials and may also be required to pay taxes upon the wages they receive.

In 2008, the British government decided to require that all performers from countries other than the United Kingdom who were engaged by festivals leave the United Kingdom immediately following their final performance. The festival producers and local council officials objected to this requirement, and it was relaxed in 2008 to allow the entertainers to remain as tourists in the United Kingdom for a specified time.

In 2009, the Western Hemisphere Travel Initiative was enacted and requires all U.S. citizens and others to have a valid U.S. passport or passport card to enter the United States from Canada, Mexico, and other countries. This includes passengers who travel by air, land, or sea.

According to the U.S. Department of Homeland Security, the following documents will be required for entry.

- *ESTA Documents:* The U.S. government requires pre-travel approval for all persons entering the United States without a visa. This documentation may be found at https://esta.cbp.dhs.gov/esta/.
- *U.S. Passport:* U.S. citizens may present a valid U.S. passport to enter or reenter the United States when traveling via air, land, or sea from Canada, Mexico, the Caribbean region, and Bermuda.
- *The U.S. Passport Card:* The passport card is only valid for reentry into the United States at land border crossings and sea ports of entry from Canada, Mexico, the Caribbean region, and Bermuda.
- *WHTI-Compliant Travel Documents for U.S. Citizen Travel via Land or Sea, updated June 1, 2009, and still effective:*
  - Trusted Traveler Cards (NEXUS, SENTRI, or FAST)
  - State-Issued Enhanced Driver's License (when available)
  - Enhanced Tribal Cards (when available)
  - U.S. Military Identification with Military Travel Orders
  - U.S. Merchant Mariner Document when traveling in conjunction with official maritime business
  - Native American Tribal Photo Identification Card
  - Form I-872 American Indian Card

Source: From U.S. Department of State Bureau of Consular Affairs. Public Domain.

International travel and entry requirements to the United States are constantly changing, so it is important to consult with a specialist or provide the most current information to event attendees and staff. The best online source is the U.S. Department of State Travel website (https://travel.state.gov/content/travel/en/international-travel.html). Therefore, as more and more events become transnational in scope, it is incumbent upon the event leader to work closely with customs and immigration officials to make certain their delegates and staff have an efficient and easy means to enter the country where the event is being conducted. Furthermore, the event leader must also work closely with departments of revenue and customs to ascertain the proper work permits full-time and temporary staff who are providing services for an event while in a foreign country.

Contracts, Permits, and Licenses: A Synergistic Relationship

Professional event leaders understand, and use to their advantage, the synergy between a well-written and executed contract and the acquisition of proper permits and licenses. All three instruments are essential for the professional operation of modern events. When developing an agreement, determine in advance who is responsible for obtaining and paying for specific permits and licenses and incorporate this language into the agreement. Failure to specify who is responsible for obtaining and paying for permits and licenses can lead to an interruption of your event and conflicts among the various stakeholders.

Therefore, conduct research carefully during the planning stage to identify all necessary permits and licenses and determine who will be responsible for coordinating this process. Include this information in your master event consulting agreement, as well as your vendor agreements. Since permits and licenses are unavoidable in most event situations, it behooves the event leader to practice the maxim that an ounce of prevention (or risk management) is worth a pound of cure. Use the planning phase to examine potential permit processes, and then use the coordination stage to link these two important steps in the event management process.

Contracts, permits, and licenses have legal, ethical, and risk management ramifications. To ensure that these impacts are positive, event leaders must understand their importance and work diligently to communicate with the required agencies, as well as to prepare and execute valid agreements.

On-Site Coordination

Once the contracts are fully executed, the event leader must commence with the formal organization of the event. This is known as the coordination phase. During event coordination, the event leader will work closely with the vendor partners to successfully manage and deliver the event according to the expectations of the client.

Catering Management

Historically, events have been associated with F&B. Here we examine how to ensure that the catering elements of an event are well coordinated.

Event caterers are usually one of three business types, and each is defined by location. First is the institutional caterer, commonly described as an in-house or on-premises caterer, who may or may not have permanent kitchens and offices at the event venue. This caterer may limit the choices for the event leader but can provide greater security by being familiar with the idiosyncrasies of the venue.

The second business type is the traditional off-premises caterer, whose clients engage him or her to cater meals at a temporary location. The location or venue may or may not have permanent kitchen facilities. However, the off-premises caterer is responsible for providing the necessary equipment and services to create an atmosphere of permanence in this temporary locale.

The third and final type of event caterer is the concessionaire. This person may use a mobile kitchen or concession trailer to dispense his or her product or may work in a fixed venue from a permanent or temporary food-and-beverage concession area. In some venues, the in-house catering operation operates all food-and-beverage concession activities simultaneously.

In actuality, although many off-premises caterers may boast of their ability to provide their services uniformly in any location in most major metropolitan areas, relatively few are able to do so. When you add multiple events on the same date, this number shrinks dramatically.

An F&B display is important in terms of teasing the eye before the palate. This seafood station appeals to eyes first with its ice-carved plates and display.

A cheese or other food-and-beverage display may also serve to promote local suppliers.

Location, Location, Location

Of the five Ws in event planning, "where" is perhaps the most critical to the on- and off-premises caterer, for a variety of reasons. First, the caterer must comply with specific health department codes and regulations that will govern where he or she may operate. Second, food-and-beverage preparation is time-dependent, and the distance between the food preparation area and the serving location can determine an entire range of quality and service issues. What happens if hot food becomes cool or even cold during transit? How will the guests feel about slow food delivery? Finally, what utilities, equipment, and other resources are available to the caterer to prepare, serve, remove, and clean up successfully?

The location of the event is, therefore, a critical consideration for the off-premises caterer. However, the on-premises caterer must also be sensitive to these issues, as even the most routine event can suffer from logistical problems. As one example, what happens in the convention center when the caterer must serve 1,000 guests on the ground floor, the kitchen is located on the second floor, and the elevator stops working? Or perhaps the event leader has asked the caterer to serve the meal in an unusual location, such as in a tent in the parking lot. Does the caterer have the necessary equipment and additional labor to accomplish this task successfully? These questions and many more must be considered well in advance of establishing the location for the catered meal.

Equipment

Obviously, tables, chairs, china, silver (cutlery), and other standard equipment will be required to serve a high-quality meal. However, the event leader must ensure that the caterer has access to the appropriate style and quantity to match the needs of the event. Some caterers own a sufficient inventory of rental equipment, while others have close relationships with party and general rental dealers to provide these

Photo by Joe Goldblatt

Food elevation is important in terms of teasing the eye before the palate.

items. The event leader must inspect the equipment to ensure not only that the caterer has sufficient quantity but also that the quality is appropriate for the event.

When considering quantity, remember that the caterer may have multiple events on the same date. Make certain that additional inventory is available in case your guest list increases at the last moment. Furthermore, make certain that, if the quantity of items is increased, the inventory will remain high quality.

In addition, it is important to keep in mind that the increased importance of suitability in F&B equipment and silverware. There are vendors that provide recyclable (paper-based or environmentally friendly, e.g., bamboo) silverware and tools (fork, spoon, and chopsticks). Especially to some clients (e.g., environment-/conservation-related clients or theme/objective of events related to sustainability), these can be a core factor of success. Beyond china and silver, some caterers also maintain a healthy inventory of tables, chairs, linens, and other serving utensils (cutlery), such as chafing dishes, props, and other elements that will provide you with a cohesive look. Some caterers stock unusual items from a specific historic period or feature items that reflect their style of catering. A caterer who primarily services the social life-cycle market may provide latticework props and gingham linens, while the caterer who works in the corporate event market may provide white linens and more traditional china and silver. The event leader must select a caterer who has equipment and experience that matches the goals and objectives of the specific event.

Utilities

As the caterer plugs in the coffee urn, the music from the band suddenly comes to a screeching halt. The guests on the dance floor look confused, but both the event leader and catering director know what has happened: an overloaded circuit caused by the coffee urn. The event leader must audit the caterer's utility needs as well as those of the other vendors to determine if the venue can support these requirements.

In addition to electricity, the caterer will require a continuous source of water. The proximity of the water will also be an important factor, as costs may increase if water must be transported from a great distance. The third and final requirement for all catering operations is waste management. The caterer must have a system for

Photo by Seungwon Shawn Lee

Chocolate fountain/display created for special occasions at events can enhance atmospheres.

disposing of waste materials. The event leader must ensure that the caterer has the necessary resources to perform professionally.

Time Constraints

Time is of the essence in most catering operations, for a variety of reasons. First, the caterer must prepare and deliver his or her product within a reasonable amount of time to ensure freshness and quality. Second, the caterer must carefully orchestrate the delivery of his or her product within a complex setting in which multiple activities are being staged. For example, a dinner dance may require that the caterer serve various courses between dance sets. At some events, the caterer must provide the entire service within a short time frame to ensure that all servers are out of the function room in time for speeches or other aspects of the program.

Service Styles

The term *service* refers to the method used for serving a catered meal. In the United States, the three most popular forms of service are the seated banquet, the standing or seated buffet, and the standing reception, where servers pass food items to guests. Each of these service types helps satisfy specific goals and objectives. Figure 6.7 (shown in the electronic appendices) provides a simple guide on when to employ a specific type of service.

In addition to these service styles, the exposition/exhibition is an important avenue for effective catering. Exposition managers know that F&B serve as a strong attraction and increase traffic greatly in an exposition hall. One of the more popular methods is to provide guests with an apron (usually donated by a sponsor and

Photo by Seungwon Shawn Lee

New trends in food (dessert) is evolving constantly. Attending food and catering-focused trade shows can help event leaders to stay current. This photo shows winners of dessert ideas at New York HX show.

imprinted with their logo) and then distribute pocket sandwiches. With this technique the guests can walk, talk shop, and eat. It is a very efficient way to provide food service for guests at an exposition and resembles a giant walking picnic.

Picnic style (also known as family style) service is also a popular technique for corporate and social reunion events. Although this style is difficult in terms of service, it is extremely popular among guests who want to sit together as one large group. This style is also popular with Oktoberfest events, as it resembles a German beer hall. This style involves placing large platters of food on the central table where guests are seated on all four sides and the guests serve themselves. Creative event leaders take this picnic style outdoors and make it a true "picnic" catering. For example, Meeting Professionals International annual convention closing ceremony held in Salt Lake City, Utah (known for its green city brand), used the picnic style setup with blankets and picnic baskets. It is a great case of combining given resources (green nature) with appropriate serving style to increase the synergy effect. Its video is available at https://www.youtube.com/watch?v=O6_pn4nKVDc.

English and Russian services, although not very popular in the United States, are two styles that may be implemented for the right occasion. English style involves serving each table from a moving cart. In Russian service, the server uses silver platters from which he or she places each course onto a guest's plate. Both styles of service may be requested, but the caterer must be equipped and schooled properly to produce an effective result.

Logistic Considerations

Proper and efficient guest flow as well as effective methods for ensuring timely delivery of F&B are essential considerations for a catered event. The event caterer may have substantial experience working in a permanent venue, but when asked to provide services off-premises, he or she may not be aware of the additional rigor required to survive in the jungle. To survive and thrive, one must know these basic laws of the event jungle:

- Determine in advance the goals and objectives of the catered event and match the logistical requirements to these objectives. For example, a brief networking event should use fewer chairs and tables, to allow guests time to mix and mingle.
- Determine the ages and types of guests and match the requirements to their needs. For example, for older guests, more chairs may be needed to provide additional comfort during an extended reception.
- Identify the food preparation and other staging areas and ensure that there is a clear passageway to the consumption area. Check the floors to make sure that they are free of debris and allow the service staff to move quickly.
- Whenever possible, use a double-buffet style for this type of service. The double buffet not only serves twice as many guests but also allows guests to interact with one another as they receive their food.
- Do not place food stations in areas that are difficult to replenish. Large crowds of guests may prevent service personnel from replenishing food stations efficiently.
- When passing food items, place a few servers at the entryway so that guests notice that food is available. This technique ensures that most guests will see and consume at least one of the food items being offered.
- Use lighting to highlight buffets, carving, and other stations. Soft, well-focused lighting directs guests' eyes to the food and makes it easier to find as well as more appetizing.
- Use servers at the entryway to pass drinks rapidly to guests as they enter, or open the bars farthest from the entrance first. For smaller events with ample time,

passing drinks may be preferable; however, for larger events where the guests must be served quickly, staggering bar openings may be beneficial. Once the distant bars begin to experience lines of 10 or more persons, succeeding bars are then immediately opened, working back toward the entryway.

- Instruct the bar captain to close all bars promptly at the appointed time. Use servers to line up at the entryway to assist in directing guests into the main function room.
- Provide return tables to accept glassware as guests go to the next event. Staff these areas to avoid too many glasses accumulating.
- Request that servers distribute welcome gifts or programs during the setup period and be staged in each dining station to assist with seating. Servers should be requested to offer chairs to guests without hesitation, to expedite seating.
- Use an invocation, moment of silence, or a simple "bon appétit" to signal the beginning of the meal.
- These service times typically should be used for catered events:
  o Cocktail reception: 30 minutes to 1 hour maximum
  o Seated banquet: 1 to 2 hours without lengthy program
  o Preset salad consumption and clearing: 15 to 20 minutes
  o Entrée delivery, consumption, and clearing: 30 to 40 minutes
  o Dessert delivery, consumption, and clearing: 20 to 30 minutes
  o Coffee and tea service: 15 to 30 minutes
  o These times may vary by country or cultural requirement.
- Make certain that all service personnel have exited the function room prior to the program or speeches. If this is not possible, make certain that front tables have been served and that servers continue service as quietly as possible in back of the function area.
- Request that servers stand at exit doors and bid guests goodbye and distribute any parting gifts from the host or hostess.

Your catering event professional will suggest other ideas to help you accomplish your goals and objectives. However, remember that you must prioritize the event's goals and objectives, and catering may or may not be high on the list. Therefore, it is important to maintain balance as you decide where to focus during specific periods of the event. Catering styles are currently in flux in the twenty-first century as many events have become more casual in nature. However, to ensure that your guest feels comfortable and confident during your catered event, it is helpful to provide some level of order and decorum such as directing the guests to the double buffet table by table (inviting them to dine) or having the servers help with seating at a seated dinner.

Once you have identified the event's goals and objectives, you choose the service style to make certain that your guests' needs are satisfied. After basic needs are satisfied, it is time to add some magic to turn an ordinary catered affair into an extraordinary special event.

Coordinating Catering Operations

As caterers assume increased responsibilities in the event planning profession, other members of the professional team will need to adjust their marketing and operations strategies to cope with this new phenomenon. "Can and will caterers charge for event planning services beyond the cost of food and service?" and "Will all future catered events place significant emphasis on food and beverage at the risk of ignoring other elements and producing a more balanced event?" are but two of numerous questions that will be raised.

Earlier, it was observed that, historically, caterers have always provided some degree of event planning services. Will caterers develop these services further to reflect full depth and breadth of resources available within the planned events industry? If they choose to broaden their education, their impact can have substantial implications within the industry. The future of event planning may include both good F&B, as well as equally excellent services managed by the caterer. This consolidation will be welcomed by some clients who desire one-stop shopping and rejected by others who may, for a variety of reasons, prefer to entrust their event to another event leader. Regardless, the future force in catering will include offering many diversified services carefully combined into a nutritious, filling, and satisfying buffet. At the center of the bountiful buffet of these diversified services may be professional event planning.

Global event leaders must also recognize that trends are typically regional and then national in scope. For example, recently we have noticed a trend that involves the elaborate design and construction of full-scale ice martini bars. These bars are constructed entirely of ice; fiber-optic lights illuminate them internally. The bartenders dispense hundreds of martinis, which are well received by baby boomers, who want to relive the classic moments from the 1930s and 1940s enjoyed by their parents. The same is true of cigars, which are very popular in many parts of the United States. In other countries, cigars and martinis are usual and customary; in North America, they are often reserved for very special occasions.

To best utilize the trends in event catering, you first should review all event literature to be sure that you are incorporating a trend that is on an upward trajectory. One very good resource is *Catering Magazine*. It is also important to pay attention to emerging food trends. Previously vegetarian and vegan menus with plant-based proteins such as lentils, tofu, and quinoa showed up on event tables. Plant-based meat emerged in 2019 and is likely to continue popularity beyond. Health-conscious and environmentally minded people welcome this new food option. Once vegetarians and vegans had to bear with a tasteless patty. Today's engineered meatless meats taste just like the real meat and even satisfy carnivores. Next, make certain that you test the trend idea with a focus panel of your event guests and others to make certain that it is appropriate and can be implemented with high quality. Finally, remember the difference between fads and trends. Fads are often short-lived. You may purchase 5,000 pairs of crocodile figure knock-offs as part of your fun Aussie-themed event, only to discover that they went out of vogue 6 months ago. Cautiously incorporate trends into your event design to enhance your plan, as these trends may in fact become fads that change rapidly.

Catering Presentation Ideas

Putting "zing" into event F&B presentation is not only creative and fun duty but also challenging duty to event leaders. Some of effective and well-adopted tactics include music, entertainment, decor, theme, dress, and layout. A wide range of inexpensive and highly effective methods for presenting F&B at your event is located below. Remember that each of these ideas must be considered first and foremost in a cultural context to make certain there is a goodness of fit between your creativity and the guests' final perception.

The Living Buffet

Effect As guests browse along a seemingly normal buffet table, they are startled as the head of lettuce suddenly starts talking to the cauliflower and the cauliflower turns to the guest for advice on how to handle the unruly lettuce.

Photo by Joe Goldblatt

The garnishing, decoration, and overall presentation of food and drink is critically important in terms of promoting the overall event theme and demonstrating customization and quality.

Method Using a standard buffet table, cut two 24-inch holes in the top. The holes should be located approximately 12 to 18 inches apart and away from the front edge of the table. Place two actors, in headpieces that resemble lettuce and cauliflower, under the table with their heads penetrating the hole. It is best if the headpiece covers the eyes or they keep their heads slightly bowed until time to speak. Elaborately garnish all the area around the fake lettuce and cauliflower. Use theatrical lighting to soften the light on this area of the buffet.

Reaction Guests will shriek with delight, and the talking lettuce and cauliflower will become one of the best memories of your catered event.

Bonus Write a brief script between the lettuce and cauliflower in which they engage in a heated discussion about health and nutrition. Have the actors turn to the guests to ask their opinions.

The Human Buffet Table

Effect A person supports an entire buffet on his or her garment.

Method Place a male or female actor in the center of two buffet tables. The buffet should be slightly elevated on platforms so that the edge of the table is at eye level. Construct a costume that appears to support the entire buffet. A woman may wear a long dress and the skirt may be supported with matching fabric used to skirt swag the front edge of the buffet table (see Figure 7.5), or a male may wear a colorful tailcoat with the tails extended with matching fabric to drape the tables. Place bright light on the actors in colors to complement their costumes and slightly softer light on the buffet tables. Match the lighting for the actor's wardrobe with softer lighting in matching colors on the buffet skirting.

Reaction Guests will ooh and ah as your elegant actors wave and invite them to dine.

Bonus Direct the actors to freeze and come to life periodically. This will create an ongoing activity for the guests to observe and enjoy.

Resource Roberts Event Group of Philadelphia offers this attraction and many other innovative entertainment ideas.

The Living Dessert Models

Effect A 10-feet-high model wears a gorgeous gown and reveals smaller models with desserts on their gowns.

Method Place a female model on stilts in the center of a giant frame. On top of the frame is a lavish costume such as a Renaissance dress or Folies Bergère style costume. Use fiber optics and other lighting such as chasing lights on the wardrobe for added effects. The center of the gown opens and reveals smaller models who emerge wearing long gowns with frames on top holding dozens of small desserts for the guests to enjoy.

Reaction Guests will first be transfixed at the stunning appearance of the models and may need encouragement or examples from your staff to step forward and help themselves to dessert.

Bonus Hide under the dress additional male models who also exit through the folds in the skirt and distribute chocolate candy on small silver trays.

Resource Champagne Showgirls: http://www.champagneshowgirls.com/
   Photo: http://photos.jonathanivyphoto.com/p995034080/h1f11a1cf#h7aaba0

That Old Black Magic

Effect Thirty servers enter once the guests are seated. Each server is carrying a silver tray with two top hats. Suddenly the entire room begins to glow in the dark.

Method Purchase 60 black-plastic top hats. Fill each top hat with 20 glow-in-the-dark bracelets and sticks. Line the waiters up outside the room service entrance of the function. Dim all the lights and instruct the servers to enter as you play music such as "Old Black Magic" or "Magic to Do." As the servers arrive at the tables and place their hats in the center, quickly turn off the lights. Instruct the servers to place their trays under their arms, clap their hands, and distribute the glow-in-the-dark pieces from inside the hats to the guests.

Reaction Your guests may first wonder why there are no centerpieces for this elaborate catered event. However, once the glow-in-the-dark gifts are distributed, the guests will applaud as they become the room decor and you produce magic at a fraction of the cost of traditional decor.

Bonus Purchase white gloves for the servers and color them with glow-in-the-dark dye. As the lights go dim, have the servers wave their hands above their heads and then clap them before producing the glow-in-the-dark gifts.

Resource The Oriental Trading Company, Inc. catalog (www.orientaltrading.com) offers hundreds of inexpensive party supplies.

The Servers Parade

Effect Your guests receive their main course and/or a unique dessert that has been created for them as your team of servers parades the dessert to their tables.

Method Use glow-in-the-dark swizzle sticks or other items to decorate the dessert trays. Play a lively march or theme music that reflects the style of the catered event as the servers march forward. Stage the servers so that they enter at the rear of the room and march through the tables holding the trays high above their heads. They may then circle the individual tables two or three times before pausing and then lowering the plates onto each place setting. Lower the lights and use follow spot-lights to sweep the room to create additional excitement. Prior to their entrance, announce: "The chef has prepared a once-in-a-lifetime dessert creation to celebrate this momentous occasion. Please welcome your servers!" The servers march (or dance) to each table and serve the main course and/or dessert.

Reaction Your guests will respond with spontaneous applause followed by clapping rhythmically to the music as your servers deliver dessert.

Bonus At the conclusion of the dessert parade line, have the servers line up in front of the stage and gesture to the left or right as the pastry chef appears for a brief bow. Make certain that the pastry chef is dressed in all white with a traditional chef's hat so that he or she is easily recognized. This will cause an additional ovation, perhaps a standing one.

Resource The Culinary Institute of America or Johnson & Wales University College of Culinary Arts may refer you to their graduates throughout the world who are among the leading pastry chefs working in the modern food-and-beverage industry.

The Incredible Edible Centerpiece

Effect Your guests will notice that their centerpiece is both beautiful and edible. They will see and smell as well as taste this delicious work of art.

Method Engage a chocolatier to carve a centerpiece out of chocolate for your guests to enjoy. The carving may represent the symbol of the event or the logo of the organization sponsoring the program. Use a pin light to illuminate each sculpture independently. Make certain the sculpture is on a raised platform, such as a gold or silver epergne. Include fresh fruit in your display to add color to your final design. One excellent subject is a large chocolate cornucopia filled with fresh red strawberries.

Reaction Your guests will soon notice the work of art gracing their table and engage in lively conversation about its origin. Some guests will take photos, and others may try to nibble.

Resource Belvedere Chocolates (www.belvederechocolates.com) and Forget Me Knot.com (www.forgetmeknot.com) have standard chocolate sculptures, such as a signature bonsai tree or magician's top hat, or they can create original designs for your event.

Champagne Vending Machine with e-card Camera

Effect This new vending machine was originally introduced when Moët & Chandon debuted its new champagne line in 2016. It became very popular at events like benefit dinners and galas. It includes a facial recognition camera, along with custom backgrounds and online connection, so guests can share e-cards with their friends. And most of all, having fun with their champagne bottle dispensed to their hands.

Method Just like any vending machine (this is special as it gives you a champagne bottle) and the installed monitor and camera allow guests to take photos with preset background.

ECOLOGIC

The additional benefit of using an edible center piece is that the decor is consumed rather than simply turned into waste matter. You may wish to add a small sign describing for the guests the environmental benefits of consuming their centerpiece decor and even remind them that although they may add a few calories they are reducing the carbon footprint of the event.

Reaction Your attendees will gather around this vending machine and watch a cute champagne bottle vending through its delivery belt (just like a Coke can). They then take a digital photo holding it in their hands or toast. An instant photo booth installed in the vending machine will provide a very special photo of a happy champagne memory—"Life is always fun with a champagne toast."

The Ice Cold Logo

Effect As your guests arrive for the cocktail reception, they observe an ice carver putting the finishing touches on an elaborate sculpture.

Method Your caterer can refer a professional ice carver who will pre-carve from a large block of ice your organization's logo, image, name, or other important and valued symbol of your group. Place the carver on a raised platform, and use rope and stanchion to provide ample working room and keep your guests from being hit by flying chips of ice. Make certain that the ice carver completes his or her work of art at the very moment your main function is to begin. Upon completion, stage several photos of your key leaders with the new work of art and then announce that the main function will begin.

Reaction Your guests will crowd around the carver and begin intense discussions with one another about the creation. At the conclusion of the carving, they will erupt into applause and begin taking numerous photos.

Bonus Ask the ice carver to use an electric chain saw, as this creates noise and excitement. In addition, the use of flame (fire and ice) is another dramatic touch that your ice carver may wish to incorporate into the final design (e.g., a dragon breathing fire).

Resource An excellent and creative resource for this type of production is called Fear No Ice. A multimedia, performance art team of professional ice carvers creates masterpieces in ice, including corporate logos, while performing to high-energy music.

Selecting the Best Caterer

The best caterer is the organization best equipped with experience, knowledge, creativity, personnel, and resources (human and actual equipment) to achieve your goals and objectives. In each community, there may be several full-service off-premises caterers with excellent reputations. However, you can narrow the list to one, two, or perhaps three by using these 20 criteria:

1. Find out how many years the company has been in business and the size of events it has catered.
2. Ensure that caterer has health and occupancy permits (and all other necessary permits).
3. If serving alcohol, make sure that caterer has on- and off-premises alcoholic beverage permits.

4. If permits are in order, make sure that caterer has liquor liability insurance.
5. Ask to see references and/or client letters.
6. Ask to see pictures of past events—look for professionalism and setup of kitchen/staging area.
7. Identify past and present events that caterer has handled and find out maximum and minimum sizes.
8. Check to see if site meets the Americans with Disabilities Act requirements and complies with laws.
9. Find out policies on client tastings.
10. Review printed materials—menu descriptions will tell about the level of professionalism.
11. Ask to see design equipment and/or in-house rentals—look for innovation and cleanliness.
12. Leave messages with the company receptionist—see how long it takes them to return your calls.
13. If on-premises, make sure that any electronic or live music complies with Broadcast Music, Inc. (BMI) or American Society of Composers, Authors, and Publishers (ASCAP) regulations.
14. Check for their membership in professional organizations (i.e., National Association of Catering Executives [NACE] and ISES).
15. Find out where the executive chef received his or her training.
16. Find out how waiters are attired for different levels of service.
17. Find out if servers are proficient in French service, modified French service, or plated service.
18. Find out deposit requirements and terms.
19. Review and analyze contracts and cancellation agreements.
20. Call the local party-equipment rental company and find out about its historic working relationship with the caterer.

Catering Coordination

The event leader must closely coordinate all event activities with the director of catering or other catering team leader. Within the catering team, each member has particular responsibilities:

- *Director of catering:* The senior catering official, who coordinates sales and operations
- *Catering manager:* Coordinates individual catered events, including sales and operations
- *Banquet manager/captain:* Manages specific catered functions; servers report to banquet manager
- *Server:* Person responsible for serving the guests
- *Bartender:* Person responsible for mixing, pouring, and serving alcoholic and nonalcoholic beverages

To ensure that you are coordinating each element effectively with your catering team, make certain that you hold a series of telephone or in-person meetings to review the various elements that will be included in your event. The first meeting should be used to review the proposal and answer any questions you may have about the food, beverages, equipment, or service and terms of payment. The next meeting will be held prior to signing the contract to negotiate any final terms, such as the inclusion of a complimentary food tasting. Some caterers prefer that you attend a comparable event and taste similar items that will be served at your event. However, if your event is introducing new cuisine, it is essential that you insist on a separate food tasting to ensure the quality of each item prior to serving your guests. In some instances, there will be a charge for this service; you should confirm this prior to signing the contract. The final meeting should include a thorough review of all elements, including the schedule, equipment, and service levels, and answer any final questions the caterer may have regarding delivery, utilities, or other important issues.

Reviewing Proposals Most caterers will provide a complete and detailed proposal, including the type of cuisine, number of servers, schedule, equipment rentals, payment terms, and other pertinent information. Using the next checklist will ensure that all important information is included in the catering proposal:

- History of the catering organization, including other clients of similar size and scope they have served.
- Letters of reference from other clients of similar size and scope.
- Complete description of cuisine.
- Complete description of style of service, including the number of servers/bartenders that will be provided.
- Complete description of equipment that will be provided by the caterer. Equipment may include tables, chairs, and serving utensils as well as other items. Make certain that each is described and that quantity is included.
- List of additional services to be provided by the caterer. This might include floral, entertainment, or other special requirements.
- Complete description of payment terms, including date of guarantee, taxes, gratuities, deposits, balance payments, and percentage of overage provided by the caterer.
- All schedule information concerning deliveries, setup, service, and removal of equipment through load-out.
- Insurance, bonding, and other information pertinent to managing the risk of your event.
- Any additional requirements; this might include utilities such as water, electric power, and so on.

Negotiating with the caterer is an important step in the process of selecting the best caterer. In smaller event markets, where competition is not as great as in larger markets, negotiation may be more difficult. Still, regardless of size, five areas may often be negotiated:

1. Ask to pay the lowest deposit in advance or to pay a series of smaller deposits spread evenly over a period of months. Even better, if your organization has a good credit record, ask to pay net 30 days after your event.
2. Ask for a discount for prepayment of the full amount. You may receive up to a 5 percent discount if you pay your entire bill several weeks in advance.
3. Ask for a discount if you are a not-for-profit organization. Although all not-for-profit organizations ask for this concession, you may be successful if you can convince the caterer that your guests may bring him or her additional new business. Offer to actively promote the presence of the caterer at the event to ensure high visibility.
4. Ask for a complimentary service. Some caterers will provide services ranging from a complimentary ice sculpture to a pre- or post-event reception for your guests.

5. Ask for a complimentary food tasting for yourself and your key decision makers. This should not take the form of an additional event; rather, it is a business activity for the purpose of inspecting the food presentation and taste, and other important elements of the event.

Final Step The final meeting should always if possible be held in person or through video teleconferencing. Often it is held at the event site in conjunction with the food tasting or final walk-through. This important meeting is your final opportunity to review the critical details regarding the caterer's contribution to your event. Five major points must be covered during this meeting:

1. Confirm the day, date, time, location, parking, and other critical information with the caterer.
2. Carefully coordinate all catering deliveries and access to the loading entrance with other vendors.
3. Review the times for the service, and instruct the caterer regarding the other elements of the program and how he or she will interface with these aspects.
4. Review the caterer's alcohol management program. Ask the caterer if his or her staff has received training and how they will handle guests who are obviously inebriated.
5. Review all payment terms and any elements you are required to provide as part of your agreement.

Cost-Saving Measures Increasingly, both clients and their event leaders are concerned with cost. In some corporate circles, it is not the actual cost but the perception of a high-priced event that is of greater concern. Use this list to avoid these concerns and lower your overall catering costs:

- Carefully analyze the meals that must be provided. Some meals may be taken by guests on their own, such as at networking dinners, where all guests pay their individual bills. You may also wish to substitute concessions for some meal functions. An individually priced buffet line may be a good alternative for some meal functions.
- Use buffets and boxed lunches instead of seated banquet service. Reducing labor cost may help reduce expense. However, with buffets there may be food waste, so discuss this with your caterer in advance.
- Price food items by the lowest possible unit (cup, glass, piece, or dozen) rather than by the tray or gallon. Order only the amount of food you will require based on the history of your event.
- Secure sponsors for meal functions. In a recent study, we learned that sponsors are very much interested in providing funding for meals that are related to educational programs.
- Secure in-kind sponsorships from bottlers and others in the food-and-beverage industry.
- Reduce or eliminate alcohol from your event. Many events are becoming beer-and-wine functions in place of full-open-bar affairs. This change is happening not only due to concerns about health but also because of the perceived association between heavy drinking and drunk driving.
- Serve a signature drink to everyone upon their arrival. A signature drink is an original drink that your bar manager creates for consumption by the entire group. At a catered function, the first need of most guests is to occupy

their hands with a drink. Offer your signature drink at the entrance to your event and address this need, while reducing your budget by controlling consumption.

- Allow guests to serve themselves. This is especially popular with children's events. Make-your-own-sundae bars and the making of a 5-foot-long submarine sandwich are not only entertaining but may also result in cost savings.

Catering Trends

A trend is a pattern of behavior that is likely to be sustained over time. Although the event catering profession is susceptible to shifting tastes of global-minded guests and is certainly affected by the state of the economy, several trends are emerging. Forward-thinking event leaders and caterers have been seeking catering menus that satisfy guests' palates and eyes. These five trends are well-worth noting, as they will certainly influence many of the decisions you will make.

The first trend is that nutritious and organic foods have become as much a health issue as an ethical one. Since Eric Schlosser's 2001 landmark *Fast Food Nation* exposed the perilous, unsustainable fast-food industry, the organic food market has taken off running. One direct result has been the Slow Food Movement (www.slowfood.com), which promotes using organic, locally grown, seasonal ingredients in traditional recipes. Event guests increasingly want to know the ingredients in their F&B to make wise decisions regarding menu items. Therefore, caterers will want to make available the ingredients and may even wish to list these items in a menu on signs posted near the food items. As the world's population ages (especially in the United States), guests will be more and more concerned with good health and will turn to nutritious foods as a primary means of promoting this lifestyle. Furthermore, caterers will continue the practice of promoting heart-healthy menu items, as offering these items will provide a popular alternative and also differentiate the caterer from competitors because of this attention paid to low cholesterol items. Plant-based protein and meatless meat are well aligned with these demands and growing in popularity on the tables of events catering.

A second trend is gin-flavored cocktails, Scotch whiskey as well as U.S. bourbon (served neat or in cocktails), and craft beers are current alcoholic beverage trends.

Multicultural-minded dishes and drinks: With the growing number of global-minded millennials desiring familiar and unique and local and global tastes, catering professionals create new innovative menus. Menus are customized to meet those demands such as a refreshment station preparing made-to-order crispy Japanese rice cakes topped with spicy Korean chopped kimchi or Alaskan salmon with Thai salsa. Drinks are like a Korean soju (clear rice wine) with a cocktail mixology of Maine blueberry juice and peach.

The third trend relates to the second trend in that, increasingly, caterers are seeking additional revenue streams and some are even moving from strictly food-and-beverage operations into full event planning services. This change comes with great challenge as well as potentially great opportunity. Historically, caterers have been involved in all aspects of event planning. Caterers, especially in the social life-cycle event market, have been responsible for providing or recommending the services of florists, musicians, decorators, invitation designers, and other allied professionals. Today's trend merely quantifies this historic business opportunity and repositions the caterer as an event leader who specializes in catering services. However, to take full advantage of this trend, the catering professional must be willing to round out his or her education with a rigorous course of study in event planning. In every profession, eventually, superior quality combined with good value can conquer fierce competition. Event planning is no different from other professions in this regard. If catering professionals are to expand their services to include those of event planning, they must be willing to acquire the new skills that will complement their existing talents to improve their quality and provide them with the tools to compete effectively in the event marketplace.

A fourth trend is more attention to an increasing number of dietary considerations. Caterers customize menus to any and all dietary needs without compromising flavor or variety. Tracy Stuckrath, CSEP, CMM, and VHC is the founder and chief connecting officer of Thrive! Meetings and Events, based in Atlanta, Georgia. At age 30, she discovered that she was extremely lethargic and, despite visits to numerous physicians, could not determine the cause. After visiting an ENT she was diagnosed with an allergy to wheat products. Therefore, Tracy went on a yeast-free diet, avoiding yeast, sugar, vinegar, dairy, white flour, peanuts, and mushrooms. However, as she was a professional event leader, she found it nearly impossible to avoid these products at special events. As a result of her own dietary needs, she discovered that many people also had similar food allergies. Tracy then decided to educate herself through the Institute for Integrative Nutrition and today is one of the leading authorities regarding food allergies associated with meetings and events. According to Tracy, more and more hotels and catering organizations are recognizing the need to create inclusive menus for individuals with different dietary needs. For example, Fairmont Hotels and Resorts helps guests with specific dietary conditions manage their needs while traveling by offering options for macrobiotic, vegan, and other diets. Tracy believes that all future meetings and events may be improved by being smart, green, and delicious. Her boutique consulting firm is committed to achieving this goal one meal at a time.

Fifth and finally, more and more caterers are carefully labeling their foods and the ingredients used to prepare these items on their buffet as well as on the printed menu itself. Many guests have severe allergic reactions to certain foods such as peanuts, and, therefore, it is important to provide advance notice to your guests of the ingredients of the F&B you are serving.

An overarching theme of these trends can be summarized as "mindful menus." As a culinary term, mindfulness in regard to menu design means more organic, veggie-centric dishes, plant-based proteins, sustainable meats, and expands to behaviors of conscious consumption. Therefore, these five trends—nutritious and organic menus, a wider range in alcohol service, the growing wide range of dietary needs, the need to label food items by describing their ingredients, and the expansion of the caterer's services to include those of full-service event planning—may be viewed as future economic opportunities provided that education and commitment to quality are implemented consistently.

Coordinating Technical Production Resources (Audiovisual, Lighting, Sound, and Special Effects)

The event planning profession has seen perhaps the greatest paradigm shift in the live production sector of this industry. Live production is also what differentiates events from other entertainment or creative products. Although one may argue that television specials are billed as "special events," in most instances these

Photo by Seungwon Shawn Lee

These light beams and BOGO light up any image on any surface to enhance ambience and also reduce energy costs.

Photo by Seungwon Shawn Lee

Decorated ceiling effect with LED beams and GOBO images at George Mason University Holiday party.

events are filmed or taped before a live audience. Productions ranging from the U.S. National Football League's Super Bowl half-time show to the Three Tenors concert combine live production with various audiovisual, lighting, sound, special effects, and video resources to produce a well-crafted event that ultimately is viewed by millions via television. The modern event leader cannot ignore this major shift and must understand as well as implement these resources when appropriate.

Why = What

It was previously described that, prior to selecting the most effective resources for your event, you must establish clear goals and objectives by asking why this event is necessary. Due to the myriad new technologies now offered, this question is more important than ever before. An inexperienced event leader may decide to mix and match a wide array of new technology to impress his or her guests during the event. In fact, this mixture becomes a collage of inappropriate resources that results in confusion to the guests. An award-winning designer reportedly cautioned his young apprentices that "less is indeed more." The event leader must also use caution when selecting appropriate resources to support or enhance the event to make certain that each device is well- integrated rather than extraneous. The list that follows can be used as a primary coordination tool for selecting and engaging these resources:

- *Identify the purpose of event technology for your program.* Will the event technology be used to attract attention or to improve communications?
- *Determine the size of the live audience.* The technology you select for the audience will be determined by the number of guests.
- *Identify the age, culture, and learning style of your guests.* Some guests are visual learners, while others are more attuned to audio influences. Still other audiences, due to their age, may prefer a louder or quieter sound level.
- *Inspect the venue and inventory assets.* This includes preexisting light (natural and artificial), in-house audiovisual equipment, utilities, the experience of local technical labor, and any other elements that will interact with your event.
- Sit in a guest's chair or stand in the guest's place, and try to envision the event through his or her eyes and ears. Check for obstructed views and other distractions. Identify potential solutions to develop optimum enjoyment through the entire event.

Purposes of Event Production Technology

Whether the purpose of your event is to educate or entertain or, perhaps, both, the technology that you select will help you best achieve your goals and objectives. In the conference event field, you may select slide projectors, overhead projectors, a teleprompter (in Europe this is referred to as an auto-cue), or perhaps one microphone to improve communications between the presenter and the participant. The entertainment field may require theatrical lighting and special effects, such as fog, laser, or strobe lights. Other fields will require different technologies; however, ultimately the purpose of the event will determine the final selection and coordination of the event technology. Figure 6.8 (in the electronic appendices) describes how to make the proper technology to the style of your individual event.

Audiovisual Effects

The term *audiovisual* was probably first coined in the 1950s, when schools and, later, businesses and then associations used slide and overhead projectors and sound recordings for instructional purposes. During the 1970s, this technology expanded rapidly with more sophisticated audio tools as well as video enhancement after the invention of video-projection systems. Indeed, today dozens of audiovisual tools are available for use by event leaders. Audiovisual projection is divided primarily into two projection fields: visual and audio. Audience size and distance, and the age and type of attendee are critical considerations when selecting a tool. The right tool will make your task easier and the event more enjoyable for your guests; the improper tool will cause you frustration and irritate your guests. Therefore, when selecting audiovisual tools for an event, refer to the checklist to check and balance your decision.

Digital images have replaced traditional photography in the event production industry. Yesterday's slide projector has been replaced by the notebook computer loaded or the universal serial bus (USB) storage device with hundreds of slides and entire educational programs, including music and video. Today's projectors are wireless, making installing and connecting different video/audio resources easy and fast. As mobile devices replace PCs and laptops, new projector models are capable of using an app installed on a smartphone or tablet to display presentations and documents. Monitor industry publications such as *Sound and Video Contractor (SVC)* magazine and Creative Planet Network.com to stay in touch with the latest technological advancements in the rapidly changing audiovisual field.

Conducting and Analyzing the Event Site Inspection

Site inspection occurs during both the planning and coordination phase. During the planning phase, potential sites are inspected to identify those that should receive requests for proposals. Increasingly, this task is conducted using the Internet. However, we advise you whenever possible to visit the site yourself or send a representative to inspect the physical assets. Even using three-dimensional technology on the Internet will not allow you to view every aspect of the venue. Inspections based on advanced virtual reality (VR) and augmented reality (AR) technology are in place in aviation and construction industries. The event industry is adopting the technology for site inspection, too. While technology-based inspections don't completely replace an in-person site visit, they are effective in reducing the number of initial site visits, so event leaders can filter a venue without having to go all the way to that site. AR-enhanced site inspection can be beneficial to event leaders and venues as AR can provide details on the display of AR-enabled information on real images (e.g., dimensions, capacity, and number of tables and chairs allowed and available dates and time). Therefore, a physical inspection is essential to confirm and verify the quality of the physical space.

It is particularly important that you schedule a site inspection during the coordination phase to reconfirm that there have been no changes to the site since the planning period. We recommend that you visit the site no less than 30 days prior to the event to reinspect it and make certain that you will be able to conduct the event effectively within the venue. If there have been dramatic changes, this type of lead time will give you sufficient time to rework your event design or even, if necessary, change venues.

The Site Inspection

Perhaps the most important activity involving space is the site inspection. Using a comprehensive, customized checklist will make this task efficient and thorough. It will also allow you to delegate this task to others if you are not able to travel to the site yourself.

MeetingMatrix (www.meetingmatrix.com), acquired by IT giant ORACLE, has greatly expedited this process through their development of a Web-based program that lists thousands of venues throughout the world. Their service also includes certified diagrams to further ensure the accuracy of your event design. Finally, once you locate the appropriate venue, using their exclusive computer-assisted design and drawing program, you can create original designs using tables, chairs, lecterns, drape, ice sculptures, and even the organization logo to completely outfit the room where the event will be held.

When conducting the in-person site inspection, always carry a laser measure, a digital still or video camera, notepad, and pencil. Upon arrival, note the ingress to the parking facilities for up to 1 mile away. What will be the estimated travel time in heavy to moderate traffic, and are there alternative routes if the main artery is blocked by an accident or construction? Determine where the parking area will be for your official and VIP vehicles. Find out if special identification is required for those vehicles to park in these preapproved areas. Measure the height of the loading dock (if available) from the driveway to make certain that your vehicles can deliver directly onto the dock. This knowledge alone may save you thousands of dollars in additional labor charges.

Ask the venue officials to show you the entrance door for your personnel and the walking route to the pre-event waiting area (dressing rooms, green rooms, and briefing rooms). Write down these instructions and read them back to the official. Note who supplied these instructions, as they will later be given to your personnel, and should there be a problem, you must be able to refer back to your original source for clarification.

Measure the square footage of the waiting area, and determine how many persons can be accommodated when official furnishings are included. Locate the restrooms, and note if they are adequate or require upgrading (e.g., bringing in nicer amenities, such as specialty soaps, toiletries, perfumes, full-length mirrors, and fresh flowers).

Ask the venue official to lead you from the waiting area to the location of the actual event. Thoroughly examine the event site from the perspective of the spectator or participant. Most importantly, can the spectators see and hear comfortably? Sit in the seat of the spectator farthest from the staging area. Determine how the person with the most obstructed view can best see and hear.

When possible, ask the venue official to supply you with their most recent floor plan or diagram of the site. Use this site diagram as a general blueprint, and then confirm and verify by using your measuring device to measure random locations. Note any variances for later adjustment on the final diagram.

Finally, before you leave the venue, sit for a minimum of 15 minutes in one of the chairs your spectator will occupy. Determine if it is comfortable for your guests. If not, ask if alternate seating is available, and at what cost.

Developing the Diagram

At one time transferring the results of the site inspection to a final, carefully produced diagram was a major labor-consuming operation. Using computer tools such as computer-assisted design and drawing (CADD) systems, this task has been simplified and automated. For those event leaders who are uncomfortable with computers, a manual system has been developed involving scale cutouts of magnets that correspond to the typical inventory of most venues (chairs, tables, platforms, pianos, etc.). Once assembled, the final product can be photocopied for distribution. MeetingMatrix uses a CADD system, enabling you to search for venues throughout the world and then construct a diagram and room setup using this system.

Before beginning the process of developing the diagram, audit all internal and external stakeholders and create a list of every element that must be depicted on the diagram. These elements may range from decor to catering tents and from first-aid centers to parking locations. You will later use this checklist to cross-check the diagram and make certain that every element has been included.

After the first draft diagram has been developed, it must be distributed to stakeholders for a first review. Ask the stakeholders to review the diagram for accuracy and return it within a fixed amount of time with any additions, deletions, or changes.

After you have received comprehensive input from the stakeholders, prepare a final copy for review by officials who must grant final approval for the event. These officials may include the fire marshal, transportation authorities, or others responsible for enforcing laws and regulations.

Once you have constructed a final, approved diagram, you have made the giant step forward from dream to idea to final plan. Event planning requires that you consistently implement your plan effectively.

Determining the Production Schedule

The production schedule is the primary instrument (other than the event diagram) that is used during the coordination phase. During this phase, the event leader must implement a minute-by-minute plan and monitor the tasks that lead to the ultimate conclusion of the event itself. The production schedule ensures that you will be able to achieve this goal efficiently. Figure 6.9 (shown in the electronic appendices) is an example of a typical production schedule.

As Figure 6.9 in the electronic appendices suggests, the production schedule begins with load-in and concludes with load-out (this is known as "bump in and bump out" in other parts of the world and in Scotland as "get in and get out"). The first line in the production schedule generally is "inspect venue," and the last line is "reinspect venue" to review and return the venue to the best condition. You will note that the production schedule is much more precise than the timeline and includes minute-by-minute precision. Typically, the event leader will include the production schedule in the timeline in the coordination phase and then provide a full version on-site at the event for the event coordination staff to manage the minute-by-minute operations.

The Event Industry Council has adopted the term *event specification guide* as the official standardized term for the previously used résumé or production schedule. The function schedule in this document is similar to the production schedule. To view a template of the event specification guide, visit https://insights.eventscouncil.org/Industry-insights/Additional-Resources and then click Event Industry Council Template.

Anticipating and Resolving Operational Conflicts

During the coordination phase, numerous operational conflicts will develop. The key is for the event leader to anticipate and resolve these problems quickly by practicing what is often referred to as *damage control*. Some of the typical operational conflicts that arise and how you can resolve them quickly follow:

- *Late-arriving vendor partners:* Maintain cell phone numbers and contact late-arriving vendors to determine their location.
- *Multiple vendors arriving simultaneously.* Sequence arrivals in logical order of installation.
- *Caterer running late in food delivery.* Monitor service carefully and use distractions such as dancing to cover long delays.
- *Speaker or entertainer cancels.* Use prerecorded music or video to cover.
- *Guests arrive too early.* Prepare for this and have appropriate staff greet and serve them.
- *Medical emergency.* Use standard operating procedures and work closely with venue to resolve.

As you can see, that wise event leader Murphy was prophetic when he wrote: "What can go wrong will go wrong." His cousin, O'Goldblatt of Scotland, however, was perhaps even more prophetic when some years later he wrote: "Murphy is an optimist." What can go wrong probably will go wrong and therefore it is best to prepare.

For a professional event leader, the coordination phase is the most exciting and often most grueling time during the event process. However, because you care deeply to achieve a high-quality outcome for the event, your ability to research, design, plan, and lead your team will smooth even the roughest edges during coordination of the event. The intersection of coordination can be crossed easily and safely because you are prepared, programmed, and ultimately polished in your ability to make the most difficult and intricate tasks appear easy and seamless.

Finally, during those often expectant moments before guests arrive, you may wish to add one additional ritual to your arsenal of coordination tools. A colleague who produced major events for large corporations once told Joe Goldblatt nearly 30 years ago that before she opens the doors to receive her thousands of guests, she closes her eyes for a few seconds and silently repeats three times: "This event is going to be easy, fun, and successful." This concept of contemplation and mindfulness may be effectively used with your next event to allow you to restore inner calm and create greater focus before you receive your guests. Although successful meetings and events are rarely easy, in fact your meeting or event may be more fun and successful if you are more relaxed in your approach to receiving the guests.

INSIGHTS FROM GLOBAL EVENT LEADERS

Tracy Stuckrath, CSEP, CMM, CHC

Thrive! Meetings & Events

Tracy Stuckrath is the founder and CEO of Thrive! Meetings & Events. She was named one of the Top 25 Women in the Meetings Industry by Meetings & Conventions magazine. She is a certified event planner, meetings manager, and health coach and has started Thrive! Meetings & Events in 2010, combining her expertise in producing events with her personal mission to educate and empower the hospitality industry and her clients to serve safer, more nutritious, health-enhancing foods. Tracy is involved in the Green Meetings Industry Council, National Association of Catering Executives, International Association of Culinary Professionals, Georgia Organics, and Food Allergy & Anaphylaxis Network.

- China's newly released dietary guidelines call on the nation's 1.3 billion people to reduce their meat consumption by 50 percent.
- 63 percent of consumers want to eat more sustainable, but it's hard for them to know whether the food choices they make are environmentally sustainable.
- Taste remains the top driver of food/beverage purchases; trust in a brand and recognizing the ingredients that go into a product are surprisingly impactful.
- Clean eating diets are most common. 38 percent of consumers say they followed a specific eating pattern or diet in the past year, similarly to the 36 percent who did so in 2018. While intermittent fasting continues to be a relatively common choice, clean eating (added to the survey for the first time this year) is actually the most widely cited diet that consumers say they follow.
- 25 percent consumers actively seek health benefits from foods, seeking weight loss, energy, digestive health, and heart health.
- Cannabis in food is also new and growing.

Q: What are the major trends in event catering–related nutrition?

A: Individuals are looking for transparency and clean healthier food. They want to know where their food comes from and what's in it. Food allergies, medically necessary diets, and veganism are on the rise.

- 34 percent of consumers eat plant-based proteins daily.
- 25 percent eat more plant-based proteins than they did 12 months ago.
- 32 million Americans have food allergies, almost double the amount estimated previously by FARE and the CDC.
- There is a 600 percent increase in people identifying as vegans in the United States in the last 3 years.
- In the United Kingdom, the number of people identifying as vegans has increased by 350 percent over the last decade.
- Veganism was Canada's top searched trend in 2017.

Q: How do globalized and complex event attendees affect event food and beverage planning?

A: Global attendees are definitely adding to the complexity of designing menus for event attendees. While we want to introduce new trends in food and beverage, it is also a good idea to provide comfort foods that the attendees know and are comfortable to eat.

Q: What skill sets related to catering/nutrition are required from students and young event professionals?

A: Event professionals at every level should understand dietary needs from food allergies to religious beliefs, lifestyle preferences, and medical conditions. They should know the laws that regulate food and beverage—disability laws, international labeling laws, food safety, epinephrine administration, corporate compliance, duty of care.

Q: What are risks that event professionals should know and be prepared in event catering/nutrition?

A: Risks associated with food and beverage include the following:

- Food poisoning
- Serving food allergens to a guest
- Serving nonreligious foods to strict followers
- Accessibility (lack of) into the event and via the food being served.

The Corporate Manslaughter and Corporate Homicide Act 2007 (UK)—This act regulates consequences of failing to take all reasonably practicable steps to protect the employees from its unsafe work environment. An organization is guilty of an offense if the way in which its activities are managed or organized (by its senior management) causes a person's death and this amounts to a gross breach of a relevant duty of care owed by the organization to the deceased.

Q: What is the advantage of having extensive knowledge of nutrition and catering for event professionals?

A: Increased revenue

- 91 percent of GF/AF consumers will return to a restaurant/caterer if they are provided safe meals the first time, which equals loyal repeat customers and increased revenues.
- 86 percent will NEVER return if they are not provided safe meals the first time.
- 600 percent increase in people identifying as vegans in the United States in the last 3 years.
- In the United Kingdom, the number of people identifying as vegans has increased by 350 percent over the last decade.
- Veganism was Canada's top searched trend in 2017.
- China's newly released dietary guidelines call on the nation's 1.3 billion people to reduce their meat consumption by 50 percent.
- New client base.
- Strong brand.
- Reduced risk.

Summary

Chapter 6 provided you with a comprehensive overview of the contracts, regulations, permits, and critical elements required for the successful on-site production of your event. These elements include the following key components.

1. *Contracts:* The written agreement or contract may be considered one of the primary risk avoidance, reduction, and retention tools for your event. It is important to carefully review all regulations and permits as well as licenses that will be required for your event and then construct written agreements that will protect your event organization as well as those you contract with for services.

2. *Catering:* From the very birth of human celebration, F&B has been a critical factor in the development and delivery of successful events. Many events are primarily focused upon the culinary experience such as the Taste of Chicago, Oktoberfest in Munich, or Taste of Edinburgh food festivals. Therefore, it is extremely important that you work closely and effectively with your catering professionals to align the food-and-beverage plans and operations with the overall goals of your special event.

3. *Technical production:* The third aspect of on-site production is composed of all of the technical elements, including but not limited to sound, lights, and special effects. As a result of the recent rebirth of and improvement in 3-D cinema technology, today's modern special events may be considered the ultimate 5-D spectacular by incorporating all five senses to create a memorable

experience for the guest. However, each of these technologies must be carefully selected, tested, and coordinated to once again satisfy the overall aims and objectives of the event experience.

4. *Site inspection:* The final section of this chapter explored the importance of developing a comprehensive site inspection check list for your event.

Key Terms

Audio-visual: The sound, lighting, and projection production elements used in your event.

Catering: On-premise (wherein a caterer has a permanent presence in the event venue), off-premise (wherein the caterer transports food, beverage, and their equipment to the venue), and concession (wherein a caterer serves F&B from specially designed catering vans, trucks or exhibit books [stands] at your event).

Concessionaire: A food-and-beverage provider who is mobile and serves from a truck, trailer or within a venue in a food-and-beverage concession specified area.

Contract: A written agreement between two or more parties specifying the obligations of each party in the production of the special event.

ESTA: The electronic pre-authorization required for non-U.S. citizens without official visas to enter the United States.

License: A written approval to conduct the event provided by a government or private organization. One of the typical licenses is to be able to serve alcohol at your event. A more

recent type of license is one for the use of copyrighted recorded or live music performed at your event.

Off-premises caterer: The firm or individual who generally prepares the bulk of the food in one location and then delivers it to a temporary location for the event.

On-premises caterer: The firm whose permanent catering kitchen is in the same location as the facility hosting the event.

Permit: A written approval from a local jurisdiction or other government or private organization that allows you to conduct the event. One of the key permits is occupancy, which specifies how many persons may be allowed in the event venue at one time.

Production: The technical production elements such as sound, lighting, projection, and special effects that may be used in your event.

Visa: The official document issued by a government at their consulate or embassy allowing entry into their country.

Career Connections

In order to rapidly advance your career through mastering contracts, permits, licenses, and the various vendor partners you will work with during your future events, start your research now. Through online research, contact local jurisdictions and review the key components of typical contracts for consulting and catering and licenses for alcohol, as well as permits for occupancy and other key permissions. Next,

make an appointment to meet with a local caterer and ask if you may have a tour of their operation and perhaps volunteer to help them with a future event. Use the same strategy to gain more experience with your other vendor partners. Finally, practice drafting sample agreements and contracts for hypothetical events so that you become comfortable with crafting these types of documents.

Next Steps

1. Conduct an Internet search for local caterers, lighting, sound, and special effects professionals, and review the range of their product and service offerings.

2. Develop an electronic database of future local, regional, and international vendor partners for your events.

3. Review the book *Event Entertainment and Production* by Mark Sonder (2004) to identify further resources for improving your

knowledge of the wide range of products and services available in this rapidly developing area.

4. Review the book *The 21st Century Meeting and Event Technologies* by Drs. Seungwon (Shawn) Lee, Dessislava Boshnakova, and Joe Goldblatt to catch up current trends and available technologies in production, vendor search and e-RFP procedures.

References

Black's Law Dictionary, www.blackslawdictionary.com

Bondurant, B. (2016) Improved communication = Better buying process. EIC Webminar accessed: https://insights.eventscouncil.org/Portals/0/Documents/Article%20Body/increased-communication-%3D-better-buying-process-webinar.pdf.

Event Industry Council (n.d.) https://insights.eventscouncil.org/Industry-insights/Additional-Resources.

Event Production Directory online, www.epdweb.com

InAVate. *Buckingham Palace Gets Projection Mapping Makeover for Queen's Jubilee Celebration,* accessed: May 23, 2012: http://www.inavateonthenet.net/article/50850/Buckingham-Palace-gets-projection-mapping-makeover-for-Queen-s-Jubilee-celebration.aspx.

MacCoy, P. (2004) *Essentials of Stage Management,* London, UK: Methuen Drama.

Malouf, L. (2012) *Events Exposed: Managing and Designing Special Events,* Hoboken, NJ: John Wiley & Sons.

Sonder, M. (2004) *Event Entertainment and Production,* Hoboken, NJ: John Wiley & Sons.

The Brand, the Buzz, and Better Success through Event Marketing

"Creativity is just connecting things. When you ask creative people how they did something, they feel a little guilty because they didn't really do it, they just saw something. It seemed obvious to them after a while. That's because they were able to connect experiences they've had and synthesize new things. And the reason they were able to do that was that they've had more experiences or they have thought more about their experiences than other people."

—Steve Jobs (1955–2011)

In this chapter you will learn how to:

- Conduct event marketing research
- Develop an integrated multichannel marketing program
- Develop retail marketing events
- Promote fairs and festivals
- Launch new products
- Develop, design, and execute print, electronic, and other advertising programs
- Understand the expanding role of virtual events in the event marketing.
- Identify future trends and opportunities for the marketing of events using multi on- and off-line channels.
- Develop comprehensive public relations programs
- Organize street promotions and creative stunts
- Develop and manage effective sponsorship and cause related programs
- Maximize event Internet marketing opportunities
- Use best practices in social media to promote your event

Photo by Seungwon Shawn Lee

George Mason University students successfully developed an event app for an event in Dr. Lee's course and they are holding them proudly.

The late Steve Jobs, the founder of Apple, was a rare genius who described his success as the ability to intersect design with engineering to satisfy consumer demand. However, he first and foremost had to satisfy his own demands as a creative genius. Jobs often told his employees that the customer's taste was not as important as their own. He further stated that often the customers would not see most of the component parts of the machines they were designing and building. Regardless, he said, every part must be excellent and brilliant whether it was seen or not. These same principles may be applied to modern event marketing through the use of integrated communications technology. Most of what your guests will experience will never be seen, as it is the software that will inform and drive the final hardware of your event.

Examples of modern media event phenomena are the international television programs *American Idol* and *Britain's Got Talent*, as well as Eurovision, which were described in the media as "event television," and the Broadway musical version of *Saturday Night Fever*, which was labeled "event theater" by *The Wall Street Journal* because the audience is encouraged to dance in the aisles at the conclusion of each show. It seems that, everywhere you look, someone is marketing events and events are being used to market products and services.

The first step in the event planning process—research—is mirrored in the modern marketing process. Without valid and reliable research, you may waste scarce time and resources. Therefore, the first step in the event-marketing process must be careful, thoughtful, and comprehensive research. The outcome of this research must result in the identification of measurable goals and objectives for your event-marketing campaign or program.

A campaign is usually an extended series of marketing activities designed to market an event, cause, product, or service, whereas a program may include many campaigns targeted at a wide variety of different market segments. For example, regional shopping centers design and implement annual marketing programs that may include a separate campaign for each of the four seasons or for specific events, such as the expansion of the center or introduction of a new major anchor store.

Regardless of whether you are designing a campaign or an entire program of marketing activities, the resources and channels available to you are expanding rapidly. However, with this expansion, there is also greater competition than ever before. This growth and competition is well documented.

Today's customers make a purchase decision after thorough product/service/brand research. The average number of searches made by a consumer that include interactions with a brand on various on- and off-line channels is between 9 and 16 before making a purchase decision (Starker, Wrigley, and Rosemann, 2015). To understand various marketing channels and their unique strength and limitations, event leaders should devote time to keep up with trends and new tactics in event marketing. There are numerous publications now devoted almost entirely to event management, event marketing, experiential marketing, and related subjects. Increasingly, mainstream publications such as *The Wall Street Journal* and others devote considerable editorial space to reporting events and their marketing value such as the National Football League's Super Bowl, the International Olympic Games, and other mega- and hallmark events.

The Five Ps of Marketing

Traditionally, marketing students have recognized that product, promotion, price, public relations, and place or location are critical components in the marketing process. Each of these five Ps of marketing is a catalyst for sales. Although marketing has become more sophisticated in the twenty-first century, savvy event marketers recognize that, ultimately, marketing is only a three-syllable word for sales.

Product

Successful salespeople have both expert product knowledge and effective sales skills. Expert product knowledge is essential in today's competitive environment. The expertise the salesperson demonstrates regarding the sponsorship package or other event component will differentiate this person from the competition. More important than sales skills, demonstrated product expertise shows the client that he or she is making a purchase that has added value and helps to develop confidence as well as long-term loyalty.

Every event product combines history, quality, and value to produce a unique program. Even new events may draw from the experience or history of the organizers. This demonstration of consistent capability to produce similar events will influence prospective clients to recognize the overall quality of the event organization. Finally, every event product must convey not only perceived value, such as dollar-for-dollar worth, but also added value.

Promotion

You may have the best-quality event product, but unless you have a strategic plan for promoting this product, it will remain the best-kept secret in the world. Even large, well-known mega-events such as the Super Bowl, Rose Parade, and Olympic Games require well-developed promotion strategies to achieve the success they require.

Following is a five-step list to assist you with identifying and budgeting for your event promotion:

1. Identify all event elements that require promotion, from the proposal through the final evaluation.

2. Develop strategies for allocating scarce event promotion resources with efficient methods.
3. Identify promotion partners to share costs.
4. Target your promotion carefully to those market segments that will support your event.
5. Measure and analyze your promotion efforts throughout the campaign to make corrections as required.

The promotion strategy you identify for your event requires a careful study of past or comparable efforts, expert guidance from people who have specific expertise in this field, and, most important, benchmarks for specific measurement of your individual promotion activities.

There are a variety of ways to measure promotion efforts. First, you may measure awareness by your target market. Anticipation of the event may be tantamount to ultimate participation. Next, you may measure actual attendance and the resulting investment. Finally, you may measure the post-event attitudes toward the event promotional activity. Did the promotions you designed persuade the participants or guests to attend the event?

Promotion is the engine that drives the awareness of your event. Throughout event history, legendary promoters such as Bill Veck, Joe Engel, and P. T. Barnum realized that you must shamelessly promote your event product to attract the attention of the public.

Veck did this in Major League Baseball by hiring little people (individuals under 4 feet in height) as his players. At the time of this stunt, there was no height requirement, and Veck took advantage of this oversight to promote his Chicago team.

Photo by Joe Goldblatt

Colorful and distinctive branding is critically important to advertise your event business to the widest possible audience. Marquee Events Group of Austin, Texas, maximizes their branding and advertising through systematic promotion on their vehicles.

Engel, a Minor League Baseball promoter in Chattanooga, Tennessee, staged a fake elephant hunt on the baseball diamond to generate capacity attendance for his losing team. And, of course, P. T. Barnum continually amused the public with his legendary promotions, such as the smallest man (a little person named Major Tom Thumb) and the biggest mammal (an elephant named Jumbo).

Most event marketers use a variety of media to promote their products. However, it is essential that event leaders carefully select those media outlets that will precisely target the market segments that are appropriate for their events. Targeting promotion strategies is essential to ensure the alignment of the event's attributes with the needs, wants, and desires of potential attendees.

Price

Market research will help you determine price. Part of this market research will include conducting a competitive analysis study of other organizations offering similar event products. You may initially believe that your product is uniquely different from every other event. However, when you interview potential ticket buyers or guests, you may be surprised to learn that they consider your event similar to many others. Therefore, you must carefully list all competing events and the prices being charged to help you determine the appropriate price for your event.

Typically, two factors determine price. First, the event leader must determine the financial philosophy of the event and the philosophy must be aligned with the mission, values, and vision of the sponsoring organization. For example, if the event is a not-for-profit venture, the organization may not be concerned with a large commercial yield from the event. Instead, the philosophical purpose of the event may be to generate overall awareness and support. However, if the event is a commercial venture, the goal is probably to generate the greatest potential net profit. Once the philosophy is clear, the event leader will be able to determine price. The price must reflect the cost of all goods and services required to produce the event, plus a margin of profit or retained earnings.

The second factor is the perceived competition from similar events. If your event ticket costs $100 and does not offer the same perceived value as a similar event selling for $50, your prospective guests are more likely to select the latter event. Therefore, you must be price-competitive. It is very important to distinguish price discount—based promotion versus value-based pricing promotion. Price discount—based promotion and sales strategy is considered one of the most aggressive sales approaches as it often delivers an immediate boost in sales. However, when a price-discounted promotion is implemented, event promoters and marketers must remember that they should be able to clearly explain and convince their customers when the price needs to increase later. Event customers do remember the lowered price of experiencing the event and won't be pleased to pay more for a similar level of experience later even if they can afford it. Becoming price-competitive does not mean lowering your ticket price. Rather, it may require raising the perception of value (as discussed earlier) to justify the slightly higher price.

These two factors—the cost of doing business and the marketplace competition—certainly influence price. A third area that may also influence price is the general economic conditions, not only in your area but also in the region, your country, and, increasingly, the world. During times of recession, some events with lower ticket prices will flourish, while other upscale event products may not be as successful. Keep a close eye on market economic indicators to make certain that your price matches the purchasing power of your target market.

Public Relations

Advertising is what you say about your event, whereas public relations is what others (their perceptions) are understanding and telling others about your event. Since many events require a second-party endorsement or even review to encourage people to attend, public relations is significantly more valuable and effective than traditional advertising.

In the 1930s and 1940s, public relations consisted primarily of press agents who worked diligently to convince the print media to devote editorial space to their clients. With the influence of leaders such as Edward Bernays (1891–1995), the public relations effort soon became more complex and respected. Bernays, credited as being the father of public relations, was both a blood nephew and nephew-in-law to the father of psychoanalysis, Sigmund Freud. Bernays (2004) recognized the psychological factors that govern a person's decision-making ability. Therefore, he advocated that public relations professionals first engage in research, including focus groups, to determine the values, attitudes, and lifestyles of their target markets and carefully match their messages to these important factors.

Today, in many event-marketing campaigns, public relations is at least equal to and, in many cases, even more important than traditional advertising. However, public relations involves much more than merely grinding out a short press release.

The effective event public relations campaign will involve research with event consumers as well as the media; the development of collateral materials such as media kits, fact sheets, and other tangibles; the organization and implementation of media conferences; the development of a speaker's bureau; and on-site media relations assistance at the event.

Event public relations helps create the overall impression that others will develop about your event. In that regard, it is significantly more valuable than advertising because it implies greater credibility. For that reason, the Public Relations Society of America (PRSA, www.prsa.org), an organization whose members include professionals in the public relations profession, states that public relations exposure is more valuable financially than advertising. For example:

- Half-page newspaper advertisement

Cost = $5,000

- Editorial about your event in the same space as the advertisement

Value = $15,000 to $35,000 (three to seven times more), depending on placement location

Use the power of public relations to beat the drum more loudly for your event. Carefully select those public relations tools that will most effectively and cost-efficiently help you inform and persuade others to support your event.

Place

In real estate, location is everything. In event marketing, distribution of your product may be everything as well. The location of your event often determines the channels of distribution.

If your event is located in a rural area, it may be difficult to promote the event due to limited media resources and logistical constraints. However, in the post–September 11, 2001, world, rural and local events appear to be growing in number and size in the United States and elsewhere. This may be due to the perception of

All staff and volunteers should be professionally uniformed with the event company branding to promote the event.

safety and security and convenience of local guests. Therefore, despite the limitations, demand has overcome these obstacles. According to a recent Eventbrite survey (2018), using a nontraditional space to host an event is a rising trend. People preferring a nontraditional space for an event has increased by 3.8 percent in 2017. Nontraditional event spaces are being considered for pop- up events, testing events for expanding in a new market, off-site receptions, and supporting ancillary needs for a larger event.

There are several event industry publications that specialize in introducing unique event places to those who try to provide unique spaces to create unforgettable experiences for their customers. They include Unique Venues (https://www.uniquevenues.com/) and BizBash.

The place where you locate your event ultimately will determine the marketing efforts you must exert to drive sales. For example, it has been shown that those events that are close to inexpensive, safe public transportation or those events that feature closed-in reasonably priced parking will attract more guests than those that do not offer these amenities. Furthermore, those events that are connected to other nearby attractions or infrastructures (such as shopping malls) may also draw more attendees due to the time efficiency of the destination. For upscale events, the addition of valet parking may improve the chances of attracting guests to a new or nontraditional location.

The event leader must seriously consider place when designing the marketing program for the event. Place does not only imply the taste or style of the event; it also, in large part, defines the type of person that will be persuaded to invest in the event. In this regard, the event marketer must determine the place in the early stages through research and design. This is the perfect time to convene a focus group or conduct a survey to determine who is likely to attend your event when they are given a variety of location choices. Making certain you have thoughtfully analyzed this important issue will save you time and money throughout the entire event-marketing process.

A Sixth P for Event Marketing: Positioning

According to Christopher Preston in his book *Event Marketing* (2011), there is an additional P that is critical to the marketing mix. Hoyle describes *positioning* as follows: "Positioning is the strategy of determining through intuition, research, and evaluation those areas of consumer need that your event can fulfill." He further states that the five key considerations when positioning an event include location, attention span, competitive costs, the program, and the simplicity of the marketing plan.

Experiential Event Marketing and Touchpoints

Experiential Event Marketing

Events are often delivered with a pleasant "surprise." Merchandise/tangible product marketers do their best to let potential buyers experience their products in advance to increase customers' purchase intention. And risk-free trials are often utilized. For example, mattress promotion includes 90-day trials and grocery markets offer free samples. Experiential marketing allows pre-experience of products or services, and it is proved that experiential marketing often outperforms single-use traditional marketing techniques. Experiential event marketing should use immersive event experiences to market a brand or product to potential event buyers.

Experiential marketing has a variety of channels to implement it and in terms of consumer satisfaction, engagement, and brand loyalty, it is considered highly effective.

Here is how experiential event marketing can be more effective:

1. Where traditional marketing is one-way communication driven to consumers, experiential marketing creates a two-way conversation with consumers. The opinions of consumers and conversations initiated from customer experiences create more interactive and appealing brand perception.
2. Experiential marketing is more interactive and engaging, and it results in a more memorable experience to event consumers.
3. Engagement-based data can be created from experiential marketing and those data are more valuable since they are of a more personal experience.

Therefore, event leaders should make efforts to accomplish memorable moments, high-quality engagement, and open conversation through experiential marketing for their target consumers.

In another example, Ford, which launched an experiential new product event to encourage consumers who don't want to visit a dealership to conduct test-drives at schools, then donated funds to school programs for each test drive.

For more examples, check out the annual Ex Awards (https://2020emsummit. eventmarketer.com/ex-awards/) that shares a glimpse of the creative processes.

Attendee Touchpoints

One-way digital media, like videos and e-mail marketing, provide event marketers a channel to establish an event brand and to cross with the **attendee journey**.

Attendee journey is a marketing term that means how many touchpoints a customer has with a brand/product before making a decision. In the event industry, it can be interpreted as how many event attendees or sponsors encounter with an event brand before making a decision to register or sponsor your event.

At the beginning of this chapter, we discussed that at least nine different interactions with an event prospectus via on- and off-line marketing channels before they register their event. And it means that event leaders should have extensive marketing strategies, tactics, and tools to bring attendees to those touchpoints. Therefore, identifying start and end points of attendee journey and what is done between through on- and off-line channels are very critical information to event marketers. Before, during, and post event surveys and follow-ups can contribute to building up this knowledge for your events. And evaluating those touchpoints and recording which ones are major and minor and their impact on buying decisions of your event attendees and sponsors are crucial.

Internal versus External Event Marketing

Event leaders may use an event or a series of events as one of the marketing methods to promote external events, products, or services, such as shopping malls, tourist destinations, or attractions (e.g., amusement parks or zoos), or any entity that is appropriately promoted through events.

However, in most cases, event leaders use marketing forces such as advertising, public relations, promotion, advertising specialties, stunts, and other techniques to promote individual events. These traditional marketing techniques should be used to inform, attract, persuade, sustain, and retain potential customers for your event.

Increasingly, a blend of internal and external event marketing is being utilized to promote events. In some cases, event leaders use miniature events as a means of promoting major events. The Sydney Organizing Committee for the Olympic Games (SOCOG) staged a major fireworks display to celebrate the decision by the International Olympic Committee to stage the games in Sydney, Australia. The fireworks spectacular began the marketing process of identifying Sydney as the city of the next Olympic Games. Smaller events, such as a torch run, were used throughout the days preceding the opening ceremonies to promote this event.

External Event Marketing

Using events to market products and services is increasing. Well-respected marketing professional publications such as *Advertising Age* argue that events are now critical in the total marketing effort. Therefore, although using an event-marketing strategy may be more costly due to the additional labor required, it must be considered seriously when promoting products and services.

Retail Events

The special events firm The Wonder Company, Inc., founded by Joe Goldblatt and Nancy Lynner in the 1970s, began by producing fashion shows, petting zoos, Santa

Claus appearances, and other retail events for local shopping centers throughout the United States. During this period, regional mega–shopping centers opened throughout the United States, and mall developers such as the Rouse Company and Homart recognized that they were the new Main Streets of America. To attract the appropriate target market, a series of events was developed and implemented to position the shopping mall as an attraction.

Using the fashion show as one example, shopping mall management could satisfy the needs of both its internal and external customers. First, the store owners and managers could showcase their goods and services to a highly targeted audience in a cost-effective manner. Second, the external customer—the shopper himself or herself—would be held captive during the 20- to 30-minute production and then directed to visit each store for special discounts immediately following the show. According to the International Council of Shopping Centers, the trade association that educates and promotes the shopping center industry, many marketing directors are earning the Certified Marketing Director (CMD) designation to develop specialized knowledge of this increasingly complex and competitive profession.

Figure 7.1 shown in the electronic appendices lists several retail events that have proven successful and the market to which they are best targeted. You will note that most of these events target women, as historically women have been the largest customer bases for retail businesses. However, these demographics are shifting as two-income families have emerged in the United States, and now both men and women increasingly share the responsibilities and pleasures of shopping. Therefore, successful event leaders will look for events that they may use to develop other markets with disposable income, such as men, teenage boys, and even senior citizens.

Timing is everything when developing and producing the retail event. To allow the consumer to devote as much time as possible to spending money, the live event should be brief in duration (under 20 minutes) and be offered frequently throughout the day to allow a variety of customers to experience the event activity. Obviously, due to the increase in working adults, weekdays during normal working hours should be avoided so that the most consumers can witness the event. Finally, many retail events are tied directly to paydays. Find out what the pay period is from large organizations such as factories, government, or other sources of large numbers of consumers, and then time your event to coincide with this window when there will be a large amount of expendable income available.

Fairs and Festivals

Fairs, festivals, and other public events may also serve as temporary retail locations (TRLs). These events often contract space to vendors, craftspeople, and others to demonstrate and sell their products and services. However, like their permanent retail counterparts, to be successful such events must be marketed aggressively through both internal and external event-marketing efforts.

A media preview event is an excellent way to inform the media about the size, scope, and excitement being offered at your fair or festival. Designing a ribbon-cutting event featuring prominent local citizens along with celebrities is an important way to announce "open for business." Finally, a series of ongoing ancillary events held at other public venues, such as sporting event halftime shows, is an important form of external marketing to introduce and remind other market segments of your event's importance.

Launching New Products

Perhaps one of the more important activities within the event-marketing area is that of launching new products developed by corporations. Each year in the United States and other countries, billions of dollars are invested in advertising to promote new products. Before these products are introduced to the general public, they are usually showcased to retailers or dealers. An event such as the launch of a new automobile serves several constituent groups. The trade media may be invited to promote the product to others. Next, the general media (newspapers, radio, and television) may be invited to help make the general public aware of the new product benefits and features. Finally, and perhaps most important, the product launch must target those people who will either sell the item to others or purchase it themselves.

The organization and presentation of the product launch event may be one of the most important steps in the overall marketing effort. Whether introducing the latest software or an attraction such as a new hotel resort, great thought must be given to the goals, objectives, and desired outcomes to create a successful event.

The following is a 10-step list for developing and producing consistently successful product-launch events.

1. Determine the goals and objectives of the product-launch event.
2. Identify the target market(s).
3. Coordinate planning with sales promotion, public relations, human resource development, and other critical departments.
4. Conduct research to refine your general production plans.
5. Use creativity to introduce your product in a nontraditional yet attractive manner.
6. Use creativity to unveil a new product.
7. Identify who will speak, for what length of time, and why.
8. Identify ways to reach those who could not attend the event (e.g., through a video program or satellite presentation).
9. Measure and analyze your results by how sales are affected.
10. Develop opportunities for added value the next time you produce a similar event.

Lavish plans for product-launch events sometimes are foiled by circumstances beyond the control of the event planner. However, most circumstances can be controlled easily through close communication with other parties. Make certain that you contact the corporate communications or public relations department early in the process to identify their goals and incorporate them into your plans. Next, and equally important, make certain that the vice president or director of sales is closely involved in your planning, as your activities will directly affect his or her efforts. Finally, ensure that senior management, including the chief executive and operating officers, understands, supports, and is committed to your success.

However, despite all this careful interaction with other stakeholders, sometimes Murphy's Law (which states that anything that can go wrong will go wrong) is invoked and subsequently problems arise. We prefer to update Murphy with O'Goldblatt's Law, which states "Murphy was an optimist." One example of this occurred in 2008, in the early days of the global financial crisis in the United States and other countries. Several key meeting industry organizations released recommended voluntary guidelines and standards for organizations that were conducting product launch events. The generally accepted purposes of these events as agreed upon by these organizations included "effective product launches to educate the sales force, channel partners and customers." However, the same organizations recommended as well that the investment in these events, if they involved incentive travel, shall not exceed 15 percent of the total sales and marketing spend. Furthermore, according to U.S. Travel Association, the recommendations also stated that any expenditure of $75,000 or greater must have a corresponding document that the event is for a legitimate business purpose.

Therefore, as a direct result of the global financial crisis experienced in 2008, corporations and other organizations are practicing greater due diligence and care when it comes to the approval of incentive travel, meetings, conferences, and product launch programs. Even though the 2008–2009 global financial crisis has passed, spending in the corporate world is still reflecting its lingering impact. Many companies have implemented policies that restrict spending. Most employees feel that they have to "save their company money" while traveling and attending meetings or conferences. Many companies utilize corporate rates with travel companies to obtain the best price. In addition to saving money, many companies use technology such as Skype to hold meetings, thereby reducing the need for travel all together. In order to improve the chances of your product launch event being approved and fully funded, you should develop a legitimate business case, demonstrating the purpose and outcome as related to the organization's return on investment (ROI), return on marketing investment (ROMI), and return on objective (ROO). The modern event marketer must be ready for any and every change imposed by local and central government, trade and professional associations (such as in the pharmaceutical field) as well as changing public taste.

Event Promotion Techniques

Five typical or traditional techniques are used to promote events: advertising, public relations, cross-promotions, street promotions, and stunts. Some events use only one of these techniques; others may use all of them to ensure that their message is received and acted on by their target market.

Advertising

Advertising includes print and electronic media, transportation media (such as bus and rail), advertising specialties (calendars, key rings, coffee mugs, and other products), and outdoor media (billboards). Larger events may use many of these media resources, while smaller events may carefully target their message to one or two media.

Print advertising is not limited to magazines and newspapers. It may also include membership directories, inserts in local newspapers, flyers (sometimes called one sheets), posters, church and synagogue newsletters, brochures, and virtually any printed media. When analyzing your print advertising needs, make certain that you test your advertising product in advance with a small distribution to test its effectiveness. Specialists in direct mail recommend that you use a split-test approach. This requires that you mail one type of advertising printed matter to one group and a different type to another to test the best response from both types. Varying items such as the color of the ink, copy, type, and weight of the paper, or other decisions may produce different results. Test your print advertising using focus groups to make certain that your event product is well-positioned for success.

Classic advertising terms such as "free," "discount," "now," "sale," and "new" may help you influence the consumer to invest in your event. Clever graphics, endorsements, testimonials, and other credibility-building devices will help differentiate your event product from others.

Electronic media include radio, television, the Internet, and any form of advertising that involves electronic delivery. Radio advertising is typically used to remind the listener about the event, whereas television is used to build excitement. The Internet is an excellent means with which to reach upscale consumers and those who are interested in science, technology, and travel. Before you select electronic media as a means to advertise your event, examine all potential media outlets.

Within television media, you may elect to cast your event broadly through major networks or narrowly cast by selecting a finely targeted cable station. For example, if you are promoting an arts-related event, you may select a cable station with arts programming. Selecting the appropriate media outlet may require the assistance of experts in media buying or from an advertising agency specializing in radio or television media.

Transportation media require that you place your message on buses, subways, and other forms of transportation. Usually these media are aimed at a very wide market and have proven effective for circuses, fairs, festivals, and other events that require large attendance from diverse groups.

Advertising specialties are those items that are usually given away or offered as a premium, as an incentive to purchase a product or service. Advertising specialties include thousands of products; however, the most typical are calendars, refrigerator magnets, coffee mugs, writing instruments, and key chains. In recent years, clothing has become popular as an advertising specialty, and some event organizers give away clothing to the media and other key constituent groups and sell the rest at souvenir stands. Once again, research this purchase carefully to ensure that the recipient values the item and will use it. Prolonged use allows it to serve as a reminder of your event.

Outdoor advertising was, at one time, one of the major forms of advertising in the United States. However, during the late 1960s, many billboards were banned in a "beautify America" campaign. Still, the outdoor billboard is an excellent way to reach large numbers of potential event participants for an extended period of time. Today, there are four states that still ban billboards: Alaska, Hawaii, Maine, and Vermont. Currently, there are 341,000 billboards across the United States. This is a decrease from 2017 when there were 368,000 billboards. New York City currently

SECUREVIEW

Via Sustainable Marketing Tools

The Edinburgh Festival Fringe annually attracts over 20,000 performers to Edinburgh, Scotland, for what they describe as the world's largest arts festival. These performers produce nearly 3,000 shows and each show may print thousands of leaflets or flyers to promote their event. The flyers are handed out on the Royal Mile in Edinburgh during the month-long festival. This flyering is historically an important cultural experience for visitors, as they have the opportunity to directly interact with the performers or representatives of each show. However, it does create a huge amount of waste. The Edinburgh Festival Fringe also produces a large paper catalog (using recycled paper) as do the other 12 major festivals in Scotland's capital city. Therefore, as more and more consumers seek to attend and experience greener events, it will be interesting to watch how the marketing culture for events such as the Edinburgh Festival Fringe carefully adapts without losing the cultural significance of the current flyering phenomena. For example, could mobile text messaging one day replace flyering?

has the most outdoor advertising in the country (https://ilsr.org/rule/billboard-bans-and-controls/).

Regardless of the type of advertising media you select, first conduct market research and follow up with tests to determine actual response. Once you have found a medium that effectively reaches your target market, use repetition to build reinforcement and retention. Finally, measure all responses to develop history and determine where your advertising dollar will pull best for each event.

Public Relations

Public relations involves informing the media and your target market about your event and persuading them to support your programs. Public relations activities for your event may include designing, printing, and distributing media kits, producing public service announcements (PSAs) for radio and television, producing and distributing audio news releases (ANRs) and video news releases (VNRs), or even producing events. In fact, according to many public relations professionals, events are the fastest-growing segment of the public relations strategy.

The media kit is typically a presentation-type folder that contains a fact sheet, request for coverage notice, media releases, and even a PSA (either written or recorded). This kit is distributed well in advance of the event to the print and electronic media to inform them of opportunities for coverage. In smaller markets, some media outlets may print your media releases word for word; in larger, more sophisticated markets, members of the media may use the kit for background information alone.

Preston suggests that media kits should include these materials:

- Press or media releases
- Photos
- Media alerts
- Requests for coverage
- Press conference announcements and invitations
- Speeches
- Background news stories
- Videotapes of the event
- CDs and DVDs of the event
- Organizational information
- Biographies of the key individuals leading the event or appearing at the event (speakers, entertainers)
- Folders, brochures, postcards
- Advertising specialty items

A PSA is a written or prerecorded audio or video announcement about your event. Broadcasters in the United States are required by federal law to allot a certain amount of time for public service announcements. In some cases, the broadcaster may provide help, as a further public service, in producing these announcements. Often a local celebrity or nationally prominent person will participate at no charge, to add credibility to your announcement.

The ANR or VNR, while a relatively new phenomenon, is one of the most effective ways to distribute your event message. ANRs and VNRs require that you prerecord a news story about your event and then, by overnight mail or use of satellite transmission, send the story to local stations that you would like to have air the story as part of their news programming. Since news programs are often the most watched segments of television programming, this type of public relations has the potential of reaching a large, well-targeted audience in a credible and cost-effective manner.

Finally, events themselves often become major public relations vehicles. To promote the effort to raise funds for Haiti relief following the January 2010 earthquake, actor George Clooney appeared on the red carpet for the Golden Globes Awards on E! TV to promote a telethon to be held the following Friday. Throughout the awards show broadcast by NBC, actors and actresses promoted the upcoming telethon and reminded people how they could contribute to the relief effort. The telethon was recorded, and further money was raised when it was offered on iTunes. In recent times, celebrities have sponsored successful telethons to benefit the Northeastern United States victims of Hurricane Sandy.

Remember that the two chief goals of public relations are to inform and persuade. Therefore, collateral materials, PSAs, and ANRs and VNRs, as well as smaller events, are excellent ways to accomplish these two important goals of an overall marketing campaign.

Cross-Promotions

To allocate market resources in the most efficient manner, you must identify and incorporate marketing partners into your campaign. These organizations may actually contribute marketing dollars or may provide in-kind services, such as providing celebrities, tagging their ads with your event date and time, or contributing other valuable components to your campaign.

When seeking marketing partners to develop a cross-promotional strategy, study the advertising and marketing activities of compatible businesses in your area. Determine which of these activities will benefit your event. Next, develop a proposal that clearly describes the resources that you can bring to the event. Finally, present the proposal to your prospective marketing partners and answer any questions they may pose.

Tagging advertising involves your marketing partner adding a line of copy to his or her regular advertising placements that promote your event. It may read "Official supporter of XYZ event" or "Meet us at XYZ event, date and time." Tag lines may appear in both print and electronic advertising.

Make certain that you chronicle all marketing activities so that you can report to your partners after the event and describe in specific detail those placements that were successful. Cross-promotions and tie-in activities are sensational ways to reach a much larger market in a cost-effective manner.

Street Promotions

This marketing activity requires that you literally take your message to the street. Street promotions may include the handing out of flyers by a clown in a high-traffic area, the appearance of a celebrity at a local mall, contests, or other promotional activities designed to draw high visibility to your event. Before leafleting (handing out flyers), make certain that this is allowed by local code. You certainly do not want to generate negative publicity by having the clown arrested for causing a disturbance. A celebrity appearance may help generate significant publicity if it is handled properly. Schedule the celebrity to include radio and television interviews, appearances at a local children's hospital or other public facility, and ceremonial events with local, state, provincial, or federal leaders. At each appearance, make certain that the celebrity is well-informed about the event and articulates your event message in a consistent manner. When selecting the celebrity to appear at your

Photo by Seungwon Shawn Lee

SPY Museum opened its doors to visitors with a special performance, a 007 movie-themed spy fighting action with wired cables from its roof.

event, you may wish to use the Performer Q rating developed by Marketing Evaluations, Inc. This rating identifies the level of recognition a celebrity has with the general public. A note of caution should be used, however, when enlisting a celebrity to help with promoting your event. Some celebrities in recent times (the cyclist Lance Armstrong, the television broadcaster Jimmy Saville) have fallen from grace in the eyes of the public. Therefore, proceed with extreme caution when selecting a celebrity to help beat the drum for your event or you may risk being drummed out of business due to their alleged or real misbehavior.

Contests and other promotional events also require analysis to ensure that they are within the bounds of the local code and that they are appropriate for your event. For instance, selling raffle tickets at a nonprofit event may require that you file legal forms and obtain a local permit.

Stunts

During the early 1950s in the United States, advertising agencies used stunts as an important method of breaking through the clutter of traditional print and electronic advertising. Today, stunts continue to be effective but must be crafted carefully to ensure that the integrity of the event is preserved. In 2018, one of the most controversial advertising "stunts" to occur was with the well-known brand Nike. Nike had teamed up with the first NFL player Colin Kaepernick to kneel during the U.S. national anthem in protest of racism and police brutality in the United States. This advertising campaign was carefully crafted as Nike had prepared to lose several loyal customers. But it was also prepared to gain new ones in support of Kaepernick's message.

A stunt involves an activity designed to generate media coverage and attendance by spectators to promote a specific event or series of events. Radio stations continue to rely heavily on stunts and will often provide remote broadcasts to cover stunts involving their on-air personalities. Stunts can be tied to charitable endeavors, such as locking up prominent officials until enough donations are raised to cover their release. Other stunts may involve creating the world's largest pizza, cake, sandwich, or other product. Before you incorporate a stunt in an event-marketing program, it is important to analyze how the stunt will further your marketing objectives and to determine all associated costs. Finally, make certain that you chronicle all media coverage that results from the stunt, distribute bounce-back coupons to attendees, and track all responses resulting from the stunt.

Getz describes one type of stunt as a flash mob. The flash mob is an event that is preplanned but appears spontaneous. One example is a crowd of dozens of individuals at Grand Central Station during rush hour in New York City who suddenly freeze for 1 or 2 minutes to draw attention to their cause or to promote a product. The participants received advance instructions, including the time, date, wardrobe, location, and other information by e-mail and then, after assembling at the venue, they are cued to begin their activity by mobile phone. If you elect to use a flash mob to draw attention to your product or cause, make certain you not only notify the

One aspect of branding is a costume element such as the Moonwalk Bra worn by the author's sister, Leah Lahasky, to promote further awareness of the need for breast cancer research and care.

media but also, to the extent possible, the venue management and other officials. It would not serve your client well if the outcome of your event were mass arrests because you and your participants were accused of disturbing the peace and disorderly conduct (Getz, 2007).

Invitation

Whether your invitation is a print or electronic advertisement, a flyer, or a formal engraved document, the copy that is composed, art that is created or selected, and paper that is chosen will greatly influence the response. The six central components of all effective invitations are as follows:

1. Name of host or event organizer
2. Date, time, and location (i.e., December 24, 2019, 15A Mulberry Street)
3. Dress requirements (i.e., black tie, business, smart casual, or cocktail)
4. Transportation and parking (local bus routes, self-park, valet)
5. Website address (URL) that includes map information for directions
6. RSVP

Six additional components may include the following:

1. Purpose of the event
2. Names of honorary board or committee members
3. Names of prominent speakers
4. Frequency or historic nature of the event (second annual, 100th anniversary celebration, or biannual event)
5. Limited supply of tickets
6. VIP status

Remember that an invitation is an official offer to the guest to participate in your event. Therefore, from a legal perspective, it is important that you choose your words carefully to reflect the actual event you are promoting.

Each of these components is designed to generate a specific response from the recipient. The most important response is to build anticipation toward acceptance followed by actual attendance.

Event Marketing with Technology

Events eMarketing

Not since the invention of the printing press has advertising been changed as dramatically as with the introduction of the Internet. In 2000, Joe Goldblatt predicted that within a decade the majority of offers and transactions would be distributed and received using online media. Almost two decades later, the 2019 Event Statistics and What They Mean for Your Events states how "78% of event creators say email marketing is their most effective marketing tactic. For those who track it, 45% of event ticket sales can be attributed to email." This shows how so many event professionals rely on the electronic media in the events industry today. The study also tells 65 percent of event workers are satisfied with e-mail performance specifically. This high percentage shows how important the usage of the Internet is in order to market to event customers. The use of the electronic platform enables them to not only automate this important process but also collect a rich database of information about their attendees. Therefore, we predict that online marketing and their resulting transactions will soon completely dominate the modern event marketing landscape throughout the world. Today, virtually every event industry worker uses the Internet to search for resources, reserve or contact vendors, and promote continuous communication. Event marketing has now fully embraced the electronic marketplace. Reggie Aggarwal, CEO of Cvent (www.cvent.com), a leading Internet event-marketing firm, told Convention Industry Council (now the Event Industry Council) Forum attendees that "the fastest, most precise, easiest, and most cost affordable way to reach prospective event attendees is through e-mail." According to Aggarwal, the penetration of the Internet will soon be 100 percent and will soon be equal to or even replace traditional television and radio in some segments as an electronic source for daily information and communications.

Cvent is one example of how the technological revolution is driving the meetings, conferences, and events industry. Aggarwal started the firm after he used e-mail invitations and reminders to promote registration for a local association that he directed. He soon discovered that he could increase the response rate significantly and better target his prospects using e-mail communications. For example, Cvent.com technology enables meeting and event leaders not only to send e-mail messages but also to note whether they have been read. Direct-mail marketers cannot monitor whether their communications are read; they can only note when a purchase or inquiry has been received. This innovation gives Cvent a competitive edge in the event market because the firm can determine quickly whether the e-mail event invitation has been opened and read. If it has been opened, the event marketer can assume that there is interest and build on that interest with follow-up communications. This customized marketing approach is one of the many benefits of the new technologies that are being developed to assist event marketers.

When developing event marketing, Internet marketing must be considered as a central part of any strategy. For example, regardless of size, all events should have a Web presence through a dedicated Web home page, a banner on an existing Web home page, or a link to a separate page. Following are points to consider when developing a comprehensive e-marketing event strategy:

- Identify your event market segments and targets.
- Design your Web strategy to reach your target market quickly, efficiently, and precisely.
- Use a focus panel of prospective event attendees to review your plans and suggest modifications to your overall design.
- Audit and evaluate the competition to determine how your Web presence can be more effective.
- Match the color scheme and design components to your printed matter.
- Determine whether you require a separate home page for your event or a link from an existing home page to a unique page.
- Identify and establish links with all marketing partners.
- Determine whether you will need a transaction page and ensure security for your ticket buyers.
- Determine whether you, your staff, or others can build the pages and/or make changes should they be needed.
- If consultants are contracted to build your site or pages, determine how they will be maintained (frequency, speed, and reliability).

- Use viral marketing (e-mails copied to prospective attendees) to promote your event.
- Use search engines to promote your event, with careful selection and registration of your URL.
- Use e-mail reminders to increase attendance during the last 2 weeks of an event.
- Use online registration systems.
- Use online evaluation systems to collect survey information before, during, and after an event.
- Use online chat rooms to create discussion areas for preregistered attendees and to generate follow-up discussion post-event.
- Carefully monitor all online activity for potential data mining to determine future needs, wants, and desires of your target audience.

The Internet will continue to drive the development of the global meetings, conferences and events industry. You must use this dynamic technology quickly and accurately to ensure that your event remains competitive throughout the twenty-first century. The authors along with Dr. Dessislava Boshnakova argued that twenty-first-century event technologies are powerful tools for marketing and social media will lead tech-based marketing tools. And those tools profoundly affect the way the event industry consumes experiences and products (Lee, Boshnakova, and Goldblatt, 2016). Proper marketing starts from matching tools to audience and engaging audiences must include strategic reassessment of available current and popular tools.

The Internet can be a highly efficient tool in marketing events. At the same time, it can be a major financial burden if your organization does not formulate specific goals for its Internet marketing policy. The objectives for each event-management organization may vary depending on company size, dynamics of operations, financial and staff resources, location, overall development strategy, and client base. The website for a small planned events start-up will differ from that of a large multinational conglomerate. Major marketing concepts enhanced by online tools include brand building, direct marketing, online sales and online commerce, customer support, market research, and product or service development and testing.C. Preston, in *Event Marketing* (2012), states that there are six advantages of Internet marketing for your event.

1. Internet marketing can help build and extend your brand.
2. Internet marketing eliminates many of the costs customarily associated with direct mail.
3. You can immediately begin making online sales in an interactive and secure environment.
4. By posting frequently asked questions (FAQs), you can provide easy access to commonly sought information.
5. Through conducting online surveys and analyzing the data from Web visits and transactions, you may acquire valuable marketing research information.

You can use the Web to publish information that has resulted from your event (abstracts, papers, and reports).

Online Consumer-Generated Media (CGM)

Some marketing theorists observe that consumers wish to be fully engaged in the product or service experience before they will recommend or express their positive opinion to others. Therefore, a live planned event provides a tremendous opportunity to turn your prospective and actual guests into, as marketing guru Guy Kawasaki suggests, *evangelists* who will rave to others about your event.

To expose participants so that they fully are engaged and totally experience your event, you must use multiple touch points, including online consumer-generated media, to turn your casual guests into raving evangelists, who will tell everyone about your event. Thanks to social networking websites, such as Facebook, LinkedIn, Pinterest, Instagram, Tagged, Twitter, and others, this has become much easier. Furthermore, as the Internet has quickly penetrated many more channels, thanks to rapidly developing mobile technology and applications, it is infinitely more possible to stay in touch with your guest at all times, resulting in events that continue before, during and beyond live event experience.

The role of online consumer-generated media is to provide your prospective and actual guests with the opportunity to become better informed and to fully participate in your event before, during, and after the actual event experience. By creating a 180-degree online event environmental opportunity for your guests, you are literally surrounding them with opportunities to learn and grow through their own predetermined levels of participation.

Online Brand Building

Online marketing—combined with television, media, and print—is a major brand-building tool. The biggest advantage the Internet has over television and old-fashioned media is the favorable cost/benefit ratio. Events organizations can achieve a much higher return on their marketing investments in Internet promotions than in a traditional campaign. The research conducted by Millward Brown Interactive, a 20-year-old international advertising research group, found that an organization can achieve significant progress in brand recognition simply by placing its logo on banners of search engines or online databases. It is important for your organization to secure the presence of its logo on the Web. You can start simply by trading space on the banner section of your website with a partner organization. You place your logo on your partner's website and create a hyperlink from his or her website to yours, in exchange for placing your partner's information on your website. It is very important to submit your company's profile to all major search engines. A few years ago, when students were conducting a search on Yahoo! using the key words *event management*, they obtained only a few matches, whereas now there are thousands. Submitting your company's profile to most search engines is free, so there is no reason not to do it.

Use these four steps to register your website with a search engine:

1. Enter a search engine (Google, AltaVista, Dogpile, Yahoo!, Bing, etc.).
2. Go to "register your site."
3. Carefully describe your site's profile using tag words that describe you.
4. After submitting your site, test the search engine by searching for your tag words.

Raising Your Search Engine Profile

You can purchase advertising on the search engines that best represent and reach your target markets or you can also work behind the scenes to try to move your event profile to a higher listing within a search engine. Text Link Brokers.com (www.textlinkbrokers.com) has examined thousands of websites to develop the best strategies for improving your overall website optimization. This process is known as search engine optimization, or simply SEO. The first step to improve your SEO is to conduct research. Figure 7.2 in the electronic appendices provides six steps to SEO success for your event.

Although there are search engine optimization consulting firms, which may be able to help you achieve your online goals, they may be beyond the budget for your individual event or event organization. However, the six tips could be a first step in optimizing your search engine performance to boost the visibility of your events website.

Online Sales and Security

At one time, the online sales concept was more applicable to companies that sell consumer goods (such as Amazon.com), not services. However, this is rapidly changing, and there are now many consulting sites online to provide event services. Planned events organizations may still benefit greatly from online, electronic commerce features. Planned events organizations conduct registration, ticket sales, and distribution of materials over the Internet. All of these are segments of event sales. By putting them online, planned events companies achieve financial savings and preserve resources that can now be reallocated.

Among the most important problems of online commerce is the problem of security. If an event planning organization conducts financial transactions over the Internet, security of clients' personal financial information is the top priority. Data that contain such information as credit card and Social Security numbers are highly sensitive. It is important to ensure that these data are protected. Since this is a critical point, it is highly recommended that you involve security professionals in this aspect of your website development. Many smaller- and medium-sized events organizations utilize the online transaction tool PayPal (www.paypal.com) to help ensure secure transactions for their customers. PayPal uses VeriSign as its encrypted security service to protect data and transactions. Mobile payment methods are widely accepted at various event locations as well as in general commerce. In Asia, including China, Korea, and Japan, mobile payment is exponentially advancing. At the 2018 Mobile Payment Conference, it was reported that China, led by the popular mobile apps Alipay and WeChat Pay, is now the largest e-commerce market in the world. It accounts for more than 40 percent of worldwide e-commerce transactions. China has also become a major global force in mobile payments with 11 times the transaction value of the United States. Alipay entered the U.S. market in 2016, and more than 4 million U.S. merchants accept its mobile payment through the U.S. partnered service. Therefore, mobile payment is a new trend that global event professionals should monitor closely.

Furthermore, they, along with eBay and other major online sellers, use SSL (Secure Socket Layer) certificates, which allow website visitors and customers to further trust your security in three ways. First, an SSL certificate enables *encryption* of sensitive information during online transactions. Second, each SSL certificate contains unique, *authenticated* information about the certificate's owner. Finally, a certificate authority *verifies* the identity of the certificate's owner when it is issued. Therefore, it is critically important that when designing your events website that you incorporate careful preplanning to ensure financial and data security for your customers.

Customer Support

Event customer support is one of the areas where the Internet can prove truly indispensable. To date, few event companies have realized the full potential of this

TECH/APPVIEW

Beacon is a Bluetooth-enabled device that can track event attendees traffic and behavior. Location-based wristbands or name tags of attendees can be tracked throughout event locations and the collected data can be used for real-time, on-site management (registration line, F&B line management, staffing, etc.) and future event planning. Wearable beacon technology is another new trend being used at events to increase attendee engagement with event host, vendors, and sponsors.

There are beacon device providers (e.g., BeaconEx) and event apps (eventBit by Experient) that track the moves of attendees in a dashboard or on an event floor map. It can be used to create heat maps that measure traffic volumes at popular activities and sessions by attendee types. These data can be combined with attendee profile data in a wider picture to illustrate the attendee journey, giving event marketers information to use effectively for its sponsorship sales and event planning. The data can also provide details of touchpoints between event attendees and key stakeholders across multiple on- and off-line marketing channels.

opportunity. Industry analysts predict that, in coming years, many event companies will shift their telephone customer support services to the Web. This does not mean that telephone-based services will disappear, but they will become a secondary source that customers will use if they need to get a more detailed response or resolve a problem. The primary source will be the Internet.

The first step in shifting at least part of your customer support services online is to start an FAQ section of your website. Simply by adding this section to your website, you can achieve better customer service and improve efficiency.

The next step after posting an FAQ page is to personalize online customer service. This may be accomplished by adding an interactive feature to a customer-support site. A customer is asked to type his or her question and submit an e-mail address. The customer receives an answer within a certain time frame via either e-mail or telephone. By adding this feature, an event organization can achieve much more personalized customer service and can also collect valuable data about its clients. Whenever possible, it should be easy and efficient for the caller to contact a live person if they have additional questions. If this is not possible through the use of existing resources, the caller should be able to receive a return telephone call from a customer service professional within a specified period of time.

Market Research

Increasingly, events organizations are recognizing the Internet's potential for market research. Burke, Inc., a leading international market research firm with a history that spans more than 65 years, conducts online focus-group meetings for its clients in addition to face-to-face interviews and telephone surveys. Using Internet technology, the company was able to bring together participants from different parts of the world for small, real-time chat sessions. Clients can observe these chat sessions from anywhere in the world. Software such as Aptex, Autonomy, Adforce, and Accrue can monitor users' behavior constantly. This information can then be used to improve the site or services or to personalize content for users.

Your website may be used to conduct market research by surveying visitors. This information can be effective if the process is well planned. Unfortunately, many websites require users to complete online registration forms without providing incentives. As a result, users often submit incorrect information or simply ignore the forms. This behavior may be explained by the desire of users to guard their privacy online and fear that their e-mail addresses will be sold to third parties. The best way to overcome this constraint is to build a sense of trust between the event organization and clients or to compensate users for submitting their data.

Product or Service Development and Testing

The Internet is an ideal place for event companies to test new products and services before they are launched. An event organization can post information about a conference that it is planning to organize online and monitor the interest that users express toward the conference. By doing this, the organization can see a market's reaction to the conference before it invests large amounts in actual planning. This testing refers to the first stage of successful events, event research. One of the biggest advantages that the Internet has over other marketing tools is real-time contact. Marketing professionals use a number of special technical features to leverage this point. Chat rooms, live broadcasting, and time-sensitive promotions are only a small part. The Internet allows marketing professionals to change and update content in almost no time, ensuring that customers have the most recent information.

Web Design and Management

Event marketing specialists today speak about second and third generations of websites. The best definition We have heard of all three types of online marketing development comes from Jupiter Communication, a leading Internet research firm based in New York. The company's analysts describe three types of websites, from least to most effective from the Internet marketing point of view:

1. *Brochureware* is the name for the basic and least developed type of website. This type of Internet material has long been recognized as primitive and boring. Websites of this type are static and contain basic information about an organization, including its address and services. The site reflects a paper brochure placed on the Web. These sites miss the entire idea of marketing on the Web, and their effectiveness today is not very high.

2. *Show-biz* is the name for the second group of websites. These sites try to amuse visitors through interactive features, flashing pictures, news reports, streaming video and pictures, or media reviews. Although these features can serve the purpose of making an organization's website more attractive, often they are not appropriate for the content and only distract the viewer's attention.

3. *Utilitarian* is the last and most developed type of website. These sites offer viewers a unique and balanced interactive service that is both highly informative and helpful in building brand recognition and loyalty. A classic example mentioned by Rick E. Bruner in *Net Results: Web Marketing That Works* (1998) is FedEx online services. The company's website does not contain a lot of flashy effects, is easy to navigate, and contains useful features, such as shipment tracking and customer address books. The result of such a high-performing online marketing strategy is that, today, about two-thirds of all FedEx customer contacts are conducted electronically. In addition to offering great customer service via the Internet, the company's website saves millions of dollars a year in regular customer support costs and marketing expenses.

Weblogs and Podcasts

The relatively new phenomena blogs and podcasts are dramatically changing the online marketing environment for special events. These new tools are the offspring of consumer-generated media (CGM), where online content is created and managed entirely by consumers. As a result of CGM, e-pinions, or online consumer opinions, are formed. The forums for these e-pinions are often blogs. A blog is a Web log of comments and opinions created, controlled, and driven directly by consumers. Obviously, in the democratic world of the Internet, these opinions can both help and harm your ability to market your event. A site for developing a blog is www.blogger.com. You can list your blog on search engines such as www.newsgator.com or www.bloglines.com.

Additional tools that are the result of CGM include podcasts and wikis. A podcast may be audio or video or both and provides brief, high-content information for consumers through streaming on the Internet. It can be used to promote entertainers or speakers who will appear at your event, as well as to provide instructions, information, and education for your participants or volunteers. The millennial generation loves podcasts because they can download them and listen to them at a later time. For a directory of podcasts, visit www.itunes.com or www.podcastalley.com.

In 2019, industry research showed that there were more than 700,000 active podcasts and more than 29 million podcast episodes! The five most popular podcasts types are society and culture, business, comedy, news and politics, and health. Smartphones are listed as the main source that listeners use to access podcasts. The study also found out that podcast listeners are less likely to be exposed to advertisements (https://musicoomph.com/podcast-statistics/).

The wiki is perhaps best exemplified by Wikipedia (www.wikipedia.org), which is the world's largest online consumer-generated encyclopedia. You may wish to list your event on a wiki site such as Wikipedia or create a wiki of your own to direct consumers to your event.

The rapidly growing online environment for promoting events will increasingly include blogs, podcasts, and RSS technology, which means Really Simple Syndication (RSS 2.0), Rich Site Summary (RSS 0.91, RSS 1.0), or RDF Site Summary (RSS 0.9 and 1.0). This is a family of Web feed formats used to transmit frequently updated digital content such as podcasts or other published materials through the Internet, as well as other advancements. You should continue to review consumer publications such as *Advertising Age* to keep abreast of these developments. The book *How to Do Everything with Podcasting* (Holtz and Hobson, 2007) can also help event leaders expand the footprint of their events through the Internet.

Video Streaming and YouTube

The rapid expansion of global bandwidth within the Internet has greatly escalated the use of video streaming through platforms such as YouTube. Events organizations may use online video streaming before, during, and following the event to share the highlights of their program with millions of Internet users throughout the world. Figure 7.3 in the electronic appendices provides examples of how to use Internet streaming to inform, educate, and persuade online users to support your event.

Often, event leaders will shoot first rather than ready, aim, and then shoot. When producing videos or podcasts, however, it is critically important to secure permission in advance from the participants. This permission may be limited or very broad in

Photo by Seungwon Shawn Lee

A Twitter wall projects event attendees' live tweeting on the screen.

scope. Regardless, you must secure, in writing, their permission to use their image in the pod- or videocast for your event. If it is not possible to secure individual permissions, you may wish to post a sign at the entrance of your event that states that: "Video recording is taking place at this event. As a condition of entry, guests consent to being videotaped without compensation for future promotional purposes by the event." A sample photo release form may be found in the online appendices for this book.

A good source for general knowledge about the legal issues affecting photographers and photography is *The Legal Handbook for Photographers, the Rights and Liabilities of Making Images* (Krages, 2001).

Mobile/Smartphone Event Marketing

The online environment has rapidly extended to mobile phone technology. Advertisers are regularly using mobile phone technology to market directly to consumers. Text messaging is rapidly evolving into full-motion video, and you can now send streaming video of your event directly to mobile phones. This technology has enormous potential for reaching the millennial generation. However, with every advancement in communications, there is also the increasing concern about privacy issues. Make certain you thoroughly research the laws and regulations regarding sending unsolicited advertisements through telecommunications systems prior to implementing your plan.

RFID Technology and Target Marketing

This technology involves using radio-frequency identification (RFID) to track the attendance of participants. A small microchip is attached to the name badge of the event participant. This microchip contains all of their critical information. A recently conducted event industry survey of more than 5,000 people who attend festivals regularly revealed that 17 percent of them were used to wearing RFID-enabled wristbands that allow them to not have to wait in line at vendors, entry lines, and exit lines. This shows the number of people who attend festivals and how people are starting to use wristbands for extra perks. This technology is used to further target whom you will market your event to, by determining levels of interest through tracking people's engagement at your event. However, there is a privacy issue regarding tracking individuals at your event site. Recently, in the United States, a high school student sued her school district for being forced to wear an RFID tag. She said that her religion forbid this type of tracking. Therefore, make certain you offer your guests the option of not participating, and if they do choose to participate, have them sign a form declaring their informed consent.

In addition to tracking attendance and participation (or lack of attendance and participation), this technology can also be used to segment your market to provide you with better return on marketing (ROM) investment. The ability to achieve higher return on event (ROE) will be a critical measurement tool for event organizers and marketers in the future.

The examples and models just described are applicable to many different professional services, including event planning. You can visit websites of various events organizations and observe how lack of proper planning or understanding of online marketing concepts results in boring websites, useless online questionnaires, and annoying e-mail listservs. At the same time, those events organizations that carefully plan their online activities and balance design and content succeed in achieving their Internet marketing goals.

Start Your Engines: Creating Greater Marketing Thrust through Commercial Sponsorship

The late Ira Westreich, noted corporate marketing expert and eloquent professional speaker, described the word *event* as an acronym that represents "Extract Value with Every New Thrust." The purpose of your event-marketing campaign is to ensure that every decision you make provides greater value for the overall event outcome. To do this, you must carefully match the objectives to the strategies, test all ideas using feedback from actual event consumers, and, perhaps most important, use creativity and innovation to differentiate your event product as a unique and valuable investment. By integrating marketing activities such as advertising, public relations, cross-promotions, street promotions, and stunts, with commercial sponsorship you will be able to build a strong campaign that will effectively promote your event to your target audience.

Commercial Event Sponsorship

The International Events Group (IEG) of Chicago is a recognized leader in the field of sponsorship research and education. Although the vast majority of sponsorship dollars is invested in sports-related events, there is a trend to diversify funding into festivals, fairs, and cultural events. The primary reason for this diversification of investment is the need of advertisers to reach more targeted demographics. Sports have generally attracted broad demographics, whereas cultural events are able to target high-income and well-educated consumers.

However, as a result of the global financial decline first experienced in 2008, many corporations chose to cut back or eliminate their sponsorship programs. Some event organizations in the United States reported loss of sponsorship of upwards of $250,000. Therefore, while sponsorship is still a critical component of most event funding schemes, event leaders must work harder and be more clever in gaining sponsorship dollars in the future. Since the 2008–2009 global financial crisis, sponsorship spending has increased. According to current statistics, North America went from spending $16.6 billion in 2007 to spending $24.2 billion in 2018. This includes sports entertainment, arts, festivals and fairs, associations, and membership organizations (https://www.statista.com/statistics/196848/north-american-sponsorship-spending-since-2007/).

It is important to understand that the event in sponsorship language is defined as the property or sponsee. The sponsor is the commercial or other organization (usually a corporation) that provides funding or in-kind resources in exchange for specific marketing benefits. Sponsors may include both private and public organizations.

Sponsorship generally becomes more valuable if the event organization is able to offer precise targeting that matches the marketing objectives of the prospective sponsor. The growth in sponsorship is due primarily to the need of advertisers to find alternative marketing channels to inform, persuade, promote, and sell their products and services. However, the number of events that require sponsorship has also grown in recent years.

Without sponsorship, many events would not be financially feasible because the cost for tickets would be prohibitive to those who wish to attend. Other events would not be able to provide the quality expected by event participants. Still other events would not be able to achieve their specified goals and objectives. Suffice it to say that, more often than not, sponsorship provides the grease that allows the event wheel to function smoothly.

Historically, sponsorship has its earliest modern origin in professional sporting events. These events have always appealed to the widest demographics and were, therefore, perfect event products for sponsorship. Sponsorship is a uniquely American invention brought forth from the need of advertisers to reach certain markets and the need of event organizers to identify additional funding to offset costs not covered by normal revenue streams, such as ticket sales.

In recent times, there has been a noticeable shift in sponsor dollars away from sporting events and toward arts events. The reason for this shift is that sponsors are seeking more highly targeted upscale demographics, and the arts' audience delivers that market segment. Therefore, those events that deliver the higher-income demographics are predicted to benefit most from sponsorship dollars in the future.

Perhaps the best example of sport sponsorship in postmodern history is the 1984 Summer Olympic Games in Los Angeles, California. For the first time in the history of the modern Olympic Games movement, sponsors were aggressively solicited as marketing partners for this unprecedented event. Offers were made, deals were cut, and the Los Angeles Olympic Organizing Committee received net earnings of over $200 million.

From fairs to festivals to hallmark events such as a world's fair, the role of the sponsor has earned a permanent place in the marketing lexicon of events. Following are typical types of sponsors for a variety of events:

- *Fair:* Bottler, grocer, automotive, and bank
- *Festival:* Department store and record store
- *Sport:* Athletic wear manufacturer, bottler, brewery, and hospital or health-care facility

- *School program:* Children's toy stores, children's clothing stores, and amusement parks
- *Meeting/conference:* Printer, bank, insurance broker, and associate member firms

Use this list as a guide to begin to identify future sponsors for your event.

Sponsorship Needs Assessment

Although most events might benefit from sponsorship, not every event is appropriate for this component. Sponsorship is a commercial endeavor and is extremely time-consuming. Therefore, unless you are prepared to enter into a commercial relationship with other parties and have the time resources to devote to this activity, you may instead wish to solicit donations.

Many event leaders confuse sponsorship with benevolence. A fundraising event where donors contribute without any expectation of commercial benefit is a benevolent activity. Sponsorship, however, is a commercial transaction in which two parties agree by way of an offer and acceptance. The offer generally involves marketing services provided by the event organizer in exchange for the sponsor's cash or in-kind contribution to the event. The marketing services may range from advertising, to banner displays, to hospitality, to a full-blown marketing plan involving public relations, advertising, and promotion.

As you can see, these marketing services place new demands on the event organizer. Therefore, event resources may need to be reallocated to handle this new demand. Not every event is able to do this.

Before you give the green light to soliciting sponsorships, use the next checklist to determine if your event is appropriate for this activity:

1. Does the event need an infusion of sponsor dollars to achieve the quality required?
2. Are there sufficient internal and external resources to support this activity?
3. Is commercial sponsorship appropriate for the nature of the event?
4. Are there sufficient prospects for sponsorship sales, and is the timing appropriate to approach them?
5. Is this activity legal, ethical, and appropriate for the spirit of the event organization?

These questions can save many event organizations much wasted time, energy, and heartache. Examining the internal and external resources may be one of the most important aspects of this process.

Although sponsors may provide much needed funding for your event to help you achieve the quality that is required, sponsors also require that your own financial resources meet their objectives. They may, for example, require that you commit a certain amount of marketing dollars. They also may require minimal or substantial hospitality services that may amount to hundreds or thousands of dollars per day. If you are going to retain these sponsors, assign one or more people to monitor the activities, service these accounts, and develop long-term relationships. Yes, sponsors can provide needed funding; however, as in any commercial transaction, they must also receive a fair return on their investment. You are responsible for orchestrating this return.

Your event may benefit from additional exposure through sponsorships. Earlier, we discussed using tag lines in advertising as one way to increase your exposure inexpensively. Sponsors may also provide you with shelf space in their retail stores or promote your event through coupons. Your sponsors can also help you with the development of a public relations campaign or can add your message to their own public relations efforts. Some sponsors have celebrity athletes, television stars, and movie personalities on contract whom they may wish to involve in your event.

Perhaps one of the more important reasons event organizers align themselves with commercial sponsors is the opportunity to achieve greater credibility for the event. Securing the sponsorship of AT&T, IBM, Coca-Cola, or other Fortune 500 firms immediately positions your event as a major player and may help your event organization secure additional funding from other sources.

Developing Sponsors

The competition by event organizers for sponsors is keen at every level. Whether your event is a local event or a national one, you must first conduct a competitive analysis to identify all competing events and study their sponsorship history and current activities. Several suggestions on how to identify appropriate sponsors for your event follow:

1. Determine the financial level of sponsorship you require. Not every sponsor can make a five- or six-figure commitment.
2. Review trade journals such as *Advertising Age* and *Sponsorship Report* to track sponsor activities.
3. Review the local business tabloid in your area to search for prospective sponsors.
4. Network with advertising and public relations agency officials to find out if their clients have an interest in your event.
5. Conduct a focus group with prospective sponsors to solicit and later analyze their opinions and attitudes toward your event.
6. Make certain you link your sponsorship program directly to the business case the corporation has developed.

Once you have developed a list of prospective sponsors, the next step is to qualify them for solicitation. Do not waste your valuable resources by making endless presentations to sponsors who do not have the interest or resources to support your event financially. Instead, qualify your sponsors by contacting local organizations, such as the chamber of commerce, board of trade, banks, and other centers of commerce, to inquire about the financial viability of the prospective sponsor. Next, thoroughly review the sponsor's past marketing efforts to determine if its overall marketing plans are conducive to sponsoring your event. Finally, talk to advertising and public relations executives and attempt to forecast where your prospective sponsor may put its marketing dollars in the future. Perhaps the logical place for investment is your event.

Selling Sponsorships

Always do your homework regarding the sponsor's needs, wants, and desires prior to attempting to sell a sponsorship. To make the sale, the sponsorship offer must be an exact fit with the needs, expectations, goals, and objectives of the commercial sponsor. Customize the offer to achieve these goals and objectives prior to your presentation.

Constructing a successful proposal is equal parts art and science. As an artist, you must design an attractive, enticing, and aesthetically pleasing product that the sponsor will want to purchase. Therefore, describe the capability of your organization and past sponsors (if any), incorporate testimonials and references from leading individuals, and package the proposal with a professional design. Avoid being clever. Remember that the sponsor will be making an important business decision and will prefer a serious business plan to one that demonstrates cleverness. The science part involves carefully identifying your target market and linking all sponsorship activities to sales or recognition that will benefit the sponsor. List the benefits and activities that the organization will enjoy as a sponsor of your event. For example, the sponsor might be able to provide free samples of his or her product or service and conduct marketing research. The sponsor might be able to offer the company's product or service for sale and measure the results, or the sponsor may benefit from public relations exposure.

Include in the proposal sponsorship terms for payment and any requirements the sponsor may have in addition to these payments. In some events, the sponsor is allowed to provide an exhibit at its own cost. In others, the exhibit is provided as part of the sponsorship costs. Describe any additional costs or services the sponsor is required to contribute to avoid any future surprises. This list summarizes the key elements in a winning sponsorship proposal:

1. Describe the history of the event.
2. Include a capability statement about your organization's resources.
3. Incorporate testimonials and references from other sponsors.
4. Describe the benefits and features that the sponsor will receive.
5. List all financial responsibilities that the sponsor must accept.
6. Describe any additional responsibilities that the sponsor must accept.
7. Describe how you will chronicle the sponsorship activity.
8. Include a time and a date for acceptance of the offer.
9. Include a provision for renewal of the sponsorship.
10. Include an arbitration clause in case you and the sponsor disagree regarding the sponsorship activities.

One of the more effective ways to persuade sponsors to participate in an event is to organize a prospective sponsor preview program. During this program, you and your staff describe the benefits and features of your sponsorship activities to a large number of prospective sponsors. You may wish to invite a couple of previous sponsors to provide in-person testimonials about the benefits of the sponsorship. You may also wish to presell one or two sponsors so that when you ask for a reaction from those in attendance, at least two from the group will respond favorably. Their favorable response may, and usually does, influence others. Avoid trying to hard-sell during this program. Use this program to plant seeds that will be further cultivated during meetings with individual sponsors.

Overcoming Sponsor Objections

Most sponsors will want their sponsorship activities customized to achieve their specific goals and objectives. Therefore, they may have some preliminary objections after receiving your initial offer. Once you have presented the offer, ask for their reaction on each benefit and feature. Listen carefully and list these comments. Make two lists. One list is for approvals, those items that they see the value in sponsoring. The second list is for objections, those items that they cannot see the value of at this time. Your goal is to move all the items from list 2 to list 1. To do this, ask sponsors what their organization requires to overcome their objections on each point. In some cases, it might be additional exposure. In other cases, it might be the price of the sponsorship. To overcome these objections, be prepared to provide sponsors with the tools they need to make a positive decision. For example, if their objection is cost, you may be able to combine their sponsorship with others and lower their contribution. If their objection is limited exposure, you may be able to reposition their involvement inexpensively to provide them with greater and more sustained visibility. Handling objections is an integral part of the sponsorship sales process. Rehearse these discussions with your internal stakeholders to identify other common objections, and be prepared to provide the solution your sponsors need to remove these barriers.

Negotiating Your Sponsorship

Almost every sponsorship will require intense negotiations to move it to fruition. Whenever possible, conduct these negotiations in person with the decision maker. Assign a specific date and time for these negotiations and confirm that the sponsor is a feasible prospect before entering into a serious negotiation. In most negotiations, both parties desire a win–win–win outcome. In this type of negotiation, you win as the event organizer, the sponsor wins as the event funding agent, and the stakeholders of your event win from your mutual efforts to secure these dollars.

Carefully analyze what your sponsor expects from the sponsorship prior to your negotiating session. Determine in advance what additional components you may be able to offer if required. Also, list those concessions that you cannot make. Finally, list those items that may require further approval from your board or others before you agree to them. Begin the negotiation by asking the prospective sponsor to list all items that are acceptable, bundle them, and have the sponsor approve them. Now you are prepared to focus on those items that require further resolution. Ask the sponsor to describe his or her concerns about each negotiation point and take careful notes. Look at your list of concessions and decide if any item you have listed will help resolve these concerns. If it is appropriate to offer a concession, do so and ask the sponsor for his or her approval. Once the sponsor has given approval, ask him or her to provide you with an additional service, usually at modest additional cost to the sponsor, to balance his or her end of the negotiation. If the sponsor is unable to provide you with an additional service or product, determine if you are able to proceed to the next point.

Do not be afraid to walk away if the sponsor asks for concessions that could sacrifice the credibility or reputation of an event or that would undermine the financial wealth of your event. Instead, thank the sponsor for his or her time, offer to work with the sponsor in the future under different circumstances, and leave the room as quickly as possible. In some instances, event organizers have reported that this approach has forced the prospective sponsor to reexamine its position. It is not unusual to have the sponsor call the event organizer the next day and offer a greater concession to save the sponsorship.

Closing the Sponsorship Sale

You must always ask for the order when presenting your sponsorship proposal. State at least three times that you want to develop a positive relationship with the sponsor. Start your discussions by stating that your desired outcome is to ensure that the sponsor understands all the benefits and features of your event and will desire to become a sponsor.

Throughout your presentation, ask for feedback from the sponsor and build on the sponsor's positive reactions by saying that you are pleased that it recognizes the value of your event product. Finally, at the conclusion of your presentation, ask the sponsor's spokesperson for his or her overall impression and state, once again, that you would like the sponsor's business.

Unfortunately, these techniques may not be enough to get a clear answer. In some cases, you may have to say something like "So, can we count on you to sponsor our event?" Sometimes you need to secure the answer to this question in order to plan your next step in sponsorship negotiations or to decide to move forward with the next sponsor. The word *ask* is the most powerful three-letter word in sponsorship sales. Unless you ask, you will never know. Remember to ask early, often, and before leaving to confirm the sponsorship sale.

Servicing Sponsorship Sales

Once the sponsor has accepted your offer, the next task is to service the sale in order to retain the sponsor's support in the future. One of the more common reasons that sponsors fail to renew their sponsorship is poor communications. In Part 1 of this book, we discussed in great detail the importance of open and continuous communication. Make certain that you develop methods for implementing positive communications with your sponsors. Some event organizers use newsletters to update their sponsors, others provide regular briefings, and still others offer their sponsors marketing seminars to help them design a booth or target their product or service to event guests. It is wise to assign one or more persons on your staff to service all sponsorships and communicate regularly with sponsors to make certain they remain informed, excited, and committed to the event activities.

Another reason that some sponsorships go sour is the inability of the event organizers to deliver what they promise. If you promise that the sponsor's banner will be suspended on the main stage above the head of the performing artist, you must first confirm with the artist that this is acceptable. It is unacceptable to renege later on your commitment to the sponsor. It is always best to underpromise and overdeliver when stating the benefits of sponsorship. Exceeding the sponsor's expectations is how you turn a 1-year sponsorship into a 5-year plan with options to renew forever.

Every sponsor has a hidden agenda. It can be as simple as the chair of the board wanting to meet his or her favorite celebrity or as complex as the sales manager's bonus and promotion decision resting on this particular sponsorship activity. Ask the sponsor's representative what else you need to know about the needs of his or her organization as you design the sponsorship measurement system. For example, if the sponsor's representative is in the public relations department, his or her interest may be in seeing lots of ink and television time devoted to the name of the sponsor. Therefore, you will want to measure these outcomes carefully to assist your sponsor. Remember that you may sign a sponsorship agreement with a large corporation or organization, but the day-to-day management of this agreement is between people. Find out what these people desire and try to provide them with these outcomes.

Although communication between you and your sponsors is critical to your success, perhaps even more important are the internal communications between the event leader and his or her operations personnel. You must first confirm that your personnel will be able to support sponsorship activities at the level required by the individual sponsors. Determine if you have sufficient internal resources to satisfy the requirements both in contract as well as implied to ensure the well-being of your sponsor's investment. For example, if your sponsor wants a hospitality setup arranged at the last minute, do you have a catering operation that can handle this request? One way to ensure that the sponsors' needs are handled expeditiously is to create a written system of orders, changes, and other instructions that clearly communicates those activities required by your sponsors. Prior to distribution of these forms, have the sponsor's representative sign one copy. Then have the event's representative initial approval before forwarding it to the appropriate department or team leader.

Evaluating Sponsorships

To secure multiple-year sponsorships, it is important that you develop and implement a system for measuring the sponsor's activities. First, decide what needs to be evaluated and why. The answers to these questions typically may be found in the goals and objectives of the sponsorship agreement.

To collect these data, conduct sponsorship evaluations that are comprehensive in scope. You may wish to interview the sponsors, your own staff, the sponsor's target market, and others to solicit a wide range of opinions regarding the effectiveness of the sponsorship. Furthermore, you may wish to include in the event survey-specific questions about the sponsor's participation. Finally, ask the sponsor for tracking information regarding sales that have resulted from the sponsor's participation in your event.

You may measure the sponsor's public relations benefits by measuring the number of minutes of television and/or radio time, as well as the number of inches and columns of print media, that was devoted to the sponsor's products or name. List the comparable value using the 3:1 ratio provided by the Public Relations Society of America.

Ask the sponsor how the data you have measured should be presented. Some may prefer an elaborate in-person presentation using video clips and slides; others will prefer a simple summary of the goals, objectives, and outcomes that were achieved. Make certain that you present this information in a manner that is useful to the sponsor and that you take the time to prepare this presentation professionally to address the sponsor's needs. All future sponsorship activities will come from this important presentation.

Timing Is Everything

The process for identifying, soliciting, negotiating, securing, servicing, and evaluating sponsorships is a complex one. However, as is true with most things, timing is everything. Allow a minimum of 12 to 18 months to formulate and consummate a successful sponsorship program. A typical timeline for the various stages just described follows here:

At least 18 months in advance	Conduct needs assessment and research to identify sponsorship requirements for your event.
16 months in advance	Identify prospective sponsors for your event.
14 months in advance	Develop and present sponsorship proposals.
12 months in advance	Negotiate proposals and sign sponsorship agreements.
9 months in advance	Implement the sponsorship operations plan.
6 months in advance	Review sponsor's changes and additions as received.
4 months in advance	Review changes and additions with event marketing staff.
2 months in advance	Meet with sponsor to provide update on event progress (ticket sales, media plan).
1 month in advance	Begin sponsor public relations campaign.
1 month after event	Meet with sponsor to provide analysis of results.

Although this schedule may be effective for most event sponsorship programs, there are exceptions that should be noted. For example, macroeconomic changes, such as the recent financial crisis, provide new short-term opportunities for some event organizers to approach certain organizations (banks and financial services providers) to continue their sponsorship through the internal community relations budget rather than their traditional marketing spend. This will allow those organizations that could greatly benefit from positive public relations to continue their investment and make the decision short term, albeit for a smaller amount of money, so the event continues to benefit from support.

Some event organizers have come to see sponsorship as the goose with the golden egg. However, while specific benefits come from individual sponsorships, prior to engaging in this time-consuming and expense-laden activity, an event leader must audit for each event the needs, resources available, and benefits offered. When developing sponsorship activities, always start small and build a base of sponsors year by year or event by event from your ability to deliver high-quality and successful events consistently. This is the best way to make sure that your goose lays a golden egg, not a rotten one, for your event organization.

Evaluating Your Event Marketing Campaign

Reggie Aggarwal of CVENT.com and Professor Joe Goldblatt coined the term *return on event* (ROE) in 2000 to identify the percentage of earnings returned to an event organization sponsoring the event based on marketing efforts. The ROE is an important concept for all event marketers, regardless of event size. For example, if you are marketing a small event for 100 persons and you increase attendance by 25 percent due to your new e-marketing strategies, you may, in fact, not only have saved a significant amount of money but also have generated a sizable net profit that may be directly attributable to this marketing activity. Figure 7.4 in the electronic appendices outlines how this formula may be used to identify the ROE.

The income statement shows a significant increase in total revenues in Year 2 as well as a slight increase in net income. Now we measure the increase in return on marketing and see how the marketing function performed as part of the overall financial analysis (Figure 7.5 in the electronic appendices.) By careful monitoring, tracking, and measuring of each marketing activity, you are able to identify that in Year 2, your event generated a 160 percent return on marketing investment as compared to Year 1, with only 39 percent. To monitor, track, and measure each of these separate marketing functions, you need to use a variety of simple but effective systems.

Coding Your Event Marketing Materials

Make certain that you assign a unique code to each marketing response item. For example, if you allow your attendees to register by mail, phone, newspaper, radio, and Internet, each marketing channel should have a separate code. Figure 7.6 in the appendices demonstrates how to code and track each response. By identifying the response ratios from each marketing channel, you are better able to adjust your marketing efforts during the promotional period prior to the event and evaluate where to place your marketing dollars in the future.

Determining the ROE accomplishes three fundamental goals that are critical to your future marketing success:

1. You are able to track where your responses are being generated.
2. You are able to compare investment versus actual marketing performance for each channel.
3. You are able to compare return on marketing with other economic performance indicators, such as risk management, labor, and utilities, on an annual basis and determine whether you need to increase or reduce the budget accordingly to achieve your revenue targets in future years.

Online versus Other Event Marketing Channels

The online marketing environment that seems to permeate most marketing decisions today must be seen as one, not the only, form of attracting, persuading, and converting customers to attend your event. Too often, some event organizers solely rely on one marketing channel such as e-mail promotion to drive attendance at their event. In fact, most event attendees require multiple touch points to ensure that there is sufficient opportunity to reach the potential event attendee. Therefore, the process shown in Figure 7.7 demonstrates how to reach the event guests through multiple touch points to increase the likelihood of their participation in your event.

Other Marketing Evaluation Tools

The ROE is a quantitative system for evaluating marketing response. However, in addition to quantifying your responses, you must also qualify them. Using a focus panel to review marketing promotional campaigns, including ink colors, logo design, and copy, will help you fine-tune your material's visual impressions to match the tastes of your prospective event attendees.

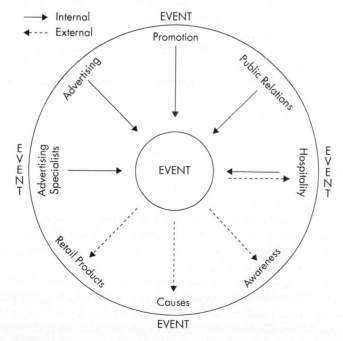

FIGURE 7.7 Internal and external event-marketing model.

You may also wish to use personal interviews to determine why nonattendees refuse to accept your invitation to participate in your event offer. These telephonic interviews can reveal important information that will help you in marketing your event in the future. For example, a nonattendee may reveal that he has trouble finding a babysitter. If this comment is replicated with a large enough sample, you may wish to consider offering on-site child care to increase attendance by families with young children or add more children's activities to your event programming.

The overall benefits associated with marketing should not be focused solely on the economic performance of an event. Remember, even if someone did not attend your event, he or she may have recommended it to others. Furthermore, he or she may be positively influenced to attend in the future. Following are some of the qualitative areas you may wish to measure in your marketing analysis and measuring techniques for each:

- *Image improvement*: Survey, interviews, focus panel
- *Recall of event name*: Interviews, focus panel
- *Recall of event slogan*: Interviews, focus panel
- *Increase in number of volunteers*: Survey, focus panel
- *Increase in sponsorship*: Focus panel, survey
- *Increase in gifts (philanthropy)*: Interviews, survey
- *Improved political relations*: Interviews
- *Improved media relations*: Interviews, clipping, and clip monitoring
- *Improved community relations*: Interviews, focus panel

The overall purpose of marketing analysis and evaluation is to provide you with the essential information you need to make better decisions in the future. Whether your event is one that recurs year after year or is a one-time affair, the data you collect from your marketing analysis will help you in the development of many different types of future events. Make certain that you assign a line item in the event budget for marketing evaluation. Some of the typical costs include: survey development and printing; focus panel facilitation; interviewer fees; data collection, tabulation, and analysis; and report writing. In addition, you may wish to contract with third parties, such as a clipping services firm, to track the media generated about your event. Your ability to measure the return on marketing for your event comprehensively will provide you with dividends for many years to come. Do not miss this opportunity to improve your competitiveness, your event's image, and your profitability now and in the years to come.

Preston suggests that the following trends will influence event marketing in the near future:

1. Through improved technological delivery, such as greater mobile connectivity, you will be able to better promote your event in real time through cell/mobile phones and other wireless systems.
2. Through faster technology (broadband), you will be able to send much more information to potential attendees at faster and faster speeds.
3. A wide range of new media outlets (including schools, colleges, clubs, amusement parks, and other locations) will develop where your potential target market can receive your message.
4. Your advertising copywriters will need to develop a new vocabulary to communicate effectively with new event consumers, including generations X and Y. This vocabulary will include text messaging.
5. Event marketers will be able to achieve greater success if they emphasize the health benefits associated with attending their events as the baby boomers age and because generations X and Y have greater interest in health and wellness.

6. A seamless registration system, wherein the consumer can arrange transportation, registration, accommodation, tours, restaurant reservations, and much more with a visit to one Internet site, will be essential for event marketers to remain competitive.
7. As the multicultural trend continues to escalate, it is essential that event marketers use multiple languages to communicate with their constituencies.
8. Due to heightened concerns about terrorism, event marketers must focus their messages on safety and security and also emphasize the need to be there to benefit fully from the event.

In addition to Preston's points, it is increasingly important for event leaders to embrace yield management in their pricing. As event tickets are perishable and individuals may have fewer dollars due to redundancies, layoffs, and long-time unemployment, the event organization that offers discounts and even free tickets for certain groups may win in two big ways. First, they will increase their overall attendance, which may lead to greater per capita spending, and second, they will be growing their audiences for the future because these individuals who are now receiving discounts or free admission will one day be ticket buyers and even potential future sponsors.

INSIGHTS FROM GLOBAL EVENT LEADERS

DEBORAH BORSUM, CSEP, CERP, CMD, CEO

Executive Vice President, SBR Events Group, Past International President, International Live Events Association and

ROBERT SIVEK, CSEP, CERP, COO

Former executive at The Meetinghouse Companies, Inc. and Past International President, International Live Events Association.

(Note: To see the complete video interview, visit the Book Companion Site for this book at www.wiley.com/go/goldblatt/specialevents8e.)

Deborah Borsum began her career by doing marketing and special events for a shopping center where she met her partner, Robert Sivek. She began to produce events with Robert and soon joined his firm.

Robert Sivek started in special events through his love of technical production and entertainment and soon expanded his career by forming his own firm, Events and Entertainment. Another local company Meetinghouse Display would hire Events and Entertainment. Each company continued to grow and, as the years moved forward, the companies became one another's

http://goo.gl/Yt62hL

biggest customers. Due to an illness of the owner of Meetinghouse Display, the two companies merged.

Q: What advice would you offer to someone who wants to enter the special event industry?

A: (Deborah) I first question them to make sure they understand what is involved. Through movies and television, being an event planner has been glamorized way beyond the real truth of late nights, hard work, and broken fingernails. If having a great manicure and cute outfit and going to a great party is what you have in mind, it is not at all what it is about. I want to know if you are interested in the work behind it, which means [what] both the creative as well as the business development side. If you are willing to work hard and gain experience from setup to technical production and other tasks, there is still a lot of opportunity for you.

Q: How important is technology today in building a special events career?

A: (Deborah) It is extremely important in terms of building connections all over the world. We often go online to find the exact resource we need. The Internet has so changed our access to anything and everything you need. The challenge in that is to make certain you are finding qualified suppliers, vendor partners, and products.

Q: How has environmental sustainability affected your special events business?

A: (Deborah) We definitely see that clients have an interest in sustainable events and producing events that reflect positively on their company.

(Robert) We have to reevaluate how we do things, what products we use, how we present products, recycling flowers, reusing things that come back to our warehouse. On the other hand, the rental business, our business, does not get much greener because we are constantly recycling and reusing and repurposing products for special events.

Q: What are some of the key attributes of successful Event Leaders?

A: (Deborah) I think you have to be visionary but also practical about the approach. I think it is important to have a goal and then decide how you are going to impart that vision to other people. I also think it is important to connect with and understand your team to make certain you inspire and motivate and provide the kind of leadership that gives them confidence that they are on a good path.

(Robert) I would add that it is important to be a good listener. It is tough to be a good leader without being a good listener. I think a lot of problems are solved in discussing them. Sometimes people just want to talk and be heard, and if you can just sit and listen, that is just plain good leadership, in my book.

Q: What do you see as one of your successes of which you are most proud?

A: (Deborah) We are lucky to have built a large company and had many employees who have grown and developed, some have even gone onto other companies and made great contributions to the special events industry.

Q: What do you see as the future for the special events industry?

A: (Deborah) I have compared the special events industry to the fashion industry. It is one that is constantly growing and changing. What was done yesterday nobody is interested in. This provides an opportunity for us to do amazing things differently every day.

Q: How can others be successful in the future?

A: (Deborah) It is important to be fresh and creative but also to use your business skills to help the industry to positively evolve and change for the better. I do not think we will even recognize this industry 10 years from today.

Q: If you were to write a LinkedIn recommendation for the special events industry 25 years from now, what might you say?

A: (Robert) We made a lot of people very, very happy and that is a good thing. When people are happy it is transmitted to others. People come away from events with a great attitude.

Q: How can events help change the world?

A: (Deborah) The London 2012 Olympic Games are a great example of bringing people together for a common goal. Events are vital in this regard. And as Robert mentioned, usually people are happier following an event. Therefore, absolutely, events can have a positive impact upon the world.

(Robert) I think when two people walk into a room and turn to one another, they may not know one another, but they say "Wow!" upon experiencing the special event; it animates them and is contagious. The borders between people dissolve as events bring people together. We use events for charitable fundraising purposes. Events bring people together.

(Deborah) Yes, events are a wonderful way to celebrate and connect with mankind.

Summary

Chapter 7 provided you with a comprehensive overview of the elements of modern event marketing including the vast array of opportunities for you to exploit new online distribution channels and expand your event marketing to maximize multiple channel marketing that will provide as many as possible touchpoints with event consumers. These elements include the following key components.

1. *Marketing research:* This research must be carefully conducted prior to developing your marketing plan to ensure that your plan aligns with the needs, wants, and desires of your future event guests.
2. *The Six Ps:* Product, place, promotion, price, public relations, and positioning must be carefully considered in the design of your marketing campaign.
3. *Online consumer-generated media:* From wikis to blogs to smartphones, it is essential that you maximize every digital opportunity to inform, remind, and promote a response from your target audience.
4. *Event marketing evaluation:* Throughout the event marketing campaign and in the summative stage, you have the opportunity to analyze all of the marketing data you have collected to continually reduce your marketing costs and improve your reach and sales in the future.
5. *More attractive sponsorship/exhibitor packages enhanced by an attendee tracking system:* This technology can allow sponsors/exhibitors to utilize push notifications and alerts by using wearable beacons to track movements of attendees. This allows sponsors/exhibitors opportunities to monitor attendee visits to their booths in real time and develop a dynamic alert invitation during slow times. This can be also helpful when staff of the sponsoring organization cannot be on-site. Increased visibility and attendees traffic to the sponsoring event and booth activity are what sponsors want to measure to evaluate the value of their sponsorship investment.

Key Terms

Event marketing: The process through which you use research, design, planning, coordination and evaluation to market your special event.

Experiential event marketing: A marketing method that uses immersive event experiences to market an event brand or experience to potential event buyers.

Online consumer-generated media: Media that is directly generated by your guests and posted to social media websites such as TripAdvisor.com, Facebook, and others.

Promotion: Advertising where you control the message, the placement, the frequency, and pay for the costs.

Public relations: The opportunity to generate third-person commentary about your event through the use of media releases, audio and video news releases, stunts, and promotions.

Sponsorship: A commercial relationship wherein one party (the event property) receives money or in-kind products and services from a public or private sponsor and in return provides promotional opportunities for the sponsor.

Career Connections

In order to rapidly advance your career through mastering the principles of event marketing, volunteer to design a marketing campaign for a local event. Develop a series of strategies and tactics that will promote sales for this event. Create a systematic system for measuring your return on marketing investment. Include in your résumé or curriculum vitae how your efforts increased overall ticket or sponsorship sales for this event. Become increasingly more skilled at using tools such as Google Analytics to measure, evaluate, and report your online marketing activities.

Next Steps

1. Use MeetingMetrics or SurveyMonkey to conduct marketing research for your event.
2. Design a website for your event.
3. Create and populate a blog about your event.
4. Use Google Analytics to measure and evaluate your website traffic.
5. Create a social media presence for your event and measure your performance.

References

Aventri (2017) The future of event marketing: An outlook on the tech and social tools to use for the future. Accessed June 2019: https://offers.etouches.com/hubfs/Aventri%20Content/Aventri%20Ebooks+Whitepapers/Aventri_The_Future_Of_Event_Marketing_Ebook.pdf?__hstc=235756254.90c8db3567d2f1a845a68dd74d574780.1560651770005.1560651770005.1560651770005.1&__hssc=235756254.1.1560651770006&__hsfp=1214103919.

Bernays, E. (2004) *Propaganda*, Brooklyn, NY: Ig Publishing.

Bruner, R. E. (1998) *Net Results: Web Marketing That Works*, IN, USA: New Riders.

Eventbrite (2018) 2018 Event trends you need do. Accessed May 2019: https://www.eventbrite.com/blog/2018-event-trends-you-need-ds00.

Getz, D. (2007) *Event Studies*, Oxford, UK: Routledge.

Lee, S., Bashnakova, D. and Goldblatt, J. (2016) *The 21st Century Meeting and Event Technologies: Powerful Tools for Better Planning, Marketing, and Evaluation*, Waretown, NJ: Apple Academic Press.

Preston, C. (2012) *Event Marketing, Second Edition*, Hoboken, NJ: John Wiley & Sons.

Straker, K. Wrigley, C., and Rosemann, M. (2015) Typologies and touchpoints: Designing multichannel digital strategies, *Journal of Research in Interactive Marketing*, Vol. 9 Iss: 2, pp. 110–128.

CHAPTER 8

Ensuring a Safer and More Secure Event Environment

> *"The hope is that public awareness of human rights standards will eventually encompass all of the rights in the United Nations Universal Declaration of Human Rights."*
>
> —*Joseph M. Wronka (1998)*

In this chapter you will learn how to:

- Recognize and comply with standard and customary event regulations and procedures
- Access, plan, manage, and control potential event liabilities
- Obtain necessary permits and licenses to operate events
- Develop and manage risk-management procedures
- Understand and comply with environmental regulations governing events
- Comply with regulations governing sponsorship of conferences and meetings
- Comply with the U.S. Americans with Disabilities Act and other International Equal Access/Human Rights Regulations
- Identify and reduce common ethical problems in the special events industry
- Measure and evaluate your event's social responsibility index
- Create socially responsible programs for conventions, festivals, meetings, and other events
- Promote your socially responsible outcomes to others

Photo by Seungwon Shawn Lee

Rolling out the red carpet enhances the ambience at an expo, and also requires safety procedures to insure the surface is even and edges are well-installed and securely taped.

Introduction

The opening lines of the United States Declaration of Independence, drafted by Thomas Jefferson in 1776, state that human rights are inalienable and include life, liberty, and the pursuit of happiness. Special events certainly help provide happiness for millions of people each year throughout the world. However, do they also help guarantee life and liberty for all people who attend, participate, or are stakeholders in some dimension of the planned event experience?

The profound belief and promise of human rights for all people was later encompassed in the language of the United Nations University Declaration of Human Rights in 1948 as a result of the atrocities experienced during World War II. Its preamble is similar to that of the U.S. Declaration of Independence and states that "Whereas recognition of the inherent dignity and of the equal and inalienable rights of all members of the human family is the foundation of freedom, justice and peace in the world . . ." (United Nations 1948).

Therefore, although every planned event that you organize may certainly contain potential risks, it is your responsibility as the host to ensure, to the best of your ability, the safety of your guests. Gerry Reynolds, Events Manager for the Highland Games in Inverness, Scotland, states that it is the responsibility of the event management to make certain that every guest returns home safely from the event.

Frank Supovitz, former Senior Vice President for Events for the U.S. National Football League, recalls a time when during the preparations for the Super Bowl he was notified that a disgruntled individual planned on using an assault weapon on fans waiting in line outside the metal detectors. His director of security, a former FBI official, later stated that if the individual had begun firing he might have killed 30 or more people and injured many more before he was himself "taken out" (killed) by snipers present at the event.

The recent increased number of mass shootings in the United States provide a sobering reminder of the importance of considering the worst-case scenario for every event and then working with key partners to help insure a safe outcome. Furthermore, it is your responsibility as the professional event leader, to the best of your ability, to protect and preserve their human rights. Finally, perhaps in the not-too-distant future, your planned event may even be the catalyst for promoting, as the framers of the U.N. Universal Declaration of Human Rights intended, freedom, justice, and peace throughout the world.

Whether you are the event leader for a wedding, the Super Bowl, or the Olympic Games, according to risk management and safety expert Dr. Peter Tarlow, author of *Event Risk Management and Safety* (2002), "All events carry two risks, (1) the risk of a negative occurrence both on site and off site, and (2) the negative publicity that comes from this negative occurrence." Tarlow, a sociologist and rabbi who has studied tourism and other types of events throughout the world, realizes that whenever we bring people together, there is an element of risk.

Most modern events have a potential for negligent activity that can lead to long and costly litigation. As the number of professionally managed events has increased, so has the concern for risk management and other legal and ethical issues. During the mid-1970s in the United States, many events were held to celebrate the 200th anniversary of American independence. During this period most events were organized by amateurs. As a result of a lack of understanding or training in risk management, there was a corresponding interest by the legal profession in bringing litigation against negligent event managers. This relationship continues today, with one notable difference. Event leaders are becoming smarter with regard to legal, ethical, and risk-management issues.

Attorney James Goldberg, the author of *The Meeting Planners Legal Handbook* (1996), addresses in this book critical issues for association meeting and event specialists such as taxation, antitrust issues, tort liability, and intellectual property challenges. Courses are also being offered throughout the United States covering recent developments in the areas of legal, ethical, and risk-management and Sarbanes–Oxley issues relating to event planning. Perhaps the best evidence of this change has been the development of alternative dispute resolution (ADR) programs to avoid lengthy and expensive litigation. Indeed, the paradigm has shifted dramatically from an environment governed by ignorance to one where education and proactive measures may reduce the level of risk and the resulting cost to event organizers.

Ensuring the Safety and Security of Event Stakeholders

A safe event environment is one that is free from hazards. A secure environment is one that is protected from future harm. The event leader is responsible for constructing a safe, secure environment, and sustaining it during the course of an event. Do not transfer this responsibility to others. The event leader either extends the invitation or coordinates the event at the invitation of others. You have both a legal and an ethical responsibility to event stakeholders to design and maintain a safe and secure event environment.

An event venue with a balcony overlooking a river: A beautiful view but event leaders should require additional risk management.

Protecting Your Financial Investment

The legal, ethical, and safety-security aspects of an event can affect the bottom line dramatically. Therefore, every decision you make that is proactive may reduce your risk of unforeseen financial impacts. Practicing thorough proactive legal, ethical, and risk-management measures may actually help your event produce greater revenues.

Although not every contingency can be anticipated, the more adept you are at strategically planning preemptive measures to prevent contingencies, the better your balance sheet will likely look at the end of the event. Lapses in legal, ethical, and risk-management judgment may cause not only loss of property, life, and money but also loss of your event's good name.

Risk-Averse Procedures

"100 die in nightclub event," screamed the headlines and television newscasters in Providence, Rhode Island, immediately after the tragic 2003 Station nightclub fire. This news story became an international incident and profoundly affected the laws regarding fire and public assembly in Rhode Island. Furthermore, every year on the anniversary of this tragedy, the newspapers and television stations remind local citizens of this terrible loss of life, and this will probably continue for many years to come.

Governor Donald Carceri of Rhode Island appointed Joe Goldblatt as chair of a task force to determine how the new regulations that would inevitably be developed could be implemented in a manner so as not to inhibit or impede the development of the events industry. After several hearings, including testimony from experts in event risk management, it was determined that, as a direct result of this tragic incident, the fire and public assembly regulations in Rhode Island would need to be

> ▼ **SECUREVIEW**
>
> Consult with your event stakeholders and find out if there is an opportunity to reduce injury by reducing the activities conducted within your event. For example, does it really make sense to offer an outdoor race across a city park when the pedal impact of the runners will damage the turf? Does it make sense to erect gigantic tents on the park land grass once again damaging the turf and requiring reseeding after the event. Whenever possible, ask yourself how you might reduce the scope of your events damage to the natural environment without sacrificing the overall quality or experience received by your guests.

greatly strengthened. These changes affected small, medium, and large businesses and resulted in direct costs of hundreds of millions of dollars.

The most recent event where a large number of event attendees were killed was the Las Vegas shooting in 2017. A lone gunman unleashed a rapid-fire barrage of bullets from the 32nd floor of the Las Vegas Mandalay Bay Hotel, killing at least 59 people and injuring more than 500 others attending a country music festival. It was the deadliest and the worst mass shooting tragedy in modern American history. Its impact on the event industry has been significant, whenever human beings assemble for the purposes of entertainment, celebration, education, marketing, or reunion, there is an increased risk of loss of life or property. This has been proven many times, as similar newspaper headlines have reported regarding accidents that have occurred at events.

With increased injuries, thefts, and other misfortunes come, of course, increased expense. This may stem from two sources: the loss of revenue resulting directly from the occurrence and increased insurance premiums when underwriters are forced to pay large settlements as a result of negligence. Perhaps the most profound loss is the loss of business opportunity that results from the bad publicity attached to such tragedies. After all, who wants to visit an event where a tent might collapse and injure people or where there is a risk of food poisoning?

Alexander Berlonghi, an early and well-respected expert in the field of risk assessment and risk management, has devised a method for attempting to identify and contain the many risks associated with events. Berlonghi (1990) describes the first step in the risk-assessment process as that of holding a risk-assessment meeting. A step-by-step guide to holding such a meeting follows. We suggest that you use it for each of your events—it could be a lifesaver.

Organizing a Risk-Assessment Meeting

The first question to ask when organizing a risk-assessment meeting is: Who should attend? Ideally, all key event stakeholders should be involved in this meeting, and you may wish to use a written survey to audit their opinions regarding risks associated with an event. However, for practical purposes, you must first identify those event team leaders who can bring you the best information from which to manage present and future risks associated with your events. These event team leaders should be included in the risk-assessment meeting:

- Admissions manager
- Advertising manager
- Animal handler
- Box office manager

- Broadcast manager
- Catering manager
- Comptroller
- Computer or data processing manager
- Convention center safety director
- Customs officials
- Department of Homeland Security representative
- Electrician
- Entertainment specialist
- Environment safety specialist
- Federal Bureau of Investigation (FBI) representative
- Fire department liaison
- Food and beverage manager
- Health and safety coordinator
- Hotel security director
- Human resources director
- Immigration officials
- Insurance broker
- Laser specialist
- Lighting specialist
- Office manager
- Parking specialist
- Police liaison
- Public relations manager
- Pyrotechnic specialist
- Security director
- Sound specialist
- Special-effects specialist
- Transportation specialist
- U.S. Homeland Security liaison
- U.S. Homeland Security official
- Venue safety director
- Weather and meteorological experts

Before the Meeting

Once you have identified the participants for a risk-assessment meeting, it is time to put them to work. Assigning prework helps meeting participants focus on the seriousness of the meeting and will probably improve the efficiency of the meeting. Figure 8.1 demonstrates a typical risk-assessment meeting announcement that you may customize for your own use.

Make sure that you follow up with meeting participants to ensure that all lists have been returned and that you understand the risks they have identified as important to their area. Once you have received responses, it is time to compile a master list of all risks that have been identified. You may list these risks in alphabetical order or subdivide them by event area.

The final step in preparing for a risk-assessment meeting is to prepare a detailed agenda that may be used to conduct the meeting. Prior to the meeting, circulate the agenda and seek feedback from the participants. Figure 8.2 provides a sample agenda and pre-meeting announcement that you may customize for a risk-assessment meeting.

TO: Event Risk-Assessment Team

FROM: Event Leader

SUBJECT: Meeting Announcement and Instructions

DATE: May 15, 2020

ACTION REQUIRED: Return your list of potential risks by July 15, 2020.

A risk-assessment meeting will be held on July 20, 2020, at 1 P.M. for the purpose of identifying and managing the major risks associated with this event. Prior to this meeting, you should audit your area and prepare a comprehensive list of risks associated with your event responsibilities.

Interview the team members in your area and ask them to assist you in this important task. Risks may involve potential injuries, loss of life or property, or other risks.

Submit this list to me by the close of business on July 15, 2020. Thank you for your contribution to this important process.

FIGURE 8.1 Risk-assessment meeting announcement.

TO: Event Team Leaders
FROM: Event Leader
SUBJECT: Event Risk-Assessment Meeting Agenda
DATE: July 15, 2020
ACTION REQUIRED: Return the enclosed agenda to me with your
                        comments by July 18, 2020

Tentative Agenda

   I. Welcome and introduction
  II. Explanation of purposes, event leader
  III. Comprehensive risk review, all participants
  IV. Additional risks not covered in listing, all participants
  V. Recommendations for risk management, all participants
  VI. Economic impacts of risk management, all participants, comptroller
  VII. Post-meeting work assignment, event leader
  VIII. Record and document meeting outcomes
  IX. Note follow-up actions from the meeting and persons responsible for these actions
  X. Adjournment

FIGURE 8.2 Risk-assessment meeting sample agenda/ announcement.

Conducting the Meeting After the agenda has been distributed, corrected, and approved, it is time to convene the risk-assessment meeting. Use a hollow square seating design and prepare tent cards for each participant, listing his or her name and event area of responsibility. A flip chart displayed on an easel stand should list the agenda for the meeting, and subsequent pages should list the risks previously identified by meeting participants. In addition, participants should receive a typed copy of the agenda and the comprehensive list of risks, along with any other collateral material that will help them make the important decisions that will be required during the meeting.

As the event leader, you are also the meeting facilitator. To facilitate the participation of all, first welcome the participants and explain that the meeting will be successful only if they participate actively by offering their expert opinions and engaging in a lively discussion concerning recommendations for reducing or alleviating the risks that have been identified.

After you have set the tone for the meeting, review the list of risks, and ask the meeting participants to study them for a few moments and identify any gaps. What risks have been overlooked?

The next stage of the meeting is to begin discussions on how to reduce, control, transfer, or eliminate the risks that have been identified. This is a good time to ask the participants to form small groups that represent cross-disciplinary task forces. For example, you may ask the admissions, box office, and comptroller team members to work on reducing the risk of theft from the box office or eliminating the risk of gate crashing. Allow 15 to 30 minutes for this activity.

When you reconvene the group, ask participants to communicate their recommendations to the entire group, and try to seek consensus from group members. Do not rush this process. During these discussions, important concerns may be expressed. You must make sure that you address and attempt to satisfy these concerns before moving on to the next stage.

Every risk decision will have corresponding financial impacts. This is a good time to use a Likert scale to rate the importance of each risk in terms of the overall event. For example, to identify risks that should receive the greatest consideration when considering the financial impact on your event, ask each participant to assign a number to each risk, with 1 representing least concern and 5 representing most concern. Theft from the box office might rate a 5, while rain might receive a 1. Once you have reached consensus on the level of importance of each risk, you may concentrate the discussion on risks that the group deems most important.

Documenting the Meeting's Recommendations The final stage of a risk-assessment meeting is to document your recommendations and assign post-meeting work groups to continue to address the important issues covered in the meeting. Assign one person as a scribe during the meeting and ask him or her to prepare review notes to be circulated within three business days. The notes should reflect the substance and content of the discussion and list the recommendations the group has agreed to pursue.

The work groups are responsible for conducting additional research to identify ways in which to better manage the risks that were discussed and perhaps lower the cost of the event. Their work may include interviewing external experts or brainstorming with their fellow event stakeholders to seek better solutions.

The review notes also serve the important purpose of preserving the history of the meeting. Should there be an incident at your event that requires evidence that you conducted risk-assessment and- management procedures to attempt to prevent this occurrence, the review notes may serve as valuable proof documenting your proactive stance.

Safety Meeting and Other Considerations

Before you allow vendors to install the various event elements, you must conduct a brief safety meeting to alert all event stakeholders to the standards your organization has established with regard to safety. Notify the event stakeholders in writing, and explain that this meeting is required for participation in the event. Usually, the meeting is held prior to installation and is conducted by the event leader. Survey the event stakeholders to determine if they have particular expertise in event safety. You may wish to call on this expertise during the safety meeting.

Use a checklist or written agenda distributed to each participant at the meeting to remain focused on the goals and objectives of the meeting. Detail your expectations of minimum safety requirements for the event. These may include taping or ramping of exposed cables, grounding all electric power, keeping the work areas cleared of debris, nonsmoking policies, and other important issues.

Ask those assembled if they have been trained in the Heimlich maneuver or cardiopulmonary resuscitation (CPR) during the past 3 years. Ask those who have been trained to serve as first responders for the event if someone requires this level of response. The event leader should be trained in both the Heimlich maneuver and CPR and be prepared to use these techniques to sustain or save lives, if required. Make certain that you ask each person to sign in when he or she attends the meeting. This will provide you with a record of those who participated and may be helpful if there is a later claim against the event. Conclude the meeting by reminding all participants that the overall goal of this event is zero percent tolerance of unsafe working conditions.

Inspections

Prior to opening the doors to admit guests to your event, conduct a final inspection. Walk the entire event site and note any last-minute corrections that must be made to ensure the safety of guests. Walk-throughs are best conducted by a team that includes your client, key vendors, key event team leaders, and, when possible, police, fire, and other officials.

During the walk-through, use a digital camera and/or video camera to record corrections you have made, and post caution signs where appropriate to notify guests of possible risks.

Photo by Joe Goldblatt

This annual Beltane May Day fire festival event in Edinburgh, Scotland, requires careful coordination with the local fire department.

These areas must be reviewed when conducting a walk-through prior to admitting guests to your event:

- Accreditation/credentialing systems are in working order.
- Admissions personnel are in place.
- Air walls are in working order in case of evacuation.
- Bar personnel have received alcohol management training.
- Doors are unlocked from inside the venue in case of evacuation.
- Edge of stage is marked with safety tape.
- Electric boxes are labeled with caution signs.
- Electric cables are grounded.
- Electric cables traversing public areas are taped or ramped.
- Elevators are working.
- Light level is sufficient for safe ingress and egress.
- Lighting has been properly secured with safety chains.
- Metal detectors are in place and operational for VIP appearances.
- Raised areas inspected to eliminate access by potential snipers.
- Ramps are in place for the disabled.
- Security personnel are posted.
- Signs are visible and well secured.
- The staging has chair- and handrails.
- Stairs have handrails, and individual steps are marked with safety tape to highlight the edges.
- Ushering personnel are in place.
- Final visual inspection of all areas and verbal confirmation with support staff and volunteers prior to opening doors/admitting guests has been conducted.

These are but a few of the areas that must be inspected prior to admitting guests. You may wish to prepare a checklist to inspect each area systematically or simply use a small pad of paper and note areas that must be corrected prior to the event. The walk-through should be conducted 1 to 2 hours prior to the official start time of an event. This will give you time to make any minor corrections that are required.

Documentation and Due Diligence

Each of the steps included in the walk-through demonstrates to officials, and perhaps one day to a jury, that you have attempted to do what a reasonable person would be expected to do under these circumstances to ensure the safety of guests. Documenting your risk-assessment, -management, and -prevention steps may assist you in demonstrating that you have practiced due diligence for your event. The goal is to achieve or exceed the standard of care normally associated with an event of this size and type. The steps just listed will help you move rapidly toward this goal.

Obtaining Insurance

Insurance is used by event leaders to transfer the risk to a third party: the insurance underwriter. Many venues require that the event leader or event organization maintain in full force a minimum of $1 million per occurrence of comprehensive general liability insurance. Some municipalities require similar limits of insurance for events to be held in their jurisdiction. Events that are more complex and pose greater risks may be required to have higher limits of insurance.

Identifying a properly qualified insurance broker is an important first step in receiving expert advice regarding the types of insurance that may be required for your event. After checking with the venue and municipality to determine the level of insurance required, you will need a well-trained specialty insurance broker to advise you further on coverage available.

A specialty insurance broker has insurance products and services specifically relevant for the Event Leadership profession. For example, large firms such as Arthur J. Gallagher & Co. or K & K Insurance provide products for clients ranging from the National Football League's Super Bowl to local parades and festivals. They are experienced experts in providing advice and counsel for the unique risks associated with events.

Identifying the Appropriate Premium After you have contacted two or more specialty insurance brokers and determined the type of insurance products that may be required for your event, you will request quotes from each broker. The brokers will ask you to complete a detailed form listing the history of the event, specific hazards that may be involved (e.g., pyrotechnics), and other critical information. The broker will submit this information to several underwriters and present you with a quote for coverage.

The most cost-effective premium is an annual policy known as comprehensive general liability insurance. Some event leaders pay as little as $2,000 annually for liability coverage for a variety of risks. Other event leaders pay their premiums on a per-event basis. Your insurance broker will help you decide what the best system is for you.

For example, the Summer Olympic Games in Athens, Greece, reportedly paid, according to Bloomberg News Service, over $30 million for insurance coverage for the first 2004 Summer Olympic Games following the tragedy of September 11, 2001. According to the insurers of PyeongChang 2018 Winter Olympic Games, South Korea, the premium to cover the event ranged between $16 and $24 million. Considering smaller scales of Winter Olympic Games, compared to the Summer Games, the insurance premium was relatively high because, several weeks before the opening of the largest winter sporting event, there was high tension in the Korean Peninsula due to North Korea's long range missile threats to both the United States and South Korea. The premium of insurance guarantees included the risk of war, declaration of war, and damage caused by acts of war. Therefore, it is critically important for you to carefully assess your potential risks and work closely with your insurance professionals to purchase sufficient insurance coverage.

These insurance products are typically associated with events:

- Automotive liability
- Business interruption
- Cancellation
- Comprehensive general liability insurance
- Director's and officers liability
- Disability
- Earthquake
- Errors and omissions
- Fire
- Flood
- Health
- Hurricane
- Key person

- Life
- Nonappearance
- Office contents
- Officers
- Performer no show
- Rain
- Terrorism
- Workers' compensation

Your client or others involved with your event may ask that they be named as an additional insured on your policy. The term *additional insured* means that, if for any reason there is an incident, your insurance policy will cover claims against those listed as additionally insured. Before agreeing to name the other party or parties as additional insured, check with your insurance broker to find out if there is an additional charge or if this is appropriate. You may also want to ask the other parties to name you as additional insured on their policies.

Exclusions Every insurance policy will list certain hazards that are excluded from coverage. Make certain that you check with your broker and review your policy carefully to make sure that there are no gaps in coverage for your event. For example, if your event is using pyrotechnics and they are excluded specifically from your current coverage, you may wish to purchase additional coverage to protect your event. Often, especially during the Y2K period of 2000, a typical insurance exclusion included computer systems. Today, some policies may exclude terrorist acts. Make certain you carefully review all exclusions to eliminate any gaps in coverage. Terrorism insurance is not typically part of a special events insurance policy. In fact, most business policies—here, special events policies—specifically exclude terrorism from coverage. Terrorism insurance can be purchased, however, and is commonly offered as a special addition or endorsement to standard business policies. It is estimated that 60 percent of all U.S.-based businesses have some form of terrorism insurance policies (https://www.usrisk.com/2018/05/does-special-events-insurance-cover-terrorism/).

Preexisting Coverage Before purchasing any coverage, audit your existing coverage to check for gaps regarding your event. Your event organization may already have in force specific coverage related to the risks associated with your event. Once you have conducted this audit, your specialty insurance broker can advise you with regard to additional coverage for your event.

Risk Control

Theft Prevention The best strategy for theft prevention is segregation of duties. All transactions that involve cash handling, returns, and deposits should have at least two employees performing that transaction.

Cash Cash must be handled accurately. We encourage you to establish a special cash log, where all cash transactions should be recorded. Even small petty cash numbers add up to a substantial amount, so if you think that $20 cash expense is not worth recording, you are wrong; $20 per week turns into $1,080 per year. Anyone who handles cash should be given occasional unscheduled vacation days to check his or her cash-handling practice. While an employee is away, a replacement is in a very good position to catch all illegal activities set up by the employee.

Inventory One of the more important tools in preventing theft of inventory is incorporation of special procedures for inventory management. Storage facilities should be monitored. Two people should be involved in storage operations. All records of inventory disbursement should be stored and checked on a random basis. In a real-time computer system, inventory should have bar codes that have to be entered into the system as soon as inventory is disbursed.

As an event leader and supervisor, you should approve all equipment breakdowns and/or replacements. Management of event planning organizations should analyze the level of breakage that is typical for their operations. Any constant abnormalities should be investigated in more depth. Physical inventory counts should be taken regularly. Shortages should be reviewed, comparing them to acceptable loss levels.

Copyright Some planned events organizations have their brand names listed separately in their assets. This is an important part of their goodwill. Any event planning organization should protect its brand. Event professionals should consult copyright and intellectual property specialists to evaluate copyright areas where an organization can have potential problems. All brand names and logos of event organizations should contain clear copyright marks and warning statements. The universal symbol for copyrighted material is ©.

Trademark, Service Mark, and Registered Mark A trademark is a symbol used to indicate that the product or service is from a unique source and to distinguish it from other entities. The symbol ™ is an unregistered mark used to promote brands or brand products. The symbol (SM) is a service mark used to promote bands or brand services. Finally, the symbol ® is a registered mark for a registered product or service. Trademark is used to protect a type of intellectual property. For example, if your event name or logo (visual identity) is unique, you may wish to register it as an official trademark to protect it from being used by others without your permission.

Terrorism and Biochemical Risk Dr. Peter Tarlow, the author of *Event Risk Management and Safety* (2002), advises soberly, "It takes only small amounts of a biochemical substance to murder hundreds of people, including those in charge." He advises that personnel should know when to enter and when to avoid possibly contaminated areas, types of equipment to use, and what the signs of a biochemical attack might be.

SECUREVIEW

Global Peace Index (GPI) is an objective and comprehensive index of a country's safety for hosting global events. The GPI ranks 163 independent states and territories according to their level of peacefulness. Produced by the Institute for Economics and Peace (IEP), its report presents the most comprehensive data-driven analysis on trends in peace and its economic value. Three domains are measured to provide a quantified score of the state of peace. They include the level of Societal Safety and Security, the extent of Ongoing Domestic and International Conflict, and the degree of Militarization.

The 10-year trend in GPI shows that global peace has steadily decreased by 2.38 percent since 2008. According to the latest GPI report, the three most peaceful regions are Europe, North America, and Asia-Pacific. Iceland remains the most peaceful country in the world, a position it has been holding since 2008, followed by New Zealand, Austria, Portugal, and Denmark.

More details of GPI can be accessed at http://visionofhumanity.org/app/uploads/2018/06/Global-Peace-Index-2018-2.pdf.

Events are often considered soft targets for terrorists. A soft target is one that is easily penetrated due to many different vulnerabilities. Tarlow has identified eight reasons for the interaction between terrorism and events and why terrorists see them as soft targets:

1. Events are often close to major transportation centers.
2. Events are big business.
3. Events have an impact on other industries, such as restaurants, hotels, and entertainment.
4. Events draw media coverage.
5. Events require tranquility or places where business can be conducted in a peaceful manner.
6. Events must deal with people who have no history; thus, risk managers often do not have databases on delegates or attendees.
7. Events are based on a constant flow of guests; thus, it is hard to know who is and who is not a terrorist.
8. Events are the point where business and relaxation converge, and, therefore, guests often let down their guard.

Managing Risk: Everyone's Responsibility The field of event risk management has grown so rapidly that there is emerging a specialization within the profession for risk experts such as Alexander Berlonghi and others. Larger events, such as the Pope's visit to Colorado, may require a risk manager. However, for most events, the event manager is also the risk manager.

To improve your event operations, as the risk manager, you must assemble a risk-management team that will assist you in identifying and managing risks. You must communicate to all event stakeholders that event risk management is everyone's responsibility.

Attractive accreditation is required for all stakeholders working at your event.

Documentation, Discovery, and Disclosure Some members of the legal profession will caution event leaders about maintaining documentation of all risk procedures because they may be subpoenaed if there is an act of negligence associated with the event. However, it has been our experience as an expert witness at numerous trials where event leaders are accused to negligence that having sufficient documentation to demonstrate having met the minimum duty and standard of care will help reduce damages or even lead to a dismissal of the case.

Therefore, we recommend that event leaders document risk procedures and be prepared to surrender the following documents associated with the event if necessary:

1. Contracts
2. Organizational chart
3. Risk-assessment procedures and risk-management plans
4. Insurance policies and certificates
5. Budgets, if required, to demonstrate investment in risk-management recommendations

Although you may produce sufficient documentation of your good judgment and planning as well as actions before, during, and after the event, you and your event may still be subject to litigation. Therefore, the real test you must pass is one that is quite ancient and, some would suggest, even simple. Ask yourself, did you perform your event planning duties in a manner to not cause harm to others? If the answer is honestly and confidently affirmative, then you have succeeded in helping advance your profession and industry into the future, while simultaneously advancing through a new frontier that is expanding every day with newer and perhaps greater challenges. Many of these challenges will relate to your ethical decisions.

Differences among Morals, Laws, and Ethics

Etymologically, the term *moral* is derived from the Latin term *moralis*, which is related to the word *custom*, or right or wrong in terms of behavior. When, according to the Old Testament, the prophet Moses received the original 613 commandments, he may have also realized that, if he or his followers disobeyed, there would be individual consequences. Morals are personal and individual decisions that have personal consequences for right or wrong behavior. The legal system is a series of laws (many based on the Mosaic code) that are linked to specific punishments. Laws are enacted by groups, and punishment is imposed by peers (juries) or judges. Unlike morals, laws use third parties to enforce them and issue the punishment based on the degree of the violation. Professional ethics are, however, neither morals nor laws. Some argue that professional ethics incorporate both law and morals, but in actuality, ethics are the principles of conduct governing individuals or groups. These principles are based on the business culture that is accepted at the time of the action. Although ethics are personal decisions, they are guided by group behavior and group acceptance.

To better understand the interrelatedness of morals, laws, and ethics, ask yourself a series of questions. Let us start with a moral question: "Would you kill another person?" A moral person would immediately answer, "No, never." However, what if your children were being attacked by a violent person and the only way to stop the attack would be to kill the assailant? "Would you steal?" Once again most people would answer, "No." However, let us suppose that your children are starving and their very lives are threatened unless they receive some food to nourish them. Now what would you do?

"Would you attack someone?" Most of us would answer negatively. However, if your country was attacked, and you were part of the army that must defend your nation, you would answer in the affirmative or face serious punishment.

As you can see, many moral questions also have legal and ethical repercussions. Most of us will not be confronted on a daily basis with serious moral or legal decisions; however, many members of this profession regularly face serious ethical dilemmas.

Common Ethical Challenges in the Special Events Industry

Ethical problems often vary according to type of industry and geographic location. In the special events industry, some ethical problems faced by hoteliers may or may not affect those in the party rental industry. The same may be said about the event leader in Brazil versus the event leader in the United States. For example, in the United States, the person who pours the alcohol may be legally responsible if a person being served overindulges and causes injury to others. In Brazil, just the opposite is true. The legal system of Brazil places the responsibility on the drinker rather than on the server. This has important ethical ramifications. If you are serving alcohol in Brazil, is it ethical to allow your guests to drink until they are inebriated and capable of causing injury to others? As you can see, the type of industry (or industry segment) and the geographic location often dictate the customs, practices, and values that are practiced by members of that community. These customs, practices, and values of the industry and local culture often drive the ethical decision-making within the event organization.

Numerous typical ethical issues are addressed on a regular basis by members of the planned events industry. Figure 8.3 in the electronic appendices lists some of the ethical issues that you will encounter most often.

Avoiding or Addressing Ethical Problems

The proactive methods described in Figure 8.3 illustrate some of the simple and practical steps that you can take to avoid the pitfalls of unethical behavior. Realistically, you cannot predict every ethical dilemma that may arise. You can, however, be prepared to resolve these problems with a proven three-step process: admission, remorse, and correction.

Despite your best efforts to avoid ethical misconduct, you can always recognize the mistake and notify the person or persons who may have been affected and tell them, "I made a mistake. I'm sorry. I will try not to let it happen again." Too often, individuals and organizations attempt to avoid confronting the problem of ethical misconduct, and the misdeed festers like a wound that never heals. From the highest office in the land to local places of worship, most of us know far too many examples of ethical violations that are swept under the rug with the supposition that they will go unnoticed. Despite the rug, these ethical infractions continue to smell, and the small lump under the rug may grow and trip others in the future unless you address the problem promptly.

There are numerous successful examples of the three-step process for handling the problem of ethical violations. This is why it is important that you and your organization develop policies, procedures, and practices to address ethical issues when they arise. One of the best examples of professional handling of a major ethical situation is the 1982 Tylenol tampering incident. Johnson & Johnson, the maker of Tylenol, immediately withdrew the product from all shelves world-wide and issued a statement describing its plans for researching the problem and improving the safety measures for its products. As a result of its response, Johnson & Johnson received plaudits from the media and customers, and sales remain strong today.

How did Johnson & Johnson know to respond to this ethical issue? The Johnson & Johnson credo states in the first paragraph that its company exists for the purpose of providing safe products and services: "We believe that our first responsibility is to the doctors, nurses and patients, to mothers and fathers and all others who use our products and services." You can create your own credo to guide you as you face the many ethical decisions you will encounter in your career. Important facets of the Johnson & Johnson credo are the statements: "We must constantly strive to reduce our costs . . . We must be good citizens. . . ." These statements not only reflect the credo of the organization but also address the operational aspects to enable managers and other employees to make decisions on a daily basis that are congruent with the values of Johnson & Johnson. When you draft your credo, make certain that it is more than cold type on a page; instead, it should burn like a branding iron into the hearts and minds of all persons who are responsible for serving as the stewards of your organization's good name. One of the many ways that Johnson & Johnson communicated its strong ethical message was through a series of internal events produced by one of the leading firms in the industry: Jack Morton Worldwide (www.jackmorton.com).

According to Bill Morton, chairman of Jack Morton Worldwide, "We were given a very small window to develop and produce these events. However, Johnson & Johnson entrusted us with their brand because of our long relationship with them. And ultimately, we were successful, despite the short time frame for development and production." Jack Morton Worldwide also has a strong credo that is based on integrity. It is a credo first solidified by the founder Jack Morton in 1939. And this is one of many reasons why the Athens, Greece, Olympic Games Organizing Committee (ATHOC) selected Jack Morton Worldwide to produce the opening and closing ceremonies of the 2004 Summer Olympic Games.

Nearly 50 years ago, Joe's father opened his small hardware store in Dallas, Texas. Instead of hanging a grand opening banner or blowing up balloons, he sat down and composed a simple but profound message to his customers. The message was then transformed into elegant calligraphy and displayed just inside the front door of his store, where it greeted customers for almost 50 years. As Joe write these lines, that message faces him, and it reads:

> *Once upon a time, I met a stranger . . . not so many years ago . . . in a distant city. When he learned that he knew my grandfather, the stranger looked at me and said, "You have a good name." He went on to explain that my grandfather held the respect and esteem of his fellow businessmen, his customers bestowed their confidence upon him, and his compassion and service for others was an inspiration to all. It is the hope of this business that we will so conduct our affairs that someday, somewhere one of our descendants will meet a stranger who will say, "You have a good name."*

> —*Max B. Goldblatt (1911–1995)*

Establishing Policies and Procedures for Ethical Issues

The Code of Ethics of the International Special Events Society (ISES) is one example of how an industry establishes standards for ethical behavior. Some ways to avoid or resolve many of the issues within the code of ethics follow:

- Do not accept expensive gifts. Ban or set a financial limit on gifts from vendor partners or clients.
- Avoid confusion regarding a change in an agreement. Put all agreements (and changes) in writing and have both parties' initial acceptance.
- Avoid improper promotion of your services. Seek written authority while working for another event leader.
- Avoid claiming credit for an event you produced while working for another firm. Clearly disclose the circumstances concerning the production of the event.
- Avoid submitting photos of an event as an example of your work. Clearly disclose that you helped produce your specific contributions to this event. Figure 8.3 in the electronic appendices describes some typical event industry ethical issues and proactive measures you may take to minimize disruption for your event.

Inclusiveness Is an Ethical Responsibility

Perhaps one day the ISES Code of Ethics will be further amended to reflect the growing importance of promoting and achieving diversity and inclusiveness within event organizations. The statistics in the event industry reflect that women continue to outnumber men. What is not evident unless you attend industry conventions is that the percentage of minorities is relatively small as compared to the general population. While many industry organizations have made significant strides in promoting minority participation at the top level of their organizations, many minorities still prefer to form their own independent organizations that may more closely address their own needs and issues.

In the late 1990s, the Washington, D.C., chapter of ISES (now ILEA) held its annual awards event at the television studios of Black Entertainment Television. As a result of this decision, the percentage of African Americans attending this event was much greater than that in previous years.

This is one example of how traditional members of this profession must rethink their locations, programming choices, and other considerations to promote and achieve diversity and inclusiveness. Without diversity and inclusiveness within our events, they and the entire profession will not be as successful and may, in fact, fail to be sustainable. While looking through ILEA's website, the local chapter events show a focus on a more diverse audience, including the millennial crowd. Every living system requires diversity to ensure sustainability. The event industry is no different. Through active and effective programs promoting diversity and inclusiveness, you can expand your event market rapidly. To do this effectively, you must regularly look beyond your own sphere of knowledge to find out what you are missing.

For example, although in 1999, nearly 25 percent of the students in The George Washington University Event Management Program were African American females, no photographs of African American females appeared in the catalog used to promote the program. When an African American staff member brought this to Joe's attention, Joe wondered what other groups might also be underrepresented. In 2019 (20 years later), we can inform you that the program brochure does in fact represent a diverse crowd: old, young, black, white, Hispanic, and Asian, and mostly women.

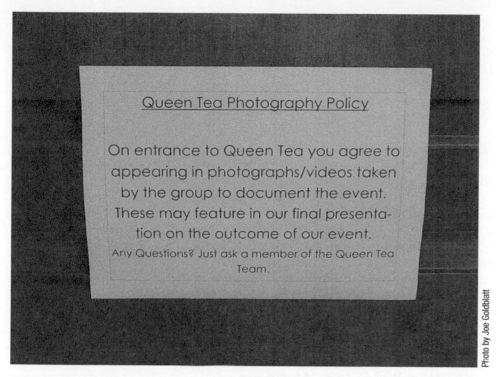

Photography requires informed consent from participants at this Queen Margaret University student event as demonstrated by this sign at the entrance.

As Gene Columbus, the longtime manager of entertainment casting for Walt Disney World, stated, it is time for event leaders to ensure "places for everyone" and make certain that every possible opportunity is developed within the events industry to create a future that is both inclusive and representative of the diversity within the new world of events. Figure 8.4 in electronic appendices demonstrates how to incorporate persons with different abilities into your event.

Identifying and Using Industry Ethical Guidelines

In addition to the ILEA, many related industry organizations use guidelines for professional practice or ethical beliefs to guide decision-making. One criterion that you may wish to use for joining a professional organization is whether it has established a strong code of ethics, along with appropriate enforcement procedures. Although these guidelines are at best guideposts rather than firm edicts, they will be useful not only to you but also to your clients as they raise the image of your profession.

Appointing an Ethical Brain Trust to Guide Your Ethical Decision-Making

We have always relied on wise counselors and advisors to help us when faced with making a difficult ethical decision. Instead of assembling this brain trust at the last minute or on a case-by-case basis, we recommend that you identify people who know you well enough to provide you with critical input during times of ethical decision-making.

According to the *Washington Post*, the Washington, D.C., Millennium-Bicentennial Celebration in 2000 resulted in $290,500 in unpaid bills. The *Post* also reported that there were questions of ethics violations. The District of Columbia established a not-for-profit organization for the purpose of raising funds to plan and coordinate the millennium and bicentennial celebrations for the District. However, there were questions about whether the organization used DC government employees to raise money for the event.

Polly A. Rich, at that time the ethics counselor in the District of Columbia corporation counsel's office, wrote in a memo that city employees should not raise money for nonprofits or solicit contributions from companies and individuals who do business in the District. Anthony W. Williams, former mayor of the District of Columbia, responded to the criticism by stating: "Clearly, the lesson from the millennium-bicentennial events and the loss of a substantial amount of money from a lot of this nonprofit fund-raising is: 'What is the proper mechanism to do it?'" The question of appropriateness is not solely moral or legal but also an ethical dilemma that every event leader must address.

Furthermore, the event leader must realize that his or her event is only as good as its ability to include everyone in the process. Therefore, it is critically important that event leaders carefully analyze their board, planning committee, volunteers, and staff to ensure that they have attempted to include as many diverse opinions and groups as possible.

Including Everyone: Arranging and Organizing Activities

Many events use tours and other off-site visits to expand the educational value of the program. Other events regularly incorporate tours of the destination and its attractions to provide guests with added value. Finally, some event organizers incorporate tours to offer diversions for accompanying persons, such as spouses, partners, friends, or young people attending with their parents. Regardless of the reason, increasingly, the arrangement and organization of tours is a critical component of most conferences, conventions, reunions, and even weddings.

There are three steps to consider when planning and coordinating tours for your event:

1. You must conduct an audit of the destination to determine if there are attractions or activities that are of interest to your guests. You can obtain this information from the local convention and visitors' association or from the chamber of commerce. Make certain that you ask the providers of this information which programs are most appropriate for specific market segments (females, males, children, mature guests, etc.).

2. Use this research to begin to assess the interest levels of your prospective guests with a brief survey of their interests. If you can match their strong interests with the best attractions and activities in the destination, you are well on your way to finding a winning combination guaranteed to increase attendance and produce excellent reviews.

3. Find a price point that will be acceptable to your guests and perhaps provide excess revenues for your organization. To do this, you will need to obtain bids from local providers. In many destinations, a for-profit organization known as a Destination Management Company (DMC) provides tour services. These services are generally priced on a per-person basis and require a minimum number of participants to operate the program successfully.

In addition to tours, the DMC may provide services such as planning and coordinating local transportation, receptions, parties, and other events within your large event, as well as a wide range of other services. Outside the United States, the term *Professional Congress Organizer* (PCO) is often used to refer to DMCs. The PCO generally provides an even greater range of services than the DMC. In addition to tours and events, the PCO may provide travel bookings, marketing of the event, and registration services, among many other services.

Two organizations represent the top DMC and PCO organizations. In the United States, the Association of Destination Management Executives (ADME) represents the leading destination management companies, and in Europe, the International Association of Professional Congress Organizers (IAPCO) represents the most respected PCO firms.

Developing Special Events within Events

The event professional is often required to organize numerous individual events within a larger special event. In fact, this is so prevalent that the certified special events professional programs require that candidates understand and be able to coordinate accompanying person events, tours, and other auxiliary programs related to special event management. Typical activities that often help form the context of a larger special event are shown in Figure 8.5 in the electronic appendices.

You must assess, through research, how the internal or external events will support the overall goals and objectives of the total event. These events should be seen as the frame of a large umbrella. Each spoke or event must carefully support the individual objectives of the overall event. If any one event is poorly planned or weakly coordinated, the entire structure may weaken. Therefore, you should conduct an audit of typical event guests, as well as those who are atypical and nonattendees, to determine their interests, needs, wants, and desires. This data can be very helpful in determining which events to offer and during which times they will be most popular.

Once the audit is completed, you will usually contact a third party, such as an entertainment, production, or other professional company, to obtain proposals to present the type of event or attraction that is required. Make certain that you encourage the proposers to use their creativity to develop your event ideas further. For example, a game show requested by a major corporation became a special event when the game company supplier suggested a hostess who was a U.S. television game show *Wheel of Fortune* Vanna White look-alike and a set that reflected the popular game show *Wheel of Fortune*. The creativity of others can quickly embellish your event design and bring added value without additional cost. Figure 8.4 in the electronic appendices describes a wide range of ancillary programs you may wish to incorporate within your event.

The final consideration when selecting the events that will compose your larger event is to confirm the reliability of the vendor-partners. Too often, event organizations driven by committees will develop extraordinary ideas with ordinary budgets and resources. It is much better to select those event elements that will bring high quality and consistent excellence to your event than to stretch the event to the breaking point. To confirm the reliability of individual vendors, it is best to inspect the event during operation before a similar group of guests or to seek references from organizers of events that are similar to the one you are producing.

Clearly marked egress (exit) ways are essential for effective way finding, as shown at the Edinburgh Moonwalk, where 10,000 participants raised nearly one million dollars for breast cancer research.

Organizing and Conducting Spouse and Partner Programs

One of the key competencies in the coordination knowledge domain of the certified special events professional program is the organization and coordination of spouse and partner programs. The term *spouse* is actually somewhat antiquated and has been replaced with the term *accompanying person* to reflect the broader spectrum of persons who are attending an event with the invited guest. The actual taxonomy of the guest list is:

1. Delegate or principal invitee or guest (often this person is eligible to vote if there is a need for the election of officers or amending the constitution of the sponsoring organization)
2. Guest of principal invitee or accompanying person (usually a nonvoting attendee)
3. Observer (usually nonvoting attendee)

The accompanying person may have a wide range of interests that must be satisfied during the overall event experience. Typically, the accompanying person will be invited to all social events with the principal invitee, delegate, or guest. In addition, special programming as discussed earlier may be organized to provide diversions while the delegate, principal invitee, or guest is involved in official functions, such as education, governance (debate, discussion, elections), or other similar activities that generally are not of interest to the accompanying person.

The event leader must strike a balance between diverting the accompanying person and totally disengaging him or her from the basic goals and objectives of the overall event. To ensure that the accompanying person is fully engaged and recognized, the person should be identified through credentials as a guest, accompanying person, or observer. In addition, an orientation program should be organized at the beginning of a conference or other multiday event to help accompanying persons to understand the opportunities available during the larger event, as well as to make them feel welcome and answer any pertinent questions.

The accompanying person very often influences the principal guest or delegate as to whether or not to return to an event year after year, so it is critically important that this person has an excellent experience that is equal to, although different from, that of the person he or she is accompanying. To monitor the experience, it is important that accompanying persons be surveyed directly or through a focus group to thoroughly analyze their event experience to allow you to improve your practice continually in the future.

Complying with the Americans with Disabilities Act and Similar International Laws and Regulations

It is projected that the number of persons in North America with disabilities will grow exponentially in the next several years as the baby boomers show natural signs of the aging process. As a result, the large number of persons with visual, auditory, and physical disabilities will significantly affect the research, planning, design, and coordination phases of twenty-first-century event planning.

During the research phase, the event leader must assess the types of disabilities that are most likely to be reflected by event participants. These important data may be obtained through historical information or through a survey of potential guests. Research will include learning about individual disabilities in order to best prepare for and serve the population that will be attending your event.

The design phase enables the event leader to work closely with the disabled community to determine the services and accommodations that must be implemented to ensure the comfort and satisfaction of all guests. During the design phase, many creative solutions may be suggested by members of the disabled population to help the event organizer satisfy his or her needs with little or no additional investment.

During the planning and coordination phases, the event leader fine-tunes the recommendations proposed by the disabled community and works with event vendors and staff to implement the best ideas to achieve the best outcomes for the overall event. These two phases should include the identification of contingency plans for serving disabled individuals who were not identified previously but must be accommodated once they arrive at the event. Figure 8.6 in the electronic appendices provides guidance on configuring a parking lot that is accessible.

Ensuring accessibility for all at an annual agricultural fair in the Yucatan, Mexico.

Joe Goldblatt abseils 300 feet from the Forth Rail Bridge to the ground to raise money for chest, heart, and stroke research and care in Scotland. Events such as this one require extensive safety protocols.

Future Trends in CSR

In 2009, six event management students from Queen Margaret University in Edinburgh, Scotland, traveled to New Orleans, Louisiana, to attend the Professional Convention Management Association's (PCMA) annual conference. The students, with financial support from VisitScotland, the national tourism agency, agreed to help rebuild and renovate one of the historic cemeteries in New Orleans that had been badly damaged by Hurricane Katrina.

Although the students arrived at midnight the previous evening, they promptly reported for duty at 8 A.M. to help restore the cemetery. Their duties included sanding and repainting the historic and ornate gates to this sacred burial ground. During their work, several local residents approached them and offered them local coffee and drinks to thank them for the efforts they were expending to help rebuild their city.

Why did the students decide to do this work? The simple answer is their personal and collective sense of responsibility. However, in fact they were part of a group of several hundred PCMA volunteers that annually provide assistance to the destinations where their annual convention is held. The PCMA Hospitality Helping Hands, a Network for the Needy program, began in 1990 as a simple program to donate food leftover from conventions to needy individuals. In the past two decades, the program has expanded to include projects such as the one that greatly benefited the city of New Orleans.

When asked why the students chose personally to participate, they said that after seeing the devastation that resulted from Hurricane Katrina, they felt like they must do something to help. For many of the students, it was their first trip to the United States. Not only did this opportunity to volunteer make a great impression on the students, but their work was featured in the local newspaper and on television, as well as in business industry reports.

The concept of corporate social responsibility (CSR) actually may have been first defined by the Scottish philosopher Adam Smith in the eighteenth century, when he stated in his classic work *The Wealth of Nations* that work, if performed ethically, would result in personal and collective gain. He further stated that the person conducting the work was a steward of the organization and of society as well.

Geoffrey P. Lantos states that there are five critical CSR activities for hospitality managers and these must be supported by top management. These strategic activities include:

1. *Clearly communicating with stockholders.* State the causes that they support in investment prospectuses, annual reports, and other corporate communications and provide a breakout of the costs and benefits of various CSR efforts. This will give potential and current investors "informed consent" in deciding to purchase shares.
2. *Investing time and money in good employee relations.* The firm benefits from more dedicated employees, less turnover of staff, and workers advocating for the firm.
3. *Investing in social programs that support the local community.* The returns include patronage by local shoppers and a steady stream of good workers recruited through employee-training programs. For example, Victorguard, a UK care home operator, used a local recruitment strategy during construction of a new home. Not only was good publicity obtained from recruiting local unemployed people, but the approach also helped to almost eliminate vandalism and theft during the construction period.

4. *Philanthropic giving, which should be viewed as a type of investment from which the corporation can expect a future return.* The firm will get the most bang for its altruistic buck if it supports causes that relate closely to its mission and core competencies and that are of interest to its target market. For instance, Avon, whose primary target market is women, sponsors Breast Cancer Crusade, whereby breast cancer education and early detection services are offered to low-income, minority, and elderly women for a nominal charge or even gratis. Avon believes that this has resulted in sales spikes and more enthusiastic support among the firm's female sales force.

5. *Sponsoring worthy causes.* For example, Walt Disney's sponsorship of the Special Olympics has helped boost its image as a family-friendly company (Lantos, 2013).

However, Lantos and others further recognize that since the Industrial Revolution, although business has been focused on economic generation, its responsibilities have expanded to serve the other interests of greater society. Prior to the 1960s, in North America and other parts of the world, ethics was not widely discussed in the business literature. In the 1960s and 1970s, society began, especially through human resources and consumer action, to place greater responsibilities on corporations to become stewards of greater society.

Despite these pressures, and the resulting changes that brought about mission, vision, and values statements from thousands of corporations, many businesses continued to suffer from public distrust. The business literature is filled with tragic case studies of once formidable and well-respected corporate citizens such as Arthur Andersen LLC, Enron, Lehman Brothers, and many others whose public statements regarding CSR did not accurately reflect their private actions.

Therefore, you may ask, how does a special events organization for the next generation and new frontier ensure that these mistakes of the past are not repeated? One way to do this is to establish a strong credo for your organization and then let this credo serve as your guide for strategic planning as well as day-to-day decision-making.

Johnson & Johnson, the global health care products company, created the credo shown in Figure 8.7 in the electronic appendices, over 60 years ago, and it is still used today to ensure that the company does not veer from its original values.

According to Johnson & Johnson officials, the credo serves as a strong moral compass. It was crafted by the former chairman of their firm, Robert Wood Johnson, in 1943, before the company went public and before the term *CSR* entered the business lexicon. Does your special events organization have a credo?

Why Is CSR Important in the Special Events Industry?

According to the *CSR Monitor*, in wealthy countries, individuals make their purchasing decisions based upon their perception of the level of CSR exhibited by corporations. This report also states that, in North America alone, 42 percent of individuals who do not practice CSR will be punished by customers who will take their business elsewhere. In North America, customers who support corporations with strong social responsibility programs are called *conventional activists,* and in Europe they are referred to as *demanding disgruntleds* (www.bsdglobal.com).

It may be argued that since the first traders crossed the great trade routes of Europe, practicing strong CSR behavior has not only been good for society but also good for business. In fact, that has long been the argument within certain business sectors. Many business leaders and philosophers such as Adam Smith agree that businesses that do not look out for the greater good of society cannot expect society to look out for them.

How You May Contribute to the Evolution of CSR with Your Future Events

According to Silberhorn and Warren, CSR is a comprehensive business strategy arising mainly from performance considerations and stakeholder pressure. Companies focus on how they interact with stakeholders and how business activities affect society. Therefore, all CSR efforts must be ultimately focused on performance (Silberhorn and Warren 2007).

One example of how disconnects between plan and performance often develop within business sectors is the information technology (IT) sector. According to Citizens Online, only one in six IT firms based in the United Kingdom support Internet activities for the disadvantaged. Furthermore, the same group identified in a study of more than 200 UK IT firms that although many firms criticize the poor philanthropy record of IT firms, most consider it fair to cut charitable giving if there is a downturn in turnover profits (Citizens Online 2001).

This is why you must recognize your core responsibilities as a member of the special events sector with regard to CSR. Sustainable development, responsible stewardship, and legacy building are key indicators for you to demonstrate not only your commitment but also your performance in each of these important areas.

Sustainable development is a term that describes development that meets the needs of the present without compromising the ability of future generations to meet their own needs. For example, when conducting a festival in a pasture, you may wish to reseed the grass at the end of the event to sustain growth in the future. In the area of human resources, you may wish to develop succession plans to ensure the special events organization will continue to operate even more efficiently in the future.

Responsible stewardship requires that you serve as a responsible custodian of the scarce resources you are using to produce your event. For example, from an environmental standpoint, ask yourself how you may reduce waste through the use of recycling systems. Conserving water, energy, electricity, and paper are all basic ways to promote responsible stewardship of your resources.

Legacy building is critically important for many destinations in the bidding process for events. London 2012 won the bid to host the International Olympic Games by presenting a strong legacy strategy to improve the social cohesion, health, sports participation, and other key performance indicators(KPIs) of the people who live in the neighborhoods where the 2012 Olympic Games were conducted. While other destinations focused upon their infrastructure, their natural beauty, and even the celebrities who endorsed their bids, London trumped all of them by focusing on the legacy of the Olympic Games. What is the legacy for your event? Will you improve the community as exemplified by PCMA's Helping Hands project in New Orleans? Figure 8.8 in the electronic appendices describes the seven economic duties of CSR for managers.

Monitor Changing Social Expectations

The expectations of generations Y and X are far different from those of the baby boomers. Do you have a plan for monitoring these changing expectations? The use of social media networking sites such as Twitter, Facebook, and others can provide you with macro social inputs. By developing a pre-event blog for your event, you can monitor in a very specific way what is in the hearts and minds of your future guests and then adapt your CSR plan to meet their expectations and needs. Rarely does a CSR plan succeed without the central buy-in of those who will be most invested. Therefore, it is important to continually monitor your core stakeholders to design and deliver programs that they are passionate about. For example, the city of Copenhagen, Denmark, has a series of programs designed to raise awareness about the plight of the homeless in their city and other destinations throughout Europe. Through sponsoring events such as a homeless football match and a homeless sculpture tour, they are not only raising funds but also awareness to address the problem of homelessness in their city and others as well. Can your next event not only entertain but also engage your publics in helping mitigate or even eliminate some of society's greatest social problems, such as homelessness?

Use the Internet to Expand Your Event's Global Social Influence

Generations X and Y are often characterized as the first completely wired workforce of tomorrow. In fact, these generations are wireless. Many cities throughout the world, including Philadelphia, Pennsylvania, are investing in Wi-Fi systems to enable wireless Internet access from almost any location throughout the city. This mobility may provide you and your staff and volunteers with new and unique opportunities to influence millions of others throughout the world. Figure 8.9 in the electronic appendices lists 10 ways to use the Internet to further promote CSR through your event.

Secure the Commitment of Your Clients, Vendors, and Sponsors to Promote Socially Responsible Events

The anthropologist Margaret Meade once remarked, "Never doubt that a small group of thoughtful, committed citizens can change the world: Indeed, it's the only thing that ever has." Your small group of clients, vendors, and sponsors should join you in aligning their activities with your CSR program.

Identify and Liaise with CSR Counterparts in Government, Nongovernmental, and Other Stakeholders

The more stakeholders you have involved in your event, the more likely you are to achieve your specified outcomes. When involving others, remember the key success factors listed in Figure 8.10.

1. Involve others in the development of these programs, and make certain your final plan matches their needs and receives their firm support.
2. Conduct research to find the natural linkages between what you want to accomplish and what others are already doing. Do not duplicate—rather, improve efficiency and reach by partnering with others.
3. Establish a system for mutually communicating your messages to all publics.
4. Establish an evaluation plan to let your partners and others know how you achieved success through your CSR program.
5. Share your success with others. Prepare a brief post-event report case study describing how you created your CSR program and activities and how these could be improved in the future.

FIGURE 8.10 Five key success factors for involving others in your CSR programs.

Ensure That Your CSR Influence Is Felt Both Internally and Externally

One of the major mistakes many corporations made in the twenty-first century is that they failed to share with their own employees, vendors, and other stakeholders the influence of their CSR programs and activities. Unless those inside as well as outside of your organization are aware of your aims, objectives, and outcomes, participation may be lacking. You may wish to develop an internal and external strategy to involve stakeholders—or in small organizations, your goals may be satisfied by combining these strategies.

First, it is important that you have support and strong buy-in at the top of your event organization. Make certain your CEO (chief event officer), board chairman, board members, and other stewards of your organizations support your approach and activities. Next, turn your attention to key sponsors and vendors and solicit not only their endorsement but also their support. Your sponsors may be delighted to raise their community relations profile through participating in your CSR program. Furthermore, your vendors may already be involved in a CSR program and may offer you invaluable advice and support.

Second, consider reducing your discussion to a formal written treatise, such as a manifesto that is signed by all parties to formalize your partnership. Finally, and most importantly, regularly update your internal and external partners regarding your plans, activities, and progress. This may be done through e-mail, a Web page, or even informal, periodic in-person meetings.

Measure and Evaluate Your Event's Social Responsibility Index

In order to manage your corporate responsibility performance, you must constantly measure your activities and your results. Measuring CSR may be simple, such as measuring the volume of recycling you have achieved from year to year at your event, or complex, such as measuring how your employees, volunteers, and others feel about their role in your program. Regardless of how you choose to measure your results, it is important that you set general or specific KPIs for each area of your CSR program, and then select the appropriate tools to measure these outcomes. Figure 8.11 lists the most common areas to measure in CSR

Outcomes	Measurement
Environmental: Recycling	Measure volume increase.
Social: Cohesion	Measure post-event increase in online community activity.
Education: New skills	Measure increase in job performance.
Health: Wellness activity participation	Measure increased physical fitness activities.
Economic: Fairness	Measure increase in dispersion of economic influence of your event throughout various sectors and communities.

FIGURE 8.11 Special event CSR outcomes and measurement strategies.

programs and the tools you may use to provide valid and reliable results for wider distribution.

Measuring your CSR performance through a comprehensive index not only allows you to see where improvement is required but also lets you track from year to year the success you are achieving and to share this good news with external stakeholders such as the media to further improve the profile of your event.

Create Socially Responsible Programs for Conventions, Festivals, Meetings, and Other Events

Although the special events industry comprises many sectors, many would agree that conventions, festivals, and meetings represent three of the largest in terms of total attendance. Figure 8.12 in the electronic appendices lists examples of best practices in CSR in each of these sectors.

Conduct Social Responsibility Orientation and Training Programs for Your Event Staff and Volunteers

To be fully engaged in your CSR programs, your staff and volunteers must first be informed, then understand, become better educated, and then become committed to the ideals of your program. The information and understanding phase begins with a comprehensive orientation program that may include first an online e-mail message that links to a website. This could later be followed up with an in-person meeting at which you show a video of the benefiting organization. Finally, training should be provided to educate your staff and volunteers. This could also be provided through the Internet or in person, and there should also be an assessment component to let your participants know that they are able to fully benefit from their engagement in your program.

Special Events and Human Rights

Dr. Rebecca Finkel of Queen Margaret University is the author of *Human Rights and Global Events* (2014). Her research provides strong arguments that special events are no longer viewed solely as activities to be produced and consumed as ritually repeated activities, but can, in certain geographic and sociocultural contexts, contribute to violations of the Universal Declaration of Human Rights. In order to comprehend the complete picture of global events and fully examine the linkages between globalization processes and global events, it is necessary to look at all aspects, including the less salubrious practices often associated with the bright spectacles.

For example, many mega-events such as the Summer and Winter Olympic Games attract a disproportionate number of sex trafficking-related businesses that provide illegal services due to the demand from tourists as well as athletes. Dr. Finkel's research examines the political and social impacts of these activities and seeks to identify strategies for event leaders to anticipate and mitigate these potential negative occurrences before, during, and following the special event.

According to Finkel (2014), event managers hold much more power than they may think. By working with governments, local communities, and other organizations, they hold the power to be agents of social change at host destinations. This can be for positive social change, such as improving the lives of the people at the host destination through short-term involvement in the event and long-term investment in communities. Or, it can be for negative social change, such as turning a blind eye to human rights abuses such as displacement, corruption, and criminal activity, which can often be the result of development for the event. As more developing countries host mega-events, there is more potential for both human rights abuses and human rights advancements (2014), and event managers need to take responsibility for the power they possess by being accountable to host communities before, during, and after the event has taken place.

Promote Your Socially Responsible Outcomes to Others

Although it seems that the news media only desires to report negative stories to the general public, in fact, most news outlets allot time for feature stories such as your good news resulting from the CSR program. One way to help ensure this future coverage is to identify a media partner or partners who will help you develop public service announcements and provide free advertising space to promote your activities.

The consumer media is just one of many outlets you may use to promote your activities. You should also consider providing photos to your event stakeholders, a short fact sheet and a link to the charity benefiting from your activities so they can promote your event to their friends, family, and business associates. It is not unlikely that each of your 1,000 event volunteers, vendors, or sponsors has 200 friends and family that they may contact through e-mail. Therefore, if you give them the good news to share with others, they may reach over two million people!

Finally, it is important that you develop a comprehensive post-event communications plan for your CSR program to inform, educate, and persuade multiple publics about your activities. This type of publicity is indeed priceless, although it may be measured through comparable advertising valuation. The best advertising of all is the reputational advantage you will gain by not only producing high-quality events enjoyed by many. You may also, in a small way, improve the world with every new guest experience.

INSIGHTS FROM GLOBAL EVENT LEADERS

Frank Supovitz, President & CEO
Fast Traffic Events & Entertainment

For more than 30 years, award-winning event producer Frank Supovitz has been at the helm of some of the world's most prestigious, widely-viewed and well-attended sports and entertainment events. He who previously served as Senior Vice President, Events for National Football League (NFL), founded Fast Traffic Events & Entertainment in 2014, an event management and consulting company based in New York. He provides event, entertainment, and experience management and consulting services to world-class brands including The South Street Seaport, Indianapolis Motor Speedway, Pro Football Hall of Fame, BIG EAST Conference, Milwaukee Bucks, and National Rugby League (Australia). what went wrong/right and what we learn from them.

Q: Are we in a new era of risk management for mega events (shootings, cyber terror, etc.)?

A: Without question, we are in a new era of risk preparedness and management. That's why an event organizer like me was the natural choice to write a book on crisis management called *What to Do When Things Go Wrong* (McGraw-Hill, 2019). Events that attract any combination of masses of people, media, and broadcasters are regrettably attractive target-rich environments for those who mean to do harm. Now, with everyone's mobile phones with instant access to social platforms, getting publicity for a disturbance doesn't even require traditional media.

With guest and participant safety as the most important, nonnegotiable responsibility for any event organizer, a heightened focus on safety and security has become essential.

Q: How to train event staff for risk management and emergency planning?

A: One of the key lessons in *What to Do When Things Go Wrong* is the notion that every event staff member you empower is an early-warning system to identify problems and take responsibility for either fixing them or reporting them to someone who can. I often print a hotline or text number on the back of event credentials that staff members are encouraged to use to report anything that is wrong, out of the ordinary, or something they need help with. I also encourage staff to not just observe that something has gone wrong, but to either take steps that can fix the problem without endangering them, or to share that information with their supervisor. It doesn't have to be directly related to their job. It can be literally anything that looks wrong or suspicious.

Staff need to know what they need to do if there is an emergency. Expecting everyone to know the whole plan is not reasonable. If they need to go somewhere to help guests, they simply need to know where to go and specifically what to do.

And, they need to know where to go if there is an evacuation because we need to make sure they are out of danger.

Q: Global sporting mega-event planning: any difference when hosting one abroad?

A: Every country has different standards, rules, and laws relating to events. The custom in some countries allows gambling in their stadiums, it is illegal in others. Some allow secondary ticket sales, and others do not. For safety and security measures, some European football (soccer) stadiums control who sits in what sections of the venue to make sure that fans of one team are not intermixed with fans of the other. That makes game day sales difficult or unfeasible. Know the sports and entertainment cultures of every nation you plan events in.

Summary

Chapter 8 provided you with the knowledge required to assess, analyze, plan, manage, and control the risks associated with your special event. In addition, you have learned how to apply ethical decision-making to typical special event challenges. Finally, the concepts of CSR were examined and applied to modern event management to make certain that every event you produce in the future could, in fact, help change the world. Event leaders should possess the latest information on risk assessment, planning, and management for events. They include, but are not limited to, accreditation, establishing the balance between secure systems and guest comfort, and the use of technology in promoting safer and more secure events. This chapter also shared new material regarding how global events require global visions and strategies for inclusivity.

Key Terms

Corporate social responsibility (CSR): The strategic process through which the event organization determines how each event may build social and environmental capital and produce positive social, economic, and environmental impacts.

Ethics: The gray areas that too often result in problems for event leaders and their organization's reputation due to poor planning and decisions. Ethics may inform laws but are not always subject to legal tests. However, they must be carefully considered to build a positive reputation for the event leader.

Health and safety: The requirement that event leaders meet the standard of care customarily associated with providing a healthy and safe outcome with every special event.

Risk Management: Identifying, assessing, analyzing, planning, managing and controlling the typical risks associated with your event.

Career Connections

Review the published code of ethics for planned events-related organizations (see the ISES principles of professional conduct and ethics in the electronic appendices) and ask experienced event leaders how they interpret these guidelines within their everyday event planning processes. Review the corporate social responsibility plans of several corporations who plan or sponsor events and discuss with their human resources staff how you could best incorporate them into a future event you might plan for them. Discuss with an experienced event professional how he or she makes ethical decisions related to everyday event challenges.

Next Steps

1. Conduct a thorough risk assessment and create a health and safety plan for your event.

2. Develop corporate social responsibility guidelines for your event organization.

3. Create ethical decision-making policies for your event.

References

Berlonghi, A. (1990) *The Special Event Risk Management Manual*, Dana Point, CA: Berlonghi.

Finkel, R. (2014) *Human Rights and Global Events*, London: Routledge.

Goldberg, J. (1996) *The Meeting Planners Legal Handbook*, Washington, D.C.: Goldberg & Associates.

ILSR (2019, January 09) Billboard bans and controls, accessed May 2019: https://ilsr.org/rule/billboard-bans-and-controls/.

Lantos, G. (2013) Ethics based marketing: Corporate socialism unethically masquerades as "corporate social responsibility," accessed June 10, 2013: http://www.ethicsbasedmarketing.net/11.html.

Silberhorn, D. and Warren, R. (2007) Defining corporate social responsibility: A view from big companies in Germany and the UK, *European Business Review*, Vol. 19 Iss: 5, pp. 352–372.

Supovitz, F. (2019) *What to Do When Things Go Wrong: A Five-Step Guide to Planning for and Surviving the Inevitable—And Coming Out Ahead*, New York: McGraw-Hill Education.

Tarlow, P. (2002) *Event Risk Management and Safety*, Hoboken, NJ: John Wiley & Sons.

United Nations (1948) *Universal Declaration of Human Rights, Fiftieth Anniversary of the Declaration of Human Rights*, New York, NY: United Nations, accessed June 10, 2013: http://www.un.org/rights/50/decla.htm.

USrisk.com (n.d.) Does special events insurance cover terrorism, accessed May 2019: https://www.usrisk.com/2018/05/does-special-events-insurance-cover-terrorism/.

Wronka, J. (1998) *Human Rights and Social Justice in the 21st Century*, Lanham, MD: University Press of America.

PART FOUR

Trends and Triumphs

CHAPTER 9

The Virtual View of Live Events

> "After the Industrial Revolution, people started commuting to work and traveling to malls to go shopping, but digital technologies have brought work, hospitals, shopping centers and schools within our grasp, and our homes will become a new platform in which 60 percent to 70 percent of our work, education and medical activities could be carried out".

> Ki-Moon Ban, **Eighth Secretary-General of United Nations Secretary at 2018 Future Consensus Forum**

In this chapter you will learn how to:
- Define virtual reality for meetings and events
- Understand the historic development of digitally enhanced virtual events
- Identify the appropriate digital event platforms for your special event
- Expand the potential registration revenues from your digital events

As the keynote speaker at the 2018 Future Consensus Forum, former U.N. Secretary-General Ki-Moon Ban spoke of the future life of people in cities. He forecasts a new paradigm of living places for people who do their work, education, and medical services in urban settings. Due to heavy expenses and housing costs that come with living in a large city, many people are leaving metropolitan areas. He stated, "After the Industrial Revolution, people started commuting to work and traveling to malls to go shopping, but digital technologies have brought work, hospitals, shopping centers and schools within our grasp," and added that our homes with a fast communication connections will become the platform in which 60 to 70 percent of our work, education, and medical activities would be performed. What does this mean to our event industry? A combination of works and education is delivered in forms of conferences, seminars, workshops, and long-distance professional development

This parade celebrating a championship win was attended by 1 million people in Washington DC, and live-streamed and watched by 25 million people around the world.

programs in our event industry. Additionally, to create a more sustainable environment in line with the future, emerging technologies, including Virtual Reality (VR), are being used to enhance and lengthen the real live event experience. As high-speed bandwidth and 5G data becomes more affordable, the future will embrace remote and virtual participation. Morton Heilig is regarded by many scholars as the father of virtual reality. He was a philosopher, filmmaker, inventor, and the man who first created the Sensorama machine for 3-D film projection and the Thrillerama theater where rear projection was first used and then live actors appeared in front of the screen, interacting with the 3-D film images. One of his later inventions, in 1969, was the Experience Theater, which combined visual material, sound, and even smell to create a total environment for the audience. He was, in fact, a true visionary regarding the convergence of film and live action.

In the twenty-first century, many major motion pictures are released in 3-D as a standard format. Increasingly 3-D television is in wide use throughout the world and even Her Royal Majesty Queen Elizabeth II recently filmed her annual Christmas day message using 3-D technology. There seems to be no end to the opportunities for using technology to make the live event experience more exciting for audiences. In January 2017, U.S. President Donald Trump's inauguration became the most live-streamed event in history. And in May 2018, Warren Buffett's speech at the Berkshire Hathaway Annual Shareholder's meeting was watched via a streaming service on computers and mobile devices. These are some of the examples that tell us that the surge in VR-based events will only get bigger.

Virtual versus Live: Digital versus Live Events

Virtual reality is often a technological experience rather than a real one. Jonathan Steur of Stanford University argues that a device-driven definition of virtual reality is unacceptable. According to Steur (1992), a narrow definition that is limited to technology ignores the human contribution to this phenomenon.

Therefore, for the purposes of meetings and events production, the term *virtual reality* is more complex and includes the incorporation of creativity with technology to replicate and/or simulate the real experience. Virtual versus real can be also approached from a perspective of digital versus live experience. VR events have been used to describe the delivery channel of a real event. Since it has expanded with many different technologies and requires broader understanding of digital technologies, the event industry has started using "digital" event.

The Historic Development of Virtual Events

Education delivered by using remote technologies and other methods has been an accepted form of learning for over 50 years. The telecommunications corporation AT&T was one of the first major contributors to the teleconferencing field with the development of its product called Picturephone. During this time, travel was extremely cheap and most workers did not realize what an asset teleconferencing would be in the future as travel costs became more problematic and convenience more important. In the latter part of the twentieth century, a major international hotel brand decided to convert one or more of their meeting rooms in each of their major convention hotels into a dedicated teleconferencing space. The executives of this company believed that teleconferencing would rapidly enhance, and perhaps even to some extent replace, traditional face-to-face meetings.

During this same time, major corporations introduced intranet secure teleconferencing systems, using technology known as Codec. Joe Goldblatt was part of a meeting in Washington, D.C., with six executives from Xerox Corporation as we conducted a final planning meeting for their annual corporate event. While the technology was imperfect, it certainly eliminated travel and related expenses and, most importantly, allowed the Xerox senior executives to benefit from reduced time away from their office.

However, while there has been significant expansion of the global meeting and event footprint through distributed technologies such as teleconferencing using satellite technology and more recently, due to increased broadband capacity, the use of WebEx, BlueJeans, Skype and FaceTime, face-to-face meetings and events continue to be, for many, the primary choice for high-quality communication.

So what has changed in the past half-century in terms of our ability to meet, to learn, and to experience one another through enhanced technology systems? The simple answer may be that, in fact, everything has changed. However, we believe that the more things change, the more they remain the same, if as a professional event leader, you remain committed to high-quality experiences through communication.

Often modern communications, aided by e-mail, instant messaging, and social media, result in our opinion in *collisions* rather than *collaborations*. Joe sometimes refers to these collisions as "hit-and-run" meetings or encounters without time for explanation, analysis, or understanding. Therefore, with each advancement in modern communications, there is an increased opportunity to redouble our efforts to increase the quality and impact of our communications, knowledge, and learning opportunities.

In the early 1990s, a new cable television network decided to launch its world premiere in three cities in the United States, Joe was asked to orchestrate a satellite link between each remote city. The satellite link was tested in advance, and all systems were go. That is, until we had a major snow storm at one of the principal broadcast sites, New York City. For over 1 hour, there were no telecommunications during the live event, and in television time, 1 second of dead air time can be interminable. Therefore, when embracing new and emerging technologies, event leaders must be extremely cautious, flexible, and prepared to implement numerous contingency plans. Anyone who has had interruptions with a Skype video call knows exactly what we are talking about. Figure 9.1 depicts the historical development of digital meetings and events.

Why Produce Digital Content?

According to Johnnie White, executive director of Meetings and Educational Services for the Transcatheter Cardiovascular Therapeutics division of the Cardiovascular Research Foundation, "Fresh content is why this is important for us. So we'll continue to invest in the content portal." Since 2010, that investment has been made almost entirely in-house within his association. TCTMD (www.tctmd.com) now serves more than 60,000 subscribers in cardiovascular medicine. Mr. White is the 2012 chairman of the Professional Convention Management Association, whose members regard Virtual Edge as a cutting edge technology in effectively transmitting content beyond the convention center meeting room. (Virtual Edge 2012).

Goldman Sachs projects VR and AR to be future computing platforms beyond its current usage as applications of contents display. VR is a technology that immerse users in a virtual world; AR is a technology that overlays digital information onto the physical world. Multiple industry research forecast their market will grow up to $120 billion by 2020 and $140 billion by 2025. These trends tell the events industry it should be ready for this change that can reshape many existing ways of experiencing products and contents—from visiting exhibitors' booth, interacting with attendees from the opposite side of the globe, or watching live cultural and sport events (Goldman Sachs 2016).

One of the key VR use practices is the streaming of live events (e.g., conferences, concerts, cultural, and sporting events), which can solve problems of limited seating at events and makes more revenues by making it available to larger attendees. While there will be attendees still want to physically attend and watch events live at the venues, there are some attendees who will be satisfied with this technology. It is expected to have 28 million users in 2020 and grow to 95 million in 2025 as 30 percent of current live event attendees become VR users of events.

In summary, the advantages of VR digital events include the following:

1. Price per event: Discounted cost compared to live events (e.g., $10 per VR National Basketball Association game compared to $50 live game ticket).
2. Easy access overcomes physical limitation; makes events available to anyone and anywhere.

It is important to note some challenges to find best solutions of VR as a live event alternative. One, gaining the rights to VR streaming broadcasting is hard, and not clear in current broadcasting contracts. Two, many VR attendees wearing current models of VR headsets would have a limited interaction as many of current VR contents are consumed individually. Live events offer attendees to be lively engaged in their environment. For virtual events, creators should devote their efforts to offer effective networking and relationship building tools.

1947:	Dennis Gabor invents holography in Hungary.
1950's:	Bell Labs introduces audio teleconferencing.
1951:	First Australia School of the Air broadcasts lessons to children by shortwave radio.
1952:	Pennsylvania State University introduces closed captioning television versions of their courses to broadcast programs to remote locations on their campuses to alleviate overcrowded classrooms.
1953:	The Ford Foundation provides a major grant to help develop Educational Television stations (ETV) in the United States. The first educational television station opens in Houston, Texas.
1957:	First radio satellite communications are launched.
1962:	First satellite to relay television communications is produced.
1969:	The Open University distance learning program is founded in Great Britain.
1970s:	AT&T introduces Picturephone video teleconferencing to multiple sites.
1980s:	Digital telephony is introduced through the development of ISDN lines.
1990s:	Voice over Internet Protocol (VoIP) is introduced to enable computer-based teleconferencing.
1991:	First webcam is developed at Cambridge University.
1992:	First radio webcast. By 1996, there were 86 radio stations broadcasting on the Internet, and in 2013 there are now thousands.
1993:	"Severe Tire Damage" is the first band to perform live on the Internet from Xerox PARC, and scientists webstream the performance to Australia.
2000:	Video-telephony is introduced through programs such as Skype and iChat.
2004:	Go To Meeting™ is introduced by Citrix to allow a single desktop computer to teleconference with multiple locations.
2008:	Marriott and Hewlett-Packard sign a deal to create HP Halo Telepresence rooms in select Marriott venues.
2008:	CNN introduces hologram of reporter Jessica Yellen in a studio during U.S. presidential election coverage.
2010:	Increased use of mobile smart phone communications for videoconferencing through introduction of Apple's FaceTime application.
2012:	Tupac Shakur hologram is introduced at Coachella Music Festival and later seen by over 13 million people on YouTube.
2014:	Periscope, a video livestream platform app was developed and acquired by Twitter before it even launched.
2016:	Facebook launched Facebook Live, a live video streaming service that lets anyone broadcast from their mobile devices straight to their Facebook page. CNN streamed the first U.S. presidential debates in VR, which was watched across 121 countries.
2017:	U.S. President Donald Trump's inauguration is the most live-streamed event in the history of live streaming. First release of PlayStation VR games, where a group of people can put on headsets and be transferred into a virtual world to play the game.
2018:	Wearable glasses for image projection developed for public sales. A virtual meeting is held in VR by Oculus.

FIGURE 9.1 Historical development of digital meetings and events.

Examples of Digital Meetings and Events

Many meetings, exhibitions, and events are using VR as a channel to provide an enhanced 3D perspective of their contents. According to Future Market Insights, the global market for Augmented Reality (AR) and VR was valued at $5 billion in 2016, its market is estimated to reach $120 billion by 2025 (Future Market Research). During the 2008 United States presidential election, the television network CNN used a virtual reality holographic image of a reporter in the television studio to interact with the live television presenters. This was the first example of a holographic image being used to supplement and enhance a real reporter from the field as his or her image was projected into the study from a remote location. Later, this technology was incorporated in a major music festival in California. This very modern technology is actually a descendant of a Victorian era magical illusion.

The singer Tupac Shakur died in 1996; however, he was boldly brought back to life in 2012 at the Coachella Music Festival. The firm Digital Domain Media Group Inc. was responsible for developing the technology that created the lifelike hologram of Shakur who performed with Snoop Dog and Dr. Dre during the festival before hundreds of thousands of fans and it has been seen by over 17 million persons worldwide according to YouTube.

The company responsible for this technology produced the pioneering special effects for films such as *Titanic* was founded in 1993 by director James Cameron and movie special effects pioneer Stan Winston. However in 2012 the company filed for bankruptcy protection citing major losses. This is perhaps one example of the significant expense side effects that is associated with this emerging special effects technological revolution.

Delivery of Digital Event

Therefore, virtual content may be transmitted using the following means through a professional association website or other portals. This transmission may be either asynchronous (the participant may access the content whenever and wherever they wish) or synchronous (the participant has a scheduled time to access the content and this content is often facilitated by a live moderator).

Types of Virtual Digital Events by Delivery Technology

- Audio Conferencing
- Video Webcasting
- Webinar
- Live Streaming

Audio Conferencing

The audio webcast requires the lowest Internet bandwidth and is usually enhanced with shared documents, such as PDF or PowerPoint™ slides. When developing the audio conferencing, it is important to remember that people actually a narrator reading their text much slower that one does in a normal conversation. Therefore, the narrator should use a lower vocal tone and speak at a moderate to slow pace. It is also important repeat key phrases to make certain the listener recognizes and remembers this critical information. Weakness of an audio conference is when multiple speakers are used simultaneously, it distracts listeners. In addition, the lack of visual information (e.g., facial expressions, body language) limits a complete delivery of messages to attendees.

Video Webcasting

The video webcast requires a much higher Internet bandwidth and may not be appropriate for some countries where the local bandwidth is not sufficient to provide uninterrupted video streaming. When producing video content the key requirement is that less is more. Use simple visual images, symbols, graphs, charts, and tables and allow them remain on screen long enough for the viewer to fully grasp the content. If you use an on-camera speaker, have the speaker speak direct to the viewer and place the content over their right shoulder, similar to a television news presenter. You may also wish to superimpose key words as text over the chest of the on camera speaker (MPI Foundation 2012).

Webcast

The webcast is a one way broadcast using the Internet to transmit content to your participants. It does not include direct synchronous interaction during the program; however, some webcasts do accept e-mail questions to the presenters.

Webinar

The term *webinar* means a seminar, workshop, or lecture conducted over the Internet. The webinar is interactive and uses a moderator or facilitator to engage the individual participants in the discussion. Often, the webinar will include a white board screen, allowing the moderator to draw key models while he or she is speaking.

Regardless of which technology you select for developing the virtual platform for your event, it is important to remember that, first and foremost, the needs of the learner must be paramount in your decision-making. For example, some participants have a very low level of technological sophistication, while others may be much higher. Therefore, it is important to constantly consult with your potential participants and test you technologies prior to adopting them on a widespread level. Figure 9.2 demonstrates a typical screenshot of a webinar in progress.

Live Streaming

Live streaming allows any individual who wants to share a live event via social media networks. Today's generation, who always want to share what is happening and "cannot-miss," identify live streaming as very handy and a popular way of virtual event delivery.

The effectiveness of live streaming for getting people's attention is proven in the world of SNS. According to "MarketingProfs," Facebook users comment 10 times more on live videos than on regular videos. Other social media networks like Instagram, Twitter, and YouTube also show similar trends (Nevel 2019).

Event organizers are also increasing their adoption of live streaming for event promotion and content distribution. It gains its popularity with a proven effectiveness for event leaders to broadcast some aspect of an event onto the event's social media accounts to generate buzz when the event is in progress. Providing a well-designed live feed for keynote speeches, panel sessions, and product launches is an essential part of both hybrid and live events. These trends have led event leaders and marketers to focus on delivering a high-quality live stream.

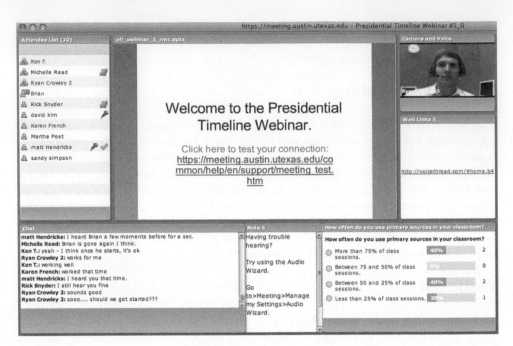

FIGURE 9.2 Webinars computer screenshots.

Distance or Blended Learning?

Some higher education institutions prefer to use the term *blended learning* rather than *distance learning*. There is a subtle but important difference between these two terms. Blended learning involves both a live event experience (face to face) and receiving information through a audio, video, pod cast, webcast, or webinar. Usually the larger percentage of educational delivery transmission is through the use of technology. However, there are no hard-and-fast rules in this rapidly evolving educational marketplace. You may find that through offering blended learning many of your participants will experience a higher-quality education experience than with technology alone, due to the opportunity for face-to-face learning. While in other cases, some participants may prefer a larger percentage of classic distance learning, using only technology to deliver content at a distance to the participants. This is another reason why it is extremely important to carefully to consult with your target market and then test their usage before you finally implement your program.

According to a American Society of Association Executives 2010 *Exploring the Decision to Learn* study of over 7,000 members of professional associations, there is a strong preference for face-to-face and blended learning versus strictly distance learning facilitated by technology. Less than 6 percent of the total respondents said they would choose distance learning through technology as their first option for adult education.

Creating New Event Revenue through Webcasts and Webinars

One of the many reasons professional associations adopt technology solutions for delivering education is the potential for reducing cost and increase new sources of revenues.

Rolfes (2009) states that professional associations currently derive less than 40 percent of their income from dues or subscriptions. Therefore, they must constantly seek alternatives for making of the remaining 60 percent of their annual budgets. Historically, the second largest source of income for many professional associations has been from annual conferences, conventions, and exhibitions. One way that associations seek to further close this revenue gap is through offering distance education programs in the form of webinars and webcasts.

However, historically associations have been somewhat smug in thinking that if they build it, they will come. In other words, the association executives and their staff believed that their association, as a representative of the industry (and therefore the stewards of its body of knowledge) was in fact operating in a monopoly environment. The rapid development of Internet-connected computer in the late twentieth century dramatically changed this paradigm.

Associations and their education managers now must compete against free high-quality education providers known as massive open online courses (MOOC). One of the best examples of this phenomena is the Khan Academy, which offers of 3,000 online courses from arithmetic to physics. The founder of the Khan Academy is Sal Khan and he argues in his book *The One World School House* that in the future education providers such as associations and universities may become assessment

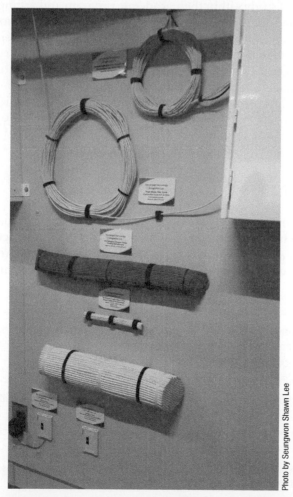

Photo by Seungwon Shawn Lee

Advancement of networking cables for effective live streaming of events: Faster, thinner, and easier to install network cables enable event venues to be ready for live event streaming and hybrid event implementation.

and credentialing providers rather than providers of actual education. According to Khan, most of the education in the future will be available for free. Therefore, as you begin to think about how you will design, market, deliver, and develop your online education component as a virtual enhancement to your live event, how do you compete with free? Today, there are as many as 11,400 courses are being offered as MOOCs (https://www.edsurge.com/news/2019-01-02-year-of-mooc-based-degrees-a-review-of-mooc-stats-and-trends-in-2018).

Figure 9.3 provides a historic timeline of the MOOC movement.

Credentials and Qualifications

One way you will be able to monetize your online education program is through offering continuing education (CE) or continuing professional development (CPD) credits. In many professions such as medicine, law, engineering, and teaching, these credits are mandatory for individuals to maintain their professional license or ability to practice. For professions that do not have CPD requirements, you may wish differentiate your program by offering a certificate of attendance or completion of a series of courses or modules. Finally, some colleges and universities may be willing to list your course of study within their academic program and arrange for academic credit to be granted. Regardless of which direction you pursue, your participants will want to know why they should invest in your programs, and often efficiency and cost is not enough to make the final sale. You will need to offer a strong carrot such as CPD credits, a certificate or even credits toward a college or university degree. However, credentials and qualifications are not the only motivation to participate in adult education. According to Albert and Dignam (2010), participants also cite that they are motivated to learn to keep up to date professionally or increase their competence at their job. Dignam and Albert surmise that they participate in education because they *want* to not just because they *have* to.

How to Charge

There are at least three ways to generate income through educational content delivered through the Internet. The first method is to charge for the actual intellectual property through a fee such as charging $39.95 for a 90-minute webinar. The second method is to offer the webinar at no charge to participants and have the cost

FIGURE 9.3 The brief history of massive open online courses, democratization of learning.

1960s:	Buckminster Fuller gives a lecture promoting the industrialization of scale of educational technology.
2006:	Khan Academy is launched.
2008:	Cormier coins term MOOC at University of Prince Edward Island.
2011:	Massachusetts Institute of Technology (MIT) announces MITx suite of free online courses and inexpensive certificates.
2011:	250,000 persons sign up for a Stanford University course on artificial intelligence.
2012:	Udacity offers MOOCs for free.
2013:	MIT developed the MITx platform for offering MOOCs, which was renamed edX after partnering with Harvard.
2016:	MOOCs are listed as an important tool to achieve Goal 4 of the UNESCO 2030 Agenda for Sustainable Development.

sponsored by a third party. In this case, the webinar is brought to the participants as a public service by a corporate entity. The third method is a hybrid of these first two options, whereby a lower price is charged for the intellectual property and sponsorship is received from a third party.

To determine how much to charge for your content, conduct a market analysis as if you were offering any other project or service. You will need to know your direct and indirect competition, your unique selling proposition, the overall state of the macro- and micro-economy, and, very importantly, the perceived value (quality) of your offering. For example, if the federal government has just announced new regulations regarding a specific product or service offered in your industry, you may be able to develop an online training program to ensure compliance with this regulation. This may increase the unique selling proposition of your training program because of the statutory requirement related to this new development.

Tracking and Encouraging the Progress of Learners

Often associations describe a member's life span within their organization as the member journey. By this, they mean that the member may join initially to network with others, then he or she will pursue professional certifications at a later stage of membership. Professional education is a lifelong pursuit; therefore, it is helpful for you to create a profile for each participant in your program and send them automatic reminders regarding their opportunities for progression through the educational services you offer. If you have received their credit card billing information, in the same manner as iTunes or Amazon, you may simply ask them to enter a password, and then they will be enrolled in the new course for their program automatically.

One of the largest providers of professional association education and training is the American Society for Association Executives (ASAE) in Washington, DC. The ASAE University online courses, facilitated webinars, and online archives provide their members and others with 24/7 access. For example they offer a 2-day virtual audio seminar for staff of small associations for $295 for ASAE members and $495 for nonmembers. This seminar results in providing the participants with 12 hours credit toward earning their Certified Association (CAE) professional designation. In addition, ASAE offers a online Membership Management Certificate Program as well as a Component Relations Management Certificate Program.

SECUREVIEW

Through Sustainability

The largest single contributor to the carbon footprint for most meetings and events is air travel. Therefore, one way you can help reduce your carbon footprint is to reduce the amount of travel that is required for your meeting or event. It is important to carefully ask your board or manager if the meeting or event could be conducted virtually and achieve the same outcomes as a face-to-face meeting. You should also include the actual participants in the meeting or event in this discussion as well. If the majority of persons with whom you consult agree that the meeting or event should be conducted in a virtual format, then find the most high-quality, efficient, and cost-effective means to achieve this. When you schedule face-to-face events, try to bundle or piggyback programs and events so that the participants do not have to travel more than once for a similar purpose.

The ASAE University online website features numerous advertisements that are of interest to association executives (hotels where their meetings may be held, audiovisual service providers, etc.). Therefore, ASAE is able to monetize their online education offering not only through course and certificate program fees but also through sponsor advertising.

New Approach to Marketing Digital and Virtual Events

The event industry, along with many businesses, is serous about how to track attendees/customers. For many years, this has been a hot topic of many business strategies in the event industry in the face of the growth of digital events.

It is often said that one of the most important benefits of virtual events over physical ones is the capacity of the former to track leads, attendee traffic patterns, and quantitatively measure event performance to calculate event ROI with immediate generated statistics. Your events website and the e-mail addresses of your participants are the primary means to disseminating information about your virtual events program.

You should use a push system to constantly inform and educate your target market about new and valuable virtual event programs that will benefit them. You should also list the cost/value benefits of the online experience versus the cost of travel, accommodation, and other related costs associated with attending in person.

The Professional Convention Management Association (PCMA) of Chicago, Illinois, uses a push system through blast e-mails to members to encourage individuals who have not registered for their convention in the final weeks to consider attending through their Virtual Edge online program. Their user-friendly website includes a Invite A Friend option to help the association build attendance by having participants recommend others to join them in the course.

TECH/APPVIEW

Virtual reality (VR) is changing many aspects of the event business. Event leaders quickly adopt VR as a way to grasp venues with its 360-degree walk-through tour and enhanced features that show different logistics (e.g., lighting, table setups, and decorations). Event venues, meanwhile, can use the technology to promote events more effectively—a much more effective marketing tool than a printed brochure or simple images posted on its online outlets.

Leading brands have been successfully using AR and VR at events to connect and activate their target audiences. In particular, new product launching events are quickly adopting VR and experience its high returns. Volvo, for example, showcased its new XC90 model to buyers with a virtual product presentation. According to *VR Vision* magazine's research, value perception in potential buyers' prospects increases by up to 33 percent when adding AR to new product launching and marketing events, and VR tools can increase buyers' confidence in products by up to stunning 135 percent.

Condor, a German airline company, also utilized VR technology for a "virtual assistant." It greets and guides travelers through the check-in process, a feature that could be transferred over to many types of events.

Many professional theater companies in the United States and Europe now automatically create a YouTube trailer to promote their upcoming shows. We recommend you consider this for your educational program or other event offering as well. You may wish to create a dedicated YouTube channel for your event as a way to organize all of your content. These trailers may help you dramatically increase the hits on your event website and also increase ticket sales.

Old Wine in New Bottles?

This chapter began with a statement that the more things change, the more they remain the same. Recently, the leading accounting and consulting firm Deloitte faced a unique challenge. Their leaders had to decide how they would take forward corporate education within their huge company. An obvious choice would be to decentralize the delivery of education through a major investment in technology-assisted learning tools. However, after consulting with their employees and their clients and examining best practice in related fields, they decided to build a new campus, called Deloitte University (DU). This is why they made this important and ultimately correct decision.

Deloitte's most tangible product is the skills of its more than 54,000 people across four disciplines–tax, audit, financial advisory, and consulting. Clients increasingly call on Deloitte professionals not only to provide a high level of service in their own specific discipline but also to advise them across the spectrum of business needs and issues. This makes it vital that Deloitte professionals be continuous learners across the full range of technical, industry, professional, and leadership disciplines in order to stay on the leading edge.

Beyond the need to continue to provide topnotch client service, Deloitte sees its commitment to talent development as fundamental to the organization's long-term competitive advantage. In an uncertain economy, it is critical that Deloitte attract and hire the right people—and the need is more urgent than ever. According to the Employment Policy Foundation, by 2025, there is expected to be a 35-million-person gap between the supply and demand of knowledge workers in the U.S. economy.

Deloitte's solution to closing this gap and developing the leaders of tomorrow? Deloitte University—a $300-million-dollar investment to build a brick-and-mortar facility with the mission to enhance leadership as a core competency at all levels, inside and outside the walls of Deloitte, and to inspire new thinking that helps clients face off against their challenges.

The Vision for Leadership Excellence

The doors of Deloitte University opened in 2011, but the vision was born in 2005, under the leadership of then-U.S. CEO Barry Salzberg, who currently serves as the global CEO of Deloitte Touche Tohmatsu Limited. At the time, a number of shifts were taking place both inside and outside the organization.

For one, Deloitte's workforce demographics were changing significantly. In 2005, Deloitte's population was approximately 43,000 employees—with continued growth, it has since reached over 54,000 employees with many of them coming to the company directly upon graduating from undergrad institutions. More than

60 percent are under the age of 35. In addition, clients were adjusting to an increasingly globalized economy with a constant stream of new and emerging technologies, including mobile devices and social media platforms, which were changing the way business is done.

These were trends that Deloitte saw coming—and the leadership team knew that generation Y had very specific values and expectations for their career development. For these reasons, Deloitte's talent and learning teams began orchestrating a wholly new approach to attracting top talent, cultivating leadership from within, and keeping up with the changing business landscape to provide better solutions for clients' most complex business needs.

To do this, Deloitte first undertook a survey of its workforce. What they found was surprising—six focus groups and over 900 survey responses from Gen Y learners revealed that not only was a commitment to learning and development important to recruiting this demographic but that live off-site learning is considered "critical" for them as well. Most of Deloitte's professionals work on-site at client businesses around the nation, working virtually with other team members. A physical facility would provide greater opportunity for face-to-face networking with peers, and more importantly, senior leaders.

After evaluating internal interests, Deloitte leaders then looked at the kinds of knowledge and skills Deloitte's well-rounded professionals would need to excel, and they found that, overwhelmingly, many skills required real-world simulations couldn't be maximized through virtual teams. For example, while updates to the tax code and certain regulatory training, such as workplace skills, can be achieved through virtual learning, complex and advanced skills require more collaborative, simulated scenarios that only a physical facility can provide.

There was another reason that a physical facility appealed to Deloitte—the opportunity to design a place that reflected and reinforced the organization's values and brand. As a strategic step in building the professional services organization of the future, it would further distinguish Deloitte's brand in the marketplace and enhance its reputation for attracting and developing top talent and enabling that talent to address clients' most complex business challenges.

Making the Case

To make this vision a reality, Salzberg had to get the approval of Deloitte's almost 3,000 partners and principals. To a large degree, the question came down to cost. A $300 million investment in a physical facility when virtual options were much cheaper would require a strong business case—and partners had many questions, including what the institution would look like, how many facilities there would be, and how it would differ from the current learning model?

Salzberg knew he had to get specific. His team visited similar institutions to learn best practices and understand the challenges ahead. Originally, the decision to build this facility was purely about ROI around the external venue spend that was generated by our learning programs. The team felt that they could build a facility and deliver training at a lower cost point than constantly contracting for external venues. However, over time, that original vision morphed into the idea that Deloitte University could and should be the heart of the company's corporate culture. Salzberg and his team realized that the opportunity they had in front of them was to combine the ideas of corporate culture with the opportunity to create business leaders at all levels of the organization. That is how Deloitte University ended up being branded the Leadership Center.

Salzberg's team envisioned a multiacre site that would have accommodations on the ground, along with amenities and restaurants, which would bring together team members from all of Deloitte's disciplines, levels, and U.S. regions in simulated real-world business scenarios as a means to increase collaboration and teamwork.

The next step was to choose a location. Multiple sites were scouted before deciding on Westlake, Texas, a neighboring town of Dallas. Centrally located between the two coasts, Westlake is not only accessible but also provides a temperate climate, a perfect combination for a year-round learning hub.

To ensure Deloitte University would be a new kind of learning facility that reflected the range of services and expertise offered by Deloitte professionals, the organization's leadership proposed a governance structure with representatives from each of Deloitte's core practices and direct lines of communication to be the learning officers from each team.

After in-depth discussions, the Deloitte partnership was fully on board and committed to the project, from the board of Directors on down.

Construction began on the 107-acre plot of land in 2009. In keeping with Deloitte's commitment to environmental sustainability and managing long-term costs, both energy and water efficiencies were top of their mind during the facility's construction. For example, approximately 50 percent of construction waste was recycled, and 90 percent of the architectural space has views of natural light, reducing the use of interior lighting.

The official opening ceremony was held in October 2011. Today, Deloitte University boasts 800 guest rooms at 300 square feet each, 35 classrooms, 36 team rooms, a 12,000 square-foot fitness center, a two-mile running/walking trail, an amphitheater that seats 176 people, a grand ballroom, full-service dining halls, and a social venue called The Barn.

A New Kind of Learning

Deloitte's leadership knew that building Deloitte University was only half the process. To maximize its potential, the firm needed to adopt an entirely new approach to talent development.

At the same time the facility was being built, Deloitte leaders, including CEO Barry Salzberg and Chief Talent Officer Bill Pelster (2012), worked to create a new kind of learning curriculum to be delivered at Deloitte University—a curriculum that was leading-edge, simulation-based, and collaborative. In June 2011, Deloitte leadership increased the amount of learning across Deloitte to 4 million hours, up from 3 million hours conducted the year prior. Those additional 1 million hours now occur at Deloitte University.

Deloitte has always invested heavily in technical and professional training, but Deloitte University has increased its capabilities to provide industry and leadership training. Most of the programs offered at Deloitte University are complex, multiday simulations built around small team interactions with a 1 to 5 facilitator-to-student ratio.

The formal, traditional lecture would have no place inside a Deloitte University classroom. Deloitte University classrooms have no "front," and there's usually not a podium in sight. Instead they employ modular furniture arranged in a number of configurations to facilitate dialogue and role-playing. Four classrooms are specifically designed as "TeleClassrooms" and are linked to other similar rooms, newly constructed, in all major offices across the country, enabling teams to come together across distances to solve problems and learn together. This network of TeleClassrooms reaches 90 percent of learners across the Deloitte U.S. organization.

Learning programs are designed to replicate the real-life situation as closely as possible. For example, while learners engage in competitive team-based business simulations, facilitators will throw them the kind of curveballs they might expect on a real project—for instance, midway through an exercise, a learner might receive an e-mail with information that completely changes the scenario, teaching him or her to make quick decisions. Faculty members also act as "cast members" and engage in one-on-one simulated conversations to give learners practice handling difficult conversations. By challenging learners in a safe environment, partners, principals, and directors can guide learners to new skills that apply to their day-to-day situations with clients.

Ninety percent of the courses are taught by senior Deloitte professionals—the very people who live Deloitte values and serve its clients each day. In other cases, outside instructors are brought in from a pool of facilitators, including retired Deloitte partners, principals, and directors; leading industry pundits; clients' CEOs; and other external experts.

In its first 3 months of operation, DU delivered 154 programs to 8,602 learners, who completed 219,320 learning hours. By the end of its first year, it was expected that more than 30,000 learners across all levels of Deloitte would attend DU. Deloitte professionals can expect to visit the center an average of every 2 to 3 years.

Even when not in Westlake, personnel will benefit from the enriched culture and collaboration that Deloitte University has catalyzed across the organization. Deloitte University is designed to allow people to network across their normal organizational boundaries. Additionally, key promotion milestone training is cross-functional, allowing team members to work on complex problems that span traditional organizational boundaries. For example, there are simulations that allow tax, consulting, and advisory professionals to work together. In the past year, nearly 4,000 promotes at Deloitte attended cross-functional training at DU and other Deloitte learning venues. This team building and networking will strengthen the collaboration of team members working together from different sites to resolve complex client issues.

The Return on Learning Investment

Leaders understood early on that Deloitte University would not be a cost-saving measure. For one, an increase in live learning means a natural increase in travel. Instead, the $300 million investment will be evaluated in terms of whether Deloitte has successfully moved the bar on learning and better prepared its professionals to serve clients with distinction. Rigorous models are in place to evaluate results of the learning across multiple dimensions—focusing on curriculum, faculty quality, and, of course, business outcomes.

To track outcomes, Deloitte has instituted a number of measurement strategies, including surveys, focus groups, interviews with learners, and social media forums to help ensure that professionals are satisfied with their learning, and, more importantly, are applying the skills they've gained on the job. Deloitte conducts learning assessments on key programs and has seen a significant jump in responses around how and when what individuals have learned at Deloitte University is being applied back on the job. Depending on the assessment model, there is a follow-up survey on select programs 90 days post-training, which will go to either the individual or their respective manager.

With the official opening in October 2011, the testimonials from feedback surveys thus far are entirely positive, with the focus areas of leadership development, culture, networking/social events, and overall experience all rated as "excellent." The most recent feedback survey conducted found an average rating of 4.8 out of 5 on the overall experience. In addition to this, in one of the recent focus groups conducted participants said that, after attending Deloitte University, they now have a more positive perception of Deloitte due to the firm's investment in its people and learning.

Overall, the investment in the facility and the 25 percent increase in annual training have allowed Deloitte to differentiate itself in the market for talent. The Kirkpatrick level one analysis has jumped from an average of 4.2 to 4.8. Additionally, Deloitte University's strategy is directly linked to Deloitte's business strategy to create world-class business leaders. This summer, for the first time, it will roll out Industry Mastery level programs for all 20 of its industry sectors. This will significantly increase the core skills of all of Deloitte professionals.

Deloitte University is affirming its commitment to the growth and success of its people, clients, and the global business community. In 2017, Deloitte launched Deloitte University North (DU North), a learning and leadership development center in Toronto, Canada. Over 8,000 key clients, community leaders, and Deloitte practitioners from across the Americas and around the world participated in DU North's programming. Its global leadership centers are now located in Westlake, Texas; Deloitte University Asia Pacific in Singapore; Deloitte University Europe, the Middle East and Africa in La Hulpe, Belgium and Chantilly, France; and Deloitte University, Hyderabad, India.

Beyond Deloitte

Ultimately, the mission of Deloitte University is to enhance the skills and competencies of all Deloitte employees in order to prepare them to be world-class leaders, no matter if they finish their careers at Deloitte or eventually join other organizations. The experiences and skills they gain at the Leadership Center will contribute to the kind of professionals they become and the decisions they make, which has the potential to affect the future of business practices.

In the short-term, as long as clients and stakeholders, such as regulators, can see the impact in their own business and the way Deloitte conducts business, Deloitte University will be considered a great success.

The Future of Virtual and Live Events

Virtual event technology is revolutionizing the world of events in their delivery to and accessibility by attendees. Forward-moving event organizations and leaders recognize virtual digital event technology is essential to engage today's attendees who seek unique, personalized experiences. AR/VR and live streaming via mobile devices are among many tools available to create entrancing event experiences. What technologies event leaders should use and how they obtain the necessary skills and information to capture their attendees' attention and differentiate their event will be key tasks for event leaders of today and tomorrow. The speed of technological progress through the development of mobile computing devices such as the iPhone, iPad, and other tablets is dramatically

VR is the new platform of computing and the event industry will embrace it in many creative ways into live events. A young boy tries a VR head set during a product demonstration at an event.

changing the way we seek, find, and consume education and culture. Therefore, we predict the following changes on the horizon for meetings and events in the next 5 years.

First, there will be a rapid expansion of live streaming designed for mobile devices for special event promotions, cultural and sports programs. This will be to stimulate potential attendees and supply of event seats that are often unfilled during various times of the day and year. Event leaders will seek more product to place bums in seats and live streaming events may be just the ticket.

Second, Lee, Boshnakova, and Goldblatt (2016) stated in their book *The 21st Century Meeting and Event Technology* that more and more conferences and exhibitions will utilize VR as a way to give attendees a 3D perspective of their products or contents. Considering the global market for AR and VR that is expected to grow up to $120 billion by 2025 (Future Market Insights 2017) and the comfort attendees have with such technologies, it is clear that the widespread of VR and AR in future events.

Third, live educational programs will continue to be offered at conferences, conventions, and exhibitions. However, these programs will be primarily focused upon dialogue, discourse, and debate rather than monologue. Online-based educational programs will excel in areas of technical trainings, certificates, and professional development that focus on a delivery of contents and examinations. The classic talking heads of the twentieth century will give way to the power of the group dynamic in the twenty-first century.

Third, there will be more meetings, conferences, and live events than ever before as individuals experience a taster on the Internet and then seek the real experience through the face-to-face opportunities provided by event leaders such as yourself.

The new virtual events and fast advancing technologies will create new markets and may disrupt current markets. The good news is that the number of events worldwide and the demand for these events will dramatically increase, especially as the baby boomers retire and have more leisure time. However, the other news is that the competition will be far greater due to major improvements in Internet technology. To be successful in the future, you must not only be able to conceive and produce a high-quality event but you also must be increasingly able to harness the power of the Internet to deliver your event to the widest possible audience through the local cinema or the personal tablet.

For 2019 and beyond, it is expected that attendee tracking at events results in decreased costs by adopting radio-frequency ID (RFID) and will gain more popularity in on-demand content subscription. These tools are proven to be very effective in digital/virtual event environments and will contribute to track and forecast event attendees' consumption of contents, digital traffic patterns, and pre-/during/post-event engagement activities. Event leaders of digital/virtual events can access statistics easier than ever, which can result in dynamic measuring of real-time event ROI. The most recent technological advancement of bringing Tupac Shakur back to life is, in fact, one that has its roots in the theater as well. The effect that made Shakur seem lifelike is a derivative of a Victorian magic show illusion called Pepper's Ghost! It actually has its roots in Italy when a sixteenth-century Neapolitan scientist named Giambattista della Porta created an illusion entitled "How we may see things in a chamber that are not actually there." Later in London in 1862, John Pepper and his colleague Henry Dircks developed the Dirksian Phantasmogoria to make ghosts appear on stage. The technology was rather simple and is still used today, albeit with advanced digital imaging.

Therefore, before you look too far into the future for the new big idea for improving learning, entertainment, and the overall experiences that may be gained through special events, we recommend you first look to the past, which has many wonderful ghosts such as Mr. Pepper that may inspire you to create your own future phantasmagoric solutions to enhance the learning outcomes and entertainment experiences, and generate wonder and even astonishment from your future audiences.

Summary

Chapter 9 explored how the traditional live event has rapidly become a blended live and virtual event reality. This paradigm shift is greater in speed and breadth than the historic development of teleconferencing in the latter part of the twentieth century. The following key points underpin this significant change in terms of developing and delivering content for meetings and events.

First, the demand for education and entertainment is growing, and consumers wish to have this type of experience available 24/7.

Second, competition for audiences is also growing, and consumers have a wide range of choices available and seek value-added education and entertainment experience.

Third, the potential distribution channels for education and entertainment range from local cinema theaters to the personal tablet computer, and this will also increase demand for attending live events in the future. In conclusion, the importance of using digital enhancement to support and provide efficiencies is well proved, but event leaders agree on that it will never completely replace face-to-face communications with unique experiences of in-person live events (i.e., body language, context, interaction, scalability, and more). There will be types of face-to-face interactions that are preferable over a strictly virtual meeting or event.

INSIGHTS FROM GLOBAL EVENT LEADERS

Corbin Ball, CSP, CMP, DES

Corbin Ball & Co.

Corbin Ball is an international speaker, consultant, and writer helping clients worldwide use technology to save time and improve productivity. He is a highly acclaimed speaker with the ability to make complex subjects understandable and fun. Corbin is a 2018 inductee into the Event Industry Council's Hall of Leaders. Corbin has been named as one of "The 25 Most Influential People in the Meetings Industry" five times by *Successful Meetings/MeetingNews* magazines.

Q: How will virtual events affect live event sectors?

A: Webinars and other virtual meetings are great for short information exchange. However, in today's multitasking and often distracting work environment, attention spans are short. Thirty minutes to an hour is usually the maximum you can expect someone to pay attention sitting in front of a monitor.

Face-to-face meetings, on the other hand, take people to a more focused location with fewer distractions. As long as people are informed, entertained, and fed, event hosts can keep people engaged for days. At the minimum, there is a social contract to at least look like you are paying attention at an event. This is very different than most virtual events. The opportunities for networking, brainstorming, and relationship building are usually far greater at face-to-face events than online. To put it succinctly, there is no such thing as a virtual beer!

Q: What sectors will be created and what sectors in event industry disrupted by virtual event technology?

A: Virtual meetings are an alternative communication medium, as mentioned, good for short information exchange. It is simply another tool in the meeting planner's box to bring people together. I don't think that it will create new sectors or significantly disrupt existing ones.

Q: Please name top 5 technology skill sets that students who majoring event management while they are in school?

A: Technology will continue to remain a rapidly changing field. It is likely that much still has not been invented. The important thing is to adopt a mindset to embrace technology change. I am not certain about specific technology skill sets that apply. It is more about being technology literate and aware of the options that become available. The good news is that, as technology advances, it becomes easier to use.

Q: How to stay current with event technology?

A: There are many sources: newsletters, publications, events, tradeshows. There is a plethora of sources about new technology trends and how they apply to events.

Q: How powerful tool will VR/AR be for new generations of event industry?

A: AR/VR will likely have a significant impact on the event industry. See the following article for details: https://www.corbinball.com/article/36-mobile-and-wireless-technology/243-vrvsar.

Key Terms

Asynchronous transmission: An Internet transmission of a educational program where the participant may join whenever and wherever he or she desires. This is often a prerecorded webcast versus a webinar.

Augmented Reality (AR): A technology that superimposes a computer-generated image on a user's view of the real world, thus providing a composite view.

Audio webcast: A low-bandwidth alternative for transmitting information using the Internet.

High definition: A television resolution significantly higher than standard definition television (when projected in high definition it projects five times as many pixels as standard definition television).

Live streaming: A live video streaming service that lets anyone broadcast from their mobile devices straight to their SNS account.

MOOC: Massive Open O Courses, educational programs offered free on the Internet and attended by large numbers of learners.

Synchronous transmission: An Internet transmission of a educational program that is prescheduled for a specific date and time and often involves a moderator and/or facilitator.

Video delayed webcast: A video (often with audio) of a live event shown after the live event has concluded.

Video Web simulcast: A video (often with audio) of a simultaneous live event.

Virtual Reality: The incorporation of creativity with technology to replicate and/or simulate the live experience.

Webcast: A usually one-way webstream of a program with limited interaction.

Webinar: A synchronous seminar, workshop, or lecture with the opportunity for participation by all attendees and facilitated by a moderator.

Webstreaming: Where audio and/or video files are compressed and delivered through the Internet.

Career Connections

To increase your opportunities gaining lucrative employment, it is critical that you understand and embrace the various technologies that will be used to develop and deliver content to the widest audiences. Therefore, you must become proficient at using products such as Windows MovieMaker, and SNS live streaming production tools to create short video trailers to promote your event and upload these trailers to YouTube and other social media websites. In addition, use professional equipment to create your video clips as the quality of promotional video production creates the first impression of your event. You should also continually examine how best to lower the cost for distribution of your live event and use the Internet to increase attendance to live events in the future.

Next Steps

1. Create a one to two minute trailer promoting your event and upload it to YouTube.
2. Develop a content distribution plan for your education program by using either a webinar, webcast, webstream, audiocast, or videocast of your program.
3. Conduct market research to determine the right price point for your online educational offering.

References

Albert, L. and Dignam, M. (2010) *The Decision to Learn*, Washington, D.C.: American Society of Association Executives.

Future Market Insights (2017) Augmented reality and virtual reality market - global industry analysis & forecast, 2017–2025.

Goldman Sachs (2016) *Profiles in Innovations: Virtual and Augmented Reality*, New York: Goldman Sachs.

Lee, S. S., Boshnakova, D., and Goldblatt, J. (2016) *The 21st Century Meeting and Event Technology: Powerful Tools for Better Planning, Marketing, and Evaluation*, Oakville, Canada: Apple Academic Press.

MPI Foundation (2012) The strategic value of virtual meetings and events, accessed March 22, 2019: http://www.mpiweb.org/Portal/VirtualEvents.

Nevel, J. https://www.marketingprofs.com/articles/2019/40433/eight-tips-to-maximize-your-video-marketing-efforts-on-facebook.

Nyheim, P. and Connolly, D. (2011) *Technology Strategies for the Hospitality Industry*, 2nd edition, Upper Saddle River, NJ: Prentice Hall.

O'Brien, D. and Pelster, B. (2012) Case study, Deloitte University: A career-long investment in leadership excellence, accessed September 2012: https://www.3blmedia.com/News/CASE-STUDY-Deloitte-University-Career-Long-Investment-Leadership-Excellence.

Professional Convention Management Association, How technology is changing the meeting space, VR being used to scout venues and debut products. Will that hurt F2F?, accessed spring 2019: https://www.pcma.org/how-technology-is-changing-the-meeting-space/.

Rolfes, R. (2009) *The Competition Within: How Members Will Reinvent Associations*, Bloomington, IN: Imagination Publishing.

Steur, J. (1992) Defining virtual reality: Dimensions determining telepresence. *Journal of Communication*, Vol. 42 Iss: 4, pp. 73–93, Hoboken, NJ: John Wiley & Sons.

Virtual Edge (2012) Professional Convention Management Association, Convene Magazine.

Virtual Edge Institute (2012) Cardiovascular Research Foundation takes in-house approach to digital event strategy, accessed December 10, 2019: www.virtualedgeinstitute.com.

CHAPTER 10

Reinventing a Joyful and Sustainable Career

"You can never have an impact on society if you have not changed yourself."

—*Nelson Mandela,* **former president of South Africa (1918–2013)**

In this chapter you will learn how to:

- Advance your event planning career through formal and informal education and experience
- Identify internal and external environments and forecast their impact on career development
- Recognize emerging careers for event professionals
- Gain more professional experience to build your résumé
- Become a Certified Special Event Professional (CSEP), Certified Meeting Professional (CMP), and Digital Events Strategist (DES)
- Earn the credentials you need for employment, promotion, and long-term success
- Incorporate principles of sustainable development into your business and career

During the final days of 2012, the U.S. government, according to news reports, was teetering upon a fiscal cliff. The two major political parties could not agree upon how to create a sustainable economic future. During the long sweep of human history, the United States and other countries have also wrestled with how to achieve long-term social, economic, and more recently environmental success through small changes and compromises that must be made in the short and midterm. President Mandela well understood this conundrum and walked his talk by refusing to have his heart hardened from over 30 years of imprisonment.

We live in a time of rapid and constant change. The main catalysts for these changes are shifting demographics, accelerating technology, and increasing

Event career advancement through mege event volunteering: George Mason and Virginia Tech students volunteering at 2018 Winter Olympics in Pyeongchang, South Korea.

environmental awareness. Therefore, one may ask, what is the role of the professional event planning during this extraordinary time in our human history?

In this chapter, we will expand the discussion by updating the listing of emerging careers for event professionals and provide a career blueprint from pre-college through late career reinvention. This chapter will include a section on volunteering, interning, and using emerging tools such as LinkedIn and the creation of video résumés. Finally, this chapter includes a section entitled "Earning a Qualification and Achieving Professional Certification" that details how to select an appropriate qualification, how to study for the certification examinations, and other key information to expedite the certification process. We will also argue that now, more than ever before, professional event leaders must embrace the long view of how planned events can embolden, inform, and expand our humanity. In order for event leaders to achieve a successful and sustainable career through changing the world, they must change themselves, their way of viewing the world, and their way of acting, just as President Mandela envisioned. Probably the most admired tech company in the world, Apple CEO Tim Cook spoke to 2019 college graduates and delivered a somewhat surprising statement, but one well-aligned with what President Mandela said. Mr. Cook stated, "There are some who would like to believe that the only way you can be strong is by bulldozing those who disagree with you . . . We forget sometimes that our pre-existing beliefs have their own force of gravity. Today, certain algorithms pull toward you things that you already know, believe or like. And they push away everything else. Push back! It shouldn't be this way."

This is also a time of rapid growth for the professional planned events. As noted in Chapter 9, due to the intersection of the virtual and the live event, face-to-face communication has the greatest opportunity, since the time when it first developed around the prehistoric camp fire, to reach more people and do more good. It is, therefore, critically important that you be ready to embrace this threshold moment in the history of our profession by making certain you have developed a sustainable skill set. Fortunately for all of us, there are innumerable opportunities to do this.

Environmental Sustainability

One of the major trends in modern society is the concept of "greener event." Thanks in large part to pioneers in the hospitality industry such as the Saunders Hotel Group of Boston, Massachusetts, guests throughout the world became aware in the early 1990s of their role in the sustainability of the spaceship called Earth. Tedd Saunders launched the hotel industry's first Green Team in 1989 and helped develop the common practice of inviting hotel guests to reuse their towels and linens in order to reduce the waste water and energy required for daily laundering. Joe Goldblatt met Tedd in the mid-1990s when he invited him to serve as the keynote speaker for a conference he chaired in Oracle, Arizona, at the Biosphere environmental research center. Many of the participants were highly skeptical regarding the concepts discussed by Tedd, which included climate change and global warming. However, by the end of the 3-day retreat, the 30 international leaders from the meetings and events industry who had come together to explore the future of events management agreed that sustainable environmental development was one of the most critical challenges and opportunities for the approaching twenty-first century.

The conference concluded with the adoption of a manifesto that outlined the mission for the twenty-first-century events industry, as shown in Figure 10.1.

In only 30 years time, we have seen climatological evidence of many of the concerns identified in this manifesto. Therefore, if the event planning industry is to achieve a sustainable future, it is essential that we first address the key environmental challenges that may either inhibit or accelerate our success in the future.

Former U.S. Vice President Al Gore's film *An Inconvenient Truth* demonstrated that the excessive burning of coal, gas, and oil has overpowered the Earth's atmosphere with greenhouse gases such as carbon dioxide (CO_2). Mass deforestation has limited the environment's ability to absorb these greenhouse gases, allowing them to pollute the atmosphere. This pollution causes increasing temperatures, known as global warming, and abnormal weather patterns, known as climate change, and, according to the National Geographic Society, the symptoms are as follows:

- The last two decades of the twentieth century were the hottest on record in 400 years.
- Montana's Glacier National Park, which had 150 glaciers in 1910, now has only 27.
- By the end of the twenty-first century, sea level may rise between 7 and 23 inches. Rises of just 4 inches could flood many South Sea islands and large parts of Southeast Asia.
- More than a million species face extinction (National Geographic Society 2009).

Mission

To accept environmental, technological, and economic change in order to ensure a successful and enduring industry we must:
1. **Serve** as responsible custodians of the natural environment and educate others to understand this value and financial benefit.
2. **Improve** our technological capabilities to simultaneously reduce cost and improve quality.
3. **Establish** strong mutually beneficial strategic alliances for educational, social, and economic benefits worldwide.

FIGURE 10.1 The Future of Event Management charter, May 8, 1998, The Columbia University Biosphere, Oracle, Arizona.

Gore has championed the environment in public debate, but aside from his role as a political leader, he is a Greener Events Leader. His now famous 2007 Live Earth concert series featured mega-concerts on seven continents, and was broadcast around the world to teach an estimated 2 billion people about climate change (Live Earth 2009). Gore also organized 2009's most notable greener event, the Green Ball, celebrating the inauguration of President Barack Obama. In many ways, the Green Ball, which featured e-mail invites (to avoid paper waste), a green carpet made from recycled materials, and organic food sourced from local farms, was a model greener event (BizBash 2009).

The global events industry is following Gore's example. Event leaders and customers demand environmentally sound venues and materials more than ever. For example, finding an event venue that aligns with eco-friendly practices is much easier now. There are growing programs that help event leaders make better environmental friendly event operating decisions. Certifications such as Leadership in Energy and Environmental Design (LEED) certifications are widely accepted, and event leaders can conveniently select their event venues based on needs in silver, gold, or platinum levels.

The website of *Special Events* magazine features dedicated sections of greener events. Event industry is paying attention to green event by streamlining its information and education for event leaders by Event Industry Council, formerly known as Convention Industry Council, that now includes Green Meeting Industry Council.

The U.S. Environmental Protection Agency (EPA) has established the Green Meeting/Conference Initiative to promote environmentally friendly practices in the events sector and share samples of green meeting policy for event leaders on its website (https://www.epa.gov/fgc/sample-green-meetings-and-events-policy; EPA 2019).

We can learn from Gore's example. As world leaders create green policies and industry leaders set green initiatives, so too will twenty-first century event leaders need to pioneer within the new field of greener events.

Defining "Greener"

- *Carbon footprint*: The total combined CO_2 emissions of your event
- *Carbon offsetting*: Financial investment toward CO_2-reducing projects, such as renewable energy or forestry, measured as 1 offset = 1 metric ton of CO_2
- *Climate change*: Abnormal deviations in the weather and other meteorological factors
- *Environmentally friendly practice (EFP)*: An action designed to minimize negative impact and/or promote positive impact on the environment
- *Global warming*: The increase in the Earth's average temperature since the mid-twentieth-century and its projected continuing rise
- *Greenhouse gases*: Water vapor, CO_2, methane, nitrous oxide, and other gases, the excessive use of which contributes to global warming and climate change.
- *Organic*: Foods or natural products made without the use of pesticides or other artificial or chemical agents
- *Renewable energy*: Energy generated from recurring natural resources such the sun (solar), wind, and water (hydro)

Defining "Greener Events"

As Thomas Friedman argues in *Hot, Flat, and Crowded*, rising oil prices and war in the Middle East have fed a geopolitical energy crisis, thus contributing to a growing public focus on alternative energy solutions, a focus sharpened by President Barack Obama, who promised to invest heavily in green technologies as part of a new vision for America (Friedman 2008).

As diverse businesses seek to apply eco-friendly strategies to their industry practices, many predict a green boom similar to the 1990s Web boom (Esty and Winston 2009).

According to Samuel deBlanc Goldblatt, author of *Greener Meetings and Events* (2012), *greener events* can be defined as special events that continually endeavor to provide superior experiences through environmentally friendly strategies.

In accordance with his definition, greener events promote three core values: innovation, conservation, and education.

1. *Innovation*: Creatively harnessing emerging strategies and green technology for increased energy efficiency and environmentalism
2. *Conservation*: Using the Earth's natural resources and waste minimization in a responsible manner
3. *Education*: Promoting ethical behavior toward energy and the environment by creating memorable event experiences.

About 30 years later, Dr. Lee attended an inaugural Sustainable Meeting Planner Certificate program in Washington, DC, with 25 event industry professionals for 2 full days of the program that includes the United Nation's global sustainability initiative and a wide range of hospitality, tourism, and travel industry co-developed.

Sustainability

Sustainability derives from the theory of sustainable development created by the United Nations during the 1980s to encourage development that "meets the needs of the present without compromising the ability of future generations to meet their own needs," as stated in the UN document *Our Common Future* (2012).

Air and land pollution of an outdoor event site directly compromises the ability of future event leaders to produce events on that site. Indirectly, careless wasting of resources such as paper or gasoline compromises future generations' special events.

While the concept of sustainability allows environmentalists to communicate their green concerns in the language of strategic planning, sustainable development does not necessarily imply environmental activism. Affixing the terms "green" or "eco" to the start of a term (green energy, ecotechnology) more clearly reflects a concerted effort to reduce environmental impact and to conserve natural resources, beyond the definition of sustainable development. Responsible event leaders will always pursue sustainability in their long-term business plans. We encourage you to consider the specific ways in which green technology and environmental initiatives can sustain and improve your long-term business plans.

Ecotourism

The tourism industry, with its market for recreational air travel, is one of the world's largest gas consumers and polluters. Perhaps this is why tourism experts were quick to apply the principles of sustainable development to their field. David Fennell defines *ecotourism*, or environmentalist tourism, as

> *a sustainable, non-invasive form of nature-based tourism that focuses primarily on learning about nature first-hand, and which is ethically managed to be low-impact, non-consumptive, and locally oriented (control, benefits and scale). It typically occurs in natural areas, and should contribute to the conservation of such areas.* (Fennell 2007, p. 24)

Greener events leaders may glean much from this definition of ecotourism. Certainly event leaders recognize the value of sustainability in long-term business growth, but is this sustainability "nature-based"? No man is an island, and no event is disconnected from its natural resources and environment; think of sustaining not just your business but your event site, your resources, your energy. Similarly, all events impact the culture of their locations, and greener events must, therefore, be "locally oriented" to maintain meaningful and beneficial relationships with local culture. Lastly, event leaders can use corporate social responsibility (CSR) to "ethically" manage greener events.

What about "low-impact" and "nonconsumptive"? Should not the best events always be high-impact, offering guests a lavish feast to consume? Actually, greener events can deliver a huge, spectacular impact on patrons, complete with sights, sounds, and foods to consume. Japan's Fuji Rock Festival, known anecdotally as the world's cleanest music festival, annually presents major bands like The Red Hot Chili Peppers and The Cure in a huge outdoor environment that encompasses 10 different stages for performance, vendors offering outstanding local cuisines, sustainable campgrounds, and other attractions such as a Japanese "onsen" spa and a cable-car ride. Through rigorous recycling procedures, responsible land maintenance, and consumer education, Fuji Rock Festival gives consumers a high-impact festival experience like none other through sustainable, green practices, which minimize environmental impact. Probably no single televised special event has a bigger impact on American life than the National Football League's Super Bowl, but few Americans would have suspected that the 2008 Super Bowl XLII was 100 percent powered by renewable energy.

You, too, can make a big impact on your patrons without making a big impact on natural resources. Fennell's definition of ecotourism presents a goal for greener events pioneers to meet, a beacon of sophistication for you to labor toward. Not all events may be certified greener events, and very few events will achieve a zero carbon footprint, but all events may aspire to be a shade greener each time they are created and produced.

Fair Trade

One of the more visible trends to emerge from sustainable development is the Fair Trade movement, created to counteract unfair third world labor practices. As defined by the Fairtrade Foundation, a "fair trade" between manager and laborer means:

Fair pay
Investing in projects that enhance workers' quality of life
Partnership
Mutually beneficial long-term relationships
Social, economic, and environmental responsibility (Fairtrade Foundation 2011)

Event leaders know firsthand the importance of customer service: The greatest food on Earth feels like garbage when delivered by a grumpy waiter. Keep your staff committed to the cause and dedicated to excellence by treating them as partners in your enterprise. Offer them discounts. Keep them informed of company news. Encourage a positive employee culture. Consider an annual employee Thank You event. The Oxfam charity runs a hugely popular program for volunteers to serve as stewards at UK music festivals, picking up litter or directing crowds in exchange for free admission to concerts. The music festivals gain a free, enthusiastic workforce and the volunteers gain inspirational work and affordable recreation. Instead of seeing a sharp divide between staff and patrons, try blurring these boundaries to create a festive atmosphere that celebrates fair trade and equality. If the service staff are having fun, chances are the patrons will too.

Outgreening and Corporate Social Responsibility

CSR features strongly in this book as a charitable value for for-profit companies, and, indeed, CSR serves as motivation for many environmental initiatives. However, a growing number of forward-thinking companies are environmentally motivated by sheer profit incentives and competitive advantages. Friedman describes how green initiatives saved money and improved the performance of New York City taxicabs and how solar power gave the U.S. Army a tactical advantage in the Iraq war. He calls these strategies "outgreening," and calls for companies to not just settle for being "carbon neutral," but seek a "carbon advantage," for increased profitability and heightened performance (2008, p. 126). He makes this same argument, but in a political context, earlier in the book, quoting energy expert David Rothkopf:

"Green is not simply a new form of generating electric power. It is a new form of generating national power—period" (2008, p. 23).

Similarly, green is a new means of generating business power—period. Before even mentioning the ethical justification, Live Earth's Environmental Guidelines list six tactical advantages of greener events:

1. Attract and partner with artists. (At the Live Earth concert, more than 200 acts joined the environmental cause on a pro bono basis).
2. Be a responsible citizen and a visible environmental leader in your community.
3. Appeal to the audience that, although they may not recycle, like to know others are contributing to the good of the world.
4. A marketing and PR advantage over the competition.
5. Doing your part.
6. Knowing you and your employees make a difference every day.

Financial Savings

Financial savings come not just from accruing fewer expenses but also from government grants, which green companies are increasingly eligible for. As an event leader, you will know the iconic, unsurpassed value of a Steinway piano, but did you know that Steinways run on solar? Steinway, the world renowned piano manufacturing company, has the largest solar rooftop of its kind in the world, for which it received a $588,000 grant from the New York State Energy Research and Development Authority, and for which it expects to claim $266,000 in federal solar energy tax credits. As Steinway's vice president for manufacturing, Andrew Horbachevsky, explains, "We kind of backed into the ecological thing. Green is also the color of money" (Goldblatt 2012).

Green is certainly the color of money for billionaire media mogul Ted Turner, America's largest landowner, a committed environmentalist, and creator of the cartoon show *Captain Planet*, about an environmental superhero. At a fundraiser for the Captain Planet Foundation, the *New Yorker* quotes a conversation that Turner's daughter recalls having with her environmental activist father:

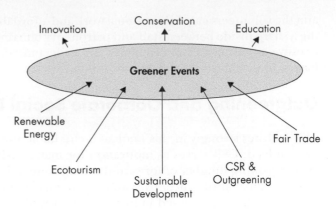

FIGURE 10.2 The Sam deBlanc Goldblatt theory of greener events. Greener events draw upon the inputs of ecotourism, sustainable development, fair trade, renewable energy, CSR, and outgreening. The three defining outputs of greener events are innovation, conservation, and education.

"He reminds me constantly, 'Do you know who Captain Planet is?' I'm like, 'No, Dad, who is he?' And he's like, 'It's me!' " (Goldblatt 2011).

As Friedman predicts, tomorrow's captains of industry may all be Captain Planets. Green business strategies of CSR and outgreening are two important aspects of emerging greener events. Figure 10.2 shows that these strategies, along with ecotourism, sustainable development, fair trade, and renewable energy (discussed later) help to define greener events. These diverse inputs form the modern definition of greener events and generate the three core outputs of innovation, conservation, and education.

Event Pollution

The 1999 Woodstock festival generated approximately 1,200 tons of landfill waste, the recycling of which would have meant the conservation of 5,100 trees, 2.1 million gallons of water, and 1.2 million KWh of electricity (Goldblatt 2011).

Twenty years later, the city of Virginia Beach, Virginia, stated in a news release that crews cleared away more than 10 tons of trash and debris left behind by "Floatopia" event attendees. Some of the items left behind included floats, beer bottles, clothes, and even some tents. The community was displeased with the total disrespect for their bay, animals, and beach (FoxNews 2019).

*Even after many efforts and increased awareness of reducing event pollutions, there are strong counterarguments for events that promote themselves as peace, love, and joy. Many of the current trends in the events industry are also unsustainable given the Earth's natural resources. Many events follow patterns of careless consumption handed down throughout society since the Industrial Revolution.

Your First Five Steps to Creating More Sustainable Events

Once you have analyzed the various kinds of pollution your event is likely to generate, it is time to create your plan of attack. A greener event's tools to minimize waste are known as **environmentally friendly practices** (EFPs), strategies that include everything from alternative energy to recycling. But Rome wasn't built in a day, and neither can events immediately turn green. Before we tackle the big EFPs, here are five small EFPs that you can employ right this minute in your home or office to drastically cut waste and conserve energy.

1. Go Paperless

Nearly all work is e-mail-based today. Think before you print: Do you really need to see it on paper? Consider the many documents distributed to clients, staff, patrons, and stakeholders that could be e-mailed instead of mailed. Make e-mail your first option, with a snail mail alternative for those who request it. Instead of keeping paper files for everything, burn digital files onto disks or portable hard drives. Of course, you will need hard-copy originals of all signed legal documents, as well as sentimental documents. The Capital Fringe Festival in Washington, D.C., annually outfits the office walls with an enormous festival calendar made from butcher paper and thousands of sticky notes, a process which encourages transparency and community within the organization. The official calendar, however, is digital, and they have recently taken the cost- and time-saving measures of going paperless with all artist applications. Remember that unimportant documents can be printed on junk paper, and other documents can be printed double-sided. Double-sided printing cuts your paper bill in half!

2. Turn Off the Lights

How many electronic devices are plugged in around you right now that are not in use? Stereos on standby, computers in screensaver mode, and fully charged cell phones that are plugged into electrical sockets are using electricity for no good reason. Turn off the stereo and computer, and unplug your fully charged cell phone. Most importantly, turn off all lights when not in use. These cost-saving measures for office and home are directly applicable to your greener events. All electronic devices and technical equipment need to be tested before the event, but, once tested and fully charged, they should be turned off until the pre-event phase. Video projectors, sound boards, spotlights, and Public Announcement systems can waste enormous amounts of electricity when left on standby. Turn them off and marvel at how low your next electricity bill is.

3. Turn Down the Heat

Insulate your building and your body. Winter is cold for a reason; if you have to wear a parka outside, you shouldn't get away with a t-shirt in the office. Outdoor heating units are increasingly popular but huge energy wasters. Instead of fighting against cold weather, capitalize on it! The 2009 London Ice Sculpting Festival brought thousands of people to the grounds of the National History Museum in chilly January 2009 with a little help from Icebox, the UK's leading ice art specialist. Challenge your patrons to embrace the cold with imaginative winter event themes. For indoor environments, double- or triple-glaze all windows and invest in better wall insulation. Germany has recently developed green buildings that are so insulated that they stay warm in the winter without any internal heating at all. How does "zero" sound for your next heating bill?

4. Buy Greener

Energy-efficient light bulbs are slightly more expensive in the short term and vastly cost-effective in the long term. Green cleaning products are competitively priced and much more pleasant to use and to smell. You can find consumer shopping guides on everything from green shoes to green furniture on *Tree Hugger*, a green lifestyle Web magazine.

5. Use Silverware

Get rid of those plastic spoons and paper cups, and treat yourself to real food and drink served with real silverware and dishes. Think about how much money you spend on Starbucks coffee, and then consider the savings of brewing your own coffee and encouraging the staff to bring in their own mugs and thermoses. If you provide coffee for event crew, consider encouraging them to bring in their own thermoses. Giving your staff opportunities to do their bit for the planet may just keep them motivated.

Cultural Sustainability

Part of greening your event is making a meaningful connection with your event site in order to ensure the preservation of its natural environment. The same goes for the inhabitants of that environment. Greener events leaders will find new and exciting ways to support *cultural sustainability*, an important principle of ecotourism, wherein the host culture is incorporated respectfully and meaningfully into the event's design. Greener events can partner with host cultures in two direct ways: culturally and economically.

Local Cultures

High in the North Sea, between Scotland and Norway, sits the Shetland Isles, the northernmost islands in the United Kingdom. Isolated from the mainland by a 12-hour ferry ride, Shetland's stunning, treeless landscape contains an exceptional culture, which combines rich nautical traditions that evolved from whaling to fishing and oil rigs, with Scottish and Viking heritage. This culture is celebrated and reinforced by Up Helly Aa, a unique Shetland event celebrated on the last Tuesday of every January. Originally a disorganized riot of marauding men firing guns and dragging flaming barrels of tar through the city streets, the event was institutionalized into a safer community heritage event around the end of the nineteenth century. Like New Orleans' Mardi Gras and the Philadelphia Mummers Parade, Up Helly Aa consists of over 40 different squads of men dressed in flamboyant costumes based on different themes. These "guizers" parade through city streets in a torchlight ceremony that culminates in the bonfire of a Viking longboat. They then spend the following 12 hours, from 8 P.M. to 8 A.M., visiting 12 separate town halls, where they regale local audiences with a brief skit or song, engage in a Scottish country dance or two, and taste the local food and drink. Although the Shetland Hotel serves as the unofficial town hall for tourists, tourism is not a core goal of Up Helly Aa. Many of the guizers' skits revolve around obscure local issues, and unlike tourist-friendly "ceilidhs" (traditional Scottish folk-dancing parties), there is no instruction on how to perform the complex group dances. This spectacular event is meticulously organized by Shetlanders, for Shetlanders, with the explicit purpose of sustaining Shetland heritage, culture, and community.

Greener event leaders will hold up this rich Viking pageant as a model of cultural sustainability. If your annual conference can connect with the Association of Dental Hygienists in just 1 percent of the meaningful cultural way that Up Helly Aa connects with Shetlanders, your event will succeed. Before arbitrarily imposing an event theme, research your patrons and discover their passions and dreams. Find unique ways to create meaningful connections between patrons. Similarly, respect the host culture of your event site location. You can win favor with the local authorities by partnering with local organizations or inviting prominent local figures to attend your event. Perhaps the Association of Dental Hygienists can donate surplus toothbrushes to a local hospital or invite students from a local dental college to attend the conference.

Local Economies

A local authority's greatest concern when reviewing an event proposal is often the potential economic impact. Destination event patrons want to experience local culture and consume local goods and services. By partnering with local businesses, you can satisfy both local stakeholders and patrons. The Connect Music Festival features diverse food stalls and bars operated by a wide variety of UK vendors. The best location and most spacious tent, however, is reserved for local distillery Loch Fyne Whisky and local seafood merchant Loch Fyne Oyster Bar. By featuring these emblematic local delicacies, Connect stands out from all other music festivals, offering patrons a uniquely Scottish highlands experience. This also supports the local economy, ensuring a stable political and economic environment for future festivals. What about the environment? By favoring local suppliers, greener events cut down on supplier transportation and, therefore, CO_2 emissions.

Promoting Your Greener Event

Marketing is one of the most important aspects of greener events, not only because it sells the event as contemporary and ethical but also because it educates patrons. Greener events pioneers should endeavor to leave every patron educated and inspired to pursue sustainability in his or her life and work. When the University of Colorado initiated a recycling program at football games, they periodically lit up the scoreboard with an "environmental savings report" to the cheers of 50,000 screaming fans (Goldblatt 2011).

Greener events can target various niche markets: Are you attracting a wild, free-spirited hippy crowd, who seek spiritual connection with nature, or are you serving ethical professionals who require modern amenities with elite environmental standards? The first group may be thrilled by composting toilets, while the second group might prefer the finest locally sourced, organic, gourmet cuisine. Regardless, events with an explicit environmental theme should publicly catalog every green initiative and strategy employed, distributing well-rounded information online, at the event, and in the press. Other events may employ more subtle themes, making artful use of the color green and employing smaller, more elegant informational signage.

Information and signage must be readily available. The same customer who complains about a cup deposit scheme may be thrilled to find that he or she is actually helping the environment. As Rego explains, "The challenge of really greening a venue is that a lot of it happens behind the scenes. What people see is the lights going on. They don't see the power that's going in from the windmills. They don't see the power from the biodiesel sitting out back behind the stage that's going into the generators" (Goldblatt 2011).

Publicize your windmill. Highlight your biodiesel. Encourage increased public discourse about greener events.

Toward a Greener Tomorrow

If the greenest event is the one that doesn't happen, why do we celebrate events? Why, for that matter, do we allow ourselves air travel when we know that the CO_2 emissions are corrupting the atmosphere? To be completely carbon neutral, must we live in thatched huts and sustain ourselves through local farming and hunting? Envisioning a completely green lifestyle can be quite scary, and too much to ask of any modern man or woman. However, thanks to constantly emerging technologies and human ingenuity, carbon efficiency is becoming attainable within our contemporary lifestyle, and for every sacrifice, there are new opportunities. Trading in your Segway for a pedicab, for example, can be viewed as either a reluctant sacrifice or an exciting opportunity. As a greener events pioneer, it is your job to harness new technologies and ideas to create your own imaginative portfolio of sustainable initiatives. These initiatives will grow a healthy business by growing a healthy environment. While you need not switch to 100 percent composting toilets, switching to energy-efficient light bulbs will save you time and money. Remember that not all events can become completely green, but all events can become greener.

SECUREVIEW

How might you apply the principles of environmental sustainability to secure a successful and sustainable career? First, ask yourself how you might work smarter rather than harder to conserve your energy. How may you use technology to advance your career in special events and create greater efficiencies? Second, subscribe to electronic-based job posting services and apply for positions electronically. You can also opt to conduct interviews using technology (e.g., Skype, WebEx). And when you are on the other side (hiring), apply the same strategies. Next, ask yourself how you may find a career position that allows you to promote green travel by using public transport. Finally, why not align yourself with a green events organization whose values you admire and want to support.

Education

While it is important for you to educate yourself and others about climate change and the value of greener events, it is also critically important for you to continually advance your career in event planning through other continuing education initiatives.

Only a few years ago, education was considered to be a minor requirement for employment as an event planning professional. Joe remembers participating in the first meeting designed to develop questions for the Certified Special Events Professional (CSEP) examination. He argued that the questions should be more rigorous. The professional educators attending this meeting reminded him that, because there was so little formal education in the field at that time, it might be difficult for even experienced Event Leaders to pass the test.

A few months later, a brave group of industry veterans sat for the first CSEP examination. They literally trembled as they walked into the examination room. Although combined they represented hundreds of years of professional experience, none had the benefit of formal education in the special events field.

Today, the landscape is dramatically different. According to studies conducted by Temple University, 172 colleges and universities throughout the world offer curricula, certificates, and/or degrees in planned-events-related fields. And the numbers continue to grow. A partial listing of these institutions is listed in the electronic appendix that accompanies this book.

These courses include:

- Advertising
- Anthropology
- Art
- Beverage management
- Business administration
- Catering
- Communications
- Culinary
- Design
- Education
- Floral
- Folklore
- Hospitality
- Hotel
- Information systems and information technology
- Law
- Museum studies
- Music
- Political science
- Public relations
- Recreation
- Sport management
- Television
- Theater
- Tourism
- Travel
- Web design and management

In addition to these related fields of studies, many colleges and universities offer specific programs in the field of event planning. George Mason University, Leeds Metropolitan University, Queen Margaret University, Temple University, Johnson & Wales University, Sheffield Hallam University, Bournemouth University, The George Washington University, the University of Nevada at Las Vegas, and dozens of other universities offer concentrations in special events, entertainment, and meetings and expositions. Northeastern State University in Tahlequah, Oklahoma, may have been the first college in the United States to offer specialization in the field of meeting planning and destination management. In addition, several colleges and universities throughout the world have adopted The George Washington University Certificate Program, so it is now possible to receive standardized training in this field in many different parts of the world as well as in the United States. In 2005, Temple University, School of Tourism launched the Executive Certificate in Event Leadership, a comprehensive industry certificate program linked to six interrelated event fields.

This growth in formal education for event leaders can be compared to the related field of information technology. In both areas of expertise, specific skills are required to ensure that high-quality performance is achieved consistently over time. However, unlike information technology, event leaders must also master the critical human resource skills essential for working effectively in teams. This dimension adds challenge and opportunity for educators as they work to develop a standardized field of study similar to that of medicine, law, accounting, or public relations.

In a research study by the authors, over 50 percent of festival and event leaders had earned a bachelor's degree and nearly 10 percent had a postgraduate degree. The percentage of event professionals with qualifications has continually increased, and today it is essential to have a certificate, a degree, or a professional certification for employment in planned events. Therefore, it may be assumed that professionals in this field are highly educated compared to the general working population in the United States. This means that those entering this competitive profession should expect to have a formal education plus experience in order to succeed. Increasingly, a major part of this formal education is specialized in the area of planned events studies.

A Body of Knowledge

Organizations such as the Event Industry Council, the International Association for Exhibitions and Events, the International Live Events Association, and the International Festivals and Events Association have identified specific bodies of knowledge within their industry sector. This knowledge is encapsulated in the certification programs that each organization has developed. While the body of knowledge varies according to the organization, generally each of these fields includes knowledge in these domains:

- Administration
  - Communications
  - Financial planning, management, and analysis
  - Information technology
  - Organizational development
  - Scheduling
  - Tax liabilities and regulations
  - Time management
    - Strategic planning

- Coordination
  - Amenities
  - Advertising
  - Awards
  - Catering
  - Decor
  - Entertainment
  - Etiquette
  - Human resource management
    - Conflict resolution
    - Staff recruiting, training, supervision, and reward
    - Volunteer recruiting, training, supervision, and reward
  - International customs
  - Lighting
  - Parking
  - Prizes
  - Protocol
  - Sound
  - Speakers
  - Strategic management
  - Transportation
  - Venues
- Marketing
  - Advertising
  - Analysis
  - Assessment
  - Conflict resolution
  - Evaluation
  - Negotiation
  - Planning
  - Promotion
  - Proposal development and writing
  - Public relations
  - Sales
  - Sponsorship
  - Strategic marketing
  - Stunts
- Risk management
  - Assessment
  - Compliance
  - Contracts
  - Financial impacts
  - Insurance
  - Licensing
  - Management
  - Permits
  - Planning
  - Safety
  - Security

In addition to these broad categories, each specialized field emphasizes additional requirements, such as exhibit planning and management, hotel and convention center negotiation, and catering. However, through consolidation, perhaps there will soon be an era of unprecedented collaboration among the various industry subfields. Event leaders should, in our opinion, adopt the model generated by medicine many years ago. Event leaders should be trained as general practitioners (such as the CSEP program), then earn additional certifications as specialists in individual fields. With this model, clients and employers worldwide will be able to use a global standard for event planning training and identify specialists who have advanced training in certain areas.

Education and Your Career in Planned Events

Obviously, it is important for you to obtain a strong general studies education at the undergraduate and perhaps graduate levels. In addition to general studies, you may wish to focus your education in areas where the majority of event leaders have earned degrees (business administration, education, and tourism, in that order).

Increasingly, event planning professionals are earning advanced credentials, such as professional certificates in events, meetings, expositions, and related fields. The professional certificate is often more valued by industry employers because it represents a specialized body of knowledge that is immediately useful to organizations that employ event professionals. Therefore, to be successful, it is important for event leaders to understand both the theory and practice of event planning. To sustain your career, you should carefully design an educational blueprint from

Career fair with many event organizations looking for bright event leaders.

which to construct your future career. This blueprint should include a thorough understanding of the history and theory of the profession, skill training, and practical observation and application. A model blueprint for developing your event planning education is as follows:

- General studies education: arts and sciences, business administration (observation/ internship)
- Postgraduate education: business administration, tourism, Event Leadership (practical training/externship)
- Executive development: certificate in event planning, meetings, expositions, or related field (observation/externship)
- Certification: Certified Special Events Professional (CSEP), Certified Meeting Professional (CMP), and up-and-coming Digital Event Strategist (DES), or other respected industry certification program (practical training)
- Continuing industry education: through professional associations, such as the International Live Events Association (ILEA), Meeting Professionals International (MPI), and others (observation/practice)

In addition to this formal education, successful event leaders combine classroom experience with extensive practical training. Undergraduate students at Queen Margaret University have greatly benefited from student work experience and internships and externships ranging from small event planning consulting organizations to the International Olympic Games. They have coordinated expositions for up to 40,000 people and have observed small social events. Every opportunity has provided a rich learning experience for these professionals. We strongly suggest that you invest a minimum of 15 to 30 hours per year observing or practicing under the aegis of another event organization. By observing the best (and sometimes worst) practices of others, you will find that the educational theory and skills you studied earlier will synthesize into a new foundation for future success.

Major attention and efforts have been placed on planning sustainable events over decades, and its importance will become even more prominent in the future.

It requires event leaders to possess extensive and professional training of key factors influencing sustainable event planning.

In May 2018, the Events Industry Council hosted the first Global Sustainable Event Standards Forum at IMEX Frankfurt. It brought together leaders in the sustainability community to discuss event standards and criteria and how to encourage adoption of these practices globally.

Extensive discussion and debate among eighteen representatives resulted in drafting a definition for event sustainability that included four guiding principles that the participants believe should underpin any sustainable event standards. The Events Industry Council is launching a campaign to engage event organizers, suppliers, and corporations in the cause and to make a commitment to these principles.

Professional Experience

Finding a worthwhile internship or externship may be a daunting task, especially for a newcomer to the industry. First, it is important to understand the difference between internship and externship. Generally, *internship* is used to describe a supervised experience that an undergraduate or graduate student affiliated with a college or university receives while earning academic credit. *Externship* refers to the practical experience that a senior professional employed in the event planning industry receives in an organization other than his or her own.

Internships and externships should both include a blend of observation and practice. One of the earliest descriptions of formal education is that provided by the philosopher Socrates, who described the educational process as including observation and questioning. Using the Socratic method, you should find outstanding organizations or individuals or both, observe them, ask lots of questions, and then draw your own conclusions from this experience. In the best scenario, your industry teachers or mentors will simultaneously question and challenge you (just as Socrates did with his protégés in ancient Greece).

Career Paths

Duncan Hendry is the former chief executive of the Festival and King's Theatres, two of Scotland's largest performing arts theatrical charity, presenting hundreds of performances of music, opera, dance, and theater every year. As chief executive, Duncan Hendry is not only responsible for programming these fantastic venues but also responsible for the management of two major public buildings.

According to Duncan, career paths may vary, as he illustrates with his own example.

I've been very lucky in that I've had the opportunity to pursue a career that I was really interested in and passionate about. For most of my career I've followed opportunities that have cropped up that felt exciting at the time. Only on a couple of occasions have I made what I would describe as a strategic career move—the first being when I decided to leave the uncertainty of concert promotion to run a festival funded by the local authority. The second being after I had run a festival for 10 years and it felt as if it was time to move on and perhaps move into the marginally more secure area of working in venues rather than festivals.

My most recent move from running the Aberdeen Performing Arts in the North East of Scotland to moving to the Festival and King's Theatres in Edinburgh was perhaps more of an instinctive or perhaps visceral decision—it just felt like an exciting thing to do–without making any financial sense–but I haven't regretted that decision for a second.

During his long career, Duncan has had some exciting experiences in terms of production of special events. He recalls one exciting time when he had to hire a private jet for the godfather of soul, the late James Brown.

> Then there was the time that James Brown flew himself and his entourage into different UK airports for an evening concert in Aberdeen—I had to charter a plane to go to Glasgow to fly all 32 of them to Aberdeen to get them there on time. It was a difficult experience but it was worth it to bring the Godfather of Soul to Aberdeen for one night only.

Career paths may indeed vary; however, it is important that you continually progress in your career in special events and one of the best ways to do this is with an internship or externship.

Finding an Internship or Externship

One of the easier ways to identify a high-quality practical training opportunity is through a formal institution of learning, such as a college or university. Another way is through professional networking in an industry organization. Using the auspices of a college or university may provide you with additional credibility for obtaining a high-quality practicum experience. In fact, a professor of planned event studies can help you open doors that were closed to you before. Many planned events employers may even be suspicious of persons who wish to engage in a practicum for fear that this is merely a ploy to steal ideas for use in their own companies. Therefore, the intervention of a college professor or mentor can provide an employer with reassurance that the practicum experience is required for graduation and that students will be supervised to ensure proper ethical behavior.

Once you have identified an appropriate practical experience, you should send the potential supervisor a one-page brief description of the observations, experiences, and outcomes you desire from this experience. Figure 10.3 is an example of such a document.

Some internships are paid, others include a small stipend, a few provide living expenses, and still others provide no compensation or expenses. You must determine the best setting for your needs and whether compensation is required. If you are an event leader who is providing a practical training opportunity, it is important to remember that U.S. labor laws prohibit displacing a paid employee for an unpaid intern. Therefore, event leaders and other employers may use interns to support staff but should not utilize them as a means of displacing current employees to reduce expenses.

During the internship or externship, you should exhibit good work habits (e.g., good attendance, punctuality, dress) and conduct yourself in a highly ethical manner. For example, it is important to ask your supervisor about proprietary information and then to abide absolutely by his or her requests for confidentiality. Finally, remember that you are there primarily to learn from these people, who are more experienced than you. Therefore, refrain from offering unsolicited advice. Instead, carefully write down instructions, observations, and other notes in a journal to help you document what you are learning. At the same time, note any questions and then ask for time with your supervisor to probe him or her with questions concerning any areas of the practicum where you need further clarification.

At the end of the practicum experience, both you and your supervisor should have a debriefing session to evaluate the practicum. The supervisor should complete forms describing your attendance, punctuality, performance, and learning capacity, as well as write a letter of recommendation for use with future employers.

Date

Dear Employer, Supervisor, etc.:

Your organization is one of the most respected in the special events industry and, therefore, I am requesting the opportunity to receive a practical training experience under your auspices. The training will require the following commitment from your organization:

1. Five to ten hours per week on-site at your place of business, observing your operations
2. Participation in practical experiences you design for me to enhance my learning experience
3. Your supervision of my practical training
4. Completion of a brief form evaluating my performance at the end of my practical training
5. Submission by your firm of a letter of recommendation for me (if appropriate) to assist me in career development

I will be contacting you in a few days to discuss this opportunity, and I thank you in advance for your consideration of this request.

Sincerely,

Jane Event leader

cc: Prof. Joe Goldblatt, Ed.D, FRSA, Professor and Executive Director, The International Centre for the Study of Planned Events, Queen Margaret University, Edinburgh, Scotland

FIGURE 10.3 Proposal for event planning practical experience opportunity.

You should promptly write a thank-you letter to the supervisor expressing your appreciation for this unique opportunity.

A good practicum experience requires the commitment of both a generous supervisor and a curious and loyal student. When you plan this experience carefully, you will find that you have not only established a rich learning opportunity but built a lifelong connection with mentors who will encourage your success.

Certification

Professional certification is the sign of professions that have matured and seek a uniform standard to ensure consistent levels of excellence. Most professional certification programs, such as Certified Public Accountant (CPA), were developed early in the twentieth century. One of the reasons for the development of industry standards and certification was to limit the role of government in licensing emerging professions. The event planning industry has followed this historic pattern.

ILEA (formerly known as the International Special Events Society) established the Certified Special Events Professional (CSEP) certification program, which was originally based on the empirical studies conducted by the Canadian government. ILEA elected to consolidate the Event Manager and Event Coordinator into one comprehensive vocation titled Event Manager or Special Event Professional.

According to the Canadian government and the ILEA certification committee, the vocation of event planning requires competence in four knowledge domains. These represent the body of knowledge in the field of Event Leadership and, therefore, require a high degree of competence in administration, coordination, marketing, and risk management. ILEA further ratified the findings of the Canadians by stating that the critical path for the production of a professional event required administration, followed by coordination, succeeded by marketing, and then finally reduction of exposure through well-developed risk management.

Today, hundreds of event professionals worldwide hold the title of Certified Special Events Professional (CSEP). To obtain this difficult and challenging designation, they must exhibit a high degree of professional experience, formal education, and service to the industry and must pass a two-part examination. The CSEP is considered by many as one of the most rigorous assessments in the event planning industry, and those who earn this designation are considered to be the preeminent practitioners in the industry. You should aspire to join their growing ranks. Their exam is fully automated, and you may take the examination at various locations throughout the world.

According to the Event Industry Council (EIC) more than 10,000 professionals hold the title of Certified Meeting Professional (CMP). This certification predates the CSEP and requires a point system to qualify for sitting for their multiple choice examination. One of the major benefits of this certification is that recent studies show that more and more often persons with the CMP are given hiring preference, and statistically CMPs earn significantly higher salaries than those without this certification. In addition, it is important for event leaders and students to stay focused on what new credentials or certifications are developed as the event business is changing to adapt to a new world and younger generations. One such example of an emerging certification is the Digital Event Strategist (DES) by PCMA (www.digitalexperienceinstitute.org/digital-event-certification) and Sustainable Event Professional Certificate Program (SEPC) by Event Industry Council (www.eventscouncil.org/Sustainability/SEPC).

We often point to the example of medical doctors as one reason why it is so important to ensure that professional event leaders function at a consistently high level. Doctors have the ability to save lives but also lose lives one person at a time. Event leaders, by contrast, can save or lose hundreds or thousands of lives at one event, depending on their level of training, experience, and that illusive quality called judgment. Therefore, the event leaders, in our opinion, has an even higher degree of responsibility than doctors. In addition, event leaders often organize seminars or educational programs that train current and future doctors, so our responsibility extends into their profession, as well.

Recertification

Many certification programs require that certified leaders be recertified every few years to ensure that they are currently engaged in the industry and that they remain knowledgeable about developments in the field. The process for recertification typically requires documentation of education, experience, and service to the industry. The CSEP program requires recertification every 5 years after the initial certification has been granted. Recertification is based on continuing education and continuous employment in the planned events industry.

Credentials

We are often asked by prospective students to quantify the value of a master's degree versus a certificate. Typically, the questioner asks: "What do I need to be successful in the field of planned events—a undergraduate degree, a professional certificate, a professional certification, or a master's degree?" The question automatically assumes that credentials or third-party validation is important to success in the special events industry. This is a correct assumption. Although it has not always been the case, the facts clearly indicate that, in the U.S. economy, those who have credentials earn more, are promoted more often, and enjoy more economic and career opportunities than those who do not have appropriate credentials. It is very common to see job listings in the event industry list "CMP preferred" in postings.

The type of credential you earn depends largely on which sector of the events industry you decide to enter. For example, in the government and education sectors, it is generally known that the education you attain affects the promotion or appointment by salary grade, whereas in the association sector, although education is important, it is also acceptable to obtain certification to demonstrate your training, competence, and experience level. However, in the corporate sector, increasingly, it is not unusual to find MBAs who are responsible for coordinating major events.

Bill Morton, former chairman and chief executive officer of Jack Morton Worldwide, one of the world's largest experience marketing and planned events firm, once told Joe that his firm actively recruited MBA students from leading business schools for senior management positions. He explained that the blend of strategic thinking skills, marketing analysis and execution capabilities, and financial management training and experience helped his firm ensure that strong management leaders would sustain and advance the mission of the 60-year-old firm.

It is interesting that Morton did not specifically mention the need for experience in planned events as a prerequisite for appointment as a leader in his firm. In fact, planned events experience, although important, is not essential to succeed in many organizations today. What is essential is proof or evidence that you are competent to advance the goals and objectives of your employer. Increasingly, employers are turning to third-party organizations, such as colleges, universities, and certification organizations, to vouch for this competence.

When we give references for students enrolled in planned events academic programs, potential employers ask the typical questions about persistence, punctuality, and intellectual capacity. However, ever more frequently, they ask questions about the ability of the candidate to work in a team, to communicate, and to lead an organization to accomplish specific goals and objectives. Although it is difficult to quantify, much less rate, these abilities, employers count on them to determine if the candidate they will hire will succeed quickly after he or she is appointed. This is another reason why it is important to obtain a credential. Behind every credential

TECH/APPVIEW

Make certain you are fully using the power of the Internet to promote yourself at all times. Establish your own personal wiki, website, and weblog. Use these sites to demonstrate the growth of your career by posting photos (with permission of the copyright holder) of the events you are producing, testimonials from clients and your thoughts about the future of planned events. Next, make certain you are listed on LinkedIn and participate in relevant discussions with other professionals who are at your level or slightly higher. This way others can quickly get a sense of your ability to think, analyze, and discuss key issues within the industry. Use the infobahn to accelerate your career advancement through electronic professional networking. It is very important to note that SNS, although it started as an informal method of communication mostly among friends and closed groups, is now officially requested and reviewed by employers such as governments and their agencies as a part of application review materials. As of May 2019, anyone who wants to get a U.S. visa to enter for event experiences, are now asked for their social media history by the U.S. State Department.

are people who tested, assessed, and can vouch for the integrity, persistence, communications, and leadership abilities of the person holding the credential. Whether they are former professors, industry certifiers, or even internship supervisors, each one has had a prolonged, intimate, and objective opportunity to evaluate the candidate. For this reason alone, it is important to earn a credential; with it comes references and contacts that will help you gain employment and promotion.

So you may ask what credential is most valuable. The simple answer is: all of them. We recommend that you determine what your industry sector demands in terms of a credential and, as soon as you earn it, begin exploring how you can earn the next credential. In today's competitive global business environment, you must demonstrate your competence continually. Whether you are in Asia, the Americas, Europe, Australia, or Africa, governments as well as nongovernmental organizations are developing higher standards for event leaders. For example, the governments of Great Britain, South Africa, and Australia have joined Canada in developing standards for event planning professionals. These standards require high levels of professional education, as well as experience. Therefore, to compete in the global planned events industry, you must continually seek the credentials that future employers demand to ensure your long-term success in this growing field.

Power Tools

Once you have mapped your journey, you need transportation tools to ensure that you arrive speedily at your destination. Historically, the most powerful tools have been the résumé and cover letter. We recommend that you follow these 10 steps to best apply these tools:

1. Create a preliminary list of employers who have (or are likely to have) open positions in your field.
2. From this short list of 25 to 50 people, create a computer database using Access, Excel, Filemaker Pro, or a similar contact management software program.
3. Send a cover letter to each contact, as shown in Figure 10.4. Customize the letter for each organization based on the homework you have completed to learn about the person and the organization's strengths.
4. Wait 2 weeks after the letter has been mailed, and then call each contact between 7 and 9 A.M. or between 5 and 7 P.M. These are the best times to reach your contact directly without interception by an administrative assistant.
5. When you reach the contact, reintroduce yourself and assume that the person has received your letter. ("I am calling about the letter I sent you requesting a personal interview.")
6. Ask for an interview at one or two specific times. ("Could we meet in person or by telephone on Tuesday at 10 A.M. or Thursday at 4 P.M.?")
7. If the contact agrees to meet with you in person or by telephone, thank the person immediately and reconfirm in writing via e-mail or other correspondence.
8. If the person refuses to see you, ask if there are others whom you should see or other organizations that could benefit from your skills to which the person can refer you. Get at least three to five referrals. Add these names to your database.
9. If you confirmed the meeting in person or by telephone, conduct further research about the organization so that you are prepared to ask pertinent questions.

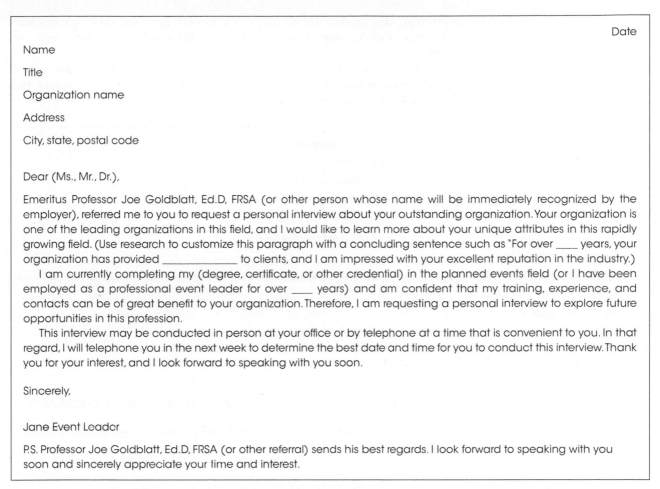

Date

Name

Title

Organization name

Address

City, state, postal code

Dear (Ms., Mr., Dr.),

Emeritus Professor Joe Goldblatt, Ed.D, FRSA (or other person whose name will be immediately recognized by the employer), referred me to you to request a personal interview about your outstanding organization. Your organization is one of the leading organizations in this field, and I would like to learn more about your unique attributes in this rapidly growing field. (Use research to customize this paragraph with a concluding sentence such as "For over ____ years, your organization has provided _____ to clients, and I am impressed with your excellent reputation in the industry.)

    I am currently completing my (degree, certificate, or other credential) in the planned events field (or I have been employed as a professional event leader for over ____ years) and am confident that my training, experience, and contacts can be of great benefit to your organization. Therefore, I am requesting a personal interview to explore future opportunities in this profession.

    This interview may be conducted in person at your office or by telephone at a time that is convenient to you. In that regard, I will telephone you in the next week to determine the best date and time for you to conduct this interview. Thank you for your interest, and I look forward to speaking with you soon.

Sincerely,

Jane Event Leader

P.S. Professor Joe Goldblatt, Ed.D, FRSA (or other referral) sends his best regards. I look forward to speaking with you soon and sincerely appreciate your time and interest.

FIGURE 10.4 Model cover letter.

10. During the personal interview session, do not offer your résumé unless requested. Instead, show your portfolio of an event or events that you have produced. Conclude the session by asking directly: "What would be necessary for me to earn the opportunity to work for your outstanding organization?" Do not speak again until the contact tells you specifically what is necessary to earn the job.

    Finding a great job in this field is a combination of timing, persistence, and talent. Timing is the most elusive part of the equation, because rarely is a job created specifically for you. Instead, you have to wait until a position needs to be filled. This is why persistence is important. You may wish to create a electronic greeting card has your photograph and a few lines about your experience, skills, and credentials, and mail this to your contact list on the same date each month as a reminder of your interest in working for them. Personalize the card with a handwritten e-mail note that says: "I am writing further to indicate my interest in working for your outstanding organization. Please let me know if there is an opportunity to work with you in the near future."

    The e-greeting card technique has been highly effective with our students for the last decade, as the tenure of employees in an organization has shrunk from 2½ years to less than 1 year. During a period of full employment, employers are constantly on the lookout for capable people able to start work immediately. Your postcard may arrive at just the right moment, and, instead of conducting a formal search for candidates, the employer may telephone you to interview for the job. You have already shown interest, enthusiasm, organization, and persistence, and these are qualities that employers value. You have also made the company's job easier by helping it find you quickly.

The two critical tools, the résumé and the cover letter, must be consistent with the standards used traditionally in the event planning field. Figures 10.4 and 10.5 provide models for you to use in the future.

Résumé

Jane Event Manager, CSEP

1234 Main Street

Celebration, Florida

Telephone: (304) 544–1234

E-mail: jem@eventsrus.net

Career Objective

To assist a leading event organization to achieve high quality and rapid growth through my contributions as an event planning professional.

Professional Experience

- Managed a 2,000-person healthcare exposition with a budget of $150,000 in March 2010
- Coordinated a 500-person legal conference with a budget of $50,000 in September 2009
- Developed and managed a 50-person executive education retreat with a budget of $19,000 in July 2009

Related Experience

- Conceived and coordinated a 1,000-person community festival with a budget (including in-kind contributions) of $50,000 in spring 2009
- Led a 25-person event planning workshop/retreat with a budget of $1,000 for the purpose of organizing an annual conference for a community-services organization

Volunteer Experience

- Founded a 500-person bazaar with 50 exhibitors and a budget of $500 for Holy Name Church
- Created and managed a 250-person banquet for Cub Scout Awards with a budget of $1,200
- Organized and managed a 100-person fundraising walking event for AIDS prevention with a budget of $3,000

Education and Training

- Candidate to receive the Queen Margaret University honors degree in Events Management (July 2020)
- Certified Special Event Professional (2013, recertified 2019)

Awards and Recognition

- International Special Events Society Volunteer of the Year, 2017
- Dean's List, George Mason University, 2018
- Employee of the Month, Regent Hotel, May 2017

Technology Skills

Access, Computer Aided Design, Excel, Word, World Wide Web, Web design (HTML), Social Network Service account maintenance and creation, Event Mobile App development

Languages

Spanish (high verbal and written)
Chinese (moderate verbal and written)
French (low to moderate verbal)

References

Available upon request

FIGURE 10.5 Model résumé/curriculum vitae.

Note: Résumé should not exceed one page.

The purpose of the résumé and the cover letter is to reduce to writing the impression you will make in person. These important tools rarely help you obtain a job unless they are supported by a good reference, your homework about the organization, and, most important, the impression you make in person. We strongly suggest that you work with a career coach through a local university or college or someone in private practice to help you optimize your abilities when you are ready to make that all-important first impression.

Gene Columbus, a veteran leader for over three decades in human resources for the Walt Disney Company, has written what we consider to be the definitive resource in career planning for event professionals and aspiring professionals, including students. This book, published by John Wiley in 2020 has hundreds of additional resources to help you launch or sustain your career. We recommend that you acquire *The Complete Guide to Careers in Special Events* by Gene Columbus.

New Hiring Practices

With the rapid development of the Internet coupled with low employment, event planning employers have been flooded with résumés through their individual websites. To overcome this burden, many employers have created electronic application systems. These systems are extremely prescriptive and leave little room for creativity or innovation to be exhibited by the event planning applicant. However, many will allow you to upload your résumé at the end of the application process. It is critically important that you include key words related to the job application in both your online application and your résumé. These words will be scanned into the computer and analyzed for candidates who match the criteria set forth in the job description. Therefore, it is important to carefully select the words and phrases you submit to improve your chances of being interviewed. Figure 10.6 provides an example of how to match your key words to the job description.

Life and Career

Too often, event planning professionals build a successful career and at the same time risk ruining their personal lives. Although mental and physical stress are not unique to the events industry, the constant demand for creativity and innovation, and the increasing speed of delivery, can cause event planning professionals to literally burn the candle at both ends until exhaustion and illness require professional intervention.

Recently, a leader in the festival industry grew irritated with Joe when he explained that many of the generation described by demographers as cuspers or busters do not want to work a traditional workweek of five 8-hour days. Instead, according to research, many prefer to work a shorter workweek with longer

Job Description:	Key Words for the Application and Résumé:
Event marketing professional with experience in sponsorship merchandising, advertising sales	Experienced, event marketing, sponsorship, merchandise sales, advertising sales, increased sales, increased sponsorship, increased advertising revenues, skilled in Adobe, Publisher, HTML, and other publishing software. Extensive experience In social media design, management and evaluation

FIGURE 10.6 Making the match: Linking your education, skills, and experience to the event planning job description.

Photo by Seungwon Shawn Lee

Dr. Goldblatt delivers the keynote speech about festival destinations and professionals development for the China event industry, Chengdu, China.

workdays. The reason for this major paradigm shift is the recognition that the 7-day workweek of preceding generations ultimately led to rapid burnout. In protest, the cuspers and busters choose to work a shorter number of days and a longer number of hours per day. This schedule permits them to separate work and leisure activity and grants them longer weekends (3 days as opposed to 1). Furthermore, they prefer to separate work from leisure in order to fully enjoy recreation, culture, and other activities.

Perhaps there is a lesson to be learned here—or several lessons. In an age defined by technology, it is often difficult to escape from the world of work. Therefore, to find a life in addition to a career, one must be ever vigilant about understanding the difference between these two values. Experts in leisure study define work as the absence of leisure. However, for work to be enjoyable, it must be rewarding and fulfilling. Therefore, to sustain life and career, it is important to understand the nuances that define the difference between each of these two similar but different states of being.

Because the special events industry is perceived by guests as "a fun business," practitioners often forget that, in fact, this is the business of fun. As a business it requires hard work, persistence, and talent. Each of these tasks is bound to deplete your energy. You must replenish this expenditure of energy with a healthy lifestyle that includes proper exercise, nutrition, and spiritual nourishment. This replenishment is essential if you are going to experience both the joy of work and the *joie de vivre* (joy of life).

From Invention to Reinvention

To achieve long-term career success, it is important to develop a historical perspective of careers in this field. Compared to other more established professions, such as medicine and law, the relatively new profession of Event Leadership is better positioned as a career for long-term sustainability and growth. At the turn of the nineteenth to twentieth century, event leaders were unknown despite the fact that many events, including world's fairs and expositions, were produced in abundance. Like many modern professions, planned events first began as a craft that was learned through an informal apprentice system. However, in the 1930s, pioneers such as Jack Morton and others used their organizational skills in music and personnel management to conduct successful social and later corporate events. As events grew in size in the 1960s (Woodstock, Hemisphere in San Antonio), there developed a need for specialists to plan and manage these large-scale events. Specialists with experience in film, television, writing, music, and public relations/communications, such as the late Robert Jani, Tommy Walker, and David Wolper, used their skills to produce many of the marquee events of the twentieth century. These events included the opening and closing ceremonies of the Los Angeles Olympic Games in 1984, the Knoxville and New Orleans World's Fairs, the 100th Anniversary of the Statue of Liberty, the inauguration of President Ronald Reagan, and the ubiquitous Super Bowl half-time spectaculars throughout the 1980s.

The Emmy Award winning producer David Wolper's autobiography, *Producer* (2003), summarizes the newness of this field. Peter Ueborroth, president of the Los Angeles Olympic Games Organizing Committee, invited Wolper to lunch and asked him to produce the opening and closing ceremonies of the 1984 Olympic Games. Wolper discussed it with his wife and she asked, "Do you know how to do something like that?" Although he had attended three previous Olympics and had received numerous awards for television and film production, he had not produced events of the magnitude of the Olympic Games opening and closing ceremonies. He spent the night convincing himself, and the next day he accepted the job.

As the twentieth century came to a close, the demand for trained, experienced event leaders grew, largely due to the need for professionals who could fill the positions that were being created in this new field. For example, in the early 1990s, there were few classified ads listed under the heading of Event Manager, Event Coordinator, or Director of Special Events. However, by the end of the century, several ads appeared under these headings on a daily basis.

The event industry is a dynamic and multidisciplinary industry, and it produces positions that cross over multiple sectors. The authors interviewed industry experts in various fields for this book to gather career advice for students and young event professionals. Mr. Frank Supovitz, CEO & Presidents of Fast Traffic Events & Entertainment, and former Senior Vice President of Events for the National Football League, has provided invaluable advice about the exciting career.

Q: Please give career advice for students who major non-sports management and who want to be in sports event & entertainment industry. And what are the current trends in the multidisciplinary sport, entertainment, and event industry?

A: The skills required for sports events are very similar to those needed for entertainment and corporate events. Most event professionals work away from the field of play, dealing with operational, logistical, and production responsibilities. Those areas of expertise are common across nearly every kind of event. The technical knowledge base to execute a sports event on the field, in the pool, on the court, on the track, or on the ice and to manage participant athletes are specific and require specialists with relevant sport experience. But, more event jobs in sports use generalists with skills that are transferable across the entire event industry.

Through the development of formal education programs such as Queen Margaret University's Executive Master's in International Planned Events Management, Temple University's School of Tourism Event Leadership Executive Certificate Program, The George Washington University Event Management Certificate and Master's Degree Program (and their licensees throughout the world), Leeds Metropolitan University Diploma in Events Management and Great Britain Center for Events Management, Northeastern Oklahoma University's Destination and Meeting Management Program, the University of Nevada at Las Vegas Tourism and Convention Administration Program, The University of Technology, Sydney, Australian Center for Event Management, and, most recently, Johnson & Wales University's master of business administration (MBA) degree concentration in Event Leadership, thousands of students throughout the world are learning prescribed systems for leading events toward success.

As a result of the rapid development of this field, many of the early pioneers may shake their heads in amazement at how far the profession has come. While the first generation of Event Leaders (Jani, Morton, Walker, Wolper, and others) might be amazed at the progress the field has made in such a short time, the current generation of educators is hopeful that, through formal education, the profession will become better respected by the general public and will encourage sustainable careers.

We characterize three periods of economic growth of this profession: First was the era of the practitioners (those who learned by doing), which was roughly from 1930 to 1980. Next came the age of the educators (those who have learned through a combination of formal education coupled with guided experience in the field), which covers the period of 1980 to the present day. However, now as we are on the cusp of the second 50 years of this young profession, we are entering the age that will be dominated by future event leaders.

In the first edition of *Special Events: The Art of Science Celebration* published in 1990, Joe interviewed the late David L. Wolper (1928–2010) and asked him how he was able to motivate 100,000 people during the closing ceremonies of the Los Angeles Olympic Games in 1984 to spontaneously join hands and sing "Reach Out and Touch (Somebody's Hand)" (Ashford & Simpson with vocals by Diana Ross), and he told Joe that a producer must "know how to use special events to produce specific emotions in people. As a producer, I know how to invoke laughter, tears, joy, and, of course, love."

Nearly 15 years after that interview, Wolper wrote his biography, which charts his successful career as one of the preeminent producers of the twentieth century. According to Wolper, "The producer is the man or woman with the dream." Wolper examines his many successes as a producer from television's *Roots* to the 100th anniversary of the Statue of Liberty, through Liberty Weekend, to hundreds of other television spectaculars and special events. In fact, Wolper's work created the term *special event television*. In his own words:

I have been successful as a producer primarily because I had the natural ability to recognize a good idea, whether it came from my mind, or someone else's. I could sell the idea: I worked as hard as I asked anyone working for me to work to bring it to fruition. I was not afraid to take risks to achieve quality, and maybe just as important, I hired good people and gave them all the responsibility they could handle. I was always there in the background. I was never afraid to dive in and get dirty, but I had the good fortune to find great people and recognize their talent. And with my banking experience, I knew finance, so I could build a company. I was the orchestra conductor who picked the music. I was the cook who mixed the ingredients. And I was the judge who made the decisions. I picked the people who worked from my documentary company. I picked the right people when I created the ceremonies for the Olympics (1984 Los Angeles Olympic Games). I picked the right people to make Roots. I suspect that not one of the hundreds of people who worked for a Wolper company would state that I was an easy person to work for; I wasn't. I demanded quality.

Future planned event professionals must now embrace the traditions and educational opportunities of the past 50 years, and simultaneously using their strategic planning skills to chart a course for the future of the profession. This merger of practice, theory, and the ability to balance life and career will be essential as event leaders address the many new and unknown challenges in the new world.

As a future planned event leader, it is important that you lead, but also record, remember, and celebrate the triumphs, joys, and even sorrows of our lives. You are responsible for leading this effort. You are a modern pioneer destined to explore, expand, and improve the global event management industry in the twenty-first century. The global technological revolution we have created can hollow us or hallow us, depending on how we embrace it. We prefer to use the metaphor that the twentieth-century scientist Albert Einstein envisioned when describing his theory of relativity. Einstein wrote that "science without religion is lame and religion without science is blind." He envisioned that, one day, he would be able to ride a laser beam of light into the twenty-first century; indeed, his theories and ideas continue to challenge and illuminate us today. Einstein continues to ride into the future, taking us along with him, as our dreams become realities, just as his theories became scientific fact.

Sometimes a lamplighter must turn his or her light toward dark places to provide greater illumination or all. Mandla Mentoor is one example of this practice with the work he is doing in Soweto, South Africa. Mentoor, a community activist, has taken one of the most impoverished areas in South Africa and helped transform it into a tourism destination by using events featuring local artisans and performers to attract economic development. Describing himself as the founder, member, and director of the Soweto Mountain of Hope, Mentoor has proven that lives and places may be transformed through events. However, numerous other lamplighters in many of the dark corners of our world are also bringing illumination through events.

How May Planned Events Help Create, Sustain, and Celebrate a New World?

Whether in Edinburgh, Scotland, or Seoul, South Korea, Stavanger, Norway, or Seattle, Washington; Alice Springs, Australia, or Almaty, Kazakhstan, there is a common purpose for perpetuating and growing these celebrations. In Joe's studies with the Batwa Pygmies of Uganda, the aboriginal tribes of Uluru, and other indigenous people throughout the world, he identified five common motivations for celebration. According to his research findings, human beings celebrate to remember their ancestors, promote kinship within their tribe, demonstrate pride in their culture, and transmit rituals to future generations. However, according to the aboriginal elders he interviewed and whose commentary he researched at the Strehlow Research Center in Ayres Rock, Australia, there is a fifth motivation that may surpass all of the others in terms of power. The aboriginal elders told him that he would perhaps never really understand why these rituals, traditions, and celebrations were so important because, indeed, they were motivated and invested with magic and mystery. As one of the elders looked penetratingly into his eyes and revealed this belief to him, he reacted in a suspicious and typically skeptical manner. Although his reaction was motivated by the requirements of scientific inquiry, for the first time in his research, he realized something more important was being revealed to him than mere opinion.

For literally thousands of years, traditional people throughout the world have preserved and transmitted their celebrations for a common purpose. There is obviously a reason for this cultivation and transmission of the cultural symbols of celebration. The reason, we have concluded, is that these celebrations imbue their very lives with meaning. In fact, without these celebrations, people lack reasons for life itself. Anthropologists and sociologists who study linguistics have learned that when a common language is removed from a tribe, the roots of civilization are also destroyed. Celebrations are a common language that is perpetuated and expanded by all people to illuminate their lives.

Many years ago Joe's family celebrated his parents' 60th wedding anniversary in a public reception. His 86-year-old father was not in good health; however, he managed to stand in a receiving line for nearly 1 hour welcoming his guests. The next night, Joe's wife and sister began frying potato pancakes for the Jewish holiday of Chanukah at their parents' home. Later that evening, his father suffered breathing problems and an ambulance was called to take him to the emergency room. Sadly, he passed away that night.

They began planning the funeral service and Joe discovered that unbeknownst to all of them, his father had recently enrolled in a course entitled "Computing for Seniors" at the local community college. Not only did he enroll, but he actually graduated and received his official certification of completion.

Later, when he delivered his father's eulogy at the funeral Joe mentioned that throughout his father's long life, his father had always reminded his family to stay green and growing. He often said, "Never ripen. When you start to ripen you start to rot."

One way his father demonstrated his philosophy was by being one of the first senior citizens to correspond with his grandchildren through e-mail in the early 1990s. When Joe asked his father why he did not simply write them a letter, he looked at him incredulously and said, "You are becoming old- fashioned. You must always look to the future. I want my grandchildren to communicate with me and e-mail is how we will do this in the future." Well, of course, he was right about this development and so many other things as well.

Therefore, perhaps your greatest challenge as an event leader is not merely to light the lamps for those who will follow you in this growing industry but also to shine your lamp into the darker corners of the world and on those who will most benefit from your talents. As you find new places to shine your light in the future, we raise our glasses in a celebratory toast to you as you begin or continue your journey in the field of eventology. The celebratory toasts that follow indicate the many global opportunities ahead of you as a professional event leader. May your celebratory roots grow stronger and your wings beat faster as they take you and others further to rapidly advance the global celebrations industry!

- *Afya!/*Vifijo! (Swahili)
- *Apki Lambi Umar Ke* Liye (Hindi)
- *À votre santé!/Santé!* (French)
- *Ba'sal'a'ma'ti!* (Farsi)
- Cheers! (Great Britain)
- *Chook-die!/ Sawasdi!* (Thai)
- *Egészségedre!* (Hungarian)
- *Fee sihetak*! (Egyptian)
- *Fi sahik!* (Arabic)
- *Gan bei!* (Mandarin)
- *Gesondheid!* (Afrikaans)
- *Gia'sou* (Greek)
- *Hipahipa!* (Hawaiian)
- *Kampai!* (Japanese)
- *Kippis!* (Finnish)
- *Konbe!* (Korean)
- *Kong chien!* (Chinese)
- *L'chaim!* (Hebrew)
- *Mabuhay!* (Tagalog)
- *Minum!* (Malaysian)
- *Na zdorov'ya!* (Ukranian)
- *Na zdrowie!* (Polish)
- *Nazdrave!* (Bulgarian)
- *Noroc!* (Romanian)
- *Nqa!* (Sesotho)
- *Oogy wawa!* (Zulu)
- *Prieka!* (Latvian)
- *Prost!* (German)
- *Prost!/ Zum Wohl!* (Austrian)
- *Proost!* (Dutch)
- *Saha wa'afiab* (Moroccan)
- *Salud!* (Creole, Spanish)
- *Sanda bashi* (Pakistani)
- *Saúde!* (Brazilian, Portuguese)
- *Salute!/ Cin cin!* (Italian)
- *Serefe!* (Turkish)
- *Skål!* (Danish, Norwegian, Swedish)
- *Sláinte!* (Irish Gaelic)
- *Slangevar* (Scottish Gaelic)
- *Vashe zdorovie!* (Russian)
- *Zivjeli!* (Bosnian)
- *Zivjeli!/ U zdravlje!* (Croatian, Serbian)

INSIGHTS FROM GLOBAL EVENT LEADERS

Michelle Russell, Editor in Chief, *CONVENE* magazine by the Professional Convention Management Association (PCMA)

Michelle Russell is the Editor-in-Chief of *CONVENE* magazine. It is published by PCMA since 1986 and the leading meetings industry publication for educational content and professional development. She is a writer, editor, and collaborator who loves leading a talented team to produce a monthly award-winning magazine that elevates the role of the meeting professional. She has an entrepreneurial mentality and believe we are at an exciting crossroads in print and digital media (from her LinkedIn introduction).

Q: What career advice for students who major event management?

A: I think the future is really bright for live events. Just one reason why: According to the World Economic Forum's Future of Jobs Report 2018, the need for a workforce that prizes lifelong learning and upskilling is going to become more critical and this is where business events can bridge the gap. Here's an excerpt from the report: "To prevent an undesirable lose-lose scenario—technological change

accompanied by talent shortages, mass unemployment and growing inequality—it is critical that businesses take an active role in supporting their existing workforces through reskilling and upskilling, that individuals take a proactive approach to their own lifelong learning and that governments create an enabling environment, rapidly and creatively, to assist in these efforts." The challenge for event organizers will be to create environments and educational formats that are innovative and foster learning, making connections with peers, and building communities. And to think about these communities as being year-round, not just coming together physically once or twice a year.

Q: How does emphasis of sustainable and technology enhanced events affect career development of current event professionals?

A: Unfortunately, live events take a toll on the environment. Event professionals today must learn what they can do to minimize the environmental footprint, to offset carbon use, to avoid food waste, to recycle, reuse, and design events that keep sustainability top of mind. Event organizers tell us that they are overwhelmed by event technology. Business event strategists today and tomorrow must be technologically savvy, understanding what platforms and tools will make for effective events, gather the most insightful data, and deliver the best results while safeguarding attendee privacy.

Q: How valuable are the industry certificates/designations for career advancement?

A: Certifications and designations are highly valuable to help event professionals stay at the top of their game. In addition, *Convene* surveys indicate that those event professionals who obtain the CMP designation earn in the neighborhood of $10,000 USD more per year than their peers who do not.

Q: New skills that event professionals should refine/possess for next 10 years

A: To be strategic as well as understand logistics, to be knowledgeable about how adults learn best, to understand and accommodate a growing diverse attendee base's needs in terms of religious dietary preferences, cultural expectations (e.g., prayer rooms), to pay attention to wellness initiatives—in essence, to understand human needs and balance them with growing technology. This is a human-centered business, built on relationships and making connections, negotiations, and collaboration.

Q: How to become a global event leader? (e.g. education, experiences, skill sets . . .)

A: Understand cultural expectations. Diversity is having a seat at the table (bringing many different people together), inclusion is having a voice (making sure your speakers reflect a mix of genders/races/backgrounds/ages), and belonging is having that voice be heard. Event designers will need to create spaces where people of all different backgrounds feel that they belong in this community.

Summary

Chapter 10 explored the role of sustainable development from a environmental perspective as one example of how you can ensure you are developing a sustainable career in special events. The three great forces of global change include changing demographics, environmental awareness, and rapidly expanding technologies. Therefore, it is critical that you embrace these changes and respond appropriate with events and career decisions that will be sustainable in the future. One of the keys to sustainable development is to create a extensive program of continuing education, resulting in new experiences, education, skills, and qualifications such as professional certifications. You must continually look to the future and focus on remaining green and growing to seize the many new opportunities that are being created within the special events industry every day. It is critical to be updated with emerging careers for event leaders and provide a career blueprint from pre-college through late career reinvention. Volunteering, interning, and using emerging tools such as LinkedIn and the creation of video résumés can be good tools to explore throughout your career journey.

Key Terms

Electronic employment application: A prescriptive electronic portal wherein you must only apply by completing specific fields within a online application and uploading your résumé to a prospective future special events employer.

Fair trade: Fair pay, investing in projects that enhance workers' quality of life, partnership, mutually beneficial long-term relationships and social, economic and environmental responsibility

Greener events: Special events that continually endeavor to provide superior experiences through environmentally friendly strategies.

Key employment application terms: The use of key terms such as marketing, sales, sponsorship, production, design

that will be scanned and analyzed by a prospective special events employer through your online employment application.

Outgreening: The use of greener event strategies to promote competitiveness and increase profits.

Sustainability: The ability to wisely use the resources of today to create ever stronger and more successful tomorrows.

Sustainable development: The ability to only use the resources you need today to insure that you have sufficient resources for use in the future.

Career Connections

Create a 1-, 2-, and 3-year career plan. Use the forces of change identified in this chapter as levers you push to promote the sustainable development of your career.

Identify two or three new special events job opportunities, and select the appropriate key words to use when revising your résumé and completing the online application.

Next Steps

1. Analyze how the economic, social, and environmental impacts of your next special event may be improved through more efficient and strategic planning.

2. Create a detailed greener events policy for your next event.

3. Create a comprehensive greener events information and education program for your various publics so that you are able to inform and educate your guests about the greener opportunities they are experiencing throughout your special event.

References

BizBash (2009) Green inaugural ball leaves me fuzzy on the details, accessed June 12, 2013: http://www.bizbash.com/green_inaugural_ball_leaves_me_fuzzy_on_the_details/washington/story/14106/#sthash.4kVRVBfL.dpbs.

EPA (2019) Green Meeting/Conference Initiative. Accessed June 12, 2019: https://www.epa.gov/fgc/sample-green-meetings-and-events-policy; EPA 2019/

Esty, D. and Winston, A. (2009) *Green to Gold*, New York, NY: John Wiley & Sons.

Fairtrade Foundation (2011) accessed June 12, 2013: http://www.fairtrade.org.uk/what_is_fairtrade/fairtrade_foundation.aspx

Fennell, D. (2007) *Code of Ethics in Tourism*, Multilingual Matters, Channel View Publications, Bristol, UK.

FoxNews, T. (2019) *Floatopia' event in Virginia Beach leaves over 10 tons of trash on shoreline on Memorial Day*, accessed June 2019: https://www.foxnews.com/us/virginia-beach-floatopia-tons-trash-shoreline-memorial-day.

Friedman, T. (2008) *Hot, Flat and Crowded*, New York, NY: Farrar, Strauss and Giroux.

Goldblatt, S. (2012) *Greener Meetings and Events*, Hoboken, NJ: John Wiley & Sons.

National Geographic Society (June 2013) Countdown to extinction, accessed June 12, 2013: http://ngm.nationalgeographic.com/2009/01/endangered-species/klinkenborg-text.

United Nations (2012) Our common future, accessed June 12, 2013: http://sustainabledevelop ment.un.org/content/documents/UN-DESA_Back_Common_Future_En.pdf.

Wolper, D. (2003) *The Producer: A Memoir*, New York, NY: Simon and Schuster International.

PART FIVE

Best Practices and Real World Event Experiences

Global, National, and Local Best Practices in Event Leadership

Coach Lombardi was responsible for creating one of the most successful teams in American football and Yogi Berra not only was a Major League Baseball player on the field, but his wise and often humorous aphorisms have been quoted throughout the world. Both of these men recognized that most competitions are won off the field during research, design, planning, coordination, and constant evaluation of their performance.

While there are many definitions in the business management literature of the term "best practice," I prefer to define a best practice in the field of planned events as an event organization that demonstrates one or more of seven key attributes:

1. Best practice event organizations continually, over time, advance their mission through consistent performance improvement.
2. They continually innovate to improve and enlarge their body of knowledge.
3. They create new opportunities for the expansion of the profession.
4. They seek to promote positive global impacts through their individual contributions.
5. They promote sustainability through each event.
6. They demonstrate the highest level possible of corporate social responsibility throughout their organization and with every event they design and produce.
7. They generously share their best practices with others so that the entire industry and rise and prosper and become more sustainable.

Event management is often similar to long distance running, as shown by there participants in the BUPA marathon in Edinburgh, Scotland. Event leaders must often demonstrate great stamina to complete their journey.

In this eighth edition of *Special Events* we have analyzed dozens of successful global, national, and local events and then subjectively selected three event organizations that, in our opinion, best emulate the seven characteristics of a best practice special event organization. In fact, there are perhaps thousands of best-practice event case studies to choose from each year; however, these selections represent, in our own personal and professional judgment, those that deserve recognition and meet the criteria identified above.

The South by Southwest Festival (SXSW) global event that was selected has demonstrated how an event organization that stays closely attuned to forces and trends can continually reinvent itself and grow and prosper to become an international leader in its field. SXSX is the only global event that has been selected for this honor for two consecutive edition. SXSW was selected for this edition because of the foresight, integrity and courage the organisers demonstrated in cancelling their 2020 event due to the danger of spreading the Corona virus. They were one of the few major events to very early agree to cancel their event to protect their guests, local residents and others. For this reason, we have honored them again. The Norwegian Constitution Day Events, national event selected demonstrates how traditions and history may be beautifully integrated to promote national pride and engage multiple generations of Norwegians in and outside of Norway via series of themed events. Finally, the two local events selected show how local event can increase the feeling of belongings for local community; and sensitive planning and widespread community engagement can change media perceptions from negative to positive. In addition these local based events have set a firm foundation of a future legacy for other events to improve their practice.

In future editions, we will continue to search the world for best-practice event planning organizations, and we welcome your recommendations. Only through careful scrutiny and evaluation of these and future best practices will we continually improve our profession.

Best Global Event

The SXSW Global Phenomenon of Weird Practices that Work Wonders around the Corner and throughout the World

Austin, Texas is known throughout the world for its quirky slogan "Keep Austin Weird!" This slogan reflects the ultra-liberal and creative population that has developed in the capital city of Texas over many years. Austin's rich musical history has featured major performers such as Willie Nelson and others developing their international careers from within the city limits of Austin as showcased on the popular American television music series entitled *Austin City Limits*. Add to this heritage technology pioneers such as Michael Dell, whose direct sales model revolutionized the personal computer industry, and Rick Linklater, whose debut film, *Slacker*, not only coined an immortal phrase but is honored in the Library of Congress' National Film Registry, and you get a sense of the city's leading-edge diversity. In addition, Austin recently hosted America's first Formula One race since the Grand Prix left Indianapolis in 2007.

Despite these many noteworthy milestones, Austin's greatest accomplishment may be the birth, development and legacy of an unusual event called South by Southwest, or simply SXSW.

In 1986, the organizers of New York City's New Music Seminar—a conference, trade show, and festival for music industry professionals—visited Austin with the intent of launching a Texas spin-off. When they abandoned their plans Austin's alternative newsweekly *The Austin Chronicle* joined forces with local music promoters and managers in 1987 to organize their own music event modeled on the successful northeastern seminar. The name South by Southwest (SXSW) was chosen by the *Chronicle's* cofounder Louis Black as a play off of the Alfred Hitchcock film entitled *North by Northwest*.

The first event was held in March 1987 and 150 attendees were expected. When over 700 music biz representatives showed up from all over the United States, the organizers began to think they might have started something somewhat that was, well, truly weird.

Between 1987 and 2012, SXSW has become Austin's largest event in terms of combined economic impact. The estimated economic impact in 2012 was calculated at $190 million dollars in an analysis by Austin economic consulting firm Greyhill Advisors.

Over the past 25 years, the conference and festival have grown and changed by paying close attention to numerous macro-trends. In 1994, the festival added a film component that included a multimedia track, which proved so popular that in 1995 the two components were split into separate events entitled SXSW Film and SXSW Multimedia. In 1999, to once again reflect changing industry standards, Multimedia was renamed SXSW Interactive. Anticipating future trends, in 2011, SXSW launched events for the education industry (SXSW Edu) and the sustainability community (SXSW Eco), and August 2013 will see the birth of SXSW V2V in Las Vegas, a unique conference bringing together creative startups and venture capitalists.

Some people consider SXSW to be responsible for the rise of the film subgenre known as mumblecore. As has happened perhaps thousands of times in the past two decades, an origin myth came to life over drinks at SXSW, in this instance a musician who was also a sound editor is credited with coining this new term while sitting at a local bar with fellow festival goers.

Over the years, SXSW's conferences have regularly featured international trendsetters as part of their education program. For example, in 2006 SXSW Interactive featured Wikipedia founder Jimmy Wales and Craig's List founder Craig Newmark. Although the social media site Twitter was not officially launched at SXSW, it, like have many other technology platforms, gained tremendous traction in its embryonic stage as a result of participating in the festival. As one example of the power of SXSW for advancing new technology platforms, Highlight, Glancee, Sonar, Kismet and other social discovery (users finding users) mobile applications have gained instant traction during the Interactive conference. Although all of the SXSW events continue to grow, the Interactive conference attendance has more than doubled in the past few years to become the largest of them all.

Imitation is indeed the greatest form of flattery, and the SXSW format has been replicated throughout the world. However, the Austin, Texas festival continues to hold the preeminent position with its innovative decision to feature the music, film, and interactive industries within a single event for the creative industries. It is considered by most industry insiders to be the single best investment in terms of professional industry networking, introducing new products, and making important business deals as well as career connections. In this regard, SXSW is similar to the 65-year-old Edinburgh International Festivals that combine several different event genres within the same time period (Edinburgh International Festival of Music, Dance and Drama, Edinburgh Festival Fringe, Edinburgh International Book Festival, Edinburgh Mela, and more) to create a highly successful kaleidoscope of complementary programming for multiple audiences.

As a result of SXSW's significant long-term success and exponential growth, the City of Austin is facing challenges with developing ordinances and infrastructure to facilitate the growth of the event, which now spans 9 days and features over 2,200 musical acts, 425 film screenings, 500-plus trade show exhibitors, and 147,000 participants from all over the world. For example, in 2012 the city council considered ordinances that would strengthen safety and occupancy regulations and permit requirements for special events, especially at venues not typically used for public gatherings such as parking lots or retail establishments. According to City of Austin Music Program Manager Don Pitts, "We obviously want to keep the maverick feel of the city during SXSW, and our approach acknowledges that. The focus was planning, and then plan some more, and be prepared for anything to happen."

In 2012, SXSW became a Gold Green Business Leader in the City of Austin. With growth, the SXSW organizers recognize that they must take responsibility for their environmental impacts. One way they do this is though an innovative bike share program.

The year 2012 saw the creation of SXSW's first ever bike share program, SXcycles. According to many members of the bike industry, SXcycles was one of the largest free bike shares ever executed in the country. Open to all Film, Interactive, Gold and Platinum registrants, this program provided free bicycles for daily use courtesy of HBO's newest series, *GIRLS*. These Tern Link D8 folding bicycles were seen all over the city during SXSW Film and Interactive, and proved to be a fun, easy, and eco-friendly alternative for getting around downtown. During the beautiful Austin weather, all 150 bikes were checked out within 2 hours of opening! As SXSW programming grows to include more satellite campuses, we hope that SXcycles will play an integral role in helping registrants get where they need to go.

Mike Shea was not only a professional musician but also partner in a trade association management company 23 years ago when he first became a consultant to SXSW. Now, as executive director, he helps run the show. He describes SXSW as a global marketplace for ideas. One of the major challenges his event faces year upon year is the need for more accommodations—in 2012, SXSW's Housing Department booked nearly 11,000 hotel reservations totaling more than 50,000 room nights. As often happens with mega-events such as SXSW, the event's growth has outpaced the ability of hotel and other accommodation suppliers to keep up with demand.

One of the unique attributes of SXSW is that, despite its size, it retains a feeling of intimacy, as many business deals are conducted not in gigantic meeting halls but rather in official SXSW lounges or local bars and restaurants. In addition, SXSW producers developed a start up village concept wherein new developers can hone their entrepreneurial skills through contacts made in smaller, more intimate settings among strategically targeted like-minded persons.

In just over a quarter of a century, the SXSW Conferences and Festivals have demonstrated that sometimes in weird and wonderful places such as Austin, Texas, great ideas may take root, flourish, and grow. Perhaps, most importantly, this uniquely successful event has also demonstrated that the better a event organizer becomes at listening to his or her customers and anticipating local, national, and global emerging trends and forces, the greater sustainable success they will achieve over the long term.

SXSW
Roland Swenson, Cofounder and Managing Director
Nick Barbaro, Cofounder
Louis Black, Cofounder
Brent Grulke (1961–2012), Creative Director
Hugh Forrest, Interactive Director
Mike Shea, Executive Director

Best National Event

Norwegian Constitution Day Events, Oslo, Norway, and More

Norwegian Constitution Day is the national day of Norway observed every May 17. Among Norwegians, it is the biggest national holiday, referred to as *syttende mai* (meaning Seventeenth May), *Nasjonaldagen* (The National Day), or *Grunnlovsdagen*. While Independence Day is celebrated in other countries, Norway celebrates Constitution Day.

It is necessary to review the history of Norway's independence to understand how Constitution Day has become so important to Norwegian's celebration.

History of the Norway Constitution Day

The Constitution of Norway was signed at Eidsvoll on May 17, 1814. The constitution declared Norway as an independent kingdom after the Napoleonic Wars.

Originally, the celebration of this day began among students. However, it didn't continue. Norway was at that time in a union with Sweden, and the celebrations were banned between 1820 and 1829 by King Karl Johan of Sweden, believing that celebrations as a kind of protest and disregard against the union.

It finally became an endorsed and established tradition in 1833 when poet Henrik Wergeland gave a public patriotic speech to support reform of Norwegian government minister Christian Krohg.

The Highlight: Children's Parades and More

While the Norway Constitution Day events are related to its independence, they are nonmilitary in nature. And this is what makes this eventful day to standout compared

Norway's Constitution Day parade.

to many other countries' independence-themed events/parades. Norway's Constitution Day, rather, is all about children. There are children's parades all over Norway. Norwegian author Bjornstjerne Bjornson, who wrote the national anthem, came up with an idea of staging a parade just for primary school children, representing Norway's bright future. The first children's parade, for boys only, was conducted in 1864; girls were allowed to join in the parade for the first time in 1899. This parade is a patriotic spectacular of red and blue flags flying and marching bands. Each elementary school district arranges its own parade with an abundance of flags and marching bands between schools. The parade takes the children through the community, often making stops at homes of senior citizens, war memorials, etc.

Constitution Day's close association with children has continued on since then.

This holiday celebration brings a festive mood throughout the country, especially in Oslo, the capital. The festivities begin very early for adults with a 7 A.M. champagne Norwegian-style breakfast, comprised of scrambled eggs, salmon, and fresh bread. This breakfast is held early to allow people to attend late morning main children's parades and many more. Another special characteristic that contributes to making Constitution Day a unique holiday is all the beautiful *bunads* (the traditional Norwegian costumes) that the locals wear. Some 100,000 people travel to Oslo city center to participate in the main parade and festivities.

The magnificent Oslo parade includes some 100 schools and marching bands and passes the royal palace where the royal family waves and greets the people from the main balcony. During the parade, a marching band will play and the children will sing lyrics about the celebration of the National Day. The children also make a lot of noise shouting "Hurrah!", singing, blowing whistles, and shaking rattles. The parade concludes with the singing of the national anthem *Ja, vi elsker dette landet* and the royal anthem *Kongesangen*. After the parades, there are games for the children, and often a lot of ice cream, soda, sweets, and hot dogs are served—what a sweet finale for the children!

The parade is broadcast on TV and streamed online every year. You can watch its latest parade on Facebook :https://www.facebook.com/KOMONews/videos/live-its-syttende-mai-in-ballard-the-annual-parade-and-festival-celebrates-norwa/1837982846270039/.

In addition to the children's parades, there are other parades for citizens, which are led by marching bands and often local boy scouts and girl guides, local choirs, NGOs, etc. This takes place before or after the school's parade.

Brief Timeline of a Full Day of National Day Events (in Oslo)

- The Morning parade: Starts at Dreggen 7 A.M.
- The first parade takes place already at 7 A.M. from Mariakirken (St. Mary's Church), with a salute, the national anthem, and, of course, the Bergen song. The Morning parade ends with a speech at the Festival Square.
- The main parade: Departure from Koengen at 10:15 A.M. The main parade is one of the biggest events on 17th of May. It involves the city's "associations, corporations, and government agencies." The parade ends at the Festival Square.
- The Flag Parade (the Children's Parade): Starts at the Festival Square at 10:45 A.M. The Flag Parade starts from different schools and marches to the gathering at Festival Square. The route goes through the city center and passes the main parade and ends at Torgallmenningen.
- Fireworks round off the day at Festplassen at approximately 11:15 P.M. The firework starts relatively late considering Norway's long daylight time in May.

Celebration across the Country

It is a day full of national pride and festivities across Norway. In the municipality of Asker, the children gather in the morning outside Skaugum, the residence of the Crown Prince and Princess.

Bergen has its own traditions for the parade, including comic troupes, various local organizations, and a children's parade. A unique feature in Bergen is the city's many traditional and special *Buekorps*—the traditional drummer brigades.

In Trondheim, children from all the city's schools parade the streets of Trondheim in the morning. Later in the afternoon, the "Citizens Parade" (Borgertoget) starts. This is a parade in which firefighters, sports teams, students associations, and other associations are represented.

In Stavanger, the day starts with salute at 7 A.M. Later, there are the Children's Parade, Russ Parade, and finally Citizens' Parade. The British school has since the 1970s, later followed up by the Dutch school and the American school, carried flags from a number of countries from all over the world.

Kristiansand, in addition to parades of school children and citizens earlier that day, is known for its conclusion of National Day with dancing in the streets (*tapto*) and spectacular fireworks. For those who want to continue the party until midnight, a jazz band with local touches plays until midnight in front of the Christiansholm Fortress.

Celebration of Norway Constitution Day Abroad

Norway's Constitution Day is also an important event day for Norwegians living abroad to gather and celebrate. May 17 dinner is celebrated by many Norwegian immigrant communities throughout the world with traditional foods.

Since 1952, the Bay Ridge neighborhood in Brooklyn, New York, has had an annual May 17 Parade. The celebration is well attended and celebrated by Norwegian-Americans who immigrated to Brooklyn.

Petersburg, Alaska, also known as "Little Norway," is a Norwegian settlement with strong roots to its home country. The festival occurs in the weekend closest to May 17 and includes a parade, Leikarring dancers, herring toss, and even a pack of Vikings and Valkyries.

The largest Norway Constitution Day celebration festivities in the United States occurs in Stoughton, Wisconsin. The celebration includes canoe racing, two parades, an art fair, and a 20-mile run that starts in Madison, Wisconsin.

The Norwegian community in London holds a May 17 celebration each year in Southwark Park. The celebration is attended by a large number of Norwegians abroad and includes a small parade, a traditional service in the church, and the selling of traditional Norwegian goods, and a lot of Norwegian flags for Norwegians who have left theirs at home.

In Glasgow, Scotland, the 17th of May is celebrated at Murano Street Student Village where Norwegians enjoy the traditional festivities of the day with Norwegian traditional colors.

Stockholm, Sweden, has a large celebration with a parade starting at Engelbrektsplan and ending at Skansen with more than 10,000 participants.

Be Aware: Closures of Businesses

For foreign travelers visiting Norway on or around this annual holiday, most businesses/shops will not be open outside of some gas stations, hotels, and many restaurants. But even with restaurants, it is better to double check by calling ahead and asking whether they are open, to be on the safe side.

Best Local Event

Celebrate Fairfax! Festival, Fairfax, VA, USA

About the Hosting Place and Surrounding Areas

The hosting place of the Celebrate Fairfax! Festival, County of Fairfax is a county located in the Commonwealth of Virginia in the United States. It borders with surrounding counties and is a part of the Metropolitan Washington, D.C. area. With 1.1 million population, it is most populous and ethnically diverse jurisdiction in Virginia.

Overview of the Festival

Celebrate Fairfax! Festival is the Northern Virginia's largest community-wide celebration, known as simply "The Fair!" It takes place in every summer, the second weekend after Memorial Day (Monday of the last week of May, a national holiday). Its marketing phrase is "Summer Starts Here." It is hosted at the 25-acre Fairfax County Government Center. This annual festival entertains more than 70,000 attendees with more than 300 exhibitors, food vendors, and interactive activities during its 3-day event. The festival features live concerts on multiple stages, carnival rides, children's activities including a petting zoo and train ride as well as the Fairfax County Karaoke Championship. With multiple stages of entertainment, music, a showcase of arts and education with a mix of agricultural and high-tech, it has become a significant focal point of annual gathering and celebration of the community. Fireworks bright up the sky of Fairfax County nightly.

History of the Celebrate Fairfax! Festival and Its Organizing Bodies

The Celebrate Fairfax! Festival is a combination of a music festival and a county fair. It first opened its door in 1982 as the Fairfax Fair at a nearby university campus, George Mason University. As a fast-growing county, there was a growing need to create an event that unites growing population. Therefore, its goal was to be established as a major event to reach all of Fairfax's communities. Its inaugural planning committee was a blue ribbon commission comprising elected officials and community leaders. Its early version included commercial and county government exhibits, a cook-off, and carnival.

Initially, the festival was planned by the Fairfax County's office, the Fairfax County Extension Office. As its size and responsibilities grew, the festival was coordinated by the nonprofit Faxfair Corporation, and the university campus no longer could accommodate it. Then-brand new Fairfax County Government Center, the current venue, replaced its location and allowed to add more featured events including county government exhibits and additional programs such as the SciTech Center, which is a science, technology, and engineering focused 10,000 square foot pavilion of interactive science-based activities.

In 1996, Faxfair changed its name as Celebrate Fairfax, Inc. It enforced its mission "The Celebration of Fairfax County and Its Communities," and its vision was to be a key stakeholder of the festival. In 2000, Celebrate Fairfax, Inc., permanently changed the name of the Fair as the Celebrate Fairfax! Festival.

Highlights of the Festival

The Sunday Brew features local and regional breweries with multiple stages of non-stop entertainment and beer-themed activities and exhibits. In the United States, only people who are 21 years or older with a ticket can enjoy this fun and beer-filled event. The popularity of this event and increased sales of beer and alcohol allow the festival to have high-cost headliner entertainers on its program.

The Celebrate Fairfax! Festival is a highly experiential event with many interactive programs. VIP experience packages offer the individual guest access to sponsor-like benefits with the front of the stage viewing for headliner shows. Other highlights include Tastes of Virginia Wine Bar, Celebrate Fairfax 5k Race, and Robotics Pavilion.

Best Practice with Think-out-of-the-box Ideas

The Celebrate Fairfax! is an outdoor festival with an ongoing threat of inclement weather. It has come up with innovative programs to resolve such threats and to have a sustainable success.

There are 22 different ticket types, offering various choices for festival-goers. They include a general admission to VIP admissions with Gold, Platinum, and Titanium tiers, which include an access to every events and pavilions. Other examples of ticket choices are a Family VIP, special Sunday Festival Admission & General Sunday Brew Admission, and a 5K Race registration package. Since more than 40 percent of ticket sales are through online and available on the day of festival, it helps festival-goers to make choices even on rainy or windy days

Its increased online ticket sales are an outcome of strategically orchestrated digital-driven marketing. Celebrate Fairfax! does ZERO newspaper advertising. Its main marketing channels are social media and its website. Other advertising channels such as sandwich board, television, and radio are all designed to direct potential attendees to its website, where they can purchase various types of ticket packages.

Recognition and Awards

The Celebrate Fairfax! Festival was awarded with a Bronze Pinnacle Award winner by the International Festivals and Events Association for its quality and success in 2005. The festival was recognized as one of the Top 20 events in the Southeastern United States in 2006. It was also featured as the Best of Nova: Kid-friendly Festival by *Northern Virginia Magazine* in 2015 and 2016.

Year-long Celebrations

As the Celebrate Fairfax! Festival continues its success, the CFI produces a series of events to make Fairfax County to be filled with year-long celebrations, including the Workhouse Brewfest, Fall for Fairfax KidsFest, and Celebrate Fairfax CV+ Event Training Program.

For example, the Fall for Fairfax KidsFest is held on the grounds of the Fairfax County Government Center as a 2-day run weekend event in October. This family festival is full of activities including pumpkin painting, petting zoo, hayrides, kids crafts, and stage entertainment.

More updated event schedules can be found at http://celebratefairfax.com.

INSIGHTS FROM GLOBAL EVENT LEADERS

PETER CWALINO

Hospitality Sales Executive

http://goo.gl/AJT9ky

(Note: To see the complete video interview, visit the Book Companion Site for this book at www.wiley.com/go/goldblatt/specialevents8e.)

Peter Cwalino attended hotel school in Virginia and then transferred to the University of Nevada in Las Vegas and worked at the Flamingo Hilton hotel. Late he helped open the Rio Suites hotel and the moved to Dallas, Texas, 21 years ago. According to Peter, during his early career in Dallas he worked for some great companies including Mary Kay, the cosmetics giant, and Cadbury Schweppes, and now is the senior catering manager of the Fairmont Dallas hotel.

Q: What do you recommend for these individuals who are starting their career in special events?

A: Get involved by volunteering with events on a larger scale. The U.S. NFL Super Bowl was in Dallas in 2011 and was a great opportunity for volunteers. This will give you a good insight of what it takes to put on an event of that magnitude. Then I recommend you earn a degree from some [of the] incredible schools and programs that are currently available. You should also obtain a professional certification or certifications in this field such as Certified Meeting Professional (CMP) or Certified Special Events Professional (CSEP).

Q: What changes have you seen in our career regarding technology?

A: Two decades ago you saw the typewriter, a land line telephone, and today it is all about advanced technologies such as smart phones, and I think this is a huge change. From the Internet and the smart phone, you can Skype to conduct a meeting, and the audiovisual technology that is now available is incredible. Customers today expect quick responses and today through technology this is possible. For example, my goal at the Fairmont Hotel Dallas is to satisfy the client's request within 1 hour, and today's technology helps me achieve this goal moving rapidly from a inquiry to a request to a formal proposal.

Q: How has environmental sustainability affected the modern special events industry?

A: Fairmont Hotels and Resorts is one of the pioneers in eco-friendly green meeting initiatives. For example, when dispensing water we do not use plastic bottles, we offer water in pitchers, and in this way you eliminate the recycling and the plastic bottles. In terms of reduction, we do not place pens and papers at each chair for meetings, rather we make them available at the back of the room for those who need these supplies, so you are reducing waste. We are a locally based company and we source products locally as well as having our own 3,000 square foot rooftop herb garden, where the chef selects [herbs] for his menus.

Q: If you could have made any changes in your career, what would they have been?

A: Twenty years ago when I arrived in Dallas my first job interview was at the Fairmont Dallas hotel, and now I am employed here. Since then I have worked for some incredible companies. I have been given great opportunities working with some incredible people. I truly believe things happen for a reason. I would not have made any changes, as I believe one's career comes full circle and that circle for me is now complete at the Fairmont Dallas.

Q: What is your secret for developing a sustainable career?

A: I am a firm believer in building client relationships that have actually turned into friendships. I have coordinated events from small to large, from no money to lots of money, and I can say that over those years I have built a great circle of friendships.

Q: What do you believe will be the biggest changes in the future of special events?

A: Change is happening every day due to the passionate people you work with in this industry. Therefore, I believe than in 50 years we will see more and more change because this is a truly dynamic and rapidly evolving industry.

CHAPTER 12

Twenty Real-World Event Management Experiences and Mini Case Studies

"Life can only be understood backwards; but it must be lived forwards."

—*Soren Kierkegaard* **(1813–1855)**

During Kiergegaard's brief life, the controversial Danish philosopher, theologian, poet, and religious author wrote many official texts on organized religion, Christendom, morality, and ethics among other subjects. His nephew caused a disturbance at his funeral while protesting the role of the church in conducting his uncle's funeral. He was later fined for causing a public disturbance at a funeral. His uncle

Photo by Seungwon Shawn Lee

Brave new world will require event leaders to create memorable experience integrating themes and unique venues for both live and virtual events with or without face to face attendees.

would have liked this, as he continually fought with church officials, and this final controversy was in keeping with his short but well-lived and well-documented life.

Therefore, this final chapter provides you with 20 major and mini case studies to enable you to enjoy a well-lived life in special events by first looking backward to avoid the mistakes of others and also to improve your professional practice as you go forward. At the conclusion of each of the mini case studies is a series of discussion questions that will require you to further ponder how you might address these problems in the future.

Advertising and Marketing

Events are a critical marketing tool for any success of business. In fact, 31 percent of marketers believe events are more significant than digital advertising, e-mail marketing, and even content marketing, according to Bizzabo (www.bizzabo.com). So it's no surprise that events are getting bigger every year with more expenses. Apple has created high-impact product showcase events by leveraging the power of clear messaging and simple elements. The company has successfully combined small theaters, brief videos, and leaders who are passionate to share their products.

- What are some ideas for affordable yet impactful events for business marketing?
- If you were marketing an event and you are required to measure its return on investment, how do you measure tangible and intangible returns?

Attractions

The world-famous San Diego Zoo is a major venue for meetings, events, and corporate programs. To capitalize upon their over-100-year history, the San Diego Zoo has created a Zoofari Party Area to host social events for up to 500 guests. During the Zoofari experience, guests may actually have a close encounter with one of the wild animals (under the close eye of a trained keeper) and even have their photo snapped as a special memory of this once-in-a-lifetime experience. The zoo staff invite their special corporate guests to go behind the scenes and onto the rooftop of the gorilla house to learn how gorilla families bond with one another and see how these principles may be transferred to human organizations.

The San Diego Zoo also attracts many weddings to their exotic venue in a themed approach, called Weddings in the Wild. The wedding business for the zoo continues to grow year upon year, as more and more brides and grooms seek unusual destination locations for their nuptials without the cost or time required for travel to far-flung locations such as Africa. The San Diego Zoo desires to continue to increase both its social and corporate group business and more closely link these visitors to their overall mission of education and conservation.

- How can the current members of the San Diego Zoo and Safari Park be encouraged to hold their future weddings and corporate events at the venue?
- How might the wedding and corporate clients who hold events at the San Diego Zoo and Safari Park be encouraged to become members?
- How might casual visitors to the San Diego Zoo and Safari Park be encouraged to hold their future weddings, corporate, and other events within the venue and to become members and supporters in the future?

Corporate Social Responsibility (CSR)

The Super Bowl and other large-scale events have a unique opportunity to make an impact on host cities, and also on humans in general. The Super Bowl is one example. Not only does it have the ear of millions of people every year but also has the connections, the money, and the power to create initiatives such as Legacy 53.

The Atlanta Super Bowl Host Committee exists, in part, to create a lasting legacy for the city of Atlanta. The foundation of Legacy 53 is built on five pillars: Business Connect, a Capital Improvement Project, Civil Rights and Social Justice, Sustainability, and Youth Engagement. Each pillar is guided by communities of influential local leaders and experts and includes programs with partners in the community.

- In what ways are large-scale events such as the Super Bowl making contributions to society and local communities?
- Of all the Legacy 53 initiatives, which one do you feel is the most important? Explain why.

Education

Manila, the Philippines, suffered a tsunami a few days before the conference was scheduled to begin. Therefore, attendance at the conference was lower than expected. Due to lower attendance, some education programs were consolidated to ensure that the meeting rooms would have more attendance. One of the ways the event leaders added value to the final program was by using the existing speakers to form a panel and discuss major trends occurring in the industry.

- How would you replace a speaker or program that was canceled due to low attendance or travel disruption and achieve the same educational outcomes?
- What alternative educational programming formats could you offer to ensure high-quality despite having limited resources in your speaker budget?
- How will you measure and evaluate the success of your educational program in real time to ensure your attendees were benefitting from your speakers?

Entertainment

In San Diego, California, a convention closed two entire city blocks and erected portable stages at each end. The age level for the audience was primarily baby boomers. The closing act was the 1980s rock and roll band *Kool and the Gang*. When the band performed their popular hit "Celebrate," the entire street erupted into dancing, and the band was forced to perform numerous encores.

- How do you determine the genre of music for your audience?
- What are the advantages of including a well-recognized musical act in your event, and what are the challenges of making such a decision?
- How do you safely control the crowd for a performance in the middle of a downtown street that has been closed when people begin dancing spontaneously?

Environmental Sustainability

There is a food and entertainment festival similar to many of its kind, but there won't be any animal products served up on a plate. All the food is vegan, and the festival celebrates the plant-based lifestyle. The annual VegFest will be held in a beautiful outdoor park, drawing vegans, vegetarians, and the veg-curious with food and other vendors, and live music.

- How can this festival be used to support a greater cause/message such as "environmental sustainability" beyond just good tasting cuisine?
- While this festival will target vegans, how can this festival attract a wider range of attendees?
- What opportunities are there within your event planning process to reduce some resources, but ensure the same overall quality for your guests?

Expositions and Exhibitions

The World Expo is considered as one of the oldest and biggest global events. Every 5 years, a city takes its turn to host the World Expo—ever since London's Great Exhibition in 1851. The World Expo lasts 6 months and any country can take part. Its purpose is to showcase what each country has to offer to help the rest of the world learn about other country's innovation in various industry sectors including culture, technology, and architecture. More information about World Expo can be found at https://www.bie-paris.org/site/en/what-is-an-expo.

Busan is the second largest city in South Korea, just 2½ hours south of Seoul by high-speed train. It is also one of the largest ports in the world. Busan is the host city of the prestigious Busan International Film Festival along with many international events. Its event infrastructure includes BEXCO, the country's second-largest exhibition facility with two exhibition centers, a convention center, and an auditorium. Within a short distance of Busan, there are abundant hotels, restaurants, and beautiful beaches. Busan cinema center offers 4,000-seat outdoor theater covered by the world's longest cantilever roof. The city is actively promoting itself to host the 2030 World Expo.

- What is your first impression of Busan (based on this case description and further your search on the Internet) as an event leader?
- What are expected qualities of host city of World Expo in general?
- To host World Expo 2030, what soft and/or hard infrastructure Busan needs to add?

Festivals

The Edinburgh International Book Festival invites thousands of school children to participate in free programs with children's book authors during the final week of the festival. The children cultivate a love of reading, the authors reach and meet many more potential readers, and some of the children are even inspired to become writers themselves through interactive workshops with the authors.

- How may you target a specific audience segment for your event to increase your events' capacity in the future?

- What additional resources will be required when you invite a large group of children to be your guests at an upcoming special event?
- How might you promote this activity to inform the public of your efforts to provide a quality program for young children and encourage their future financial support for these types of programs?

Finance

A music festival was slated to take place this weekend. It promised eight stages and performances by more than 100 artists. Days before the start of the show, however, several artists dropped out of the lineup citing incomplete or missing payments, and area news outlets reported that other musicians were increasingly worried about whether the festival was still taking place. Then the festival's venue suddenly released a statement canceling the festival entirely "due to the promoters lack of fulfilling contractual obligations." This event was now canceled and hit with similar allegations of deceiving and misleading fans. There were signs of this coming. Reports began to emerge months earlier about the festival's uncommunicative planning and potentially instable financials, which organizers denied until the moment of the show's cancelation.

- What do you think could have been executed better to ensure a better cash flow for the events production?
- How could event stakeholders have noticed the insecure financial status of the event organizer and acted to protect themselves?

Gaming

A casino decided that it wanted to attract high rollers to its New Year's Eve event featuring the legendary jazz vocalist Tony Bennett. The casino sent a CD of Tony's greatest hits to the prospective guests along with the formal invitation. The casino show room could only accommodate 300 persons, but more than five hundred people responded to the invitation.

- How do you notify those persons who were unsuccessful in receiving tickets for the show and still encourage them to come to the casino to gamble both on New Year's Eve and in the future?
- What alternatives may you offer those people who were not successful in obtaining tickets for Tony's show?
- How may you cultivate the customers who were successful in obtaining tickets so that they will become more engaged in your total casino operations?

Government

The U.S. federal government held a conference in Las Vegas that was severely criticized by national media and even by the president of the United States. As a result of this negative publicity, many government agencies canceled upcoming conferences, especially those that would be held in leisure destinations such as Las Vegas.

- How do you justify holding a government meeting in a leisure destination?
- What type of approvals should you receive in advance before scheduling a government meeting?
- Who should attend a government meeting in a leisure destination and who should not?

Hotels

Radisson Blu sponsored a research project to measure the impact of new foodservice styles in its restaurant. The hotel in Zurich, Switzerland, launched a new breakfast buffet for group and individual guests called Super Breakfast. It is described with four themes: great presentation, seasonally updated menus, local ingredients, and health-conscious options designed within its standard core breakfast elements. The research showed a 27 percent reduction in food waste compared to pre-Super Breakfast foodservice. The hotel believes the reduction was a result of quality over quantity of Super Breakfast buffet.

- As an event leader, would you willing to pay more for your group breakfast for less waste and a smaller carbon footprint?
- What type of event/attendees do you think fit well with the Super Breakfast–like meal option?

Incentive

Your incentive travel event is being held in Mexico and includes 500 travel executives who have qualified for award travel due to their sales records. Your event includes a tour of the Yucatan and a gala dinner where awards will be presented.

- How do you notify guests in advance regarding travel precautions they should be aware of prior to their departure?
- How do you further ensure the safety of your guests upon arrival within the destination?
- How do you ensure guests will have positive memories of their incentive travel experience and especially their award presentation?

Information Technology

Every event leader knows that social media is an integral part of each event. However, small event management companies still hand responsibilities of the maintenance of social media content to the youngest in the team or student interns who have good knowledge of new social media. But, the hindsight of this work assignment is that those young and inexperienced staff may not have experience in creating a brand reflecting content during the event. Today, people expect to receive content through social media nearly simultaneously while the event is ongoing. That means that, depending on the size of the event, you should dedicate staff from your event team who understand the event and will make content (including text and visuals) for social media and at what intervals they will be uploaded.

- What are solutions for small event companies with a small staff and no full-time social media technology staff to handle social media management?

- What does this mean to the career development of event management students or young professionals who are just getting into the event industry?

Meetings

A group of LinkedIn members have found they have a common interest in for cultural events. This group decides they like to meet as soon as possible face to face to further exchange information and best practices.

- How do you determine whom should be invited to attend this meeting?
- Where should the meeting be held, and how do you determine the individual costs for attendees?
- How will you measure the outcomes from this meeting to determine your level of success?

Responding to Requests for Proposals (RFPs) for Independent Event Managers

On Monday morning at 9 A.M., you check your e-mail and there are five requests for proposals in your mail box. Each of the RFPs would like a quote for you to provide event planning services for meetings to be held in the next 30 days.

- How do you determine which of the events to respond to first and which ones to decline?
- What resources will be required for you to respond to these requests?
- When do you need to respond to these requests to meet the deadline of the requestors?

Safety, Security, and Terrorism

A false active shooter report temporarily caused panic at a music-themed event as some festivalgoers were injured as they quickly fled the venue. A witness said, "There was a disturbance that led a large group of attendees to believe there was an active shooter within the venue." This resulted in these attendees running out of the venue, some of whom were injured and scared in the process.

Soon after a call was received, security and public authorities immediately sprang into action, established it was a false alarm, and there was no threat. Then the event organizer allowed those fans who fled the venue to return, and the event proceeded as planned with slight delays. It's unclear what caused the panic among event participants.

- How important is it to have procedures and policies set in case of an emergency like this?
- Based on this case, how well did the event organizer respond to the problem and what could have been done better/differently?
- What procedure should be put in place to calm a crowd when something like this happens?

Satisfying the Various Players in a Corporation

The regional vice president of sales for a retail organization is hosting an awards ceremony for key staff event in New York City. The wife of the regional vice president has great influence with her husband and insists that all key staff attend every event. The vice president does not feel as though this is critical, and, therefore, there is confusion among the staff as to which events need to be attended.

- How does the regional vice president establish a suitable policy regarding attendance at the events?
- How do you ensure the needs and concerns of the wife of the vice president are being considered?
- Who should attend which event, and who is the official decision-maker regarding attendance?

Social Event (Wedding)

A mixed-faith wedding is being held in Scotland. The bride wishes to honor the religious and cultural traditions of her non-Scottish groom. However, due to the location, it may be difficult to identify and obtain the services of a proper religious official and also to incorporate the appropriate musical resources to participate in some of the traditional rituals.

- How do you determine in advance the religious and cultural sensitivities of the bride and groom?
- How do you identify the resources needed to perform an official ceremony that incorporates all traditions?
- What other resources may be needed to ensure that the bride and groom's traditions are being incorporated in the ceremony and party?

Virtual Event

You have elected to host a virtual event with participants from 30 different destinations, using Microsoft GoToMeeting as your online technology platform. Several of the participants are having connection problems during the meeting. Other participants wish to expedite the decision-making and move the meeting along to a swifter conclusion.

- How do you help the participants overcome their connection problems through better preplanning?
- How do you organize the agenda to satisfy the time frame for all the participants so that you are able to achieve the goals of the majority of attendees?
- How will you know if your virtual meeting was successful?

INSIGHTS FROM GLOBAL EVENT LEADERS

TIM LUNDY, CSEP

Events Entrepreneur, Distinctive Design Events, Past President, International Live Events Association

(Note: To see the complete video interview, visit the Book Companion Site for this book at www.wiley.com/go/goldblatt/specialevents8e.)

Tim Lundy's career started in New York City where he trained as a professional chef. He then returned to his roots in the southern part of the United States. He continued to work as a chef and then segued into off-premise catering and says he "fell in love with the special events industry." He soon opened his own event design business in Atlanta, Georgia, and later added catering services, thus effectively marrying these two fields within his firm. Mr. Lundy has served as international president of both the International Special Events Society and the International Caterers Association and is the recipient of the Klaus Inkamp award for lifetime achievement in the special events industry.

Q: How has the special events industry changed since you began your career?.

A: One of the things that is different today is that we did not have formal education in special events when I started my career. However, one of the problems I sometimes see with graduates is that they do not have any experience. Therefore, I think it is important that you have both formal education as well as extensive experience to be successful. It is important that you follow a caterer, lighting designer, and others to observe and participate and that will make a world of difference in your future career and how you progress.

Q: How has technology affected your career in special events?

A: The Internet especially has enabled me to be a better chef, event planner, and designer because I can instantly source through the Internet the menus and décor items I need to satisfy my client's dreams.

Q: How important will environmental sustainability be in the events industry in the future?

A: It will be huge! Even brides are now asking for greener weddings by using natural fabrics for the

http://goo.gl/dcWUAV

table linens, using live plants and even biodegradable disposables. I think within 10 to 20 years almost all events will be environmentally sustainable.

Q: What is required to be an effective Event Leader?

A: You have to listen carefully to your group, stakeholders, and constituents. You must also be flexible in your thinking. In my 30 years of being in this industry, I have seen many people who only experience the world as black and white. In this industry it is not always black and white, there are always these gray areas where you have to be willing to bend and be flexible.

Q: Why are you so passionate about special events?

A: I am passionate about this industry and therefore I spend so much time making sure every event can be the best that it can be for my customers.

Q: If you were to write a recommendation for the special events industry 25 years in the future on LinkedIn, what might you say about the industry you helped create?

A: If I was to write a recommendation on LinkedIn about the special events industry 25 years from now, I would say that all of the professionals within the industry were team players and that everybody worked together to create the very best they could create the best events and that would be such an incredible goal for the entire industry.

Q: How can the events industry truly change the world?

A: I would think that anyway we can use the events industry to help educate others even in far-reaching parts of the world, to promote environmental sustainability as part of that education and creating a better place in the world for everyone. We see so much strife every day across the world and I am one of those that thinks, let us just all get along. I think we can definitely use events to help us all get along in the future.

INSIGHTS FROM GLOBAL EVENT LEADERS

JOE VAN ERON, CSEP

Past International President, International Live Events Association

(Note: To see the complete video interview, visit the Book Companion Site for this book at www.wiley.com/go/goldblatt/specialevents8e.)

Joe Van Eron's introduction into the special events industry started at 11 years old. He was one of six children and they had lost their father and three of the children had to go to work. Joe's first job was as a bus boy in a country club, where he worked for 7 years. He believes hospitality is part of his DNA because of the beauty and the service where magic could be created. In his early twenties, he worked in the temporary services industry in New York. In his mid-twenties, he stumbled back into the catering business. One of his early clients was the retailer Bloomingdale's, where he hosted an event for HRM Queen Elizabeth II during the U.S. Bicentennial. That period of time he describes as the birth of retail as theater, where they used events to promote their store and sell their products.

Q: What does it take to become a leader in the special events industry?

http://goo.gl/N2OEmv

A: Being a leader does not mean you have to be the best at what you do, but you must have an overall knowledge of the special events industry, including planning, execution, and budgeting. Even more important is sharing your knowledge with others and inspiring people through your leadership. Leadership is an intangible skill.

Q: If you were to write a recommending for the special events industry on LinkedIn 25 years from now, what might you say?

A: The same mechanics may still be there, including the basic skills, but you must never forget to be true to who you are: be honest and sincere in delivering a memorable event.

Q: Will special events continue to improve the world in the future?

A: Yes, they will always continue to improve the world because they promote a sense of place, a sense of history, and really allow people to have a hope for the future and a wonderful experience to open their eyes to the world.

GLOSSARY

3-D Digital Mapping: The use of computer technology to precisely map a surface such as the exterior of building and then project video images to create a 3-D visual effect.

Accessibility: Ensuring equal accessibility for individuals with disabilities so that they can attend and participate in your event.

Account codes: The enumeration system listed in the far-left column of the budget to allow you to easily track income and expense.

Accounts payable: Funds that are due from you to others for work orders, products delivered, or work performed.

Accounts receivable: Funds due to you from others for work you have agreed to perform or have performed.

Administration: The planning, management, and control of the event outcomes by the event leader.

Audiovisual: The sound, lighting, and projection production elements used in an event.

Audio Webcast: A low-bandwidth alternative for transmitting information using the Internet.

Augmented reality (AR): A technology that superimposes a live direct or indirect view of a physical, real-world environment, often across multiple sensory modalities.

Autocratic leadership: Top-down leadership, whereby the majority of the power is concentrated in one individual.

Balloon drop: A net or bag suspended from the ceiling containing balloons filled with air, sometimes mixed with helium, to be dropped onto the audience below as a surprise.

Banquet event order (BEO)/function sheet: Also called a "Program Execution Order" (PEO), this order of instructions outlines all event logistics and instructions a venue needs to successfully execute an event. This document details the timings of the event, space or room setup, menu selections, audiovisual requirements, and how the event will be run.

Barter: When the event company accepts a in-kind equivalent product or service in lieu of cash. In the case of a hotel client, this may mean rooms or food and beverage credit.

Bottom-up structure: Used most often in the not-for-profit sector, where the bottom of the pyramid comprises volunteers, who democratically control the governance and decision-making for the event.

Budget: The tool that forecasts, manages, and helps control income and expenditure for an event.

Catering: On-premise (whereby a caterer has a permanent presence in the event venue), off-premise (whereby the caterer transports food, beverages, and their equipment to the venue), and concession (wherein a caterer serves food and beverage from specially designed catering vans, trucks, or exhibit books [stands)] at your event.

Concessionaire: A food and beverage provider who is mobile and serves from a truck, from a trailer, or within a venue in a food and beverage concession–specified area.

Contract: A written agreement between two or more parties specifying the obligations of each party in the production of the special event.

Corporate social responsibility (CSR): Commitment to social or environmental charitable causes on the part of a corporation, and the strategic process through which the event organization determines how each event can build social and environmental capital and produce positive social, economic, environmental impacts.

Customer relationship management (CRM): A shared online database system that stores a major list of contacts and their details. This system allows companies to manage their interaction, event attendance history, and communications with their clients in an organized way.

Decor: The elements that create and sustain the atmosphere of the event.

Democratic leadership: Method of leaderships in which the decision-making for the event is spread throughout the majority of the stakeholders, and their consent is needed to make decisions. The event leader becomes a facilitator of this discussion, deliberation, and decision-making.

Deposit: A portion (usually 75 to 90 percent) of the total final amount due to the event planning company.

Dynamic structure: The expansion and contraction of an event organization, whereby an event may begin with a small group of stakeholders, expand during the life cycle of the event, and then contract as the event nears completion.

Electronic employment application: A prescriptive electronic portal through which job candidates must apply only by completing specific fields within a online application and uploading their resume to a prospective future special events employer.

E-mail etiquette: The proper way to communicate with clients, vendor partners, and other professional stakeholders electronically during your event.

EMBOK: The Event Management Body of Knowledge Project, which seeks to standardize event management practices.

EMICS: Event Management International Competency Standards, developed by Meeting Professionals International and the Canadian Tourism and Hospitality Resource Council.

Environmental sustainability: The use of decor items that provide sustainable strategies and superior experiences for guests.

Epergne: A pedestal for a table centerpiece upon which flowers are displayed.

ESTA: The electronic preauthorization required for non–U.S. citizens without official visas to enter the United States.

Ethics: Correct conduct when faced with the gray areas that too often result in problems for event leaders and their organizations reputation due to poor planning and decisions. Ethics may inform laws but are not always subject to legal tests. However, they must be carefully considered to build a positive reputation for the event leader.

Event marketing: The process through which one uses research, design, planning, coordination, and evaluation to market a special event.

Event leader: One who is responsible for researching, designing, planning, coordinating, and evaluating a planned event.

Event studies: An emerging academic field of study and research comprising foundational academic research and theorems from anthropology, psychology, sociology, technology, and tourism.

Event: From the Latin term *e-venire*, meaning *outcome*.

Fair trade: An approach that includes fair pay, investing in projects that enhance workers' quality of life, partnership, mutually beneficial long-term relationships, and social, economic, and environmental responsibility.

Float: A moving display piece either self-motorized, pulled by a motorized vehicle, or drawn by a horse and used in a parade to promote a cause or product, or to entertain.

Force Majeure Clause: This clause is included in most venue contracts to prevent the facility from being held liable should it not be able to hold up to their end of the agreement due to circumstances that are not within the venue's control. These circumstances include events such as a natural disaster or other 'Acts of God'.

Gap analysis: Highlighting those areas of the event you may have overlooked in your research.

Greener events: Special events that continually endeavor to provide superior experiences through environmentally friendly strategies.

Health and safety: The requirement that event leaders meet the standard of care customarily associated with provided a healthy and safety outcome with every special event.

High definition: A television resolution significantly higher than standard definition television (when projected in high definition, it projects five times as many pixels as standard definition television).

Holdback: A small portion (usually 10 percent or less) held back from the total fee due to the event planning company until the work is performed.

Hybrid event: A conference, tradeshow, seminar, workshop, or other meeting that combines a live, in-person audience with a virtual, online audience.

IEMS: International Event Management Standards, developed by the Canadian Tourism and Hospitality Resource Council.

JPEG: A file format that requires less memory than PowerPoint and is easily downloaded by participants.

Key employment application terms: The use of key terms, such as marketing, sales, sponsorship, production, design and others, that will be scanned and analyzed by a prospective special events employer through an online employment application.

Laissez-faire leadership: The leadership style whereby the stakeholders are free to make their decisions without facilitation from a chosen leader. Open discussion is encouraged, and eventually the event stakeholders will move from forming and storming to norming, where decisions are made.

License: A written approval to conduct the event provided by a government or private organization. One of the typical licenses is one authorizing the serving of alcohol at an event. A more recent type of license is one for the use of copyrighted recorded or live music performed at an event.

Livestream: Coverage of an event broadcast live over the Internet, often via social media channels.

Master account: An account set up to which all charges for a specified group should be applied (often by the host or event leader).

Mind mapping: A brainstorming exercise that links ideas to a core concept.

Mirror etiquette: The process whereby the event leader mirrors the behavior or others to fit in socially and professionally.

MOOC: Massive open online courses, educational programs offered free on the Internet and attended by large numbers of learners.

Off-premise caterer: A firm or individual who generally prepares the bulk of the food in one location and then delivers it to a temporary location for the event.

Online consumer-generated media: Media that is directly generated by your guests, on social media websites such as TripAdvisor.com, Facebook, and others.

On-premise caterer: The firm whose permanent catering kitchen is in the same location as the facility hosting the event.

Organizational chart: A system for organizing the role and scope of each member of staff and volunteer. A flat organization is one in which roles are consolidated to reduce hierarchy. The organization or individual at the top of the organization chart is generally considered to be the one with the ultimate fiscal decision-making responsibility for the event.

Outgreening: The use of greener event strategies to promote competitiveness and increase profits.

PA System: Shorthand for 'Public Address System'. A device that amplifies sound in one large area or throughout several rooms through speakers so that messages can be shared.

Parade: A moving pageant or procession involving self-powered and motorized floats, automobiles, animals such as horses, large inflated balloons, and individuals dressed in colorful costumes.

Payables and receivables: Money that is due to others such as suppliers and money that is due to the event organization such as sponsorship fees, registration and advertising income, respectively.

PDF: A file format that requires less memory than PowerPoint and is easily downloaded by participants.

Permit: A written approval from a local jurisdiction or other government or private organization that allows one to conduct an event. One of the key permits is occupancy, which specifies how many persons are allowed in the event venue at one time.

Planned events: Events that are planned in advance to achieve specific outcomes.

PowerPoint: A Microsoft application used for presentations that enables to use of transitions and special effects.

Production: The technical production elements, such as sound, lighting, projection, and special effects, that might be used in your event.

Project management: A planning system useful for any business activity.

Promotion: Advertising where you control the message, the placement, and the frequency and pay the costs.

Public relations: The opportunity to generate third-person commentary about your event through the use of media releases, audio and video news releases, stunts, and promotions.

Qualitative research: Subjective assessment of language or other non-numerical data.

Quantitative research: Numerical measurement of data.

Reliability: The extent to which your research is accurate.

Request for proposal (RFP): A formal request by an event or meeting planner, which lists/details all of the specifications required for the event, sent to suppliers in order for the companies to draw up a proposal of their services and bid for the business.

Return on event: The profit or other gain an event generates for organizers. With the 'Return on event' phrase, ROE can refer to the value brand awareness exercises bring, and not just the contribution to sales volume.

Risk management: Identifying, assessing, analyzing, planning, managing, and controlling the typical risks associated with your event.

Special events: A unique moment in time celebrated with ceremony and ritual to achieve specific outcomes.

Sponsorship: A commercial relationship wherein one party (the event property) receives money or in-kind products and services from a public or private company and in return provides promotional opportunities for the sponsor.

Sustainability: The ability to wisely use the resources of today to create ever stronger and more successful tomorrows.

Sustainable development: The ability to only use the resources you need today to ensure that you have sufficient resources for use in the future.

SWOT analysis: Assessment of the strengths, weaknesses, opportunities, and threats of your project.

Synchronous transmission: An Internet transmission of a educational program that is prescheduled for a specific date and time and often involves a moderator and/or facilitator.

Tempo: The pace of the event schedule.

Temporary employee: An employee who by the nature of his or her role and scope is appointed for a limited period (hourly, daily, weekly, yearly, etc.)

Time management: A system for improving efficiency by using time-saving methods and devices.

Top-down structure: An organizational structure that is generally used in larger hierarchal organizations such as the military or government to ensure command and control.

Traffic flow: In terms of events, "traffic flow" refers to the movement of visitors through an exhibition. It can also refer to how attendees move from one area, hall, or room to another.

Triple bottom line: The financial, cultural, and environmental impact of an event.

Validity: The extent to which your research measures what it purports to measure.

Venture philanthropy: Investment from private organizations that desire a social return on their investment rather than a financial one. Therefore, if a venture philanthropist provides your event organization with $10,000, they may desire evidence that you have made a significant contribution to the social welfare of your stakeholders.

Video/Web conferencing: Using video technology to broadcast an event or meeting to participants who are unable to attend in person.

Video delayed Webcast: A video (often with audio) of a live event shown after the live event has concluded.

Video Web simulcast: A video (often with audio) of a simultaneous live event.

Virtual reality: The combination of creativity with technology to replicate and/or simulate the live experience.

Visa: The official document issued by a government at their consulate or embassy, allowing entry into their country.

Volunteer: An individual who offers to participate in your event due to specific rewards (that are often intangible) he or she will receive.

Webcast: A usually one-way Webstream of a program with limited interaction.

Webinar: A synchronous seminar, workshop, or lecture with the opportunity for participation by all attendees and facilitated by a moderator.

Webstreaming: A process in which audio and/or video files are compressed and delivered through the Internet.

INDEX